Trappers, Hunters 'n' Co

Trappers, Hunters 'n' Co

Wayne Blake

The Halcyon Press

Published by

The Halcyon Press

A division of

Halcyon Publishing Ltd

P.O. Box 360, Auckland, New Zealand

Printed through
Bookprint International Limited
Hong Kong

ISBN 978-1-877256-79-0
Copyright © 2008 Wayne Blake
First Published 2008
All Rights Reserved

Contents

Shanghaied

Billowing winds howled mournfully round the eaves of the old wooden cottage rattling the cobwebs hanging from the windows and sending a cloud of smoke backsliding down the kitchen chimney. Rain. Sheet upon sheet of torrential rain pelted against the aging rustic weatherboards. The river was rising, trees were down, roads awash, bridges gone; mud, slush and bog. It was mid summer on a meat shooting block and this was the mighty West Coast.

. . .

The sun was shining, skies were blue, the smell of macrocarpa hung heavy on the air. Tucked well beneath the shelter of the overhanging hedge a chunky little Border Collie dog uncurled himself, stretched three ways, and wandered over to his boss's sleeping bag. For a minute he sat there undecided. Then he stuck a cold wet nose in the boss's eye to get him moving.

Bob sat up in his sleeping bag and looked around. Up on the rise, outside the Queenstown Forestry Office, several other bods were lying beneath the macrocarpa hedge, dead to the world in their sleeping bags.

"C'mon, you bunch," Bob called. "Rise and shine. Time to get moving."

The Christmas break had come and gone. Deer cullers were already back on their blocks. It was time meat shooters were too.

Most meat shooters of the day had begun their careers as deer cullers. But as venison recovery picked up steam there was a gradual exodus of shooters from the Forest Service. Some became ground shooters, working valley and bush from Land Rovers and jet boats. Others teamed up with helicopter gangs. By the mid 1960's large numbers of ex-deer cullers had become meat shooters and there was a shortage of qualified men to fill the ranks of Government hunters employed to control introduced animals in protection forest areas. The New Zealand Forest Service was desperately endeavouring to recruit experienced men.

There was always a bit of mileage to be had pulling the leg of a Forestry boss. Before checking out of town we would drop into the office, make out we were sick of meat shooting and were seeking re-employment with the Forest Service. We would get them all worked up and excited in there, then we would tell him that we had suddenly had second thoughts and had decided to stick with meat shooting after all.

. . .

Jock Fisher welcomed us into his office and quickly found chairs enough for all to be seated.

"Nice to have you boys drop round," he said shaking each one warmly by the hand. "I hear it's a bit washed out over on the Coast."

"Hardly stopped raining in weeks," Dale replied..

"Can't tell me anything new about the Coast," Jock rejoined. He had been a West Coast culler himself for years prior to being appointed senior field officer in Hokitika. "So when are you planning on heading back?"

"If you had a nice dry block offering, loaded with game, I might be tempted to not go back," said Bob.

Jock spun round in his chair and pointing to a map on the wall said, "How about that? One of the best blocks in Southern Lakes Conservancy. The Dobson. Fantastic country. Tahr, chamois, deer. Dry as a bone most of the time. You can have that one if you want it."

"What about me?" asked Denny. "I'm a starter too."

"Next door block is the Hopkins. Needing shooters there too.

Shanghaied (photo Bob Hannigan)

Another mighty piece of country. Plenty of deer, and no shortage of chamois and tahr there either."

We all knew of Jock as a genuine bloke. Serious about his job, and not inclined to overrate the country he would be sending his men into. Heck, after the mud and slush of South Westland it looked pretty enticing. Bonus shooting at $3.50 a tail plus 3 rounds for every animal dropped. Jock didn't say much more. Before we even knew what was happening, Bob Hannigan and Denny Black had signed away their freedom on the dotted line.

"So what have you got for me, Jock?" I asked, not wanting to be left out. "I wouldn't mind a job to fill in the rest of the summer."

And thus, before the morepork squawked 3 times that very night, three slightly impercipient souls, along with Kim the dog, were levered into service and hustled out of town. Signed, sealed and contracted, back in the Forest Service; deep in the headwaters of the Waitaki Catchment — somewhere beyond the shores of Lake Ohau.

Shanghaied!

"Anyone else?" asked Jock.

But the others were already gone. Travelling fast out of town. Heading in the general direction of the mighty West Coast.

CHAPTER 1

Hut Builder

Ohau Base (photo Bob Hannigan)

Shades of twilight trickling off the Main Divide, tumbled down the valley slopes and spread across the vast expanse of boulders, gravel and quicksand at the confluence of the Hopkins and Dobson rivers. It was the time of day when your average normal bloke would have been relaxing with the wife and kids, day's work done, nothing left to do other than eat, relax, put the feet up....Yeah, right!.

Things were not quite like that in the Waitaki Animal Control Centre. Field officer Reardon hovered about the bunk room door watching much as a gecko watches a fly as I rummaged through my gear, bundling essentials into my frame pack.... Sleeping bag, spare clothing, hut building tools, ammo, fishing gear.... Suddenly his eyes latched onto the fishing gear... a neat little four piece rod, complete with spinning reel and zeddies.... just as it was disappearing into the pack

"That's a handy looking piece of fishing equipment you have there, fellow" noted Johnny Reardon. "And just what," he demanded, "do you aim on doing with it?" .

"I will probably use it for catching fish," I replied, feigning innocence. "You ever noticed any nice fat trout while you was wandering about in the Hopkins?" I asked.

"Have you got a fishing licence?" he glowered, ignoring my query. "In case you are not already aware of it, apart from being your field officer I am also *the* Forest Ranger, and poaching and poachers are two things I do not tolerate in my territory."

"Good job you mentioned it. Fancy me forgetting about a licence. You know, I probably would have wandered off up the river without even giving it a thought if you hadn't brought the matter up. And we certainly wouldn't want to go mooching about the block reducing Forestry food bills with illegally caught trout now, would we!"

Johnny stood there silently sizing me up for a minute or two, trying to figure out whether I was just plain cheeky or just plain stupid, while I mumbled in an undertone and pushed more gear into my pack.

"Licence my ass," I muttered. "What difference is a licence going to make to a trout when it's hooked,"

"Ay? What's that you said?" asked Johnny.

"Just thinking aloud how you need a licence if you don't want to

Looking up the Hopkins from Ohau Base (photo John Fleming)

get booked," I replied

"That's right," said Johnny. "You can't fish round here without one. The licences are back in the office at Omarama. But I'll make one out for you and bring it in next time I come. It will be docked off your pay. Get your gear into the Land Rover. If we don't get moving we won't make it to the Forks before dark."

We drove away from the base camp, along the Hopkins river flats, Johnny driving, me opening and closing gates. And as we drove off into the gathering twilight I got to pondering on the ways and means of hunters, and bosses and such. It didn't matter whether you were a shooter, a track cutter, a hut builder or what, it was not uncommon for the field officer to try and make some sort of an impression as soon as he laid hands upon you. He was the boss, you were the underdog and first impressions meant a lot. In a way it was a sort of a game, but having once before been employed by the Forestry I knew how to play.

Ordering me up the valley with a full load of gear right on last light was not untypical under the circumstances. But having just arrived on the block, tired and dusty, after a long drive from Queenstown, I was hardly in the right frame of mind to be embarking on a five mile trek up the Huxley River loaded down with a heavy pack merely because someone needed to make his impression. In reality there was no reason why we could not have waited until after breakfast the following day. But I had my suspicions what all the urgency was about. These would be duly confirmed shortly after daybreak the next day when others would also be duly impressed upon.

About five miles up river from the Ohau Base, we left the Land Rover at the end of a rough track and took off frenetically into the beech forest.

"You guys are going to be building a hut right here," said Johnny, as we near ran through the bush, "once you've finished the Broderick Hut."

"The man's got to be a nut case," I thought, "It's okay for him with just a sleeping bag and a loaf of bread in his pikau. But if he thinks I'm going to keep this up for the next hour and a half with a pack full of hammers, bullets, rifle and gear he must think we're all a bit stupid round here."

In a short while we had ploughed through a mile or so of forest, just about galloped up a bit of a rise and come out on a bluff above the Huxley River. I waited while Johnny went first across the swing bridge, almost bouncing the stays off their moorings as he went. He cleared the bridge and without looking back to see if I was following, took off into the forest on the north bank.

While it was true that we needed to set a good pace to get to the Huxley Forks before nightfall, it seemed more likely that all the rush and tear was to the end of losing me in his dust. The field officer would get there first, get a fire started with a billy on the boil, then when I finally turned up the stage would be set for bawling me out. No doubt en route there would also have been one or two deer out on the river flats that got away because I had not kept up with him.

While I could not be sure that that was what Johnny Reardon was trying to do, nor could I be sure it wasn't. The bridge was left rollicking crazily on it's cables as I charged off into the forest in pursuit.

Johnny was about ten years older than me, so perhaps he had slowed just enough to get his second wind, but anyway, I managed to catch up with him half a mile upstream, and from there on I hung tenaciously on his heals as we maintained our ridiculous pace. By now he must have realized he was not likely to lose me. So the next play in this stupid game was to be first to sight a deer. However, with all the racket we were raising between the two of us, rattling boulders and bush, all we managed do was spook two or three deer from up in the bush above us without sighting any of them, and it so happened that there was nothing out on the river flats for either one of us to gloatingly point out to the opposition anyway. Without establishing anything of great significance we ploughed on into the fast approaching dusk.

Right on last light we climbed out of the riverbed, topped a small rise below the Forks Hut, and there close up to the bush edge and all but blending into the backdrop of the forest stood a beautiful big

Lower Huxley River (photo Barry Thomson)

stag. Johnny and I were neck to neck as we topped the rise, but he was looking somewhere else and I was the one to see the stag. I snapped my rifle to my shoulder and the animal came up bright and clear in the scope. Johnny never even saw it go down. He spun on me and demanded my reason for loosing off a shot.

"You have to do that to shoot deer," I said, as I started off in the direction.

Johnny looked at me incredulously.

"I'm telling you that's what I just did. Come on." And I took off with Johnny looking half angry and full of disbelief in my tracks. And that was the turning point when Johnny's attitude toward me changed. He wasn't very impressed when I, out of habit, attempted to remove the stag's velvet antlers, reminding me, as he slashed the antlers to shreds with his skinning knife, that I was now in the employ of the New Zealand Forest Service, and perking such things as velvet antlers and carcasses and such like off the block was forbidden and definitely not allowed. But he was quite taken with the perfect neck shot of a deer that he hadn't even seen. And from there on we came a lot closer to being good mates, and with a whole lot more mutual respect accorded than had been apparent just a short while earlier.

We dined on venison stew.... Chopped up chewy back steaks, so fresh they weren't even nice, braised in thickened gravy with onions, tinned peas, and bread. Then downed a tin of Wattie's Bartlett pears sloshed all over with insipid watery custard. Hunched over a brew

Huxley Forks Hut (photo John Fleming)

before the fire, we swapped yarns about various shooters and field officers whom we knew in common, and talked about protection forests and erosion, regeneration and possum damage, meat shooting and fur trapping, and as we crawled into our sleeping bags for the night and Johnny snuffed out the solitary hut candle, I breathed one more sigh of relief that I had managed to pull off a good shot and hadn't blown it by missing that one and only chance I was going to get to establish my own credentials.

It seemed like I had barely snuggled down into my sleeping bag when Reardon shattered my dreams, bouncing off his bunk and pulling on his pants by candlelight. Pitch black night beamed in through the hut window.

"C'mon, it's time to get going."

Somewhere out in the vast Pacific, several hundred miles east of the Southern Alps, daybreak was still searching out the Chatham Islands, so I doubted very much that it was likely to be stumbling across Huxley Forks in the immediate future. But Johnny reckoned we had about an hour's travel to where the lads were building the Broderick hut and he wanted to be there in time for breakfast. I loaded a haunch from the previous night's stag on top of my already overloaded pack, while Reardon hung the other in a tree to be picked up on his way back down river (so much for the rules regarding Forestry employees perking such like off the block), and we slogged off into the predawn chill.

The Broderick hut was only partially constructed and there wasn't much sign of early morning life, let alone breakfast having already been cooked and eaten before we got there. Field Officer Reardon was in his element. This, I had rightly suspected, was part of the motivating factor behind the previous night's twilight jaunt. Signalling for quiet he all but tippy-toed the last thirty yards to the site.

"What in the hell are you two doing," he bawled at the top of his voice, **"still in the sack at this time of the morning?"**

His day was made. It had certainly all been worthwhile.... Leaving Ohau Base already knackered and racing against time to reach the next hut before nightfall; scattering deer through the bush as we went, then forsaking a good night's sleep to be away before first light in order to catch the boys still in their sleeping bags... and here was us, already travelled between huts while they were still sleeping.... Yep! I was back in the Forestry alright, and nothing much had changed in the interim. I guessed a field officer's lot would have been a dreary lot indeed without such moments as these.

Doug Ford was head man, and he was the one who knew what dwang fitted where, and what was a purlin and what was a stud, mainly because he had pre-cut and bundled all the bits and pieces back in the Blue Mountains Forestry Camp before they had been airdropped into the head of the Huxley. I took an instant liking to Doug, but he had his problem... he was totally blind in one eye and had failing eyesight in the other. But that made no difference to his being a really good bloke.

Les Stanley was the off-shoot, and he was a good bloke too. A year or two younger than Doug and me. I do not think he had been working for the Forestry for long. He could not have been going by the way he got visibly shaken by Johnny Reardon's bawling him out of bed. Most blokes who had been around for awhile would not have been overly concerned at all the noise, realizing that it wasn't nothing unusual for field officers to go charging round blocks frightening all the handy deer into the next watershed.

Johnny hung around long enough to have breakfast and get into a heated argument with Doug over what was jam and what was not.

"Why are there two tins of jam opened at once?" demanded JR, looking over the heap of supplies stacked neatly in amongst the building materials.

"There's only one been opened," replied Doug.

"Two!" said Johnny.

"One!" said Doug.

"Well what's this then?" said Johnny, holding up an opened tin of strawberry jam.

"That is strawberry jam," said Doug.

"And this?" asked Johnny, holding up an opened tin of marmalade.

"That is marmalade," said Doug.

"So then, why the hell have you opened two tins of jam at once?" demanded Johnny.

"There is only one tin of jam open," said Doug.

Johnny looked as if he was starting to get mad. But so did Doug.

"This?" he asked lifting up the strawberry jam once more.

"Strawberry jam," said Doug.

"And this?" he asked, now holding up the marmalade.

"Marmalade," said Doug, " and marmalade ain't jam."

"So what the hell do you call it if it isn't jam?"

"Marmalade's marmalade, and it ain't jam."

"Of course it's jam," rejoined Johnny, voice rising an octave or two.

"Then you show me where on the tin it says anything about marmalade being jam," said Doug.

Johnny wasn't looking too happy as he strode off down the track that morning. All his good work bawling the boys out of bed completely undone over one lousy tin of marmalade that someone had forgotten to label "Marmalade Jam".

The Broderick Hut was perched on a spur a short climb above the

North Branch of the Huxley River, right in the thick of good hunting country. Red deer were well dispersed throughout the bush and open tops, chamois hung out in the alpine meadows and tahr were to be found inhabiting the upper levels in those sorts of places that one

Looking into the headwaters of the Huxley
(photo John Fleming)

Temptation! Through the Broderick into the Lansborough

expects to find tahr inhabiting. All around we were boxed in by a series of rugged mountain peaks that rose above seven thousand feet. Some two thousand five hundred feet above the hut, slung between 7,500 foot Mt Strauchon and 7,125 foot Mt McKenzie, the Broderick Pass cut through the Main Divide and dropped away on the other side to the Landsborough River... handy access for any enthusiastic cullers wishing to boost the tally in a bit of unshot poaching territory. Beyond the hut site, we looked straight into the head of the Huxley, an awesome mass of sheer bluffs, ancient glaciers and eternal snow fields.... A great location for a culler's hut, with plenty of animals, beautiful scenery, poaching territory just yonder through the pass and all.

The foundations of the hut had already been completed and the floor nailed down. Doug reckoned that given three good days the job would be all cleaned up. "But," he added, "the hardest part was yet to come." He was referring to building the concrete hearth and fire surround and I was soon to discover what he meant.

Prior to working on the Broderick, I had never given much thought to the amount of effort that goes into building a mountain hut. Trekking up to three hours between back country huts over rugged terrain in adverse weather, pushing through saturated bush, rock hopping slippery river boulders and fording icy mountain streams weighed down with pack and rifle, one is usually close to poked and more than a little thankful to arrive at the welcoming shelter of the next hut. But who ever stops to spare a thought for the blokes who built it, and the sweat and hard yakker they expended in so doing?

Knocking framework together with hammer and nails isn't nothing much to write home about. But lugging pack loads of waterlogged gravel and sand up steep inclines from the nearest source of supply, invariably located half a mile down the slopes in some mountain stream, is. Staggering and crawling, literally on hands and knees out of the stream up to the hut site, the three of us spent the better part of a morning slugging it out load for load. And then, just about the time of day when we should have been resting up under a shady tree, we had to start all over, hauling eighty pound loads of water for the mix; eight gallons per trip, two biscuit tins slung with number eight fencing wire for handles that dug deep into your palms and sloshed cold water down your boots. And at the end of it all, after several more hours hand mixing concrete, I sat on a stump to one side of the hut surveying the sheer tops hemming us in and silently hoped that one day an avalanche would not come crashing down the slopes and sweep all our sweat and hard work into the Huxley way below.

But aside from the occasional heavy going, such as doing a pack horse out of a job carting sand, gravel and water for fire surrounds, and digging deep holes for long drop toilets in amongst the rocks and

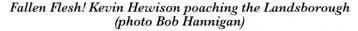

*Fallen Flesh! Kevin Hewison poaching the Landsborough
(photo Bob Hannigan)*

goolies, hut building was a fairly cushy sort of a job. We were given
one week to assemble each hut but with three of us on the job it only
took four or five days, and the rest of the time was ours to do as we
pleased.

Some blokes liked to spend their leisure hours lazing about reading
books and doing as little as possible, but I loved hunting. There wasn't
much else came into my mind other than grabbing my rifle and
pulling on a pair of boots. If I wasn't already climbing about in the
tops I was probably thinking about it checking them out from the hut
doorway with a pair of binoculars.

I was doing just that, scanning the tops with my binoculars soon
after my arrival at the Broderick site, and I picked out a chamois
doe and her joey reclining on a rocky outcrop close to the Broderick
Pass some 2,000 yards in a straight line from the hut. Chamois have
brilliant eyesight and I got the impression that they were sitting there
surveying the activity that was going on down at the site. Each day
they would be there, reclining on the same vantage point, taking us
and all the surrounding countryside in.

As deer cullers and such, we had all been well indoctrinated by the
Noxious Animals Act to believe that every moving thing, other than
native species and naturalized citizens needed total demolishing. And
even some of the natives were taking their share of the flack. Keas,
parry's and Pukekos for example. Interestingly, the numberless hoards
of tussock chomping high country sheep, bush ravaging cattle that

churned there way through leasehold land, spiflicating chainsaws, bulldozers and Department of Public Works in general, were given the wink of approval and, for some inexplicable reason, counted in with the naturalized citizens as not to be shot.

Naturally, with due consideration to the order of the day, I felt it my duty to contribute my patriotic bit and go demolish joey and his mum. So just after breakfast one morning I set out on the long haul up to the Broderick Pass. I estimated about two hours climbing and sidling would get me within shooting distance. Late that afternoon when I finally got back to the hut, Les told me that the chamois must have been watching me as I took off from the hut and dropped into the cover of the adjacent stream bed. Because after some time and I still had not returned to the hut they suddenly got up and hightailed it through the pass.

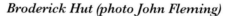

Broderick Hut (photo John Fleming)

I wasn't so stupid as to climb all that way without sneaking the odd peek at the quarry. But thinking, when I could not see them perched on their outcrop, that they were probably browsing some alpine herbage just out of sight, I plodded on regardless. Which just goes to show you your average Hopkins chamois isn't quite as stupid as your average Hopkins hut builder.

Having completed the Broderick Hut, Doug and I were commissioned to build a couple of deer exclusion plots. One was high above the mouth of the Huxley, in amongst stunted mountain beech just below the open tops. The other was above the bush edge on the opposite side of the Hopkins, close to Cullers Bivvy on the Neumann Range. Les went off with Johnny somewhere to work on something else for a couple of weeks.

The idea of a deer exclusion plot was to completely fence off a small area of bush or grassland so that no browsing animal could gain access. Observations could then be made of the depredations on the outside compared to the regeneration on the inside. It was a brilliantly contrived scheme that allowed for the fact that deer don't climb fences while disregarding the fact that possums do. Nevertheless, there were, scattered around the mountains and bush of New Zealand dozens, possibly hundreds, of such plots and many a "junior woodchuck" ranger trainee and his field officer superior merrily frittered away the hours of their day crawling about on hands and knees counting, measuring, tabulating and tenderly coaxing the individual "frangiposia rangitatuses" and "blechnum disorderlies" inside their personal little plots.

A typical Deer Enclosure (photo Les Pracy)

I was entrusted with a four pound Kelly axe and told to blaze a trail and, where necessary, cut a track up through the bush to the plot site above the Huxley. This I was to do following the easiest possible gradient, and with blaze marks that would be clearly discernable to even the greenest of "junior woodchucks", fresh out of Ranger Trainee School, that might be sent in to visit the plot

Going uphill following the general outline of a ridge the going is fairly straight forward. As long as you are heading up you are naturally going in the direction you are aiming for and, as long as you stick to the ridge, you are going to come out round about where you want. I fair steamed up through the bush blazing and cutting as I went and before long the track was finished.

On the way back down though, I got the impression that certain portions of the track would have been easier going if I had initially taken a slightly different course and sidled more to the left, or in other places more to the right. A few extra blaze marks soon sorted that one out. However, there is nothing more confusing than having two sets of blaze marks where there is only supposed to be one. So to avoid any confusion I grabbed a handful of moss, tied it over the original blaze with a piece of vine, then hacked and blazed my way down what now seemed to be the better course.

The first time I did this I managed a few hundred feet of descent into a blind gully before conceding that the original track was really the only way to go. Seeing the new blaze marks did not lead to anywhere of great consequence I decided not to back blaze the trees in this area but let "junior woodchuck" figure it out for himself. — If he was stupid enough to follow the wrong set of blaze marks then serve him right if he got bushed in a blind gully. — I climbed back up to the main ridge and removed the moss from the original blaze.

This now left a choice of two trails for the downward descent. One leading back to the mouth of the Huxley, the other into the blind gully. This might all seem rather confusing to the reader (and of course to anyone travelling back down from the plot). But it was not at all confusing to me as I had just cut the track and had clearly in mind which route to follow. Nor was it going to worry Doug because he could hardly see the blazes anyway. All he had to do was follow me and he would be okay. Junior woodchuck though, fresh out of Ranger Trainee School, might have a bit of difficulty working it all out. But that didn't matter. It would be a splendid opportunity for him to test his mettle and see what he could recall regarding how to cope when one suddenly finds oneself bushed.

A bit further down I managed to do something similar, but fortunately I only cut about ten minutes worth of blazes before I realized I had lost the ridge and was sidling into the Hopkins. There was already too many trees been blazed unnecessarily, so once again I refrained from back blazing when I realized my mistake.

Further down again I cut an alternative traverse that went across the ridge and back again, ending up more or less where the traverse had begun. This one genuinely did follow a much easier course, though not to much advantage seeing you ended up more or less back where you had just come from. It was an interesting track by the time I had finished. One on which considerable fun could be had honing up one's bush craft skills. The track up to the plot was straight forward enough. But I could just imagine Johnny being tickled pink when he came to following it back down to the Hopkins.

Constructing the actual plot only took a couple of days. Bundles of Waratah standards and rolls of Hurricane fencing wire had been airdropped onto the ridge above the bush edge and after locating them and packing them down to the site we simply followed the regular pattern for such plots, drawn up on a set of plans for our convenience. There was no shortage of noise echoing through the bush as we slammed the Waratahs into position with a ten pound sledge hammer, and rattled and shook the mesh into place. But it did not seem to unduly affect the local deer and chamois population. Each morning I was up and out in the tops just as it was breaking day, and I never failed to add another two or three tails to my belt.

The Hopkins was a huge valley with lots of animals and vast shooting potential. Up here where we were building the deer plot, it was an out of the way sort of a place that the shooters probably seldom if ever shot. Fly camping right there just beneath the tops gave immediate and easy access to some great shooting. I didn't really anticipate Johnny getting too enthused over my track cutting abilities, but he was bound to be pleased about the kills.

It was drizzling rain as Doug and I trudged back down the old gravel road to Ohau Base. We had been gathering up cattle beast and pushing them ahead of us ever since we had broken clear of Teawapuhe Bush and by the time we had travelled a couple of miles there were some twenty or thirty of them ranging out ahead of us down the river flats. Suddenly Doug stopped dead in his tracks. With a startled look on his face he turned to me and said: "What's that?"

"What's what?" I replied, hair rising involuntarily up the back of my neck.

"Up on the track ahead of us? There's something moving! What is it?"

I had not noticed anything extraordinary. I glanced quickly at Doug to see where he was looking. Then I realized. A few of the cattle were only about fifty yards ahead of us and Doug had just noticed them.

" You mean those cattle beast?" I asked.

" Oh! Is that all it is?"

For the first time I realized just how poor Doug's eyesight really was. I could not help but feel a twinge of pity for him, but at the same time I was quite overcome with admiration. To be wandering around with pack and rifle in country like this with eyesight like that would take a certain type of grit and courage that you don't find every day. Who could help but love a bloke like that.

For a day or two we remained holed up in Base waiting for the weather to clear. Then our good field officer turned up and managed to convince us that just because the Hopkins was running at near flood level and the tops were still blanketed with black looking thunder clouds, and there was a bit of drizzly rain sweeping across the river flats and it wasn't far off bordering a howling gale outside, coupled up with a bitterly cold wind chill factor, that was not sufficient reason for a couple of able bodied bush carpenters the likes of us to mope around Base, hut-bound and inactive.... Our presence was required up on the Neumann Range.... If we took off now we could be there in an hour or two and that would mean no lost time when the weather finally cleared.

There wasn't much point getting all heated up and arguing about it. Inwardly fuming, we loaded our packs once more and took off into the drizzle and murk.

The river was frigid and in my estimation running high enough to be borderline, but having now abandoned Base, the next available shelter to be found was up at Cullers Bivvy and we both agreed it would be more pleasurable getting drowned than going back and telling Reardon we were not game to chance it.

We were well out into the icy current, with the bits and pieces shrivelled like a limpet, when Doug confided that he had never tried crossing a flooded river before and the water swirling beneath his eyes was making him feel giddy.

"Don't look at the water," I yelled above the rush of swirling waters. "Keep your eyes fixed on an exit point on the opposite bank."

"Well, where exactly is the opposite bank?" hollered Doug. "I can't see that far!"

About two thirds of the way across the river Doug managed to get swept off his feet and dropped and lost his axe after suddenly deciding that getting drowned wasn't going to be quite so pleasurable after all. Somehow I grabbed him by the pack straps as he swirled past, and I sort of got this feeling that when or if Reardon ever asked Doug what had happened to the axe, and if he spoke a bit too loud in Doug's ear about it, he might just end up wishing he hadn't.

Three hours later, after sploshing our way along the river flats, negotiating innumerable side creeks and finally pushing our way up through two thousand feet of saturated bush, we arrived at Cullers Bivvy, even more sour at being evicted and still none the wiser as to what all the urgency had been about, anyway.

Cullers Bivvy was a pokey little two bunk hut, but it was warm and dry, and well stocked with food and reading matter. It had not been much fun getting here, but now we had arrived we had everything we needed to make ourselves comfortable. And nor was it likely that Reardon would suddenly poke his nose in to check on our progress, so far removed from the comforts of Ohau Base, on the wrong side of a swollen river, and getting his ass all wet doing it. We settled back with our feet up, a freshly baked camp oven loaf, a billy full of tea and a couple of freshly opened tins of jam, and got stuck into whittling a few hours away browsing the pile of paper backs and comic books comprising the library.

A typical Forestry bivvy – just about had to crawl to get inside – compare door opening with rifle leaning against wall

There was a lot of fresh deer sign scattered about close to the hut. When we had done justice to the loaf, and gotten bored reading and lying about, and once the weather had cleared and we had nailed a few easy deer, and when there was nothing else left remaining to distract our attention, we might just start thinking about building that deer plot. However, from what we could make out, it wasn't really a matter of great urgency.

There had never been a track cut through the bush to Cullers Bivvy and in places the undergrowth was quite thick and tangled. Johnny Reardon, appreciating that North Island possum trappers are forever good at cutting tracks through dense vegetation, and having as yet not experienced the delights associated with the one I had just cut up above the Huxley, had once again blessed me with the privilege.

Recent experiences had taught me that life in the Waitaki Catchment was not necessarily always going to be one of wine and roses. And based on this observation I deliberated that nor did all tracks necessarily have to follow the easiest gradient. The shortest route from valley floor to open tops at Cullers was straight up, and straight up was the way my new track went. This one was not designed to test anyone's bush craft skills, but it would certainly test their fitness.

And with all that taken care of we retraced our steps back to base.

CHAPTER 2

Life in the Hopkins

With the track to Cullers Bivvy cut and the deer plot completed, Doug and I began work on the new Monument Hut. This was the one that

***Looking across the Hopkins from Near Memorial Hut
(photo Barry Thomson)***

Reardon had mentioned to me as we charged off into the twilight my first night in the Hopkins. It was sited inside Teawapuhe Bush about a mile and three quarters south of the Huxley River mouth and was quite different to all the other huts that were in the Hopkins. Whereas most were four bunkers, Monument was designed to sleep eight people, and was correspondingly bigger in area. In a short while Les was taken off whatever he had been doing and sent back in to give us a hand.

Up until now there had really been no opportunities for using that fishing rod that had got Johnny Reardon so worked up the night he saw me loading it into my pack. Way upstream where we had built the Broderick Hut, the Huxley River was little more than a creek with not a great deal of water in it. And anyway, in that sort of country I was more interested in climbing out and hunting animals rather than poking about in pools looking for trout. As for the shortage of good trout pools in the vicinity of the deer plots that Doug and I had just built up in the tops there is probably little needs to be said. There were trout to be had in the Hopkins, though, and some of them were a good size. Way down deep, beneath the Huxley swing bridge, we had stopped to watch a couple of them hovering in the current the day we trekked back to base after building the Broderick. These ones were way out of reach, but there were bound to be others in more accessible spots and now we were camped right alongside the main river I wasted no time going looking. I did not have to go very far.

Looking up the Hopkins from near the mouth of the Huxley (photo John Fleming)

Less than five minutes upstream from the building site the river had at some time or other changed its course and left behind a large land locked lagoon nestled hard up against the bush. From in amongst the beech trees you could look down into the lagoon, and I could hardly believe what I saw. There were heaps of trout idling about in it. An eroded bank sloping steeply down through the bush made much of the lagoon inaccessible, but at the northern end the bank levelled off and stepped gently onto a small sandy beach I cut back through the bush, out of sight so as not to spook them, and worked my way quietly onto the small beach. Patches of watergrass and bits of drift wood scattered through the lagoon provided reasonable cover for the fish, but there was plenty of space for casting without snagging the lure. My very first cast landed a trout big enough for all three of us. That was all I wanted. With as little disturbance as possible, I slipped quietly back into the bush and headed back to camp.

Trout – *"The first of many a feed taken from Pantry Pool"* (photo Doug Ford)

While we were building the Memorial Hut there was not much time available for shooting meat, so fresh trout was a welcome change from the tinned foods that we had been largely living on. Early next morning I was back at the pool catching another couple of fish for breakfast.

The easy way of cooking a trout is to cut it up to fit the pan. Put the pieces in a paper bag along with a little flour. Give the bag a good shake so as to thoroughly coat the fish with flour and then fry in butter, dripping or what have you.

But with just a little more effort you can do better than that.

Fillet the fish. Again, cut it into serving size pieces. Whip up an egg yoke with a fork. Smear the yoke all over the fish pieces. Roll the pieces in bread crumbs and fry in butter or margarine to golden brown, making sure the fish is cooked right through. Sprinkle with a little vinegar and salt to taste. Serve with chopped onions sautéed in butter or margarine, and a couple of fried eggs. If you have some cooked potatoes left over from a previous meal, cut these up and fry them in the pan as well.

And if you want to do something nice with left over cooked fish, flake the meat off the bones. Put it in a frying pan with a couple of knobs of butter. Add a finely chopped onion, salt and pepper. Keep stirring with a fork so the fish does not stick as you heat up the pan. Add in a teaspoon of curry powder (more if you like it spicy). Give it another good stir. Pour in about half a cup of milk. Reheat to simmering hot but do not boil. Thicken with cornflour and serve on buttered toast sprinkled with a little vinegar, salt and pepper to taste — scrumptious! If you do not like vinegar, use tomato sauce. And if you have cheese, grate that over the fish either in the frying pan so that it melts into the fish, or once it is on the toast.

Every day for awhile there we were having fresh caught trout for breakfast served in a variety of ways. We were doing so well out of it that Doug dubbed it the "pantry pool". But all of a sudden the fish switched off. Just like that they refused to take the lure. The odd one would trail the lure as I wound in but none of them would make a grab for it. I do not know how they twigged to it, but somehow they had grown wise to what was going on. I kept going back to the pool and trying but I didn't even get a strike.

Les reckoned that it was probably just as well, because he had once heard of a bloke who had gone fishing and got nothing but strikes and the bloke reckoned he had been wasting his time because you couldn't eat strikes. I assured Les that if that was the case if I happened to get any strikes I would not bother bringing them back to camp. Doug said that from what he knew about "strikes" there was nothing wrong with them as long as they were marinated for an hour or two first, but he thought the real reason why I was not getting anything might be something to do with the phase of the moon and the tide not being quite right.

Well I must admit, that one got me thinking a little harder than normal. I could not recall having noticed anything unusual about the tide. But in the end I decided that just like any other wild critters, these fish were not dumb. They had watched their mates getting hooked and realized what was going on. I knew that was the way it worked with everything else and I could not see why it should be any different with trout. Deer that saw their mates getting shot from a helicopter quickly cottoned on to what helicopters were all about and they only needed to hear the distant "thwack, thwack!" of a chopper to start hightailing it for the bush. And possums quickly got wise to what gin traps were for. Any trapper who knew what he was about, realized the only way to outwit the possum was to completely conceal his trap beneath the dirt. Well, that was all well and good. Outwitting a possum was one thing; but how does one outwit a trout? We all got to thinking about it. And then Doug remembered something he had once heard.

An Acclimatisation Society ranger had once told him how some "unscrupulous individuals" actually sunk so low as to rub Chesdale cheese on their lures to entice a trout. I thought that this was about the most ridiculous thing I had ever heard. Why waste time rubbing a piece of cheese on your lure when you could just as easily remove the lure and plonk a dob of cheese right there on the hook? And it worked like a charm. Once again we were back in business and dining on trout for breakfast.

But it was not long and they twigged to the cheese too. Up they would come, taking turns, moseying up to the bait. They would eyeball it, give it a sniff, then with obvious deliberation would knock it off the hook before picking it up and swallowing it down. But the amazing thing was, everyone of them seemed to know exactly how to go about it, almost as if there had been some sort of universal instruction on the matter. It was almost unbelievable but I watched them do it. Every time I lobbed a piece of cheese into the pool a different fish would edge up and take his turn knocking it off the hook.

When I was just a lad at school back in Wellington, I remember being taught in biology lessons that fish were hovering somewhere round the bottom rung of the intelligence ladder. Could well be! But wisdom is applied knowledge, and when it came to applying knowledge this lot would have been several rungs higher up the ladder than some of them biology teachers. Don't ever let anyone try telling you fish can't think. When it comes to survival they are no different to any other wild critter.

After what Doug had said, about "unscrupulous individuals", I was a little wary about letting on that I was putting cheese on my hook Besides, there did not seem to be much point in cluttering up their already overworked brains with such trivial details; they needed all the space they had for hut construction. When no one was looking I would sneak into the food cupboard, whip a small piece out of the packet, and away I would go. They knew where the bait was coming from, but they never were able to figure out just what it was. Doug was the one who seemed most bemused. From time to time he would stand in front of the food cupboard squinting along the shelves with his one good eye sizing up the various ingredients, but it never did register that I might be using cheese. Incredible, considering it was Doug who had come up with the Chesdale notion in the first place.

Now though, with the Chesdale no longer working, I felt that a bit of collaboration might prove useful. Anyway, they had spent more time than I had studying the food cupboard considering all the alternatives, so I felt that it was quite feasible that they could well come up with something new. Naturally, this meant that I now had to divulge what I had been using: "Anyway, it was pretty useless," I told them. "And nor does it work any more."

Obviously my two mates had given considerable thought to the matter during the time that the cheese had been working, and there was no shortage of helpful offerings as to what might work... camp oven bread, pancakes, date scones, potatoes, carrots, onions, lumps of dough, golden syrup, macaroni, condensed milk.... I was open to suggestions and anything short of ridiculous was given a shot. But nothing worked. With numbers already drastically reduced, the trout still remaining in "pantry pool" were really clued up. If the bait proved interesting, they would always figure out a way to knock it off the hook before taking it.

I had just about run the gamut when out of exasperation I tried sticking a piece of raisin loaf onto the hook anchored by the raisin... and, bingo! we were back in business. It is probably a play on words to say that trout get "hooked" on raisins. But, sniff, study, mesmerise or knock, do as they might, no way did they ever work out how to get that piece of raisin off the hook before they found they was whipped out of the pool and on their way to Monument for breakfast.

I never bothered to tell Doug and Les what I had just come up with. What with "Chesdale cheese" and construction details already taking up most of the available space, it just didn't seem right adding to their burden with such irrelevancies. It was enough that they were back to having fresh fish for breakfast.

One morning Johnny Reardon turned up just in time for breakfast. He came in to drop off Denny Black, deliver the mail and a cabbage, and inspect the progress, though not necessarily in that order. His timing was perfect. The daily fillets were just being served. Johnny sat down and a plate full of trout and a slice of camp oven bread was placed before him. Suddenly everything went dead. It was almost as if the sound had been switched off. Johnny just sat there silently staring at his plate. Then slowly, almost reluctantly, he lifted his fork and ventured the first dainty morsel into his mouth. With obvious discomfort, he did justice to his vittles, then looking up and staring me straight in the eye demanded: "Who caught this fish?"

"I did," I replied.

"Have you got a fishing licence?" he asked with more than just a trace of anger in his voice.

"Well, I think so. If I remember right, you said you would sort one out for me when you got back to Omarama from the Broderick."

"I don't remember anything of the sort," said Johnny. "So if you don't have a licence that means you have been poaching trout."

I could see Reardon was getting all worked up, and with a hut full of impressionable onlookers taking it all in he was not likely to back off too quickly. This, I sensed, was it. Reardon was about to tell me to pack my gear and get off the block. Then an interesting thought suddenly crossed my mind....

"Hey, you know what!" I said. "I bet those acclimatisation mates of yours would really get a kick out of it if they ever heard that you had been eating poached trout up the Hopkins."

I never did see that licence that ranger Reardon was going to make out for me. Nor was the subject ever mentioned again. So don't ever let anyone try telling you hut builders can't think. When it comes to survival they are no different to any other wild critter.

Ranger Reardon's embarrassing breakfast (photo Doug Ford)

Up to now Denny had been shooting the Hopkins with a bloke called Ringo (so named because the first chamois he ever bowled he shot it clear up the ring) and another bloke (who had not done anything as spectacular as Ringo, and so his name is thus lost to posterity). Prior to the Hopkins, all of Denny's previous shooting experience had been gained in the North Island riding bicycles and Land Rovers up and down forestry roads in Kaingaroa Forest. And compared to the Kaingaroa Plains he was finding the enormity and sheer drop-offs associated with massive mountain peaks and hanging glaciers a bit daunting. Some blokes were like that. They could not handle being suspended above space or finding themselves in tricky places. I had heard of one of the Hopkins shooters getting himself into a sweat when he got caught out on a tight ledge and next thing he started imagining that the weight of his rifle was dragging him off the bluff. In a panic he hurled his rifle out into space. It smashed to pieces on the rocks a thousand feet below. He later recovered the rifle and patched it up, but he found that after what it had gone through it was only ever good for shooting round corners. Blokes who suffered vertigo never did too well in this sort of country.

Denny was a welcome addition to the team. He was a big solid fellow and having a good strong labourer to help cart the sand and dig the long drop toilets was okay by us. With three of us building and Denny helping out with some of the dirty work, it still took a little over two weeks to complete Monument Hut. It was spacious, well built, comfortable and warm and we were all proud of it. Unfortunately it only stood for about twelve months before some irresponsible lout set fire to it and burned it to the ground. I believe a second Monument Hut was built to replace it, but I doubt that the hut builders would have been eating trout every morning for breakfast. By the time I left the Hopkins the "pantry" was all but bare.

Sixteen miles up the Hopkins, almost in the headwaters, another hut was waiting on the list to be built. This was the Erceg Hut, which was named after Frank Erceg, one of New Zealand's top hunters, who had been tragically killed nine months earlier in mid 1965 when he and another shooter were struck by a helicopter rotor while dragging deer off the Matukituki tops — the first of many venison helicopter fatalities.

The building materials had been air dropped to the vicinity of the new hut, but there was still shovels, hammers and tools to be packed in and it was a long hike getting them there. About ten miles up the valley, we decided to take a break at Dodger Hut, spend a couple of days there and continue on after the weekend. We arrived at Dodger about mid afternoon with drizzle and mists swirling down through the gullies and the weather not knowing what it wanted to do.

Conditions were still looking a little uncertain the following morning, but the mist had lifted and was now clinging high up in the tops. My three mates said they had nothing planned other than to hang round the hut, sleeping and eating and brewing billies of tea. But I took off straight up behind the hut and out into the open tops.

These were creamy days for deer cullers and ground shooters. When Frank Erceg had been killed just nine months earlier, he had been engaged in one of the early pioneering venison recovery campaigns. There were still only a couple of helicopter gangs operating, and they more than had their hands full working where they were in South Westland. They were still a year or two away from crossing the Alps into Canterbury and Otago. Hence there were still plenty of animals waiting to be shot if you went looking for them.

Behind Dodger Hut fifteen hundred feet of beech forest plus

another three hundred feet of stunted alpine growth brought you out onto cropped tussock lands and expansive shingle screes that reached up to the crags and snow fields above. I never knew what areas had been shot and what had not in this sort of country, but it did not really matter. There was a fair bit of leg work involved and the binoculars saved a bit on that, but if you were prepared to exert yourself there was no reason why you could not get a tail or two for the effort. I do not think anyone had been up behind Dodger for awhile for by the time I got back to the hut late that afternoon I had several tahr and chamois tails hanging from my belt and a leg of meat draped over my shoulder for the pot.

It all looked so easy that Doug determined to cover my tracks the following day and go get a few tails for himself. He set off about mid morning carrying his old Three O and a pouch full of ammo, intending to climb up to the rough stuff and look for some tahr. During the day I kept an ear out, listening for shots that might indicate he was onto something, but there were none. Then fairly late in the afternoon the weather started to turn bad. A fast moving trough poured into the valley from the south, spilling cloud half way down through the bush and sprinkling the area with isolated showers. As evening approached and Doug still hadn't returned I began getting a little anxious. Then the showers turned to sleet. By now it was almost dark and I was getting really worried. It was far too late for Doug to be still out. I fetched my rifle from the hut and fired a couple of shots into the air and we all stood around straining our ears, listening for an answering shot from Doug. There was nothing.

Half an hour later it was quite dark and I knew Doug was in serious trouble. The weather had cleared and stars filled the sky, but above the bush line a blanket of snow was now covering the tops. And if it was cold down here in the valley, it was going to be bitterly cold up there with the wind chill factor and all.

The noise from a .222 doesn't carry all that far so I asked Les to fire off a couple of rounds from his Three O. A few echoes rolled around the valley but there were no shots in return. We went back inside, stuck an extra candle in the hut window and sat around eating a fairly subdued meal. Apart from fire off the odd signal shots and listen, there was nothing much we could do until daybreak.

Travelling light and fast, I estimated it would take about five hours of tramping from Dodger to Ohau Base. One of us would have to leave at first light to raise the alarm so an official search and rescue could be put on standby. I asked Les if he would be willing to go. Denny could stay at the hut to pinpoint and answer any rifle signals he might hear. And I would climb up into the tops and begin an immediate search.

We all did it, but there were so many things that could go wrong hunting on your own in rugged mountains; bluffs, falling rocks, waterfalls, slippery streams. One could easily twist an ankle or break a leg, and with just a little carelessness or perhaps a serious misjudgement it could quickly end in death. Doug wasn't really experienced in the hills and added to that was his limited vision. I had never lost a mate like this before and I hoped that whatever I found on the morrow would not be too bad. But inwardly I had a sickening dread.

None of us felt like going to bed that night. We wiled away the hours playing cards with the billy kept on the boil, the hut door wide open, listening. And every so often one of us would wander out into the cold night air and fire a shot off into the dark, and just stand there thinking about it, straining the ears and hoping to hear a distant shot in reply that might indicate Doug was still alive.

Sometime around midnight we decided it was late enough and were just about to chuck it in for the night when Denny showed us how to play Slippery Sam. He was the banker and the three of us started betting with rounds of .303 ammunition. In a way it was good because it helped us to relax a little and take our minds off the seriousness of the situation with Doug. The only trouble was it also got a little intense and by going on 3.30am we were still playing. I was owing Denny fifteen hundred rounds of ammo and Les owed him seven hundred and fifty. I called one more hand, double or quits and told Denny I was going to bed or I'd never be able to get up at daybreak, which was now only a couple of hours away. Denny agreed. I turned up a winning hand and quickly scrambled into my sleeping bag. Les was near panicking because he didn't even own seven hundred and fifty rounds. For the sake of sleep, I told him to do what I had done, double or quits, and call it a night. Denny thought it was all terribly funny and egged poor Les along, until finally, against his better judgement Les agreed to one last hand... double or quits. Denny turned up the winner. Les looked like he was going to cry. I told him to play another hand and try again. I think he realized that sooner or later, as long as Denny didn't pull the plug, if he kept playing double or quits for long enough he was bound to win a hand. Anyway, his next hand drew the winning cards and Les was the one who quickly pulled the plug. Within seconds we were snug in our sleeping bags, snoring soundly.

I awoke with a start. There was a solid crunching out on the porchway of the hut. It was broad daylight... it was Doug. He staggered in the door, flopped on a stool, blue in the face and soaked to the skin. I looked at my watch. It was 8.30am. All our carefully laid search and rescue plans had gone by the way. Exhausted from our vigil through the night not one of us had woken early to the new day. I could only guess what must have been going through Doug's mind. For all we knew he could have been lying at the bottom of a bluff with a broken back and here we were snoozing on in our warm sleeping bags. What can you say in a case like that?

"G'day, Doug," I said, eyes just peeking out of my sleeping bag. "Where have you been?"

His teeth were chattering so audibly the poor guy could hardly answer:

"G-g-got c-c-c-caught out in the clouds, and then it g-g-got dark, and I was t-t-too frightened to work my w-w-way down through the bush in the dark in c-c-c-case I p-p-poked out my only good eye on a s-s-st-stick."

"Heck, that's not too good. You are not hurt though are you?"

"No, just b-b-bloody near froze t-t-to death."

"Didn't you hear our shots in the night?" asked Les.

"Yeah, b-b-but I was t-t-too c-c-cold to fire b-back. It s-s-snowed and I j-j-j-just lay sh-shivering up in the scrub all night w-w-w-waiting for d-d-d-daybreak."

"You probably did the right thing under the circumstances, Doug," I replied. "Now if you don't mind, seeing you're up and about and we're still in the sack, how about gathering a bit of dry firewood and swinging the billy for us. We had a pretty hard night playing cards and could do with a bit more sleep yet. Oh, and try not to make too much noise until it's ready, so that you don't disturb us."

I never was able to convince Doug that I was only pulling his leg, and that we had stayed awake most of the night worrying ourselves sick about his welfare.

Doug had really had the stuffing knocked out of him. He slept just about solid for two whole days while we plied him with hot soup and mugs of steaming sweetened tea whenever he stirred. And as soon as he was able to handle it we stuffed him full of camp oven stew. None of us knew much about hypothermia in those days, but we knew his body temperature was way down and we also instinctively knew we had to get it back up. Once Doug came right we carried on to the Erceg Hut site.

The weather was kind to us while we were building the Erceg Hut, but the heads of some of these valleys were quite regularly subject to violent conditions. Winds in excess of a hundred miles an hour shrieking over the tops from Mount Cook, hurling torrential rain and blizzards of snow were far from uncommon. And there had been situations where huts had been picked up bodily and blown right off their foundations. Anything located in this sort of environment needed to be not only constructed well but also securely anchored to the bed rock to keep it from being literally blown away. Our final job before packing up and heading back to base was to angle several Waratah standards deep into the ground either side of the hut, strain up double layers of number eight fencing wire over the roof, and securely lash down what we had just built.

Once we pulled out of Erceg, I doubted that I would ever be back this way again. Autumn was in the air and the possums would be stacking on fur in readiness for the oncoming winter. I needed to get back to the North Island and get myself organised for the new trapping season. The previous winter, Bob Hannigan and I had built a large log cabin in State Forest 90 for our trapping camp. But he was now shooting the Dobson and had indicated that he was going to stay on for the winter. We had travelled south together in his Chev 15cwt truck so if he was staying, I would have to find my own way back. There was much to be done. I had sold my ex army Quad back in Taupo, so I would need to buy another vehicle. The camp was already set up and waiting, but it would need cleaning, stores purchased, firewood gathered, traps oiled and tuned. Doug, Les and Denny loaded their packs and headed off down the river. Maybe sometime they would be back this way again. But I had no such plans and before leaving I wanted one last whack at the Hopkins.

The country was quite rugged up above Erceg Hut, with peaks rising to around seven thousand five hundred feet and plenty of rough craggy stuff scattered throughout in which tahr could hide. The Hopkins shooters had not been this way for some time, in fact maybe for a good measure of time, and some of the animals were needing educating. It was not good having complacent animals lounging round the block. Ever willing to lend myself to the cause, I set out on a one day workshop of enlightenment so that those remaining might be better equipped for survival next time shots were fired their way. Actually, I was not exaggerating about some of them being complacent. I got onto one mob of five tahr and they were not at all hassled when they saw me. I was firing shots at them before they even bothered to get to their feet. But by then it was too late and they all ended up with their tails strung on my belt.

With more time to hand I would have chosen to stay up high seeking out more tahr. But from high up on the Neumann Range I had glassed three Red deer basking on a grassy bench not very far from the terminal face of the Richardson Glacier way below.

Up on the Main Divide, thousands of feet above Richardson Glacier, deep rumbling noises like thunder were intermittently rolling around the crags, and I could see that these disturbances, not unlike muffled rifle fire, were putting the deer on edge. It took me awhile to work out where all the noise was coming from, then I noticed through my binoculars huge blocks of ice breaking off the terminal face of the Charity Glacier and avalanching into the clefts below. These animals at least knew what gunfire was all about. Every time a block of ice broke free at least one of the deer would nervously get up, ears tilted, looking down the valley. Then, as the rumblings faded away, they would slowly settle down once more. They were real toey and getting in close when your animals are already spooked takes time and patience.

Slowly I edged my way down through the boulders. Most mountains are endowed with a host of boulders, and I assumed they were put there during the creative days with future deer cullers in mind. Nevertheless, large numbers of them were incorrectly positioned and right when you need them most, they are not there. That was how it was trying to snuck up on my deer above the Richardson Glacier. For a large portion of my descent there was no cover at all and this meant slowly slipping over large rocks on my backside, trying to watch all three deer at once. Just because their heads are angled away from you does not necessarily mean they won't see you coming. With their eyes protruding out the side of their heads, deer have a wider range of vision than you might think.

The only time I will start shooting at long range is if my animals are already on the move, but as long as they are not going anywhere I want to see the whites of their eyes before I open fire. With little or no cover, you have to move very slowly, never taking your eyes off them, but if you have cover and they cannot see you then move as quickly as possible to close the gap. In this case, I was fortunate. I ran into a patch of large boulders as I was getting close which brought me to within about fifty yards of them. Two sprung to their feet in a panic with the first shot, one lay plastered on the ground. The treble two is a very fast and accurate rifle and those two deer were not going far. They were out in the open on a grassy bench and I was so close they did not have much of a chance.

From where I had just dropped the deer to Apricot Hut, was a distance of about eight miles. That was where my mates were heading for when they pulled out of Erceg, and that was where I said I would catch up with them before nightfall. I estimated it would take at least three hours solid tramping to get there… too far to pack a leg of venison on top of a pack full of tools. Instead I cut out a couple of back steaks and took off into the afternoon haze.

I stopped off at Erceg Hut just long enough to gather up my pack and secure the hut. I had been on the go for hours and a good hot brew would have been more than welcome, but lighting fires and swinging billies all takes time and with the sun getting lower I really needed to keep moving.

There were long stretches of bush edge that verged onto the river flats much of the way to Apricot Hut and I had quite fancied my chances of catching out a deer or two, but a couple of Paradise Ducks put paid to that as they took to flight at my approach and honked their noisy way up and down the valley alerting everything that I was coming. Although it was not in my make-up to go shooting native birds, I could well appreciate why some blokes made a point of eradicating the parry's from their blocks at every opportunity.

Apricot Hut – now renamed Culler's Hut (photo John Fleming)

By the time I sited Apricot, the sun was well down behind the Main Divide. I was feeling a little weary and could almost taste that welcoming brew. But even some distance before I got to it I could tell the hut was empty. Everything was dead quiet and there was that stuffy smell of a secured hut drifting up the flats. Doug had left a note on the table to let me know they were continuing on to Memorial. It made sense. Breaking the journey at Apricot Hut would have meant a lot of extra effort and lost time getting started again the next day. Besides we all liked the home comforts of our new hut at Memorial. It was going to be another fair slog and another couple of hours before I got that brew of tea, but that was okay. In the morning I would have one final whack at the "pantry". It was starting to look a little bare, but with all good fortune there might just be one last trout, compliments Ranger Reardon, to see me on my way.

CHAPTER 3

Getting There

While we had been up the valley building Erceg Hut, Johnny had decided he was going to take me off hut building and put me on shooting. However, it had never been my intention to stay on with the Forestry, and if I had wanted to get serious about it, I would have asked Jock Fisher to sign me on as a hunter in the first place. Hut building had been an enjoyable way of filling in a few summer months. But with autumn fast approaching, it was time to be back on my trapping block. I thanked Johnny for the offer, told him I was moving on nevertheless, and a few days later I was back in the North Island.

Back at Ohau Base, there had been a letter waiting for me from my bank advising that my account had recently been credited with the

Stepping stones. Wayne Blake hunting goats in the Rimutakas as a teenager (photo Bob Hannigan)

proceeds from the February 1966 fur auction in London. The prices I had realized were not quite as good as I would like to have seen, but at least I now had sufficient funds to put a deposit on a Land Rover and get started on the new season.

Aiming on a hunting career. Late 50s in the Ruahines

The type of hunting one pursued was often controlled by the seasons. Whereas deer culling was an all year round job, meat shooting was generally a spring through summer vocation, and fur trapping was for the winter months only. Trapping was my first love and I filled in the summer months waiting for the winter to roll on and usher in a new season. There was something beautiful about fur that I found hard to resist. I loved the feel of it; its softness and warmth. Its usefulness to man can be traced way back to antiquity, to the dawn of history. It would seem that the first long garments of skin were manufactured by the Creator himself, who after ordering Adam and his missus to go get their newly fashioned clothes on, booted the two of them out of their paradise garden into the real world. Bible doesn't actually say they was possum skins, but then again, it doesn't actually say they wasn't, neither.... Point is, fur trapping has been around for about as long as man his self. And that figures, because in some ways fur trapping was a site easier than deer culling or meat shooting. Then again in some ways it wasn't.

There was an element in deer culling that was not often found in other types of employment. Usually the hunting blocks were in protection forest areas... mountain ranges, water catchments and forests that were significantly important to the country they adjoined and usually these areas were at risk of serious erosion problems unless the animals within them were vigorously controlled. Most blocks covered vast tracts of land and although two men were assigned to each block, if you were working on bonus, being paid for the tails you produced, more often than not you went one way and your mate went the other. You probably had a rough idea where your mate was, but that could well be hours or days of travel away through rough mountain streams, broiling rivers and even adjacent water sheds. So when you climbed high and settled yourself down on some monolithic chunk of rock, everything out there as far as you could see, from mountain tops to valley floor and everything in between, was all yours. The bush was yours, the rivers were yours, even the animals were yours, if you could get them. Everything was yours. You were the master of all you surveyed. Well, maybe it was only yours for a season, but that's how life was. People came and people went. Never the less, there was an element about it that was not often found in other types of employment.

But all that aside, culling was also hard work, and often for not terribly good monetary return. Slogging up and down mountains day in and day out, scrambling through bluffs and bush, negotiating waterfalls and icy rivers, often struggling just to clear wages. There were good days with impressive tallies, and there were tough days with nothing to show for it. If you hoped to do good you had to work hard, fly camping beneath rock bivvies and often out in the open with no shelter at all. Trying to keep warm and dry, often cold and wet. Lugging a heavy pack on your shoulders as you slogged your way from watershed to watershed. Rationing food and living out of tins, craving fresh bread and surviving on macaroni.

Most of the blocks had been hammered for years and the office wallahs knew what sort of tallies might be achieved by a reasonable hunter. The bonus system was worked out accordingly. Hence, although a successful hunter might do reasonably well over a season, no matter how hard he worked, the Forestry made sure that no-one ever got rich from the tails he shot. That was one reason why many of the better hunters eventually left deer culling and took up meat shooting. So there was good and there was bad about culling. Generally speaking it was a young man's job. Older men had more sense.

Venison recovery by helicopter did not really get up and running until the mid sixties, although a few shooters had done a bit of preliminary experimenting with it earlier than that. But once it was under way, various companies quickly got in on the act and for a few years at least they largely controlled the business. Their shooters were often the cream of New Zealand's best, but in reality, working under the company system they were little more than cogs in a hard driving machine. If a cog wore out or broke there were plenty more waiting to be slotted into their place. In time some of the top hunters got wise, procured their own machines and a built themselves a legend. That was helicopter shooting.

Meat shooting was different, not with regard to the animals hunted, but in as much as it usually conjured up thoughts of a different type of hunter. Meat shooters, in the sense that the term is applied here, were individuals who hunted the river valleys and bush blocks from Land Rovers, jet boats, pack horses and on foot

Some trial work with the overseas marketing of venison had been done by the end of the fifties, but it was not until the early sixties that it began to gain any real impetus.

***Wayne Blake skin hunting in the Ruahines in the late 50s
(photo Bob Hannigan)***

Bob Hannigan and I were trapping possums for skins on the Wairarapa side of the Northern Tararua's. The bush was podocarp-broadleaf, full of succulent leaves and berries and the adjacent farmlands were fields of clover and paddocks of choumollier. The possums were fat and plentiful and nor was there any shortage of healthy looking deer wandering about in the bush and occasionally venturing out around the bush edges. Back in Wellington there was a ready market for undamaged deer hides in the Thorndon Quay wool stores and the Chinese merchants in Vivian Street eagerly bought all the bye products — tails, bladders and leg sinews — we procured. But as for venison, apart from the occasional back leg that we hocked off to the chef down at the Waterloo Hotel, no one really seemed interested. Our cow cocky mates were ever ready to relieve us of it for their dog tucker, but there was no way that we were ever going to lug great heavy carcasses through supple jack and bush lawyer just for the sake of feeding some cow cocky's dogs. So in those days we shot deer for the sheer heck of it and little more than their back steaks, sinews, hides and tails.

Packing deer skins from Pahongina Hut, Ruahines late 50s (photo Bob Hannigan)

Then I met up with Rex Giles. It was back in 1963 and I had been called away to the family home in Raumati owing to a family bereavement. I was impeccably dressed in a three piece charcoal grey business suit, with my polished winkle-pickers, cufflinks and tie, and about to drive into the city to call on the family lawyer when Rex came by to discuss the possibilities of my dropping off any deer I shot at the Pahiatua butcher's chiller. Rex was in the throes of establishing depots and chillers throughout the North Island and apart from the fact that he was looking for deer carcasses to fill them, he was also looking for men to help get them established and to help get his fledgling company, Consolidated Traders, up and running. I suppose he hardly expected to see some hick from the bush so well presented and during the course of conversation I was invited to join him in his venture.

Rex had this dream of placing a meat chiller in every valley wherever there was a nearby block of bush stocked with deer. My initial job would be to see those chillers positioned. I liked Rex, he was a good bloke, but he was also a glib talker.

"Within five years," he told me, "I will be a millionaire from the export of venison. You will be too if you join me now."

A million pounds was a huge sum of money and I was not convinced that it would be quite that way. Anyway, I had only been free of my carpentry apprenticeship for about eight months and the freedom I was currently enjoying suited me fine. I thanked Rex for the offer but I stuck with my hunting. Within just two years Rex Giles had made his first million pounds!

Shooting the occasional deer for pocket money was hardly meat shooting, and it was not until sometime later that I really got involved. There was nothing easy about this job. The most likely times to catch deer out of the bush was first light in the morning and last light at night. Other than that it was during the hours of darkness using a spotlight. This meant getting up well before sunup, getting back to camp after dark, and often working several hours during the night. If you were not bush stalking during the hours of daylight you were probably trying to catch up on a bit of sleep, and if you did shoot

Venison hunter Errol Brown, packing a stag
(photo courtesy Dave Richardson)

something that was when the real work began. Shouldering huge weights of carcass, knees creaking beneath the load, blood dripping down your back and into your boots, mid morning and your stomach rumbling because you still haven't stopped for breakfast.

Ray Finn wrote off his Trekka when he turned the transverse suspension inside out and broke its back under the combined weight of five massive stags he had dragged through a swamp on Te Anau Downs Station. They dressed out at close on 300 pounds each and what I wanted to know was how on earth Ray had ever managed to carry them through the swamp in the first place, because it was not just a little frog pond, it was a fair sized stretch of swamp.

"I didn't," said Ray. "I couldn't lift my boots because of the suction from the mud. So I got down into the swamp and crawled on my hands and knees with the deer draped over my shoulders."

Could you put yourself in the picture doing that? Well, Ray did it not just once, but five consecutive times. Already tired from spotlighting through the night before he began, by the time he got the first deer to the Trekka he must have been just about exhausted. Then back he would go to fetch the next one, then the next one..... Ray stood up to the strain, but it was too much for his tricky little Trekka.

Fur trapping was different. For one thing it did not entail the same amount of lifting and carrying of heavy weights as meat shooting, but it could be physically taxing nevertheless. There were traps to pack and tracks to cut through dense bush, and a lot of strain on your back bending over for lengthy periods skinning your way through heaps of dead possums. There were torn and bleeding hands from getting snagged on sharp possum claws, and cracked finger joints from working in frost and dirt. And long wearisome hours tacking out skins and clearing boards, and dressing furs. It was a seven days a week job and regardless of the weather, if you had a trap line out in the bush you also had an obligation to go tend it.

But despite having to sometimes work in rough conditions, fur trapping had its advantages. It usually meant living in a warm, dry camp, and being accessible to a store and fresh supplies, which also meant good quality food and looking after yourself. That was certainly a plus, but it was not the reason why it was my first love.

Possums are quite intelligent little animals and they catch on very quickly when they see one of their kind snared in a trap. You therefore have to fool them into believing that the area where you have set your trap is now quite safe for them to walk about. That takes an element of skill and it is known as the art of trapping. Handling and presenting fur correctly so that it becomes a highly desirable and valuable commodity fetching record breaking prices requires an even greater element of skill. It too is an art. Neither skill comes easily and trying to master both makes fur trapping not only a challenge, but also interesting and, if successful, very rewarding.

Deer culling and meat shooting certainly required skill, but in each case, once the animal was dead there wasn't much more you had to do with it other than whip off its tail and ears, or get it to the nearest meat depot.

With fur trapping though, catching the animal was only the beginning. The ultimate objective was to produce fur of such high calibre that it ended up on the catwalks of the European fashion world. And if that was where your sights were set, then you really did have a challenge and rather than being in just another type of hunting job, what you were in was more akin to a trade.

In the most general terms, possum furs were classed as either "mill" or "furrier". Mill was your average possum hunter's fur. It was nothing startling in appearance or quality and it was probably destined for use in the looms of the silk and cotton manufacturing industry. Apparently the mill type skins were cut into strips about ⅜ of an inch wide and placed beneath the shuttles of looms where they acted as a cushion that prevented the thread from breaking. They also turned up on the racks and shelves of tourist shops around the country, manufactured into middling to inferior grade garments along with bedspreads, rugs, hand muffs, soft toys, odds and ends and bric-a-brac, all of which were only as attractive as the quality of fur that went into them, and that was not terribly good.

Furrier grade fur though was something else. London was the fur centre of the world. That was where the finest furs were auctioned, and that was where manufacturing furriers from around the world would go to bid eagerly for parcels of matched and graded furs of this type. From here they might well end up in Italy, New York or Paris fashioned into a magnificent garment, adorning perhaps some gorgeous looking celebrity or draped around some pampered rich lady of the world.

In my book, "Trappers Dogs 'n' Deer (and other critters)", the art of trapping was explained at some length, but I did not explain how to produce furrier grade fur because, simply put, during the period covered in that book I had not the faintest idea how it was done. Dave Odey, an old trapper from Horopito, had got me started in the art of trapping. He also knew how to produce top quality furrier grade fur and he was consistently achieving world record prices for his furs as a result. While visiting his camp, I had seen it, handled it and fallen in love with it, but Dave Odey wasn't saying much about how to achieve it. But from the moment I first set eyes on it, I had determined that one day I too would produce fur of that quality. I realized that certain key factors were involved in its production, some of which I knew, others of which I would have to find out. It was a real challenge, but that was where my sights were set. And with that as a goal, that was what made fur trapping not only interesting but also my first love.

With the cold months of winter behind us and the possums already in full moult, Bob Hannigan and I had been idling away a bit of time waiting for the ears on our skins to dry off so we could get them baled up ready for shipping to London. The ears were left on for cosmetic reasons only. In reality they were quite worthless, but as Dave Odey had explained: "They not only look good, but the fur buyer can see at a glance the pelt is complete; nothing missing or trimmed off." If it had not been for that, we would already have been packed up and headed south for the summer. But for the sake of a few ears and improving the appearance of our skins there was an extra two to three weeks of hanging round camp at the end of the season.

We were a mile or two from Clements Camp, sitting alongside the road one afternoon, enjoying a brew of tea at Arthur Hay's batten splitting camp, when this fellow turns up hoping to talk someone into buying a Land Rover. Colin Campbell was his name, and he worked for Cable Price in Rotorua.

At the time I was getting about in a Second World War 1942 Ford V8 4 x 4 truck. Thirsty and slow, it was a real blitz of a machine, with a top speed of 28 mph and a fuel consumption of only 7 miles to the gallon. But for lumbering around the forest it was spot on. SF90 always did attract more than its fair share of townies and private shooters. Friday evenings in particular they used to come burling through the forest in their townie cars, driving like their backsides was on fire, ploughing round corners and humping rises in the road completely oblivious to anyone might be coming the other way. Sitting up high in the cab of that old World War Two Quad, strapped down safe in the driver's seat, encased in armoured steel and a huge chunk of channel iron bumper sticking out front, I wasn't overly concerned about meeting someone head-on coming round some blind corner. No one ever actually killed themselves in so doing, but from time to time, if one was looking one might notice a car load of very white faced private shooters continuing on their way at greatly reduced speed towards the Hinemaiaia. You see, Friday evenings was the usual time they drove in to the bush, and Friday evenings was also the usual time I drove out of the bush to pick up my mail down the Rangitaik' Pub. But despite its being a wholesome nice and comforting piece of machinery, the old blitz left much to be desired when it came to touring the main highways. Colin left me his contact details and I told him I would get in touch if I ever earned enough money from my skins.

That was the end of the previous winter, and now I was back in the North Island with Colin Campbell and he was demonstrating a Land Rover that he thought would suit me and my somewhat limited budget just fine.

Looking at it from the financial angle he was probably right, but sitting in the yard at a somewhat higher price, there was something else had caught my eye. A neat little '63 SWB Safari Wagon that was only two and a bit years old, had been owned since new by some old fellow who used it to do his shopping in, and its upholstery still smelled like it was new. At $1,650 it was considerably more than I could afford, but having sat in it, and driven it, and checked it out, it was no longer so much a matter of whether or not I could afford to buy it, but more a matter of feeling I could not afford not to buy it. The deal was done. Colin shouted me out to dinner in a swank downtown restaurant, and early next morning I started off for the long haul back to Omarama to go pick up my tool kit and hunting gear where I had left them in Johnny Reardon's safe keeping.

The Chinese merchants in Vivian Street had been crying out for deer sinews. The last time I had dropped a few off to them they were very pleased and gave me the best price they had ever given. Apparently there was a shortage of deer bye-products back in China and my Chinese friends assured me they would pay "Velly good money," for all that I could bring them. Most meat shooters whipped the dewclaws and sinews off the legs of their carcasses and I knew that with the increased meat shooting activity now under way every meat shooter's camp would be bound to have heaps of them hanging up to dry. At the prices my Chinese friends were indicating, I should be able to offer the shooters a better price than they would otherwise be likely to get, and make enough out of it for myself to pay for my trip down South.

At the beginning of the summer there had been only two helicopter gangs operating in South Westland, but things were hotting up. More people were getting in on the act. Big money was involved and wherever that is so, trouble is never far behind. There were vast amounts of unshot territory throughout the ranges and in the headwaters of all the valleys, but just about everywhere I went, as I drove through Westland and into Otago, I heard stories of choppers encroaching on one another's territory, and valley shooters getting anxious about the impact the choppers were having, or were going to have, on their means of income.

There was a dispute in full swing as I passed through the Makarora Valley. A meat shooter was airing his grievances with the resident helicopter pilot and, for possibly the first time there was someone threatening: "If it ever happens again, I'll put a bullet through your bubble!"

By now I had a fair stock of sinews piled up in the back of the Land Rover. I decided to call it a day, head for Omarama by way of the Lindis Pass and then north to my trapping camp at Clements.

The winds were howling through Cook Strait by the time I reached Marlborough. The bloke at the terminal in Picton reckoned that it was marginal whether the "Aramoana" would be sailing, but they loaded us on anyway, and we ploughed through Tory channel and out into the murk and froth of a filthy black night.

People sprawled in companionways and huddled on floors wherever they found room enough as we heaved and lurched our way into the storm, and in a short while the sour stench of vomit filled the ship from end to end. I think if they were not throwing up from the violent movement as the ship pitched and rolled and tossed about, then they were doing so out of fear as she creaked and groaned, her bow buried deep in a trough with her stern rising out of the wake, screws screaming in the froth and bubbles. They were not a very communicative bunch, all scattered about the decks like a bunch of dead chickens as I made my way round the ship a couple of times looking for someone to talk to.

Sea sickness had never been one of my weaker points, but you couldn't get away from the stench of it and the smell was getting at me and starting to make me feel crook too. Then as I wandered past the salon for about the third time, I poked my head in and noticed one solitary passenger propping up the bar with a mug of beer. I think there was only he, the steward and me left standing, and the steward said he was just about to close up for the night, but he wouldn't mind staying open for a bit longer if I wanted to join them for a beer. And while he plied us with meat pies and scrambled egg sandwiches which no one else seemed very interested in, my shipboard mate introduced himself as Robbie Ballantyne, owner of a crayfishing boat down Bluff. Well, that accounted for why a bit of a storm in Cook Strait was not upsetting him too much. Where he worked, down there in the Roaring Forties, was one of the wildest stretches of water in the world. While we was eating and talking, and pouring beer down I got to learning that when the cray season started next summer, Robbie Ballantyne planned on taking his ship, the "F.V. Tarawai", round the coast to Fiordland and working pots off Charles and Caswell Sounds. I had always fancied the idea of working on a crayfishing boat. The thought of working on a crayfishing boat right in the thick of Wapiti country was almost unreal. We kept on eating and talking, and pouring beer down, and before we had parted company that night I had extracted a promise that next summer, when Robbie sailed out of Bluff heading for Fiordland, I would be crewing for him as third hand on his good ship the "Tarawai".

As we sailed up through the relative calm of Wellington Harbour a few of the dead chickens started perking up a little and looking as if they might have received a second chance at life. Feeling good from the beer I had drunk, and exuberant at the promise of not only a job on a cray boat but also the opportunity of working in a part of the country that very few people ever got to seeing, I wandered about the deck full of good cheer, offering scrambled egg sandwiches to anyone whom I thought might be feeling peckish after losing it out in Cook Strait. They was a weird bunch on board that night. A little old lady, who just didn't look the sort, said a very rude word at me, and a bloke who didn't look all that seedy started spewing all over the deck once more. So let them starve. I sat down where they could all watch and began stuffing scrambled egg sandwiches into my own mouth.

I learned a valuable lesson in Wellington.... Never trust a Chinese merchant. Well, never trust a cunning old Chinese merchant anyway. Apparently, in the short time that I had spent driving round the South Island, an amazing thing had happened. Mainland China had become swamped with deer sinews. They were everywhere. No one wanted them any more. But just to help me out, my merchant friends would buy all that I had, but for only about half the price they had been paying previously.

I stocked up with food and supplies from the wholesalers and took off out of Wellington as quick as I could. Never did care very much for cities. Besides time was flying. Easter was already upon us and had it not been for all the wasted time travelling round the country qualifying my name and exploits for tabulating in Confucius' book of Chinese proverbs, I could already have been fetching furs into the log cabin. In the colder areas possums usually came into good fur in March, and March was been and gone.

CHAPTER 4

Back at Clements

It was Easter Thursday, going on midnight, when I pulled up outside Chief Ranger Lou Scudder's residence in the Forestry Camp of Sixty Bar Eight, sixteen miles down the Napier-Taupo Highway. The pines of Kaingaroa were glistening with frost beneath a near perfect moon, the Sika stags were rutting and roaring and SF90 was fair crawling with highly strung private shooters, fresh from the city, all itching to lob shots at what-so-ever twitched, identified or not.

SF90 was, and most likely still is, notoriously known as the most accident prone block of bush in all of New Zealand, and as delighted as Lou was to see me after my summer's absence, there was no way that he was going to issue me with a permit to enter the forest until after Easter weekend was gone and so were the townies with their empty ammunition packets and their billies full of bullet holes. He needed a little coaxing.

"What a helluva time to turn up for a permit." Lou muttered through gritted teeth when he saw it was only me who had dragged him out of his nice warm bed, and not some townie blowing the whistle because his mate had just got shot. "Come back after the weekend. Some time after the sun's up and we've all had breakfast."

"Sorry Lou," I returned, "But I just had to see you right away. I have an important message for you from one of your mates down Harihari."

"Yeah! What's that?"

"You remember Lester Bell? Well he told me to be sure to say 'G'day' to you next time I was passing through Sixty Bar Eight."

"Damn it all man. Do you mean to say that you woke me up in the middle of the night just to tell me that?"

"No, not really. Actually I woke you up so as you can make me out a permit to head back into Clements and keep an eye on my gear in case some loopy breaks into my camp during the long weekend," I replied.

"There's been a whole summer during which time someone might have broken into your camp," Lou rejoined.

"Thanks Lou. Greatly appreciate your having looked after it for me. I was actually heading back in that way, so I can take over from here. Now if you'll just make out that permit, then you can go hop back into bed."

"Next time you come waking me up in the middle of the night just for a permit," Lou growled, "I will have you blacklisted from every block of bush in the Conservancy." And then in a softer tone: "You remember when you first came into my office last year what I told you and your mate about accidents in that forest. Well Easter weekend is the worst possible time to be in there. I'll make you out a permit, but it is going to be conditional. I want your word that you will stay in your camp until Tuesday morning when most of the private shooters should be gone. If they want to shoot themselves that's their affair, but I don't want one of you young fellows stopping a bullet."

"That's fine, Lou. I'll probably have my work cut out chopping firewood and getting the camp reorganized. And thanks for the permit."

Home sweet home. Back at Clements (photo Bob Hannigan)

The rickety old hut on Clements Clearing, that had been our home during the previous winter, was just as we had left it. We had not even bothered putting a lock on the door before driving out of the forest, feeling that no one would want to use it anyway. If someone needed a roof over their head, there were better huts lying abandoned around

Trappers Camp at Clements (photo Bob Hannigan)

the clearing than my clapped out old shack. But the log cabin we had
built for a skin shelter had attracted somebody's interest. The solid
brass padlock securing it had been smashed off the chain and the
door left swinging. We had not left anything of much value in the
shelter apart from our traps and tack out boards, and thankfully they
were still there. If anything had been stolen it would have been some
item of little value, but the real loss was realising that the days of
trusting and believing in people, something that had always been part
of back country life, were quickly coming to an end.

The hut had collected that stuffy musty smell about it that huts do
when they have been closed up for awhile, but that soon disappears
once the door and windows are left open to air it out and the wood
range is fired up and left burning for an hour or two. The log cabin
had been built solely for use as a skin shelter, and although it had a
door either end, there were no windows built into it, making it quite
dark and closed in. This was ideal for keeping out the damp and
holding in the heat when drying skins, but it too needed a good airing
out and fires lit in the two fireplaces either end of the building to chase
out any mould that may have accumulated since it was last used.

Up until sometime during the previous winter, Clements Camp
had been Hurlihy's batten splitters' camp. And Arthur Hay and his
sons were still working the forest, felling and splitting red beech for
posts and battens. There were huge heaps of rejects piled up and
scattered about the forest wherever the gangs had worked and Bob
and I had collected heaps of these rejects back to our camp by the

truck load the previous winter for firewood for the log cabin. There were still large heaps of it outside the log cabin waiting to be used, but the kindling bin needed replenishing. The camp also needed a good scrubbing and the bulk stores I had purchased on my way through Wellington needed to be stacked on shelves and under the bunks. Then my traps needed checking and tuning; the notch into which the trip-piece slotted needed to be checked for wear and if necessary filed nice and square, the plate realigned level with the top of the jaws when the trap was loaded. Most of my traps were fine, but they all needed checking anyway.

Tuning traps. Trap plate on the left is too low and needs raising. Trap plate on the right is too high and needs lowering

Raising the trip plate

Lowering the trip plate

The trip notch has been filed nice and square

A perfectly tuned trap, plate level with the top of the jaw

True to my word, there was enough to do cleaning and maintaining gear and generally preparing for the new season to keep me occupied close to camp for the weekend. And as I pottered about, preparing and thinking about the new season, a couple of pertinent points came to mind.

First, gathering limited amounts of firewood in the back of a short wheel base Land Rover was not going to be anywhere near as convenient as throwing a couple of tons at a time on the back of the old 4 x 4 Quad had been the previous winter. Now that I no longer had the old truck for doing all the dirty work I really needed a trailer to take its place.

And second, driving round SF90 in a nice shiny Land Rover was leaving me a sight more vulnerable than had been the case when I had been perched up nice and high in the old blitz wagon, encased in armoured steel and with a great chunk of channel iron bumper sticking out the front. For peace of mind and an element of security I needed a solid galvanised crash rack bolted securely on the front of the Land Rover. Both matters would need attending to before the winter got too far underway.

I had trapped my way through a reasonably large tract of bush during the previous winter, but the amount of country still unworked was huge. And with Bob not going to be around to work his block

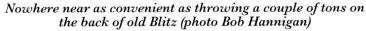

Nowhere near as convenient as throwing a couple of tons on the back of old Blitz (photo Bob Hannigan)

that made the available territory far greater than I could ever get through in the course of a winter. In effect, with the exception of Jack Bramley's block that took in the area from the Army Road to the Hinemaiaia Stream, I had the whole of SF90 to myself. But the area that I favoured the most was up on the big broad ridges above Mill Road, and that was where I planned on getting started

The handiest to camp piece of unworked territory was not far along the road from Clements Clearing — a ridge that climbed out of Jack South's watershed towards the Te Iringa track. The stream draining the watershed was actually called the Waiharuru, so I suppose the real name of the watershed was also the Waiharuru. But Jack South had been splitting battens and living there in an old bush hut, long enough for it to be called after him. To my knowledge, he was not under contract to anyone in particular, but he was a handy old fellow with an axe. The battens he split were true and straight and Hurlihy seemed happy enough getting them. Jack was quite happy with his own company and he used to keep pretty much to himself, but I took a liking to him, and if there was smoke coming out of his chimney as I drove past I usually stopped off to see how he was getting on and have a bit of a chat. Jack told me he did not care too much for one or two of Hurlihy's younger batten splitters. Reckoned they were a bunch of loud mouthed cowboys. But he took a shine to me and one day he gave me a light weight splitting axe that he said I might find useful. I never told Jack, but I had no real use for it and I ended up giving it to

Bob, who still has it tucked away in his garden shed to this day.

For old Jack, the watershed was merely the place where he felled and split huge old red beech giants of the forest. He never knew that Bob and I called the watershed after him. And it probably would not have meant anything to him if he had. I never saw him again after the winter of '65. Unfortunately, when Hurlihy's splitting gang pulled out of SF90 sometime during that winter, the old timers like Jack South drifted away too. Looking back, I wish now that I had spent much more time talking and drawing him out. Old timers like Jack, were living history. They had been working bush back in the days of bullock teams and horse drawn bush trams. Once they were gone, the forest was no longer the same without them.

There was a bit of a snig track that ran alongside the stream a short distance into the watershed just up from Jack South's hut. It was a good place for parking the Land Rover out of sight, because if no one ever told you, neither would you know there was a track there. Most townies were not necessarily prone to reading roads and few of them would ever have noticed the wheel marks ducking in behind the scrub. But living in the forest and wanting to know what was going on, reading roads was the natural thing for me to do. I wanted to know whether any vehicles had passed along before me, whether they had been and gone or whether they were still down the road. If you knew someone else was in there, you also knew there was a possibility of being shot at. So for me, reading roads wasn't just a hobby, it was a necessity. And that was a point that even my old mate Jack Bramley might have missed.

One evening Bob, me and Kim the dog were driving back into the forest in Bob's Chev 15cwt after doing a bit of shopping in Taupo. Coming or going, we usually timed it to get to the edge of the forest just about last light as, often as not there would be a Sika deer or two had wandered down off Cherry ridge and was out grazing the flats where Sika Lodge now stands. Jack Bramley and his mate, Gorgeous Gordy, were parked in Gordy's station wagon on a pumice siding with their parking lights lit up making themselves obvious and drinking a flask of hot coffee just about the spot where Clements Road starts climbing out of the monoao and into the bush.

There wasn't much got past our eyes, and as we pulled alongside to say "G'day!" the first thing we noticed was Gordy had a spotlight plugged into the dashboard and Jack had his rifle propped between his knees.

"We were going to do a bit of spotlighting," Gordy said, when Bob raised the subject, "but a car load of townies got ahead of us. Ruined the place flashing their spot all over the flats before we could get here, then shot off into the forest."

"Shooting's stuffed for the night," said Jack. "We're just finishing our coffee then we'll be heading in to the Rabbit Patch."

None of us cared too much for private shooters spoiling our territory. A few comments were passed regarding the indeterminable ancestry of private shooters in general, "Goodnights" were said, and we started into the forest.

Without even thinking about it we were looking for the "townie's" fresh tyre prints on the road in front of us. Interesting. There were none to be seen. It wasn't hard working out what Gordy and Jack had in mind. Bob and I looked at each other at the same time and start to laugh. "Don't slow down," I said. "Keep going 'til we get to the top of the ridge."

At the top we were already out of ear shot and there was room to turn the Chev. Quickly Bob plugged his spot into the dash, while I hopped out and began rolling the canopy back. Then while he finished off tying everything down I loaded up my Sako Vixen and climbed up behind the cab. We came charging back out of the forest, careered past Gordy and Jack still draining the dregs out of their coffee, enveloping them in a cloud of pumice dust as we tore by. I was set up to go with the treble two cradled across the spot and Bob knew exactly where to slam on the brakes to give me a clear view across the flats. I bowled two deer straight away. We slowed down just long enough to mentally mark where they had gone down, and took off into the night once more, this time heading for the back road to Woody Collin's and the clearings leading to the Pirua Gorge. We picked up a couple more on the way. Later we back-tracked and using Kim's infallible doggy nose located and collected the two deer we had earlier bowled off Sika Flats.

Meanwhile Gordy's tracks on the road read that "someone had gone ahead of him and ruined the place flashing their spot all over the flats before he could get there", the "Shooting was stuffed for the night," and "he and Jack had packed up their coffee and headed off into the Rabbit Patch to retire early for the night."

Back in Jack South's watershed, I parked my Land Rover at the end of the snig track and pushed into the forest carrying forty traps and a slasher. Generally speaking the slasher did not get much use. There were not many places where you had to cut tracks in SF90, and I preferred leaving the bush the way it was. But here and there thick patches of horopito needed a way cleared through them.

Down through the course of time, old Jack South had felled a good number of big old trees in his watershed, but there were still plenty left standing. Possums always work their way through the forest travelling from big tree to big tree, and that was also the way I worked when setting my traps. It did not pay to rush once you started laying them out. If you took your time you didn't miss much, and the sets you chose would more likely be productive. That was because if you weren't charging through the bush like an idiot you had more time to decide what was likely to be a good set and what was not. It also meant you had time to become familiar with the distinguishing features of the various trees where your traps were placed thus reducing the likelihood of misplacing any. Just about any of the forest giants were potentially good sets for traps. Red beech, silver beech, miro, matai, kahikatea, totara, rimu, it did not matter much. If there was a possum pad going past it was a good place for setting a trap. Quite often if big trees were close together and possum pads ran past all of them I did not waste time trying to make a decision. I simply loaded a trap at each tree and let it sort itself out. Within a few days it would be apparent which pads were not regularly being travelled and I would pull the traps out from those sets and move them on to the end of the line. But of all the various species in the forest, my most successful sets were often on the ancient old red beech trees. For some reason the possums seemed to favour these trees and night after night they would produce kills.

Forty traps was not very many. Within a few days the line would consist of eighty to a hundred. But ensuring they were on good sets and nicely covered with clean, soft humus took time. So getting forty into the bush on the first day was a reasonably satisfying effort.

I began my line at the first big old tree I came to. It was good practice to remove all the unwanted rubbish, bits of pumice and loose sticks a trap chain length and an outstretched possum, from

Dirt is chopped out of the pad and removed so trap can be lowered and positioned beneath the surface. (Trap setting sequence next 7 photos by Lance Keightley)

the vicinity of the set. It was not always practicable to do so, but you could be sure that if you did not, the first possum you caught would drag everything within reach back onto the set, possibly damaging his fur on the bits and pieces in the process.

The trap needed to be quite close in to the trunk of the tree. Possums, being nocturnal, have good night vision, but they also have strategically placed touch hairs on their faces, wrists and even their ears, which help them navigate through the night. As they travel, these touch hairs brush past the buttresses and root systems of the

Gather a good handful of humus from beneath a rotting log

Plate supported with a stick, humus positioned close to front of trap

trees telling them where they are in relation to the tree and ensuring that they do not go dragging their fur out on bits of bark as they move about. This factor needed to be taken into account when setting traps. In other words when possums travel, they travel close enough to the trunk of trees to allow their touch hairs to brush the tree. That is also how close the trap plate needed to be to the trunk.

Possums are very intelligent animals and once one has been seen by his mates caught in a trap, not many others are silly enough to want to go playing round with one. For this reason the only effective way to set traps is to bury them completely out of sight. Each trap needs to be set down into the ground so that once it is covered there is no irregularity in the pad surface that might discourage a wary possum from stepping on it. This becomes more important as the nights progress, the set has been catching for awhile and the possums become more spooked. If possible the handle of the trap should be tucked in out of the way, so that any possum using the pad will not get put off by stepping on it. If there is a buttress in the trunk then I would usually tuck the handle in behind it. With everything roughly positioned, I stapled the end of the chain as low as possible to the trunk, again taking care to make it as inconspicuous as possible. I loaded the trap, positioned it where I wanted it to be, then went looking for some good healthy humus to cover the trap.

The dirt that had just been chopped out of the pad was no good for covering the trap and I never used it for that purpose. Bits of pumice, bits of stick, lumps, stones and all sorts of rubbish could be mixed up with it. Somewhere nearby there would always be an old rotting log, and if you dug beneath this you would find all the rich black humus you required. Once more the tomahawk was brought into play to thoroughly chop up a good handful of it which I then carried back to the set. Carefully I placed the humus as close to the front of the trap as possible and, supporting the plate so that the trap did not spring on me, I then spread it neatly over the trap, covering everything in the process... plate, jaws. handle and as much of the chain as possible. To finish off, I levelled everything off with a little stick that I had cut from a horopito for the purpose. The next large tree in the general direction that I wished to travel would be my next set.

Travelling thus, taking my time, getting to recognize the peculiarities and distinguishing features of each tree as I went, I could set as many traps as I liked out in the forest and it would be rare indeed to lose even one of them. The limiting factor was the time it took to work a large number of traps, not the likelihood of misplacing any of them.

The first day of a new trap line was not such a big day. But after this, for a few days at least, each consecutive day became progressively heavier going.

In order to get off to a good start with my tallies, I needed a further

Spread the humus evenly over the trap with one sweeping movement.
Totally cover all parts of the trap.
A covered trap should be absolutely undetectable

Tidy the set by gently smoothing the surface with your stick

thirty or forty traps out in the bush the following day. The first night's return off the initial forty traps would likely produce somewhere around 35 possums. But they would not all be worth keeping. Probably there would be a few roughies with "windows", or patches of missing fur, as well as the odd "kittens", or young undersized possums, amongst them. Some trappers let these go in order to catch them some other time when the quality of their fur had improved or when they had grown to maturity. But I found that often as not, if you released a useless possum one night you ended up catching him further down your line a night or two later. Perhaps this was not the case with uncovered traps, for a recently released possum with a bruised leg was not normally silly enough to go stepping onto another trap sitting on top of the ground too quickly. But when your traps were undetectable beneath a layer of dirt, it took a smarter than average animal to figure out that a bit of soft dirt might also be associated with another trap. Catching useless possums the first night was bad enough. I did not want them coming back for a second time round. So I never released them.

I worked my way along the line from trap to trap, killing animals and resetting traps as I went. Warm possums tend to lose their fur very readily, so they have to be left until they are cold before skinning them. I carried them by their tails, five or more in each hand, to a convenient site close to the line and cached them beneath tree fern fronds until the following day. On an average line I probably cached every fifteen or so traps.

Carrying dead possums by their tails

The second day out on a new trap line, because there was only freshly killed animals that were too warm to skin, there was time available to start pushing in the next thirty or forty traps. Third day out, there was now the previous day's cooled down catch to skin, eighty traps to work, and if time allowed, ten or twenty more traps to push in. Somewhere about the middle of the day I usually took time out to polish off a flask of tea and a few sandwiches. Working head down bum up all day was heavy going, and you needed something under your belt to keep working on.

From here on the work load did not finish out in the bush. Now there was also possuming work to be handled back at the camp. The day's skins needed to be tacked out, and every day from here on was going to be solid going. Up to a hundred traps to work, heaps of possums to skin, hands scratched and bleeding from sharp claws, thumbnails bruised from skinning tough animals, and traps that were not doing well pulled out and continued on at the end of the line.

Back at camp the work would be mounting too. As soon as the skins were dry enough they had to be removed from the boards and stacked over wires to air out. This meant pulling out nails, scraping off fat and oil, rubbing the skins with bits of sacking, trimming them off the board, cutting open the tails. Then when you had cleared enough boards for tacking out the new lot of skins, away you went again, tacking out the new lot.

Back at Clements, there were not many days where I was cleaned up and finished before ten o'clock at night. Often, I would still be going early hours of the morning trying to get everything done and out of the way so that I could start afresh the new day.

As previously mentioned, in some ways fur trapping was a site easier than culling or meat shooting... then again in some ways it wasn't.

Fresh killed possums are cached to be skinned the following day. Completely cover with ferns to protect from hawk, stoat and fly damage

CHAPTER 5

Guns 'n' Tallies

Jack South reckoned there was a wild cat "bigger than a cocker-spaniel dog" used to live up in his watershed. Gave him "the woollies, prowling about in the shadows" close to his hut some nights. There was something odd about it, he said. "It ain't no normal cat. Ordinary cats don't come as big as that. Nor do their eyes light up luminous green even when there's no light reflecting off them." Like most bushmen's yarns, I took it with a grain of salt.

From time to time I caught wild cats in my traps, along with an assortment of other unwanted vermin such as hares, hedgehogs, stoats, fitches, rats... even caught a tourist once when he started poking round in the dirt where I had set my trap under a big old rimu up in the Te Ponanga Saddle between Tongariro and Turangi. But they were all much the ordinary sort of rubbish that one might expect to find cluttering up one's traps any old day of the week. Prior to working in Jack South's watershed though I had never snared a demon. It gave me one heck of a fright!

I was working my way up through the bush, nothing much different to any other run of the mill day. Trap line had been producing well and rotting carcasses were mounting up in heaps where I had been skinning out my caches. My next set was a big old totara with a trap placed on the top side as the spur went. So I had to come in from the blind side of the tree to check the trap. I noticed that there seemed to be an unusual amount of shredded bark as I approached the tree, but I was hardly expecting to be suddenly set upon.

Next instant this huge snarling black critter comes burling out from behind the tree, eyes blazing, spitting and hissing like a snake. I think if his back leg had not been anchored to the tree, he would have had me in little bits and pieces. He recoiled back on the trap chain, then came lunging again, chain taught, clawing the air trying to get at me. Most wild cats caught in a trap, tried to take off in the opposite direction when they saw you coming. But not this one. He was mean and nasty, and about as big as a cocker spaniel dog. Can't say his eyes were actually lit up like fluorescent tubes, but they were certainly blazing. I reacted just like I would have if some private shooter had come jumping out of the bush levelling his rifle at me. I charged in with my tomahawk and whacked him fair between the ears. He went down with blood trickling all over the ground, but I wasn't taking any chances with this demon having maybe eight or nine more lives up his sleeve. I thumped him several more times just to make sure.

Where he came from and why he was so huge, I do not know, but the following day, when I left my Land Rover parked at the end of the snig track, I was carrying my Jungle Carbine just in case his mum was up there contemplating pay back.

Following that little episode I fell back into the habit of packing my carbine out on the trap line. Not because I anticipated being attacked by wild cats, but because of the numbers of private shooters poking round in the bush.

I had been given a shake up the previous season when a couple of privatees had come snucking up on me unannounced, and after that it never happened again because in that environment you only needed one wake up call to put you in a state of constant alert. Henceforth I always kept the carbine nearby, because it was my policy that if anyone ever fired a shot in my direction and missed, they would not get a second chance. It was the fellow that might not miss with his first shot that worried me.

Weekends had gotten particularly bad. Droves of privatees were finding their way into the forest, and eventually it reached the point where I felt I was better off hanging around camp during the weekend rather than risk my neck out on the trap line. Naturally this had a detrimental effect on my tallies. In retrospect though, I probably should have just carried on out in the bush. In those days, shooting a privatee was not terribly expensive. You got fined more for shooting a native pigeon than for shooting one of your hunting mates. But there was time loss involved convincing the judge you had mistaken him for a deer. From what I had observed that was simple enough. All you needed to do was say, "Sorry Judge, I mistook him for a deer!" The judge would tell you to be more careful next time and not to do it again, and fine you about $100. But it meant a trip to town, and I couldn't really be bothered with all the hassle. So weekends I hung around the log cabin working on my skins and getting madder and madder at the private shooters who had gotten to so effectively disrupting my routine.

Some weekends I would take off out of the bush altogether and drive up to Rotorua to get away from it all.

Harry Vipond, who was the NZFS Senior Ranger in Rotorua, reckoned I was living dangerously trapping possums in SF90. At one time he used to hunt Sika in there, but not any more. It had gotten too dangerous. Apparently Harry regarded me as not only reckless, but also amusing. "Why come out of your block for a break if you're going to come straight round to my office asking for another one to go back shooting into?" he used to laugh. But Harry knew I was no different from most other young hunters. Usually he had some development forestry block or other locked away where he knew there were likely to be a few easy deer wandering about and he was always happy to give me the key to the gate and leave me to it. Sad to say, a few years down the track, in a "safer" block of bush than he imagined SF90 to be, whilst sitting on a log taking a break, Harry was shot and killed by a private shooter who "mistook him for a deer".

Harry was not the only one of my mates who got taken out that way. Norm Ridge, co-owner of the River-Ridge meat packing plant in Taupo, was another. He was in the Waipakihi during the roar, dragging out venison on a tractor, when he copped it.

A few months earlier, in the spring and early summer, Bob Hannigan and I had been floating carcasses out of the same valley on inflated tractor tubes and when it got around that that was where Hannigan and Blake had been getting trailer loads of deer from, Norm and another fellow decided to work the valley during the roar.

At the inquest the judge seemed quite satisfied with the explanations, but I recall the story that emerged had one or two professional hunters raising their eyebrows.

Apparently Norm had chosen one side of the valley to hunt and his mate was supposed to stay on the other. Norm had shot a roaring stag and was dressing it for dragging down to the river flats when his mate comes along and "mistakes him for a deer". As the story went.... After Norm shot his deer, he removed the head and stuck it up on the bank close by. He may have given a roar or two to try and entice another deer to roar back. Meanwhile the other fellow, for some inexplicable reason, crossed the river to where he knew Norm was hunting, and came snucking up on him. He claimed he saw the deer head sitting on the bank, noticed movement below, where Norm was still gutting the carcass, imagined the head and movement belonged to a living deer, let drive and nailed Norm. The fine was the customary "somewhat less than for shooting native pigeons" and the fellow was admonished to "be more careful next time and see that you do not do it again."

Carrying the carbine around the trap line was insurance but it was also a bit of a nuisance, and nor was it likely to produce any deer. After wandering about in the same patch of bush for two or three weeks, rattling traps and thumping possum heads, there were not usually any deer still hanging about. But that was not necessarily always the case.

One night I was loaded to the gunnels pulling out all my traps and loading them into my Mountain Mule frame pack as I came back down the ridge. It was getting towards last light and I did not want to have to come back the following day so I was packing everything into the one load. If you bundle loose traps into a pack they take up a lot of space, but threading nine of them neatly onto the chain of the tenth there was not much problem getting eighty traps plus a few skins into my Mountain Mule. That was a pretty good load in itself, but I also had another chain of traps for either hand and fifteen fresh possums as well.

Thread nine traps, alternately face up and face down, onto the chain of a tenth trap. This way none will slip from your grip and get lost (photo Lance Keightley)

Earlier in the day I had deposited the first two chains of uplifted traps on top of a log, for picking up last as I worked my way back downhill to the Land Rover. The fifteen fresh possums were the final kill off the line and again, I did not want to go back the following day just for them. So they too were included in the load.

Carrying possums by their tails fur to fur with your hand wrapping the prehensile bit, it is possible to carry quite a few at a time. In this case I had eight in one hand and seven in the other, leaving just one place left for the Jungle Carbine — swinging in front of my chest with the sling draped around the back of my neck.

The final haul to the Land Rover was only a couple of hundred yards, but the weight I was struggling under was just a bit more than I could handle. The only way I could get moving was to hoist my pack on top of the log, position the dead possums and two lots of traps to each side in such a way that I was able to move off from a more or less standing start. Somehow I managed to get mobile and shuffling under the strain I started off in the failing light towards the road. About fifty yards of agony later, I came into an open patch and walked straight into two deer. Sometimes you have to wonder just how smart some animals really are. Sika do not usually hang around for long. But these two just stood there looking at me, almost as if they realized that loaded up the way I was there was no way I could get at my rifle. I also knew that once I dropped everything I was carrying I would never be able to get started again. The seconds ticked away while I stood there looking at them and they stood there looking back. Finally I could bear it no longer. All that venison just standing there on the hoof, and so close to the road was too much. I dropped the possums and chains of traps to the leaf mould, grabbed for the carbine, and both deer melted into the forest and disappeared. It was already dark by the time I got to the road with just my rifle and pack load of traps. I am sure those two deer were still grinning next morning as I drove back through the forest making a special trip for two chains of traps and a couple of handfuls of dead possums.

Sometimes before starting a new trap line I would cruise the area with the treble two looking for any easy deer that might be hanging out in the area. But this time I blew it. I had a beautiful little stag lined up in my sights and still do not know how I missed. All I could come up with by way of an excuse was the bullet must have deflected on a twig. But nor could I really be sure that I had not simply thrown the shot. I felt that a bit of off hand shooting practice was needed to get my confidence back and make sure my eye was right.

From my hut doorway to the sign post gracing the entrance to Clements Camp was approximately fifty paces. An ideal distance for the sort of off-hand shooting practice that I had in mind. The idea was to get straight out of bed in the morning, grab the carbine and fire three off-hand shots at a tin hanging beneath the road sign, followed immediately with another three shots from the treble two. No matter whether I hit the target or missed, three reasonably rapid fire shots from each rifle was all I would have any one morning. I started with a milk powder tin filled with dry pumice dust.

When I first bought the carbine, it was in its original military condition. I wanted it for close range bush shooting, so I immediately set about hacking it down to size. Only the barest of essentials were required, so all the military encumbrances, such as the bayonet connection and flash guard, were removed. The barrel was shortened by a further one and a half inches and the timber was tuned back to a wisp along the forearm. There was supposed to be about 2,400 foot

Never noticed anything extraordinary about the old carbine in the heat of battle

pounds of energy propelling the bullet as it left the muzzle, but by the time I had finished whittling it down there was probably only about 1,200 foot pounds of energy expended out the front of the rifle, the remaining 1,200 pounds came out the butt end in the form of recoil. With real close range shooting it did not really matter whether you hit the deer or not, the bang was enough to frighten anything to death. It also permanently deafened my dog and gave me inner ear deafness. Other than that, it was just about perfect.

Trouble was, and I only learned this when I began target shooting from the hut doorway, it also had me near frightened to death just using it. It was the same weapon I had used three years earlier when culling goats in the Kaikouras, and back there, in the heat of battle, I had not noticed anything extraordinary about it. But standing in the hut doorway, gently taking up tension on the trigger, waiting for that moment of shoulder wrenching, deafening concussion... well it was different. A little bit of self discipline is good for you though, and I needed plenty of that each morning to force myself to fire off those three shots one after another. In comparison, firing the treble two was just a dream.

It is amazing how quickly one gets one's eye in with a bit of practice. Within a few days I was hitting the tin with at least two shots out of three with the iron sighted carbine and consistently hitting it with the scope mounted Sako. In a short while there was not much tin left hanging to shoot at. I needed something a bit more challenging. I removed what was left of the milk powder tin and replaced it with a Highlander condy tin. Again, within a few days I was consistently finding the target. It was too easy. I needed more range.

From the hut doorway, angling across the clearing to the opposite side of Clements Road, I could just scrape in a hundred yards of unobstructed shooting range. Again, I started with a milk powder tin.

At a hundred yards, the front sight of the carbine completely blocked the tin from view, but as long as it remained out of sight behind the bead there was a pretty good chance of scoring a hit. The Sako Vixen, with its dead flat trajectory and fine cross hairs reticle, was far less complicated and once again, after about a week of blowing holes through the milk powder tin, I was ready for reducing the size of the target.

From here on you could forget about the carbine. For one thing, when I tried to line up I had no idea where the condy tin was in relation to the sights and further, even if I could have seen the tin, I doubted that the carbine's sawn off barrel would have grouped tightly enough to establish anything. The end of the matter was, it was a relief not having to use the old Three O any more. My nerves were frazzled from the constant concussion and I was beginning to appreciate that eighteen inches from ear drums to muzzle blast was way beyond the comfort zone.

It only ever frazzled the nerves when used for target practice (photo Bob Hannigan)

The whole purpose of the exercise was to get my eye back in and rebuild my confidence after missing an easy shot, and from that point of view I had achieved what I wanted to do. I was not having much trouble consistently hitting the condy tin out at a hundred yards with the treble two, and the very next time a deer popped up in front of me in a gut high up on the mill face, I took careful aim and clean missed it at less than thirty yards.

The carbine proved just a bit too vicious for shooting tins. Using it for hunting was different because the shock waves got soaked up in the heat of the moment. Sometimes you see the shock waves ripple through a deer when it is thumped with a heavy calibre bullet. And if it has been raining and the animal is wet, as the shock travels out from the point of impact you will often see spray flying off the animals hide. That was what I felt like three shots in a row, shock waves rippling through my body, shooting at those tins with the carbine. But even that was nothing compared to the walloping I got from an elephant gun someone once gave me to play with.

I was round the back of Terraces Hotel dropping some venison off to the chef one morning when the manager came out and invited Bob and me into his office. He wanted to know if either one of us would be interested in buying an old rifle off him. His grandfather, or great uncle, or some other of equal vintage had resided in India at a point of time when it was necessary to prove one's manhood by destroying as many tigers and elephants and buffalo as time and circumstances reasonably allowed. However time and unforeseen occurrence had put paid to the era of the jolly old Raj, the old timer had hung up his pith helmet and riding boots and his jolly old bang stick had been handed down to the next generation who in turn had handed it down to the next generation who was now wondering what one does with an elephant gun in a country renowned for its dearth of wild elephants.

I did not really have much of value to offer on the subject. But I must say I was quite impressed with grandpa's piece of chosen weaponry. In layman's terms, there was room enough to lose one's little finger down the barrel. The cartridge it fired was shaped like a cigar and of somewhat similar proportions. The projectile was a huge chunk of lead, something between .550 and .575 calibre The rifling was in reasonable nick but the bore was somewhat pitted from the corrosive powders that had quite likely never been properly cleaned out after use. Having once fired the gun I could fully appreciate how such neglect could occur. One does not normally rush around looking for cleaning patches and a pull through when one is lying unconscious with a dislocated shoulder and a shattered collarbone. However, with no inkling of what I was letting myself in for I asked if I could fire off a few rounds to see how it grouped.

There was no safe place on the hotel grounds for setting up a target, but just beyond, on the side of the Napier-Taupo Highway, there was a spot where you could sit on the road edge and fire back into the bluff beneath the hotel grounds.

It was a rare occurrence indeed having something as interesting as an antique elephant gun to go firing shots through, and there was no way that either of us was going to miss out on such an opportunity. It was later that we learned no one had fired the gun since grandpa's day. No one else had ever been game to try.

Seeing I was the one most interested in buying it I had first shot — at a piece of pumice stuck in the bluff. I know there was a concussing thump as it fired. But I do not remember much after that. My right arm was completely numb and I could no longer see the target for the muzzle blast and shock waves. Bob was meant to be spotting for me, to see where the shot went.

"Shikes! What the hell happened there? Where's the target gone?" says I.

"There's a bloody great hole where it used to be," says Bob in reply. I was still a bit dazed from the concussion.

"I can't even see the bank where I was shooting at," says I.

"Well that figures," says Bob. "You wont find it looking about ninety degrees off to the right."

It was a bit too close to town for a gun of that capacity. In those days there was no armed offenders squad stationed in Taupo, but in emergencies they could always call in the army. Nevertheless, Bob insisted on having his shot at the bank. I could not believe the damage it did. With a few shots you could just about form yourself a comfortable little bivvy big enough for sleeping in. Bob reckoned one shot was enough to establish what he had thought from the beginning: "It would probably be less bloody painful just letting the wild elephant charge you down and walk all over the top of you!"

If I was considering buying it, I still wanted to know how it grouped though. The manager gave me a handful of rounds and said it would be okay to take it back into Clements. A few days later, when my vision had recovered sufficiently to see the road and my arm had regained enough feel to drive the Quad, I returned the old musket to its owner at Terraces Hotel. After the first shot there was never enough left of the target to group a second shot alongside it, and apart from that, I had come to the same conclusion as Bob, that it would be more fun being run over by an elephant than actually shooting them with a gun like that.

Enough of play. I had possums to catch and furs to ship. The first sale of the season was due in May, but having started late, there was no way I would have a representation in that one. The next was in September, and allowing for the fact that it took several weeks for each shipment to reach London, I needed my consignment dried, brushed, packed and on the wharves in Wellington no later than the end of June. I needed to keep up my tallies to meet the deadline.

Tallies were everything and I doubt there was a possum hunter did not like talking about the great tallies he took from time to time. During the summer of 1961, when I was still an apprentice carpenter and living in Wellington, a bounty hunter I met in the Urewera told me he had taken 400 possums off a poison line in just one night. At the time the Government was still paying a bounty on possum tokens; half a crown for the ears and strip of skin down the centre of the animal's back. Four hundred tokens equated to fifty pounds from the night's effort. Not too bad. At the time a fully qualified carpenter earned only twenty one pounds a week.

There used to be an old culler's hut on the side of the road right at the top of the Huiarau Summit where the Maungapohatu Road heads off along the top of the range to Rua's Stronghold. Bob and I had packed our sleeping bags and rifles and hitch-hiked from Wellington to Rotorua and into the Urewera. We had ended up staying in the old culler's hut after Russ Tulloch had driven us up there from Ruatahuna. There were no cullers using the hut at the time, but Eric Vosper, the aforementioned bounty hunter was.

Huiarau Summit deer culler's hut (photo Bob Hannigan)

According to Vos' there was no shortage of possums. There was no shortage of deer either. They were popping out of the woodwork everywhere. But Vos' said the cullers were on wages and in his opinion, culling for wages was not much of a lurk. The pay was not all that good, and he and a couple of his mates had chucked in shooting for the potentially more lucrative job of bounty hunting. Things had been going pretty well for Eric Vosper until the day he gave himself a dose of cyanide.

We were sitting in the hut one morning, having breakfast, when Allan Duncan turned up in his Land Rover. He was possuming somewhere near Lake Waikaremoana and he had driven up to check Vosper out because he had heard about the cyanide and how he had nearly karked out. We all piled in to Dunc's Land Rover and took off along the Maungapohatu Road because Eric wanted to show Dunc' where he had dosed himself. We pulled up near a set of skids and climbed out onto some logs where there was a view that went for miles

Deer were popping out of the woodwork everywhere

down a long leading ridge.

"It was way down there," said Eric. "Best line I ever laid. I'd already taken 400 off it when I copped a dose."

I remember Allan thinking it was rather amusing, but I wanted to know how it had happened.

"I'd been whipping off tokens all day and I was pretty well stuffed." he told us. "I stopped to roll a fag and there must have been a bit of powder on my fingers. Next thing I was rolling in the leaf mould, gasping for air. Fortunately I managed to break an amyl nitrate capsule or I would have been had it."

Vos' said he was so crook he just lay there for a couple of days waiting for the effects to pass off. And when he was finally able to stay on his feet without falling back down, he was still so crook it took him the best part of a day just climbing back up to the road.

"They reckon once you've had a dose, that's it," Eric went on. "You become susceptible to it, just like an allergy. And if you even get close to it, it'll get you. Right when I was really making money, too!"

About that point of the conversation we lost interest in Vosper's brush with death. Bob had noticed a deer browsing out to the right and tried to get a shot away while teetering on the end of a log. And as he fired two more deer that must have been sitting right underneath the skids we were balancing on shot off in another direction. Dunc' thought that was amusing too.

We hung around for a few more days shooting deer just for the heck of it. Then early hours of one morning, when it was still pitch black, Dunc' said he was heading back to Waikaremoana and if Bob and I wanted a lift we could come with him. It was a dead calm night and there were dozens of black possums waddling all over the road as we drove toward the lake. They probably all died of old age because not long after that the Government removed the bounty off possums and Dunc and Vos would have been out of a job.

I never ran into Eric or Dunc' again. But the last I heard of Eric he was somewhere down the West Coast. And Dunc', who is well known as one of New Zealand's top hunters, returned to culling and later shot the Wilkin for venison. In time he bought his own helicopter and also became one of the country's top chopper operators.

Anyway, Vosper's tally was about the most I ever heard of, taken in one night.... But hang on a minute Vos'. You said you whipped off tokens one day, then you lay around in the leaf mould for two days and you took another day climbing up to the road. That is not one night's effort. That is four nights.... Well, there was another bloke I heard of reckoned he took 300 in a night....

In actual fact it was not your top tallies that meant much, but your daily averages over sustained periods and ultimately the entire season. Also of course, in the final analysis, what really mattered to the fur trapper was the quality of the possums he was catching. And in this regard a whole lot of factors came to bear.

The Australasian Opossum (Trichosurus Vulpecula), as the animal's common name implies, was introduced into New Zealand from Australia where it occurs naturally throughout the mainland, Tasmania and some of the neighbouring islands. In their native land at least eight subspecies of possums have been tabled and these vary somewhat in size, colour and fur quality. Introductions to New Zealand were sourced from various Australian localities, some documented, some not. As might appear obvious from this brief resume, where the possum came from therefore, had considerable bearing on what you got once he was liberated in his new locale. But it does not end there.

To produce top quality fur the possum needs not only top quality food... of which he found no shortage in the succulent vegetation, both virgin and second growth, throughout New Zealand's indigenous forests... but also a cold and extended winter environment.

There were any amount of possums wandering about in State Forest 90, so maintaining reasonable tallies was not too difficult. But they were not a terribly good breed of possum and nor was the area as cold as some other parts of the country. Some nights fair crackled with frost and during the coldest months a good southerly blow might dump a few inches of snow, but the cold was not what you would call intense. Nor was it prolonged, and as a result the possums never really seemed to stack on fur. As well, the colour of SF90 possums was nothing startling. About sixty percent were greys, but they were not good clear greys. And the size was only middling. So the quality, at best, could only be middling.

But there is still one other factor to consider.

Even middling fur, if handled properly, can be made to look good and still fetch quite good prices. With fur, the situation is this: When a possum is wearing its fur coat it looks pretty good. For the fur trapper, the challenge is making the same fur look just as good if not better after it has been tacked out and dried. And that is not necessarily the easiest thing to do. When on the possum, the fur is distributed evenly all over the animal. After being tacked out, most trapper's furs look "all ass and pockets" — too much fur bunched around the haunches and too little around the shoulders. That was how my furs looked too. How to distribute the fur evenly was something I was yet to figure out.

Meanwhile, the weeks were slipping by. But as long as no major mishaps occurred I felt quite confident about making the September sale. Lost weekends aside, the skin shelter was looking quite healthy. Heaps of boards were swinging from the chicken mesh waiting to be stripped. Stripped furs were piling deep on the wires waiting to be brushed and combed. Brushed and combed furs were piling on the bench ready to be restacked on the wires where their ears could finish drying. And when that was done, then they could be baled ready for export. The shortest day was drawing close and everything was on cue.

CHAPTER 6

Punchy Passing Through

Thin wisps of mist swirled in confusion amongst the tops of the trees as a cold gust soughed through the clearing, preening a shower of leaves from the adjacent forest. It was late in the day, with dirty weather rolling in from the south, and I was glad to be getting back to camp where I could fire up the wood range and get a brew going.

I never used to bother locking my hut while I was out in the bush, leaving it accessible for friends to wander in and make themselves at home while they were awaiting my return. Not that a lot of friends came visiting way out in the bush, but that was the way all of us were back in those days. I was not really expecting any visitors though, so I got a bit of a surprise to see smoke wafting from the chimney as my camp came into view.

There were no new tyre marks on the road as I turned in past the Clements sign post, and I was wondering how anyone could have got here, so many miles into the bush, without a vehicle. It was still going through my mind who it could be, when this fellow must have heard my Land Rover crunching up the pumice and came out of the hut to meet me. I had only ever seen him once before, but I knew straight away who he was.

It was back at Terraces Hotel once more. The Quad was parked out back with a couple of deer and a rather large old boar lying dead with bullet holes on the tray, and I was in the kitchen talking the chef into buying them off me. There was a ready market for venison and wild pork in town at River-Ridge Game Packers, but the chef at Terraces paid better than River-Ridge, and along with the better price I also ended up perking the skins because he usually asked me to hang the deer up in the meat safe and skin them for him. The chef and me struck a deal that had us both satisfied and I wandered outside with a grin all over my face to fetch the pork. The grin quickly disappeared when I saw what was happening on the back of my truck.

This same little bloke, who was right now stepping out of my hut to greet me, was up on the back of the Quad climbing all over my

On the way to Terraces (photo Bob Hannigan)

venison and pork with a couple of frothing pig dogs. One dog was latched onto the pig's ear, trying to rip its head off one end of the body while this bloke was grabbing hold of a back trotter on the other end, violently tugging and shaking and trying to make the pork look as if it still had a bit of life in it, while at the same time sooling the other mutt, which was furiously barking and slobbering and ducking in and out doing a good job of taking pieces out of the pig's neck and nose.

Some blokes would have gone straight for their guns, but there was already enough blood on the tray, and besides that, I wasn't really sure that the judge would accept my story that I had mistaken the bloke and his two pig dogs for a mob of deer. I was unaware of anyone ever having any problems with that one out in the bush, but on the back of a truck parked almost in town outside a tourist hotel!?! Well, I couldn't be sure. I did the next best thing that came to mind:

"Hey! What the hell do you think you're doing!" I bawled out. The bloke stopped tugging on my pork.

"Is this your truck?" he asked. " We were just admiring the pig."

"That's nice," I replied. "Would you like to admire the receiving end of my Three O while you're at it?" The bloke hopped down off the Quad, called his dogs off, and smershing contentedly all over his face disappeared back into the pub while his dogs slunk beneath the hedge panting and dribbling slobbers of happiness.

"Not a bad pig," he called back at me as he disappeared from view.

Later, I was telling Jack Bramley what had happened, and when I described what the bloke looked like he said, "Sounds like Punchy! It's a wonder he didn't hang one on you for being cheeky."

"Who? Me, being cheeky? C'mon, it was my pig he was interfering with."

"Well they don't call him Punchy for nothing. He's been known to flatten people for less."

Punchy Wallace (photo courtesy of Punchy)

Punchy greeted me "as nice as pie". Came out of my cabin grinning all over his face and shaking my hand. Said his name was Punchy

Wallace and he had dropped in for a brew, and hoped I didn't mind him making himself at home and brewing up a billy.

"Na, Your welcome, " I said. "That's why the hut is left open."

"I found a tin of gingernuts and a pound of butter in the meat safe. Do you want to come in and join me for a brew?" he asked.

"Thanks a lot, Punchy. Real nice of you," I replied. "Yeah, I think I will. Haven't we met somewhere before?" I could tell as soon as he had set eyes on me that he remembered me, but he wasn't letting on.

"What was your name again?" he feigned. "No I don't think so."

Obviously Punchy wanted to forget the incident. On the day it happened, I had got a bit ruffled witnessing Punchy's dogs chewing on my pig, but after I had cooled down I saw the humour of it and got to chuckling every time it came to mind. Now that Punchy realized whose camp he had just made himself at home in, it was probably an embarrassing memory. Anyway, neither of us ever touched on the matter again.

I soon realised that there was also another reason why Punchy did not want to get me upset. He was in a wee spot of bother and he needed a friend. The police were looking for him because he had jumped alimony. He had been lying low in the Kaipo until someone had potted him, and he had only just managed to avoid being nabbed.

A couple of police officers had been sent in to arrest him, but Punchy had got wind of it and he had managed to grab his pikau and battered old Lee Enfield and had taken off down the flats heading in the direction of the Ahimanawas just ahead of them. Half an hour later he doubled back past his camp under cover of bush, this time heading for the Kaimanawas. Working his way into SF90, he snuck along the Te Iringa track then sidled down through Mill Face and set up lodgings in my camp. He was pretty sure the cops had seen him going in the direction of the Ahimanawas, so he did not think they would be looking for him around Clements.

"You know, those cops are pretty stupid if you ask me," said Punchy. "Because I have no money to pay maintenance to my missus they want to put me in the jug. If they do that then they are going to have to look after me and feed me and that is going to cost them money. It's not costing them anything while I am out here in the bush. What they should do is stop wasting their time and put the money it would cost to keep me locked up into the alimony account instead. Anyway," he added, "they will never catch me. They are too stupid for that."

I did not want to involve myself in Punchy's personal affairs, but nor could I see what advantage it would be to anyone incarcerating the poor guy. I was the sole resident at Clements Camp since Hurlihys had pulled out, and I was more or less looking after the place. I told him to make himself at home and choose whichever hut he wanted.

He said he would not be a nuisance, but he would be grateful if he could hang round for awhile until he figured things out. I told him he would be welcome to stay as long as he liked.

"I didn't have time to pack much into my pikau," Punchy told me. "If I shoot a few deer would you be able to drop them off in town when you go. All I need is a bit of bread and some tea. You can keep the rest for yourself."

"That'll be the day!" I replied indignantly. "Anything you shoot is yours. Make out a shopping list and I will get whatever you need. Hell, I wouldn't want to take any of your money."

Punchy was in quite a bad way when he turned up at my camp. Because he did not know who had potted him nor did he know who he could trust. He told me he had not eaten for a day or two and he was tired and hungry. I felt sorry for him. I told him to get stuck into the gingernut biscuits while I got a billy full of spuds and a tin of peas on the boil. There was a camp oven full of pot roasted possum legs sitting on top of the wood range. And in no time at all we would have a feed going. Even if it was not very flash, my cabin was warm and cosy. I told Punchy to bunk down for the night on Bob's old bed, and he could sort out a hut for himself in the morning

Barry Hurlihy's old hut was by far the best accommodation on the clearing. It was spacious, had a good water tank and a wood range that never smoked even in the foulest of weather. Unfortunately it was right at the opposite end of the clearing and too far from the

Across the clearing to Punchy's hut (photo Bob Hannigan)

log cabin, or I would have taken it over for myself when the splitters pulled out. Cooking food on one side of the clearing while tacking out skins on the other, and trying to get back and forth battling wind, sleet and snow in the middle of the night did not make much sense. Punchy had a quick look over the huts and said Barry's one would do just fine.

In a short time I had grown quite fond of Punchy. He and I got on well together. Most of the time he was out mooching about in the bush hunting deer, and I was out on my trap line. But when he was back at camp he spent most of his time with me, and he was a good bloke to have about the camp. He made himself useful and never had to be asked to do anything. Dishes, kindling, sweeping the floor, peeling the spuds — he just got up and did it. He knew the bush and he was quite handy with a rifle, and in a short while he had a couple of Sika carcasses hanging up in the silver beech out back of the camp waiting for my regular Friday trip to town.

Punchy was quite concerned that the cops might get wind of his batching up at Clements, and lay in wait for him while he was out in the bush. He reckoned if they started nosing around Hurlihy's huts and got to seeing his gear they would straight away start speculating that Punchy was passing through. So rather than leave it to chance, during the day while he was away hunting he would load everything into his pikau and stash it unobtrusively in the log cabin. On his return he would approach the clearing from a round about way so that he could thoroughly check everything out before venturing out into the open.

Night times he would hang around the skin shelter getting in the way, stoking the fire and watching me tacking out and working skins. And if he ran out of yarns to relate and started asking too many questions about trapping possums and handling skins I would tell him it was time we had another brew, and away he would go back into the cabin to get the billy boiling once again.

A short way out back of my cabin I had an active rubbish pit, and quite often when I got up in the morning there would be fresh pig prints around it where the resident wild scoofter had dropped in for his midnight snack. He was a cunning old devil and I never set eyes on him, nor even heard him snuffling about in the pit, but I always knew when he had been there. It wasn't long before Punchy also noticed the prints.

According to Punchy, it would be the easiest thing in the world to get this pig. All you had to do was set up a race and position a rifle in it in such away that as soon as the pig entered the race he would trigger the rifle and shoot himself in the head.

I wasn't too sure of anything quite as serious as setting up loaded rifles, but Punchy dragged me out back and explained exactly how it could be done. It certainly looked as if it would work the way he explained it.... Fence off the rubbish pit with a wooden stockade. Form a short race with a narrow entrance just big enough for the pig to get through. Bait the race with a rotting possum carcass. Position the rifle so it was aimed at where the pig's head ought to be. Tie a piece of string on the carcass that looped back to the trigger. And as soon as the pig interfered with the possum carcass.... Pork!

The idea sounded good enough, and I could not see much harm in Punchy entertaining himself with building stockades and pig races while I was out of the way working my traps so I said to go for it. The only improvement that I could offer was to make sure he lashed the rifle down firmly and pointing away from the camp, so if something went wrong no stray bullet could come flying through the walls of my hut. Having a rifle going off right outside my sleeping quarters in the middle of the night was going to be bad enough without having to duck from flying bullets as well.

Over the next couple of days he did a great job. Punchy had spent the best part of his working life out in the bush and he knew his way around with an axe and a maul. The whole thing was a work of art. Obviously it was going to take a day or two for the pig to get used to this new addition to the rubbish pit, and I remember jokingly asking Punchy what he was going to use for a rifle while his was lashed into position in the pig race and the pig was coming to terms with how he was going to snuck in for his midnight snack.

"I can't use mine. I've only got one rifle and I need that for hunting deer," he replied. "But you've got a spare one sitting in the rack. How about if we use your carbine for a couple of days?"

It is rather difficult explaining to one of your mates that you are not willing to share a commodity that you are not even using, when your mate is obviously in desperate need and he has only got one of his own which he cannot afford to be without, and now he needs a second one and your spare one is lying surplus in a gun rack gathering dust. For the second time in about as many days, but this time against my better judgement, I told him to go for it. I would make do with the Sako out on the trap line

While he was getting it rigged, I got myself preoccupied in the skin shelter, well clear of what I reckoned was the danger zone. I could somehow just imagine Punchy requesting me to juggle the possum carcass into position while he set up the string, and the holes ended up blown through the top of my head instead.

I was relieved when it was all over, with the carbine lashed securely into position, carefully aimed at where the top of the pig's head ought to be when he got interested. Punchy said we just had to wait now for a few nights while the possum got ripe and the pig got used to the change of scenery.

I guess the pig must have been a bit weary of it all because nothing exciting happened over the next few nights, and after that I didn't give it much more thought.

Most of the private shooters who came into SF90 headed straight for the Hinemaiaia Forestry Hut down the end of the road. But one day I came in off my line and there was a car load of them batched up in Punchy's residence. Of course Punchy's gear was not in it, so I suppose they did not know it was his residence. But that made little difference to Punchy. He was hopping up and down with agitation at their audacity and just itching for me to turn up so as we could go over and toss them all out on their necks. I was about as agitated as Punchy. Private shooters batched up in the Hinemaiaia Hut four and a half miles down the road was quite legal but it was still about four and a half miles too close as far as I was concerned. Having them right on your doorstep, camping on the very same clearing, was intolerable. Let them feel at home and before you knew it there would be bullets ricocheting off the frog pond while they were sighting in their rifles and goodness knows what all after that. Anyway, the huts on Clements Clearing were private property and they had no right using them. Punchy insisted that we go and confront them straight away while I was all worked up and in an agitated frame of mind, because if I stopped for a brew I might calm down and then the effect would no longer be the same.

It is not too difficult telling the difference between an angry dog and a docile one just by looking. It no doubt works the same with trappers, hunters 'n' co. The privatees realised that Punchy and me was a little ruffled before we even spoke. There was three of them met us on the doorstep and told us if we wanted to come in for a brew we could, but if we were thinking of making any trouble we could, as they put it, "turn around and piss off back to where you've just come from!"

I told them they were trespassing in private property, so they could pack their gear and they were the ones could do the "pissing off". Punchy said I was wasting valuable minutes reasoning with them and I'd got my priorities out of order. By now they should have already been dragged out of the hut and had their heads thumped. After that, says Punchy, would be soon enough for explaining what we had come for. At this, one of the townies started to give Punchy a bit of lip, and Punchy, who had one time been a pro-boxer, was just shaping up for a king hit when this other smart ass townie ups and says, "Incidentally, we've taken the number of that old .303 you guys set up on the track over there, and it's going to be handed in to the police with a formal letter of complaint about your hazardous use of firearms."

Whatever I had been about to say stopped dead on the tip of my tongue. I looked at Punchy, and Punchy looked back at me... rather sheepishly.

Then this same townie says, "It's bloody lucky we noticed the string running through the manuka when we did or we all would have had our legs blown off."

I couldn't believe it. Punchy had got sick of waiting for the pig to come to the rubbish tip, so he had decided to go meet it on its own territory. He had set up my rifle in the scrub with a string across the track so that whatever walked into the string would get blown away. Yes, it most certainly was "bloody lucky" they had noticed the string. The fight was over. We had just been felled without a blow. Utterly embarrassed I backed off. Punchy, deprived of the joy of thumping hell out of them all, toddling dejectedly in tow. The townies soon packed up and took off in the direction of the Hinemaiaia. They must have got the impression they were not too welcome. And Punchy and I sat down over a hot cup of tea and discussed some of the basic rudiments of rifle safety.... My rifle safety.

Punchy was still batched up at Clements a week or so later, when Bob Hannigan unexpectedly turned up. It was now the height of winter, and down south everything was blanketed beneath feet of snow. The last few weeks in Southern Lakes Conservancy had been all crampons and ice axes, and what with massive snowdrifts blocking the side creeks and bluffs covered in sheets of ice, wind slab snow and avalanches the conditions were too treacherous to safely continue. The shooters had pulled out for their winter break. This time when I came off the trap line and saw smoke wafting out of the chimney I wasn't left guessing as to who it was. Bob's unmistakable Chev 15cwt was parked in front of the log cabin and sitting on the woodblock, eagerly anticipating my return, was my old mate Kim, the dog.

Bob could not have turned up at a more opportune time. There were more than a thousand skins piled up in the log cabin ready for export, and if he could drop them off at the wharves as he passed through Wellington on his way back down south it would save me a trip. His timing was opportune from Punchy's viewpoint too. Ever since those private shooters had threatened to pot us with regard to the carbine incident his nerves had been all frazzled. He imagined every vehicle driving into the bush along Clements Road to be a potential raid by the local constabulary, come to arrest me because my rifle had nearly blown the legs off a bunch of dozey private shooters, and him for being party to the cause as well as jumping alimony. Punchy said Clements was getting a bit too hot and it was time he moved on. In Bob he could see a means by which to do it.

Bob could only stay a few days. I had written and told him how the influx of weekend shooters was affecting my work schedule and he realized that I may not return to SF90 once the winter was done. He had come to get his trapping gear and take it back down to

Wellington.

The days went by quickly with Bob on the block. It was good to have his company out in the bush, helping with the traps and yarning about shooting the Hunter Valley where he had been working for the last few weeks. Night times he and Punchy got the dinner going while I got on with my work in the log cabin, and when the pots were simmering he would come out and help strip boards while Punchy stoked the fire and got in the way trying to lend a hand. The three of

Bob had been working the Hunter Valley for the past few weeks (photo Bob Hannigan)

us would talk about shooting country, and Bob and I would remember something funny that had happened in the past and we would all start laughing and relating yarns about various hard case block mates we had worked with and experiences we had had. And we was usually still laughing and spinning yarns well after Punchy had gone to his hut and we had crawled into our sleeping bags and extinguished the pressure lamp for the night, until finally, the sound of snoring indicated that no one was listening any more and that was it for another day.

All too soon it was time for my old mate and his dog to be heading back to their culling block. We loaded Bob's trapping gear... tack out boards, traps, and other bits and pieces of his... out of the log cabin, along with my bales of furs, and Punchy's pikau and his battered old Lee Enfield, into the back of the Chev.

Punchy then took me to one side and confided that he was changing his identity for awhile. He said he was moving to where nobody knew him, and with an assumed name he should be alright. The name, Don Subritsky, appealed because he had never met anyone with a name like that before, and to his knowledge Don Subritsky didn't have a wife so alimony wouldn't be a problem. He said that hanging round my camp, he had learned enough about possum hunting to see him right, so he was heading off down the Wanganui River and going possuming. We all shook hands and said "Goodbye". Punchy thanked me for looking after him, and said I was a good mate and he knew he could trust me. Then he shook hands once more and re-introduced himself as "Don Subritsky". Then we had to shake hands one more time, because Don Subritsky was just passing through and I needed to say "Goodbye" to him too

Shortly after breakfast, Kim piled in on top of all the gear and the three of them drove out of the forest, Kim sitting in the back and Don Subritsky sitting up front chipper as a bird dog.

Because Punchy was a well known identity in and around Taupo, the agreed plan was to steer well clear of the town, turn south as soon as they got to the lake and get out of the district as quickly as possible. But as they drove down towards the Napier-Taupo turnoff, Punchy got to thinking about his treasured possessions he was leaving behind. Out back of a mate's house, tucked away in a garden shed, was Punchy's record Sika head, and his photo albums and things. They were almost to the turnoff when Punchy asked Bob if they could make a quick detour to his mate's place so as he could grab his photo albums before they headed south. Driving through Taupo with him sitting up front would not be a very good idea, he said, so if Bob could pull over and let him hop in the back with the dog.

Punchy gave Bob directions how to find his mate's place and added: "Back up the drive of the house next door, and keep the engine ticking over, because if you stall and can't get her started again we're dead meat."

By now Bob was getting a little edgy, wondering just what sort of a mess Punchy was getting them all into.

"As soon as you pull up," he continued, "I'll jump out the back, climb over the fence, grab what I want out of the shed, and as soon as I'm back in the truck give her the gun and don't stop 'till we get to the other end of the lake. Everything should be fine,' he reassured Bob, as he was climbing into the back, "so long as my mate's old woman isn't around. She and my missus are cobbers. She's usually out though, and she wouldn't notice your truck anyway. The old battle axe is as blind as a bat!"

It was a quiet part of Taupo, and there was no sign of life as Bob pulled up outside the neighbour's front gate and gently eased the truck into reverse. From the driver's position he could not really see what was going on in Punchy's mate's place, but he took some consolation from Punchy's assurance that the old girl's eyesight was just about shot. Slowly he backed up the drive as far as he could and as he eased the truck to a stop he felt the movement as Punchy jumped out from beneath the canopy. With one fluid movement, Punchy vaulted the fence and disappeared out of sight into the shed. And that was when Bob noticed the "old battle axe, blind as a bat" standing behind the sheets hanging from the clothesline, not missing a trick as Punchy hurdled the fence and shot into the shed.

Quick as a flash, the old girl took off for the house, presumably to either grab a shotgun or hand crank some action out of her telephone. Bob nearly jumped out of his skin. He piled out the front of the Chev to alert Punchy just as Punchy came staggering back out of the garden shed, weighed down with an arm full of photo albums and a massive eight point Sika head, all covered in dust and cobwebs.

"Get a load of this Bob," he hollered. "You ever see a Jap head like this before?"

"Pile into the bloody truck and let's get the hell out of here." Bob retorted. "Old Bungeye was standing over there watching you breaking into her shed and I think she's gone for her shotgun!".

Punchy dropped his prized deer head right where he stood and vaulted back over the fence and nose dived into the back of Bob's truck, photo albums still tucked under his arm. Franticly, he began digging around amongst the possum bales. Bob could only think he was searching for his Lee Enfield and a handful of ammo.

As deftly as his shattered nerves allowed, Bob laced up the canopy and tied the cord tight with Punchy now bailed up inside. Racing to the front, he piled back in behind the wheel and gunned the old Chev down the neighbour's drive and out onto the road. Pumice dust spurting and billowing out from the wheels he careered round the corner heading for south and as he took one last look back down the street in his rear vision mirror he saw what had to be a patrol car entering the street from the far end.

Unlawfully entering premises, burglary, Punchy in the back with a loaded gun....Bob took off out of Taupo in a panic. Somewhere beyond Hallets Bay the Chev got a flat tyre, and after a lightning pit stop he told Punchy to leave his rifle in the back and get in the front with him. One had to think of how this might be affecting the dog back there with all these bad associations forced upon him.

"Can't quite figure that out," said Punchy as they took off at high speed towards the Desert Road. "Never thought the old girl could see that well."

Bob wasn't listening. His immediate concern was getting to Wellington, and getting lost in amongst the people and the traffic.

CHAPTER 7

Fish 'n' Chips

With Bob and Punchy gone things soon settled back to normalcy. Streams of private shooters continued to buzz back and forth through the forest. Trap lines were worked out and new ones established. Once more the log cabin began piling up with work that never seemed done.... Green skins to tack out, boards to strip, dry skins to scrape and rub down, fur to brush and comb, new heaps of finished possum skins stacking up on the airing wires.... The old familiar routine, and I was right back into it. Day in and day out life seemed rather typical. Sometimes it rained and sometimes it didn't, but it didn't make much difference. The trap line still had to be attended no matter what, the previous day's caches skinned, the skins tacked out and hung up to dry, and twenty to thirty boards cleared and made ready and waiting for the next day's catch.

There were long hours involved in trapping and, because it was a winter job, no shortage of dirty weather and wet bush for floundering through. Sometimes when conditions got particularly bleak, I would give a thought to all those office wallahs back in the big smoke, with their cushy 40 hour week jobs; coffee and cakes for morning tea and bellies full of hot soup and roast lamb for lunch. But it never rained forever, and when the weather came right and the forest smelled fresh and sweet, and the song of bell birds and tuis filled the air, then I would give a fleeting thought to those same flabby office wallahs, hemmed inside their stuffy high rise buildings, breathing one another's germs through the air conditioning systems, and the hustle and bustle of traffic, and carbon monoxide filling the streets.

Trapping was long and tiresome work. As long as the trap line was producing furs the work went on. Eight or nine hours out on the trap line was only part of it. Back at camp few were the nights where I completed my work in the skin shelter before ten o'clock and often it would be midnight or after. If the catch was good there would be lots of skins to tack out, and whether it was or not there would still be lots of dried skins to strip in preparation for when it was. Tacking out and stripping boards, both jobs were time consuming and neither could be put off until later. But getting home in the evening was a natural break in the day's work and the first matter to attend would be to get the wood range fired up and a brew going, then get stuck into a thick slice of bread and honey. And once that was taken care of there would be dinner to prepare; vegetables to cut up and meat to cook. The days were too short to sit around waiting for dinner. Once on the range, most meals were left to look after themselves while I went out to the skin shelter to get a fire lit and begin turning tails with a wire spoke.

Dave Odey used to tack his skins out kneeling on the floor of his cabin in front of the wood range. Turning tails his way, he would poke a piece of wire into the ashes through the grate of his wood range then slide the wire up into the tail from the end nearest the pelt. The ashes supposedly made the inside tip of the tail grip on the wire and then Dave would draw the wire back, turning the tail inside out as he did so. I turned my tails by starting from the opposite end, the tip end, of the tail. I never could get the hang of how Odey did it. Ashes or not, I could never get the inside skin of the tail to grip on the wire. But it was easy and fast turning tails my method. Either way, Odey's or mine, first you needed to nip off the tip of the tail before getting started. So that was the first thing I did when I got into the skin shelter at night, nipping and turning tails.

The warm dry air created by the huge open fire of the log cabin was great for drying skins, but if a green skin began drying before it was tacked out it could ruin. To ensure that this did not happen I always made sure that nothing of the flesh side was exposed until it was ready for going on a board. Usually I piled them in a heap on the huge old rimu dining table I used for a workbench and systematically worked my way down through the heap. But if time was dragging on and there was a possibility of premature drying they were bundled back into the pikau, where the warm air could not get at them and they were then fished out one at a time.

A man can only work so long without a good meal before his efficiency starts dropping off. Usually, somewhere around 10 o'clock, I would start feeling that way. The fire would have burned itself out in the range, the food gone cold and I would be plodding on, tired and hungry and wishing I could call it a day. But experience had taught me that at that time of the night, if there was unfinished work still needed doing, and if you wanted to see it done, you did not stop for dinner and imagine you were going to get started again after eating. I had tried that once or twice in the past and woken up some time after midnight half eaten plate of food still in front of me and my head resting on the table. Actually, that was not such a rare event. There were many times I was so tired after finishing up in the log cabin that I fell asleep at the table before I had finished eating.

Some blokes took on a camp cook to help them out, and there were times when I considered the merits of doing the same. It would be a good feeling working out in the bush, knowing that the camp would be clean and a hot dinner waiting for you on your return. A good helper could even learn how to tack out skins and clear boards, taking a huge slice out of the work load and leaving you free to concentrate your energies on trapping and increasing your tally. But I was also aware that major pitfalls were not uncommon with these sort of arrangements.

A shooter from down south named Hank, told me what happened when one of his mates played a prank on him by placing a "domestic help wanted" advertisement in a newspaper on his behalf. Hank knew nothing about it until letters started turning up at the local Post Office. That was when he learned that his mate had advertised for a cook and housekeeper for him with a view to matrimony. Hank quickly got busy replying to each of the letters explaining that it was all a mistake. But that did not stop a young Hungarian woman turning up at his camp in a taxi late one Friday night.

"I tried to explain to her that it was some sort of a bad joke that one of my mates had played on me," Hank told me. "But she wasn't having any. She said she really wanted the job and she had spent all her money on the taxi getting here, so she would have to stay until she had earned enough money to pay her fare back to where she had just come from. She was a big woman and looked as strong as an ox, and I really didn't know what to do with her. There was no money in the camp or I would have given her some money right there and then just to get rid of her. But it looked like I was stuck with her until the Post Office opened on Monday. I told her to sleep in my room and I spent the night wrapped up in a blanket on the kitchen floor. Next morning I was up and away from camp earliest I had ever been. I tell you, it comes as quite a shock the first time a woman moves in on you.

"By the time I got back that night, the camp was barely recognisable. The old familiar atmosphere was gone. There were no dirty dishes in the sink, the charcoal was scoured off all my old black pots and billies, the floor was swept and scrubbed, cobwebs brushed off the windows. She had even boiled the copper and done a load of washing for me. And on top of all that she had cooked up this great looking exotic meal. She said it was her mother's recipe for fish and chips.

"'Hello Hank,' she says. 'Velcome home. I vass making a verry nice recipe that my mudder used to make ven I vass a liddle girl in Hungary. It is called fich cakes und chips. I vant you to sit down und try it.'

"It looked pretty good," said Hank. "So I sat down and she handed me a cup of tea, and a slice of bread, and a plate full of her special dish and I got stuck in."

"'Do you vant me to tell you how I make da fich cakes?' she asks.

"Yeah. It's pretty good," I replied. "But it has an unusual taste for fish. What did you add to it?"

"Special herbs." she says. "First I take da bone from da meat. Den I chop da meat in very small pieces und mix in da special herbs und chopped onions, before rolling in da flour und making into da cakes und dipping in da badder for flying in da fat."

"Well it tastes pretty good," I replied. "But where did you get the fish? Did you tickle a trout or something while I was out in the bush?"

"Vass is dat?" she says. "I do not know da fich called tickle-trout. Dea iss only von sort of fich dat I know, da ferret fitch. I tink dat some persons call it da polecat fitch. In Hungary dere vass no fitch so my mudder used da fox. But here dere is no fox so I taught I vud try da fitch."

"Tell you what," said Hank. "Strange how the mind works. Up until then I had really been enjoying my meal. But as soon as she told me it was polecat I took off out the door and threw up everywhere. I spent the rest of the weekend hiding out in the bush. Monday, soon as the Post Office opened, I drew some money from my account and sent her on her way. Pity in a way. She was a good worker and obviously innovative.... I never did find out how she caught that ferret. She told me if she could stay on she had another really nice recipe that her mother used to make. She called it 'curried venison cuts.' At first I thought she meant pieces of scotch fillet or something. But when she started explaining how she washed all the pieces in the creek I realized

Fitch with no chips

she wasn't talking about meat. She was referring to the entrails and guts!"

I suppose a cook around the camp would have been alright as long as she agreed to stick closely to the cook book. But then I knew of one or two other hunting mates who had started off with a cook and next thing you knew they had ended up with a wife! On thinking about it, coming home to a cold camp with dishes in the sink, and falling asleep with your face in your plate because there was so much work to do and you were too tired to eat the meal that was over-cooked and tasteless and cold, wasn't such a high price to pay. I think that worse things could have happened.

Hank told me there were ever only two things that came near to wrecking his camp. The other one was a horse.

It was the thick of winter and he was down south batched up in a small hut with a fire place and chimney constructed out of old corrugated iron tacked on the end of it. The hut was way out in the wop-wops with a smattering of snow capping the surrounding hills, and down in the valley there was a black frost colder than a boot full of icy water keeping him hut bound and huddled close to the log fire. The hut was in the middle of the horse paddock and the only warm spot in the entire district was that old corrugated iron fire surround. Hank knew that and so did his pack horse.

"Trouble was," said Hank, "the blooming horse kept backing up against the warm corrugated iron trying to soak up a bit of heat and I was not entirely sure that with all that weight against it, he wouldn't do it some damage. A couple of times I went out into the freezing cold and chased him away. But before you knew it he'd be back up against the hut, pushing his backside hard up against the chimney. Nearly drove me bonkers, rattling the billies hanging over the fire and scraping and rasping against the iron. In the end I'd had enough. I thought: 'I'll fix you, you smart overgrown ass!' So I straightens out a piece of number 8 fencing wire and got it glowing hot in the coals, then I gently poked it out through a nail hole in the corrugated iron and stuck it fair up his jacksie.

"It didn't seem to register immediately that he had a piece of hot wire sticking in his backside. He stood there for a few moments with smoke hissing out of his bum then all of a sudden it must've sunk in that something wasn't quite right. Man, did that horse take off. It worked fantastic, except for one thing. As he took off he lashed out with both hooves and kicked the bloody chimney fair off the end of my hut. Bits of burning wood, ashes and smoke went flying everywhere and I ended up wearing a camp oven of stew. So now the horse was running one way and I was running the other, racing round the hut trying to scrape hot stew off my arms and legs.

"In an emergency you don't always think straight away. Took me a few minutes of galloping up and down the hut to remember that cold water is good for burns. I makes a dash for the door and jumps straight into a 44 gallon drum of icy water and just sits there for a moment or two. Wasn't long and it starts worrying me that with all that ice floating about in the drum I might be doing irreparable damage to some of the submerged bits and pieces. So I climbed back out of the drum and started stripping off my wet clothes as I headed back into the hut. Then I saw smoke billowing out from the direction of my bunk.

"I grabbed the bucket, raced back outside the hut stark bollocky, filled it with water from the drum and ran back into the hut and emptied it all over my bunk. Damned horse had shied a chunk of burning log out of the hearth and landed it fair in the middle of my sleeping bag. So now there was a bloody great big hole burned through the middle of my sleeping bag. Good job I noticed it when I did because the log had gone right through my bunk and was sitting on the floor just about to set the rest of the hut on fire while it was at it.

"There wasn't much I could do with no fire place and my sleeping bag all burned up. So I caught the horse, loaded up the pack saddle and the two of us hobbled off down the track to the next hut; him with his backside still puffing steam and me with welts all over my arms and legs. Just as well the horse was a bit thick. If anyone had ever told him who stuck the red hot poker up his backside I reckon I would have been packing my own gear back down the track."

Open fires around huts and camps were fairly safe, as long as you were not in the habit of stuffing hot pokers up horses backsides or something similar. It was standard practice to douse the hot ashes with the dregs from the tea billy before leaving camp in case a gust of wind came down the chimney and scattered the hot coals. But the unexpected sometimes happened and I had one or two frights. In one of my trapping camps a log rolled out of the fire one night while I was sleeping in a different part of the house. The floor caught on fire and then the joists started to go. Meanwhile I was sleeping on and oblivious as to what was happening in the next room. Then for some unaccountable reason the fire died out. It was a miracle that the whole house didn't go up in flames. In the morning when I got up I was shocked to find a huge hole burned through the floor and joists in front of the hearth.

The chimney in the log cabin at Clements caught on fire also a couple of times. Gives you a bit of a fright when all your hard work is about to go up in flames. I was always alert to the danger, especially seeing that the chimney was formed of silver beech poles that were drying out more and more as time went by, so there was always a 44 gallon drum of water and an empty bucket stationed right outside the entrance to the cabin ready for just such an emergency. I always kept one full drum of water outside the door of the skin shelter and another one handy to the entrance of my cabin, and I think a lot of blokes did the same round their camps. Once the flames got a hold it would not be much use running to the creek with a bucket. Before you got back from the first trip, the camp would already be too far gone to save.

A good warm camp was essential during the winter months, but good food was equally important. Just keeping warm burns up a lot of energy, and working out in the bush all day burns up a whole heap more. I guess that was a good enough reason for some blokes having a camp cook. But Jack Bramley strongly advised against ever getting one. He reckoned that camp cooks were just a pain in the butt. They not only cluttered the place up, but they belonged in the superfluous equipment category. He reckoned that as long as you stoked up on a high protein diet that was half the battle. Plenty of eggs were all you needed. Sometimes, on his way into the bush, he would stop off for a snack bringing his own eggs with him. He would commandeer the wood range and soft boil anything up to a dozen at a time, then he'd spoon them out of their shells onto a plate, sprinkle them with salt and pepper and scoff them down, one after another.

For me, most days began with a large mug of hot sweetened tea and a huge plate of meat and vegetables. I reckoned that plenty of good red meat, potatoes and dark green vegetables was the answer. Night-times I cooked far more than I could eat at a sitting with breakfast the following morning in view. Possum legs were a delicacy and I ate heaps of them. The simplest way of preparing them was to fill the camp oven with dripping and slow deep fry them until the meat was almost falling off the bone, or alternatively simmer them in a billy full of boiling water seasoned with a touch of mixed herbs. There were lots of fancy ways of preparing them too. A large helping of precooked possum meat flaked off the bone, mixed with a helping of chopped onions and curried in white sauce, served up on a bed of steamed rice surrounded with lashings of mixed vegetables or boiled carrots doused in butter was about as scrumptious as possum legs could get. Another way was to sprinkle a few legs with a little salt, smear them with egg yolk and cover them with breadcrumbs then pan fry until done. Cauliflower or broccoli cooked in white sauce with a bit of grated cheese on top and a helping of mashed or boiled potatoes went nicely with the crumbed possum legs.

But no matter how much a delicacy or how diverse the methods of preparation, a man needed more than just one type of meat to sustain himself. They made good eating but there was no way I was going to live on possum legs alone. A feed of venison now and again would have been quite welcome, but it had effectively priced itself off the menu. Game packing plants had this thing about three legged deer. None of them wanted to buy one. Nor did they want to buy a carcass with its back steaks removed. I suppose that was fair enough, but it effectively meant that meat shooters could not afford to eat the deer they shot.

Trout was a good supplement when you could get it. But fishing could also be dangerous. Gorgeous Gordy took me and Bob Hannigan out fishing on Lake Taupo one evening and for the sake of two smallish trout I nearly got my head whipped off.

I wasn't very keen on going out fishing with Gordy in the first place because he insisted on me and Bob doing something that was against my principles. He told Bob and me to go purchase a fishing permit. Bob was keen to go fishing, and although I would never admit as much, I guess I was sort of curious about it, so I decided to tag along. Gordy had a spot around the lake edge where he could launch his fibreglass runabout off the beach and be in fishable waters almost immediately, which was pretty good. What he neglected to explain was that getting it back out of the water was not quite as easy as putting it in, and to do so it was necessary for some unsuspecting idiot to put his life on the line. We trolled up and down for about an hour during which time we hooked up the two aforementioned trout and as evening shadows settled on the lake we headed back for shore. Gordy backed his station wagon down the beach and edged the trailer into the water. Between us we guided and winched the boat into position and while Bob and I stood to one side watching, Gordy hopped back into his wagon and attempted to pull the boat out of the lake.

"Damn it!" said Gordy. "Sand's too soft. We're going to need a bit of extra weight. You guys get behind the wagon and give it a bit of a push."

So Bob and I gets our shoulders in behind the station wagon, digs our boots in and starts heaving while Gordy gives it the gun.

"No, it's not going to work," says Gordy. "What I'll do is unhitch the trailer, take the wagon up to more solid ground and pull it out with a length of rope."

With a bit more heaving and shoving, between the three of us we managed to get the station wagon clear of the soft stuff and Gordy digs out a length of nylon rope from behind the back seat. This he connects between the tow bar and the coupling and while Bob and I stand to one side watching Gordy once more gives it the gun. This time he gets the trailer clear of the water, but as soon as it comes up onto dry ground the weight of the outboard motor pulls down on the back of the boat and the coupling end of the trailer shoots up into the air.

"Damn it!" says Gordy, looking straight at me. "One of you will have to hop up on the boat and lie along the foredeck to keep the front of the trailer down while I get it clear."

So up I hops. The trailer settles nicely back into the horizontal, and Gordy once more returns to the station wagon. "Hold onto the fairlead," says Gordy as he pokes his head out the driver's window, "and you won't fall off."

Lying over the prow hanging onto the fairlead was an interesting position to be in. From there I could watch Gordy looking in his rear vision mirror as he started to take up tension on the rope. And if I looked down I could see the guide wheel on the front of the trailer digging deeper into the sand as Gordy put more tension onto the rope. And if I looked up again I could see the station wagon slowly easing forward. And if I dropped my eyes just a fraction I could also see the nylon rope starting to hum as it stretched tighter than a pair of shrunk underpants. Then suddenly I couldn't see anything at all.

Bob Hannigan with Gordy's two trout

"Damn it!" I thought I could hear Gordy saying far away in the distance. "Broke my nylon rope."

I am not too sure how Gordy and Bob got the boat clear and hitched up to the tow bar and safely back to Taupo after that. My head was still on my shoulders but the side of my face was black and my jaw nearly broken, and for some unaccountable reason I had a thumping headache. Next morning I took a photo of Bob with the two trout that nearly got my head whipped off. But after that no one could tell me that fishing wasn't a dangerous sport.

Another time I was down the West Coast, and a mate of mine and myself came close to getting shot after indulging in a spot of fishing. And it was all over something as innocuous as a single whitebait!

The Haast Road, linking the West Coast with Otago, had been officially opened at Knights Point by Sir Keith Holyoake, then Prime Minister of New Zealand in 1965. However, an hour or two earlier, on the same day, the Haast Road had been unofficially opened by Jim Barkle of Inangahua, when he drove through the ribbon in his old Bedford camper truck with his Hamilton Jet Boat towed along behind. The road either side was mud and gravel, but right at Knights Point there was a small strip of tar seal, just enough to make it all look official and pretty for the right honourable's ribbon cutting ceremony. Barkle couldn't wait for the official opening. He'd been hanging round Lake Moeraki and Paringa while the road was under construction and now he wanted to check out the Arawata. I understand that Jim Barkle stopped long enough to retie the ribbon for the official party, but there were a few red faces when the right honourable's party arrived at the scene, scissors in hand, all dressed up in their suits and ties with white carnations in their buttonholes, and there was Barkle's muddy old Bedford wheel tracks plastered indelibly right down the middle of the fresh tar seal.

By the time Bob Hannigan, Kim the dog, and I got back down the Coast after the previous season's trapping out of Clements, Dale Hunter was meat shooting the Mahitahi and the Haast Road was well and truly opened to traffic. Weather, as usual, was hosing down. So we cut arm and neck holes out of some old coal sacks, sewed up a coal sack coat for the dog to keep him dry too, and we all piled into Dale's open top Series One Land Rover and took off for a jaunt down to Jackson Bay.

There was a fishing boat tied up alongside the Jackson Bay wharf with a big haul of tarakihi spilled all over its deck and the crew were busily cleaning up prior to freezing down the catch. There were one or two other species, like the odd blue cod and some other types of fish that I did not immediately recognize scattered in amongst the tarakihi, but the one that caught my eye was a huge specimen of a ling lying in the scuppers. It must have been about 4 feet long and weighed at least 30 pounds. Fishermen and hunters are somewhat similar in some regards, so it wasn't difficult striking up a conversation.

"G'day!" I called down to the boat. "That's not a bad haul you've taken."

"Not all that good really," one of the blokes, whom I took to be the skipper, rejoined. "Fishing's been a bit off lately."

"Are you just trawling for tarakihi?" I asked.

"Yeah, that's all," he answered. "Would you like a feed of fish?"

"You guys keep it," I called back. "It's your living."

"You can take something if you like. The odds and sods aren't much use to us. We only keep the tarakihi and the cod."

"That big fish," I said, pointing to the ling. "Is that a ling?"

"Yeah, it's a ling. They're okay to eat but we'll be dumping it. You can have it if you want it."

"Are you sure? Well heck, thanks a lot," I said.

Between us, we managed to hoist it off the boat and slide it into the back of Dale's Land Rover.

"What the heck do you want this great big slimy thing for?" Dale asked as we drove off the wharf and headed back up the Coast.

"Heck, I don't want it," I said. "But I can't help thinking how similar it looks to a whitebait. Someone back in Paringa was telling me how much he loves whitebait fritters. Think of all the fritters he could make from a whitebait this size."

It was getting close to midnight, the rain was absolutely pelting down, we were soaked to the skin, and Ron Hoglund the local meat buyer was sitting in his kitchen regaling a new young shooter to the Coast with stories of great tallies and huge trophy animals when we pulled up outside his depot. By now we were almost in hysterics just thinking what Ron's reaction would be as we carried our gigantic whitebait into his kitchen and lowered it onto his table. Dale and I got on an end each of the fish and Bob went ahead and knocked loudly on the back door. It was a cow of a thing to handle it was so slippery, but being near doubled up with suppressed mirth didn't help any. Ron opens the door to see who's visiting at such an ungodly hour, and his eyes near pop out of his head as we push past him carrying this massive big piece of slimy white fish into the kitchen and place it along the length of his table.

"G'day, Ron," I greeted. "You won't believe it man. This must be the biggest whitebait that was ever hauled out of the Paringa River. Knock up a few fritters and we'll drop round for breakfast."

Ron's eyes were still popping and his expression was alternating from grins to scowls and back to grins as we took off into the night, the three of us trying to keep straight faces and not burst out laughing.

We imagined that Ron would see the funny side of our prank. But by the next morning all the grins were gone and all that was left was a very angry scowl. I got message that we had ruined his night barging in and busting up the conversation like that. The fish had left a disgusting mess on his kitchen table and he was out the back of his depot in the pouring rain at one o'clock in the morning trying to dig a hole big enough to bury it. And if anyone of us ever turned up in the middle of the night with another whitebait he would gut shoot the lot of us.

Really, I couldn't figure out what all the fuss was about. All he really had to do was drive a few hundred yards along the road and liberate it back into the river where it had supposedly come from. So from my experience, fish was okay if you could get it without endangering life and limb, but you had to be careful.

CHAPTER 8

Life on the Edge

Those coal sack jerkins that we made up for wearing down to Jackson Bay — I don't know who invented the idea. It may well have been Dale Hunter, because he was the one who introduced them to us. Anyway, they were a brilliant idea for meat shooters. All they were was a heavy duty coal sack with holes cut out for your arms and head to poke through. But water tended to run off them, so they were ideal wear for the Coast where, if it wasn't raining it had either just stopped or it was just about to start. When it came to carrying deer out of the bush they really held their own. Blood and muck soaked into your clothes and running down your back and was one of those things that meat shooters had to live with. But the coal sack jerkin did away with all that. It was quite comfortable to wear, warm, and just long enough to keep the blood off your backside.

Dale was bringing a load of deer out of the Mahitahi in his open Land Rover one day wearing nothing but a coal sack. Way up the Mahitahi in a jet boat with no one around to see you, it did not matter much whether you wore shorts under your coal sack or not. And before the Haast Road opened, when traffic was few and far between, it did not make much difference while driving about on the main road either. But times had changed. Between the river and the road there was an open paddock to drive through and then a farm gate that opened out onto the highway. Dale had just driven through the gate and was closing it behind his Land Rover when he heard a tour bus approaching from the direction of Fox Glacier.

"I had a feeling what the driver would do if he got the chance," Dale told me. "I had met him previously and I knew he was always on the look out for anything of interest to point out to his passengers.

"I should have shot back into the paddock. But instead I tried to get out on the road ahead of him and take off. I piled into the Land Rover and gunned it down the gravel, but by now the bus was so close there was not enough room to safely pull out in front of it. I had no choice but to slam on the brakes while the bus driver did the same right in front of me completely blocking my way out. Next thing I could see tourists climbing over one another to get a geek out the windows at me sitting there while the driver is announcing that the fellow down there in the land rover is a meat shooter. Then the door opens up and all these tourists pile out with their cameras and gather round the Land Rover taking pictures of me tugging on my coal sack, trying to keep all the bits covered. Two old ladies kept asking me to get out of the Land Rover and stand alongside while they took my photo.

"What did you do?" I asked.

"Sat there looking straight ahead. They must have thought I was the village idiot. I was as mad as hell. Up in the bus I could hear the driver chuckling away watching me sitting there trying to hold my sack in place squirming and refusing to speak to anyone.

"'Come on deary," the old ladies kept saying. "Get out of your car so that we can get a photo of you with your deer."

"That was the last time I ever drove out of the Mahitahi with no pants on."

One night I too nearly got caught with my pants down, only in a different sense of the word.

It was about the middle of the night and I was heading back to Clements with my shopping in the back, and as I approached the pines it brought back memories of an occasion some twelve months earlier when some deer cullers from Kaingaroa had guided us through the pines helping us to poach their block, spotlighting deer from the back of Bob's truck. We bowled a couple of deer and managed to get back to the safety of SF90 just ahead of their boss, who had been driving round much of the night trying to intercept us. It was amusing thinking back on it, but it would not have been too funny if we had been caught. The cullers would have lost their jobs for sure and Bob and I could have ended up having our hunting gear and vehicle confiscated.

Up until then, belting homeward down the Napier-Taupo Highway, I had been feeling rather drowsy, but as the Kaingaroa High Level Road came into view I started weighing up the pros and cons of ducking into the pines for a crack at a deer. It was a bit risky. I knew if I got caught I would be in deep trouble, possibly to the extent of losing my vehicle along with everything in it right down to the sausages and dripping I had just bought in Taupo. The answer then if I really wanted to eat those sausages was, "don't get caught!" Suddenly I was no longer drowsy. It all seemed like good clean fun and I decided to give it a go.

The general layout of the pines was still clear in my mind, but to get in I needed to black out the Land Rover, creep in along the High Level Road and duck off on a side road just as quickly as I could. It was not unusual for logging trucks to work right through the night and they sometimes came burling through these main roads at more than a hundred miles an hour. Getting into the forest was the scary part. If one of those fellows caught you out it could be a bit embarrassing. Most logging drivers were not too partial to poachers spotlighting their roads in the middle of the night.

Once in and away from the main roads there was not much to worry about, other than the fact that the roads were regularly patrolled by one or two over zealous forestry bods from Kaingaroa Village whose need for sleep was completely nullified by their perverted fixation for nabbing poaching meat shooters along with their equipment. There were hundreds of miles of roads in Kaingaroa Forest and the patrols could not be everywhere at once, but there were also fire lookouts with good radio communication positioned strategically about the forest. With these fellows in mind, if you really wanted to make life interesting for yourself, all you needed to do was rake the clouds once or twice with your spotlight. After that it might not pay to stay in one place for too long because there was every possibility that the patrols had been alerted and now you were the one being stalked. All things considered, with head shot venison worth only fifteen cents a pound at the time and no guarantee you were even going to set eyes on a deer, the returns hardly justified the risks. But the way I looked at it, if mercenaries really thought they were going to get shot neither would they go out to battle.

Anyway, there was not much of a battle fought on this particular occasion. There were possums and hares wandering about everywhere but not so much as a glimpse of a deer. Then, about an hour before daybreak, I caught two stags out on a large burn.

They were a long way from cover and to get to it they had to come past me. I felt a little sorry for them actually. With nowhere to run to they were as good as dead. While they milled about trying to figure out what to do I had time to climb out of the Land Rover, take a comfortable bench rest across the spare wheel on the bonnet and nail them both with a couple of head shots.

The rest was simplicity itself. The guys at Taupo Engineering had made my crash rack so that it could be lowered forward into a carrier position for just such occasions as this. Easy shooting, easy meat. I changed down to low reduction and nosed out onto the burn. They were only about a hundred yards out. Now all I had to do was lower the crash rack, load on the deer and get to heck out of it. As I worked away at gutting them in the soft glow of the parking lights, it went through my mind that this was probably the most fun I had had since Punchy shot through. Life had become a little dull without him, always living on the edge as he did.

One of the deer was a big brute and it took a bit of wrestling getting him up onto the rack. But once he was in place there was no problem heaving the other one on top. I lashed them both securely, did a final check of the load and clambered back into the wagon. Now I needed to move. It would not be long and gangs would be moving about in the forest. It was time I was no longer here. I slammed the door, turned the key and depressed the starter... half a "whirr", then nothing. Again I depressed the starter... barely a "whirr", then nothing. Once more... nothing! Driving round at slow speed with the spotlight burning all night had drained the battery, and leaving the parking lights on while gutting the deer had finished it off.

Fortunately Land Rovers came with a crank handle clipped behind the seats. Grabbing for it, I was out the door and round the front of the vehicle. Land Rovers were designed so the crank handle slotted in through the bumper, but now the crash rack was blocking the way. Frantically I worked loose the knots and tumbled the carcasses onto the pumice and dragged them out of the way. I quickly raised the rack back into its upright position and poked the crank handle into the bumper. It slotted into place, but the way the rack had been constructed no allowance had been made for turning the handle. A solid four inch plate of galvanised steel had been welded along the base of the rack to act as a brace against the bumper whilst in the lowered position. When in the upright position this plate protruded horizontally four inches in front of the bumper and the engineers had neglected lengthening the shaft of the crank handle by four inches to compensate.

Sheer fright rushed up and down my spine as I realized my predicament. Early streaks of dawn were already glimmering in the eastern skyline and anytime the early shift would be out on the roads. Pick-ups, lorries, trucks and tractors. Forestry workers would be swarming everywhere, and here was I, caught out in the middle of a burn with my pants down, so to speak. To crank the engine I would have to completely dismantle the crash rack from off the front of the vehicle, and with my Land Rover up for grabs I was near to panic. Time was against me and I was getting into a lather.

Fingers working feverishly, I attacked the bolts with a couple of Crescent spanners. Fortunately everything was still new and easy to loosen. But the rack was a dead weight. It was unbelievably heavy. Minutes were ticking away and dawn was breaking clearer by the second. Shapes and objects were coming into focus in the half light. Now the rack was off the vehicle and lying on top of the carcasses. Not too far away, out on the next road, I could hear the first sounds of heavy traffic. Slotting the handle into place, I cranked furiously. She wouldn't fire. Vehicles were likely to come driving into view at any moment Again I cranked on the handle. Still nothing....Damn it all man... turn on the key! I tried again, this time with the ignition turned on. First kick, she burst into life.

Hurling the crank handle into the cab, I raced back round to the crash rack. It was an absolute dead weight and not only did it have to be lifted onto the bumper, it also had to be juggled back and forth to line up precisely with the bolt holes. More and more vehicles were rumbling along the parallel road less than half a mile away. I needed to stay calm and work steadily. Now the rack was bolted into position and lowered. Sweat trickled down my spine. The big stag first. I managed to struggle him up onto the rack and the other stag heaved on top. Next the ropes. Lash them down tight. It would be just my luck to come sneaking out onto the Low Level Road and the load fall off.

Everything secure and I piled back into the cab. All I needed to do now was stall it and I might as well come walking out with my hands up. With low reduction and high revs, I crawled off the burn, edged onto the road and slapped it back into regular drive. Now, how to get out of the forest without being seen!?! Somehow I had to get down the Low Level Road, where all the traffic noise had been coming from, drive past the village of Iwitahi, where Lou Scudder had his office, and disappear in a cloud of dust.

Some time later, in the peace and tranquillity of my hut, I was mulling over the night's activities and I got to thinking about all that early traffic around the crack of dawn. Almost unbelievably, I had managed to come belting out of a side road, charge off down the Low Level Road and get out of Kaingaroa Forest without even glimpsing another vehicle. If I had shot those two deer, loaded them onto the rack and driven straight out onto the Low Level Road, very likely I would have come face to face with all that traffic entering the forest for the early shift. Flattening the battery and having to dismantle the crash rack had probably saved my skin. Then by nothing less than plain good fortune I had managed to get out during a lull between the contractors and the wage workers from Sixty Bar Eight who would have driven into their blocks a little later. Call it luck, or call it what you like. One thing I was sure of, poaching the pines was just too dangerous. No way would I be sticking my neck out like that again in the foreseeable future.

Not too far into the foreseeable future, as foreseeable futures go, I was back in Kaingaroa doing just that... sticking my neck out once more. It was one week to the day later. There were a few places that I had not checked out the week before piquing my curiosity.

The River Road, sidling the Rangitaiki River, contained the odd patches of interesting country. The east bank was a mixture of second growth manuka and broadleaved species, with monoao and silver tussock clearings scattered here and there. Driving along the road, which was on the west bank, afforded good clear shots at anything mooching about in the clearings on the east bank of the river.

It was somewhere round two in the morning and not a whisper

stirred the tussock. A shallow ribbon of fog suspended above the river dribbled occasional wisps through the tussocky terraces creating a surrealistic atmosphere accentuated more so by the light of a waxing moon that hung in a cloudless sky west of the midnight quarter. For about an hour I had been quietly cruising the fire breaks and side roads, with only the occasional waddling possum for company. Now I was working my way south along the edge of the Rangitaiki and was about to put out the light and head for home. I had no intention of duplicating the previous week's episode and end up running a gauntlet of forestry contractors while trying to get out of the forest. I may not be so lucky a second time.

Then, about a hundred yards across the river, a Red hind popped her head up from in amongst the monoao. And then a second one lit up in the spot. A trace of fog drifted close to the deer but the first one showed up bright and clear, big eyes shining like headlights in the dark. The treble two was strategically propped between me and the door and instantly I was out of the Land Rover, bench resting across the spare wheel with the cross hairs settled dead between her eyes. Very gently I took up on the trigger. In the stillness of the night the ensuing explosion seemed to split the air in two. Shock waves spread into the night distorting my vision. The hind was instantaneously gone from view. But I knew she was down. She had stayed staring into the light just a mite too long.

Immediately, the second one was on her feet and running, and before I could get another shot away she had slipped in behind a finger of fog and disappeared. The shock waves had broken up the night air in such a way, when I had fired, that I had not really seen the hind go down but I had heard the "thwack!" as the bullet hit and there were no doubts in my mind that she was lying there dead.

How to get over to her though was something else again. There was a thick belt of impenetrable scrub bordering a steep bank either side of the river, plus the waters were slow flowing and murky and I had no idea how deep. About a mile down the road there was a solid log bridge fording the river, but the road on that side did not turn back to the area where I had just shot the hind. From the bridge back to the monoao clearing, there was a mile or so of scrub, fog and night to negotiate. And if I managed that alright, I still had to locate the hind in the dark. I realized there was no way I was going to be able to do it. Somehow I would have to come back in the daylight.

I could just picture the scene, fronting up to Lou Scudder's office shortly after breakfast and asking him for permission to go fetch my deer. Nevertheless, I kicked a mark in the road where my feet had been as I leant across the spare wheel, so I could orientate myself when I returned in the morning for my venison.

The scene was not too far removed from what I had pictured:

"What do you mean, you want a permit to enter the forest?" he near screamed at me. "You know damned well no one gets a permit to go driving around in the pines."

"Well it's a heck of a long way round the main road through Taupo to Kaingaroa, when you can just zip up the Low Level Road and be there in a fraction of the time," I replied.

"You got urgent business in Kaingaroa, or something?" asked Lou.

"Yeah, quite urgent," I replied. "Allan Farmer would like to see me about something."

Lou sat behind his desk scrutinizing me and thinking it through. He was not so silly as to believe everything he heard. However, what I had just said was all true. It was the interpretation of what I had said that differed..... It was a long way to Kaingaroa Village along the main highway compared to driving straight through using the forestry roads, and.... I did have urgent business in Kaingaroa Forest; recovering a deer carcass before it went rotten on me, and.... If Allan Farmer, the forest ranger at Kaingaroa, had known I had spent the last two Friday nights poaching deer in the forest he most certainly would have liked to have seen me....

"Okay," Lou agreed. "You can go through, but stay on the Low Level Road all the way. I'll call through to Kaingaroa and let them know you are coming, and no ducking off on any side roads, got it!"

The hind was in the exact spot that I knew she would be, her brain lifted out of her skull as neatly as if a spoon had scooped it clean. No wonder she had dropped like a stone.

So I had my deer. But I didn't feel too good about it. Lou Scudder was a decent bloke who had always treated me well. I had been somewhat extravagant with the truth in getting his permission to enter the forest. Besides I had this feeling that even if Lou could not be certain why I wanted to enter the forest he most certainly had his suspicions. Enough was enough. Poaching was one thing, deceiving your mates was something else. Venison was cash and I needed cash to make ends meet and keep up the payments on the Land Rover until I received my next cheque from London. But not at any price. And that was the last time I ever went spotlighting for deer in Kaingaroa Forest.

One thing that was obvious during my poaching forays into Kaingaroa; there was no shortage of possums in the pines. A mate had once told me that pines possums were no good. The gum from the trees got into their fur and ruined it. Having never taken possums from a pine forest, I did not really know. But having seen so many waddling about I was interested to find out for myself just what quality of fur they did produce.

A large stretch of Taharua Road, which linked the Napier-Taupo highway and SF90, was bordered by extensive pine plantations. Some of these were relatively new plantings, some were more mature. Most likely there were a few pigs and deer living in these plantations too, although in all the time I had been coming and going I had never seen any hanging about the edges. But one little critter that never failed to make himself manifest was the ubiquitous possum. There

Lou Scudder (photo courtesy of Lou Scudder)

would always be one or two picking around or sitting back on their haunches along the roadside, waiting to be showered with pumice dust as I hurtled back to camp in the dead of night. I went and asked Lou if I could lay a couple of trial poison lines adjacent to the road and he said to go ahead.

I was a little surprised at just how much possum, and other, sign there actually was once in amongst the pines. There were droppings everywhere; possum's, rabbit's and hare's. And no shortage of well formed pads, probably travelled by all three species in the course of a night, compressed and obvious amongst the fallen needles. Locating one's bearings amongst the monotony of a radiata pine plantation was a little different to what I was used to. But with no intention of going far there was not much likelihood of becoming confused. I spent about half an hour squirting dobs of cyanide here and there and emerged from the forest feeling sticky from the gum that adhered to most everything you touched.

I never did find out how many possums died on that poison line. The next day I was back, full of eager expectation, but I was due for a big disappointment. Gum clung to the fur of the possums the same as it clung to everything else. My mate was right when he said they were no good. Not only did they feel sticky and matted, but every one of them had a mangy appearance from missing fur around the ribs. I do not know whether the stickiness irritated them and they scratched it out or whether it got lost on the bark of the trees. Nor did I waste my time trying to find out. I only picked up half a dozen. Not one of them was worth keeping and there was no point in checking out the rest of the line.

It was not really much of a loss. I had quickly realized that working amongst rows of exotic pine trees was not me.

It was vastly different working in the native with its huge variety of species, big and small. Crystal clear sparkling waters bubbled and gurgled down the clefts and gullies, ferns and mosses sprouted on rocks and banks, creepers and lianas reaching for the sky wound their strands through bark and around the trunks of forest giants. Astelias and perching lilies hung from upper limbs, scabweed, fungi, lichens, grasses, palms, coprosma and mingimingi. Then there were the birds... the robins, tuis, bellbirds, kakas, parakeets, tomtits, riflemen, long tailed cuckoos, moreporks.... that filled the trees with song. There were times, high up on the bush face above Clements Road I had stopped for a break, lain back on a carpet of moss amongst the fuschia groves, carbine resting across my knees, pikau full of possum skins for a pillow, and all but dozed off. Warm and sunny afternoons the Sika deer liked dozing off up there too. In that regard Sika deer were a bit like possum trappers and possum trappers were a bit like Sika deer. The main difference being, Sika deer had more time for doing it. Compared to all of that, wandering about amongst endless rows of neatly planted sticky pinus radiata was uninteresting to the point of boredom.

I reckoned I would stick with the native.

CHAPTER 9

Checking Out

Buds were budding on the makomako trees and blue flecks appearing down the spinal area of the pelts I was taking. And if by chance I should have failed to observe that the days were getting longer and the nights milder, the aforementioned signs would still have borne witness that the trapping season was all but over. From here on it was a matter of mopping up on the final trap line of the season. In a short while the tell-tale flecks of blue would thicken along the centre of the pelts and then spread into the haunches as the full summer moult set in. And that would be the end of that for another year, because these days there was no demand for summer grade furs.

By the end of September it was all over. I spent my last day out on the line uplifting traps and packing them down to the road.

With only a few green skins off the end of the line and no pressure to clear boards, there was not much to do back at the camp that night. Cleaning up and preparing the skins for export would drag on over the next couple of weeks, mainly because it took time for the ears to dry properly, so there was no immediate rush getting started on the boards. That could now be done more or less at my leisure as I pottered around camp keeping the fire stoked and the drying process moving along.

In the course of two winter seasons, I had run intensively worked trap lines through much of the country between Clements Camp and the Hinemaiaia Stream. Thousands of possums had been taken, but there were still thousands left behind. It was possible to thin the numbers considerably, but not possible to wipe them out. Poison lines were even less effective. From the same area of bush that one of my trap lines might take more than three hundred and fifty possums, a good poison line might take less than a hundred. I estimated that with natural breeding, the number of possums I had destroyed from my block in SF90 would all be back again within four or five years. In the meantime the areas that had been worked over would no longer produce enough skins to justify the effort required re-trapping them. So basically, it was a no win situation for the Noxious Animals

Division of the Forest Service. The elimination of possums in such a big area was a battle that could never be won by conventional means. As long as there were enough of them and the returns were good it was worthwhile hunting them. But once the numbers had been reduced to a certain level the effort required to maintain a good tally no longer justified working that area. And that gave the possum ample opportunity to get re-established. The same situation would one day apply with regard to shooting venison from helicopters.

The devastating effects that all those hungry and wasteful little animals were having on the bush each night was still a matter for conjecture. Their diet was much broader than many of the so called experts of the day would have had us believe. At the time possums were thought to be more or less entirely herbivorous. I had come to realize from observing baby possums that I had fostered back at my camp that this was not so, and in fact there was not much they would not eat. Offer them virtually anything and they would have a go at it. One thing that worried me was the way they took to raw meat and raw eggs if these were offered. Eggs especially seemed to appeal to them. That did not bode well for nesting birds. I was not sure what application the attraction to raw meat might have. I supposed given the opportunity it was always possible that they may eat newly hatched and fledgling chicks. However, before one should jump in too deep accusing the possum of further atrocities, it is good to keep in mind that possums are nocturnal animals and most birds are not. Hence at the very time of day when the possum might be out shopping for egg and baby burgers, the bird is at roost on her nest with her eggs or chicks quite adequately protected. It is also worth baring in mind that a hen protecting her brood can be a very tenacious adversary, whereas possums by nature are neither aggressive nor predacious.

That aside, it is interesting to note that for many years after they were introduced into New Zealand, it was believed that the possum would never become a nuisance. In fact the Auckland Acclimatisation Society in its annual report of 1916–17 went so far as to say: "We shall be doing a great service to the country in stocking these large areas [of rough bush hills] with this valuable and harmless animal." About ten years later a different source stated: "their skins are so valuable that at any time the animals can be reduced in numbers to the extent desired without cost."

Hanging around camp for a couple of weeks waiting for the final drying of the skins was a tedious business, but nevertheless imperative if you wanted your skins to arrive at the auctioneers in good order. The fur trapper's biggest enemy was mould. He could do what he liked with regard to brushing, and combing, and fluffing them up pretty, and sprinkling them with napthalene to keep the silverfish and bugs at bay. But if, in his haste to get cleaned up and on his way, one or two slightly green skins got packed in with a bale of otherwise nicely dried furs, things could go badly wrong — moisture, heat, fungus, slipping fur — the entire bale could turn ripe before it got there.

It was a long journey from the trapper's camp to London. Transporting them to Wellington was only the beginning. There was no saying they would not be left sitting in a wharf shed for up to a month awaiting the next available ship out, and after that they were going to be subjected to perhaps another eight weeks crammed in an ill ventilated hold, with fungal spores and festering heat, while their ship wallowed through steamy tropical seas as it crossed the Pacific Ocean, negotiated the Panama Canal, then the Atlantic. And these last furs of the season were not scheduled to go under the hammer until February which was more than four months down the track. Four months was a lot of time for problems to start developing inside a sewn up bale of furs. So there was no point trying to jump start the final drying.

Once they arrived in London though, they were in good hands. Anning, Chadwick and Kiver, were a highly reputable firm of fur brokers, that could be counted on to handle the consignment in a most responsible manner. London was the fur centre of the world, and the two leading fur brokerages were Anning Chadwick & Kiver Limited, and the Hudson Bay Fur Company. The first shipment I ever exported, went to Hudsons. And a fine old company they were too; doing their bit to reduce the number of Arctic foxes, wild mink and snow leopards still roaming free in their natural habitats. But that was no concern of mine. Possums besides being cute little critters, were an introduced pest that had become a major threat to New Zealand's native forests and their natural born inhabitants, and although I wasn't really in it for the morals, I considered every possum travelling on a sea voyage to London just one more chance for the tomtit's survival. Anning Chadwicks, I might add, was also a fine old company; turning over notable quantities of ermine, ocelot and mustelids, bless them. They also realized better prices for possum furs than Hudsons did, which was all that really counted when it came to electing one's fur broker.

One's mind tends to wander down many and varied pathways when one is standing in front of a work bench for long periods of time immersed in something as prosaic as scraping fat off skins, and rubbing them dry with rough sacking, and pulling nails, and stripping skins off boards, and stoking fires, and stacking skins on wires, and brushing, and combing, and wishing the process was already done so one can pack up and get on with the next venture. With well in excess of a thousand skins piled up around me in the log cabin, naturally enough my mind would occasionally start speculating on what sort of a return I might realize for all my hard work. Other times my mind might speculate on what it was going to be like working on a Bluff fishing boat during the oncoming summer. But more often I would be thinking about all those deer moving about in the forest with the warmer weather and the spring growth shooting up everywhere. Then I would leave off working in the skin shelter for awhile and would wander back into the cabin to check the condition of my rifles, that they were nicely oiled and ready to go, and chances were I would find that they were perfectly ready to go so I would leave off working on the furs for a few hours and I would go drop a Sika just for the hang of it. A man needed to get out of that skin shelter once in a while and get a bit of fresh air and get the circulation going.

There were times when I felt I needed to have a complete break and get right out of the forest for awhile and then I would pile into the Land Rover, and take off for Rotorua and go visit Harry Vipond, or Colin Campbell, or Rex Forrester or someone. It didn't make much difference to the furs sitting in the log cabin. The ears were going to take just as long to dry regardless of whether I was hanging round the shelter looking at them or not.

Since buying my Land Rover through him, I had struck up a warm friendship with Colin Campbell, and whenever I was in Rotorua I was always made to feel welcome and invited to stay in his flat. He was keen on shooting, and being out and about trying to sell Land Rovers all day long, he had plenty of useful connections throughout the district. Some years earlier, as a private shooter, I had once shot wallabies in the hills above Lake Rotoiti and I could recall it as having been lots of fun. Quite likely the wallabies would not have remembered it in quite the same light as me, but speaking strictly from the shooter's perspective I thought it would be rather fun to have another go at them. One of Colin's mates owned a runoff property somewhere up in the back blocks that supposedly had lots of wallabies bouncing about eating all the grass, not to mention the odd Red deer meandering in and out of the bush. Colin was given a key to the gate with directions on how to find the property and told it would be okay to do a bit of spotlighting, but under no circumstances were we to wander onto the next door neighbour's block.

"Joe reckons the fellows next door are probably growing whacky baccy back in their bush," Colin told me. "He said they're a pretty rough bunch. One of them just got out of jail after fracturing somebody's skull because he "thought" he was planning on trespassing on their land. But as long as we stay on Joe's side of the fence and do not go climbing any boundary fences we will be okay. Joe said there are no adjoining gates so we cannot really go wrong."

A few miles out of town there were the odd roads wandering back into the hills and on one of these was our farm gate. Colin asked me to unlock the gate while he drove the Land Rover through.

"You sure you gave me the right key? Doesn't seem to want to turn," I called back to him.

"Bring it here and let's have another look," said Colin. In his glove box there were several similar looking Lockwood type keys but none of them wanted to unlock the gate.

"That's a nuisance!" said Colin. "I must have left Joe's key back on the television. Well I'm not going back for it. We'll just lift the gate off its hinges and put it back on behind us. Joe won't mind."

"What is Joe using the land for?" I asked Colin as we drove down a rough track formed through the middle of a scruffy looking paddock. "He's going to have his work cut out when he gets round to grubbing out all this ragwort."

"He runs a bit of dry stock from time to time, but he said there is nothing up here at the moment. That is why it is okay to come up now and do a bit of spotlighting."

Half an hour later we were still driving slowly round in paddocks full of blackberry, gorse and ragwort, spotlight illuminating the night looking for wallabies, but there had not been much sign of wild life apart from the occasional rabbit. Then a set of eyes showed up against the bush.

"Over there," he whispered excitedly, "A deer over by the bush edge."

I was out the door and round to his side of the vehicle with my treble two in a flash. A set of whitish slightly pink tinged eyes glowed in the distant darkness.

"That's not a deer. Its a cattle beast!" I exclaimed.

"Nah!. It's a deer. Shoot it quick before it gets away."

"Colin, deer's eyes do not look like that. They shine greenish white, big and bright like the headlights of a car and nowhere near as wide. I'm telling you that is a cattle beast."

"Well at that rate it's just as well you didn't shoot it."

"I thought you said your mate had no stock up here," I said. "Are you sure we are on the right property?"

"I hope so," Colin answered. "Because if we're not we're going to end up with fractured skulls and butchered into little pieces."

"I think we had better get the hell out of it. Just in case," I replied.

Colin didn't need much prompting. We unplugged the spotlight and took off back down through those scruffy looking paddocks, down the rough track and up against the locked gate in minutes flat. We piled out and lifted the gate off its hinges, Colin jumped back into the Land Rover, gunned it through the gate and onto the road. Between us we lifted the gate back onto its hinges and had just climbed back into the Land Rover when a beat up old Land Cruiser, spotlight blazing off the roof, came charging up the middle of the road with a wild looking bunch of Maoris hanging all over it. They didn't leave us much room for going anywhere. They slammed on their brakes and came to a skidding halt hard up against the front of Colin's Land Rover.

"What are you pakehas doing up here?" one of them snarled, spotlight dazzling our eyes.

"Looking for Joe's block of land," Colin replied.

"Check the lock," one of the others growled, and the fellow with the spot spun it round to light up the gate while his mate climbed down to check the padlock.

"It's okay," he called back.

"We don't care too much for people hanging round near our land," the snarly one said. "Joe's block is half a mile up the road. Don't be still hanging round here when we get back or you'll end up with no tyres on your nice shiny wagon."

"That more than likely accounts for why the key didn't work," said Colin as we sped off in the direction of town.

"Just as well those Kumara's don't know how to read roads," I muttered half to myself.

Having shot a wallaby (photo Bob Hannigan)

"Ay? What's that you said?" asked Colin.

"Never mind," I replied. "Merely thinking aloud."

Rex Forrester, who also lived in Rotorua, had been involved with hunting and fishing one way or another all his life. At the time I doubt there was a deer culler in the country who did not know who Rex was. Most were still recuperating from the massive booze up down in Christchurch earlier that same year that had been organised by veteran Government shooters, Joff Thomson and Rex Forrester, ostensibly under the guise of a Deer Culler's Reunion. Currently Rex was employed by the Government Tourist Bureau as their Chief Advisory Officer for Hunting and Fishing in New Zealand. He was both knowledgeable and experienced and I doubt there was a man better suited to the job than he, because what he didn't know he quite adequately fabricated.

Rex was a friend and I usually dropped in to see him when I was in Rotorua. It was opening day up the Ngongotaha Stream and there he was, fishing rod to hand, flat out casting flies one direction and a load of utter bull the other. And Mr and Mrs Ben Morris were soaking it all up with their 16mm cine camera. Rex Forrester was in his element. They were shooting a documentary for their local TV channel back in the USA and Rex was their star performer.

Knowing I was about to head south for the summer and never one to miss an easy shot, Rex introduced me to the Morris' as a pro' hunter who, if they picked up the expense tab, just might be willing to let them tag along for a week or two while I worked my way down the Coast and into Queenstown.

I had only stopped off to say "G'day!" but within minutes of arriving at Ngongotaha I had been conned into taking the Morris' on a safari down South! What with hunting wallabies in a whacky baccy plot and saying "G'day!" to Rex Forrester, Rotorua wasn't a great deal safer than back on the possum block. At least back in SF90, hemmed in by trigger happy private shooters, I had a fair idea of what I was doing.

It was with somewhat mixed feelings that I loaded up my trailer with gear from the log cabin and packed the bales of possum skins into my vehicle. I knew I would not be coming back to my trapper's camp at Clements. Too much valuable time had been lost hanging round camp in the weekends owing to the large numbers of private shooters romping about in the bush. And the very ones who had screwed it up for me were now to become the beneficiaries of the hard work and effort that had been expended in building what I was leaving behind. Once they got to realizing the place had been abandoned, Clements Camp and the log cabin would become open slather. As I drove away from the clearing for the last time a melancholy mood hung about me, well anyway, for about a hundred yards or so down the road it did.

The sun was shining, there wasn't a cloud in the sky. Rays of brightness dappled outlines of undergrowth on the pumice road as they filtered down through the forest canopy. It was one very nice day as I drove out of SF90, and there was a summer full of adventure lay ahead of me. First, I had to liaise with the American cine photographer and his wife once I got to Christchurch and then safari them down the West Coast, and following that there was a job waiting for me on a Bluff crayfishing boat that was going to take me into the thick of Fiordland.

And I had already worked out what I was going to do next winter. I planned on working my way into Odey country... real fur country beneath the shadow of Mount Ruapehu. I had been working with mediocre furs long enough. It was time to get stuck into some proper possums — possums up there in the world class category. Come to think of it, those private shooters might just have done me a good turn in driving me out.

Nevertheless, it would not be the same not having Jack Bramley dropping in to commandeer the wood range and soft boil his dozen eggs for morning tea; not to mention all those times spent sitting round a blackened tea billy with Arthur, Merv and Hori Hay, spinning yarns and scoffing gunpowder loaves smeared thick with creamy butter and strawberry jam. And then there was the forest itself. You would have to travel a long way to find something prettier than a stand of ancient old red beech trees spattered with giant podocarps towering high above the lush groves of silver fern and colourful horopito the way you found them on Cherry Ridge and up on Mill Face.

Yeah, I guessed some things would not be quite the same. I supposed I might even miss it... just a little.

CHAPTER 10

Safari South

Cameras, tripods, boots, khaki shirts and trousers, rods, guns, empty suitcases, sleeping bags, day packs, hot water bottles, tins of 16mm cine film, emergency food rations, folding camp stretchers, fishing jackets, picnic baskets, inflatable air mattresses, mosquito netting... gear strewn all over the suite. Mr and Mrs Ben Morris were in the process of "sorting out the necessities" for the forthcoming safari. And with only an 88 inch Short Wheel Base Safari Wagon to pack it into, and my own gear already packed and taking precedence, there was about to become a site more sorting and a heap less "necessities" than Ben and Mrs M. may have been contemplating. It was late in the day when I had driven into Christchurch from Picton so we weren't going anywhere until the next day anyway. I suggested they leave everything right where it was and we all go have a nice quiet drink in the bar while we discuss the objectives of the Morris' safari.

Back in the States Ben had a slot on a local television channel for his hunting, fishing and outdoors movies. Rex Forrester had given him a taste of fly fishing around Rotorua, and somewhere between pub and fishing grounds had filled his head with mind boggling stories about great herds of deer, chamois and tahr roaming free and unchecked throughout the Southern Alps. Then I had happened along and new vistas were opened before the Morris' eyes. According to Rex, here was the opportunity they had been looking for to get them some amazing footage.

Knowing I was about to head south for the summer and never one to miss an easy shot, Rex introduced me to the Morris' as a pro' hunter who, if they picked up the expense tab, just might be willing to let them tag along for a week or two while I worked my way down the Coast and into Queenstown. From Queenstown, immediately after Christmas, they were planning to move on to Erewhon Station under their own steam. In a way it suited me. I was going that way, anyway.

On the side Rex had assured me that I was onto a good thing. The Morris' were loaded with money and I was about to be treated like royalty. All they wanted were a few shots of hunting territory, the odd trout rising in some West Coast lake, and some good mountain scenery.... No problem!

Not wanting to embarrass me by saying too much in my own hearing; on the side Rex had assured Ben Morris he was onto a good thing. I was a "gun" shooter, one of New Zealand's best, who was going to get the Morris' into the best this country had to offer. The Coast was my stamping ground and if any man could get them among the big herds I was he.... No problem!

Learning all these nice things about myself over a dry martini in the house bar of the White Heron Lodge was something of a revelation... not to mention a bit of a worry. Getting in amongst the herds of tahr and deer up on the West Coast tops was no easy matter; not even for fit and healthy professionals. It took hours of footslogging through rugged bush clad valleys weighed down beneath overweight packs of provisions and gear, and usually hours more solid slogging straight up ridges and bush faces before you broke out into the open tops. And even then there was no guarantee you were going to run into herds of anything.

Just a year or two earlier you possibly could have counted on it. Large herds of deer and tahr had been roaming virtually unchecked throughout the Southern Alps. But all that was changing fast. Helicopter operators had been springing up everywhere, and I had not the faintest idea where they had and had not been working. In some areas they had already greatly reduced the numbers of deer and scattered what was left back into the bush. And even if you did manage to strike it right and somehow climbed through bush into an unworked area, if the wind suddenly gusted the wrong way, the deer would be spooked and gone before you got anywhere near them. As for the tahr, they were more often than not several thousand feet higher again, amongst the inaccessible crags and rocky bluffs. And as for the chamois, although I had occasionally seen mobs with up to a dozen or so, I had never seen huge mobs of them at any time, ever. Getting an obviously unfit couple of grain fed Americans up to the tops and being there long enough to stalk and film wild animals and then getting them safely back down to the valley again before evening closed in on you, leaving the lot of you stranded in the middle of some bluff filled bush face for the night was a little daunting to say the least. Furthermore, Forrester was being more than just a little extravagant with the truth with his wild claims about my prowess as a shooter. I had never been more than average at the best of times. Not expecting more of me than Rex Forrester had assured them I was capable of delivering Ben and his good wife were only expecting me to deliver a miracle.... No problem!

Being dubbed a "gun" of the trade by Forrester did have its advantages though. For one thing it put me in good stead for sorting the essentials from the superfluous: "That 300 Weatherby Magnum with the beautifully grained American walnut stock looks interesting. We'll chuck that in the back of the Land Rover along with a handful of ammo. Don't forget your camera and a few rolls of film. Throw in a couple of sleeping bags and a change of socks, and whatever else you've got can be crammed back in your suitcases and stored here until you find your way back from Erewhon Station."

Notwithstanding my qualifications and finesse, Ben still insisted on packing a middling size suitcase with a spare set of pyjamas, shaving gear, white socks and underwear along with various bits and pieces of other unnecessary rubbish, and wifey stated quite flatly that she wasn't going anywhere unless her own personal trunk full of female unimaginables, plus her ever present handbag stuffed with make-up and powder puffs were also loaded into my Land Rover. In the end there wasn't a great deal I could do about it.

Straight after breakfast the next morning we were on our way.

I had never driven through Arthur's Pass before, so naturally that was the route to go. Soon we were passing through neatly ploughed and planted grain fields as we crossed the Canterbury Plains heading towards the Alps.

"You know, this place is just like the Wheat-belt, only on a miniature scale," noted Ben.

And Mrs M. agreed: " Yep! It sure is. But it ain't got the same scope."

Some time later we passed through a batch of tussocky low lying land prior to the foothills.

"You know what this place reminds me of?" said Ben.

"Yep!" said Mrs M. "Prairie lands, back North Dakota way."

"It sure does, but it ain't as broad and expansive as back in Dakota."

We drove on, enjoying the beautiful New Zealand scenery, until we were well clear of the plains and into the Waimakariri Valley.

"Hey now, don't this look just like Montana country," observed Ben Morris.

"Ain't never seen nothing more like it, other than back in Montana," agreed Mrs M.

"But it's on a much smaller scale," reminded Ben.

Somewhere along the way our little safari passed through bits of southern Utah, and long before we hit the Southern Alps I knew exactly where it was we were heading: "Gosh darn it! This could be plumb smack in the middle of the Rockies, 'cepting the mountains ain't as imposing like they are back home in the Rockies."

We also ventured into a slice of the Sierra Nevada's and a pocket of Alaska somewhere still to the east of Arthur's Pass, and after that I didn't really give a damn where we were, even when we got to the

Andes, because I was under the impression we were still in New Zealand, and if they tried to tell me that the West Coast was just like somewhere in Canada or Central America or some other where I was just likely to bop them one to make them put a sock in it. And anyway, I was still contemplating how I was going to go about getting these gabbling Yanks, along with their 16mm camera, powder puffs, Weatherby Magnum and all, a couple of hours up the first valley, let alone to the open tops.

We got as far as Franz the first night and dossed down in the luxury of the Franz Joseph THC Hotel. More dry martinis while lolling about on plush sofas with huge padded cushions, trolleys full of hors d'oeuvres, and then came dinner.... Prime New Zealand rack of ribs, potatoes baked in their jackets and filled with sour cream, fabulously prepared greens with garlic bread and vintage red wine. And after this the dessert. Steamed plum pudding and whipped cream sufficient to make your hair stand on end. Followed by a selection of what Ben referred to as "unassumingly good New Zealand cheeses." But not wanting to make a pig of myself I passed up on the cheeses and settled instead for a silver platter heaped high with brandy snaps filled with more whipped cream and a side plate of assorted dainties. Then came the coffee. Said to be the finest of pure Arabica coffee. A beautiful cup of hot coffee with a teaspoon of brown sugar and a measure of dark rum to neutralize the effects of the caffeine and assure a good night's sleep. And an after dinner mint chocolate put the final touch to a beautiful cholesterol free meal.

As a matter of fact cholesterol did not exist during the sixties. If it had already been invented, it was not mentioned in the better circles. Even years later, when some narrow minded persons tried to convince me of its existence I refused to believe in it. To this day I remain unconvinced and eating is much more pleasurable as a result.

That night I floated to sleep on a quilted mattress my head surrounded by half a dozen down filled pillows. Quite a contrast to the norm. Usually, when travelling down the Coast, if I got as far as Harihari I would doss down near the river beneath a bunch of willow trees. But Forrester had told me I was to be treated like royalty, and royalty could hardly be expected to doss down in some cattle paddock now, could they? Actually, once one learned how to ignore the empty talk and pointless prattle, safari guiding began shaping up into being not such a bad sort of a lurk after all.

Ben and his missus weren't in any great hurry to get started next morning. First they wanted their morning coffee. Then Ben wanted to browse the morning paper before settling into a hearty breakfast of crispy bacon with two eggs... sunny side up... and a couple of hash-browns and wholemeal toast and raspberry jelly, followed by a large helping of golden pancakes liberally drenched with genuine Canadian maple syrup. Needing sustenance for the day ahead, which I had suggested should be spent leisurely inspecting Franz Joseph Glacier then driving over the hill to Fox where there was another glacier and several other points of interest to take in, I doubled up on Ben's breakfast order and threw in a mixed grill to compliment the bacon, while Mrs M. settled for a light Continental breakfast of cereals and fruit salad. I told her that she was going to need a bit more than that to put some packing under her ribs if she ever hoped to keep up once we got rolling with the camera.

One thing I have never found difficult is instilling upon others with whom I may be associating, my enthusiasm for the West Coast's magnificent bush and mountain scenery. No other place in the world can one climb up amongst subtropical forests and look down on huge rivers of ice as one can at Franz and Fox Glaciers, and for once my glib tongued Americans had nothing to compare back home in the USA. The southern rata was ablaze with flower, imposing a gorgeous flare of crimson bloom against the deep white snow fields of Mounts Cook and Tasman. The Waiho and Fox Rivers, glacier fed and milky white, tumbled resolutely over green hued boulders sparkling with silica as they forged their way towards the not too distant coast. Native pigeons, crops full of miro berries, cooed contentedly in the bush and for the sheer joy of living tumbled their aerobatics as they moved from tree to tree. The song of bellbirds and tuis filled the air. The hugeness and awesomeness of it all, the incredible power and forces that must have been behind the creation of it all. The Morris' loved it so much they decided to book into the Fox Hotel and spend a few days exploring the area, chasing reflections in Lake Matheson, and watching silky glow worms hanging amongst the ferns beneath roadside banks.

I left them to it. Two full days of Land Rover full of silly talk and perfume had me seeking solitude. There was an old pioneer's cottage down by the Clearwater River with a couple of comfortable bunks, walls thickly insulated with still legible 19th century newspapers, and an open fireplace for swinging a billy. I told the Morris' I would be back to get them straight after breakfast on the morrow and I took off for a night of peace and seclusion. Besides I wanted to go read the wallpaper and catch up on a bit of 19th century news by candle light.

Back in the hotel, someone told the Morris' they just had to visit Lake Matheson first thing in the morning and take in the incredible reflections of Mount Cook and Mount Tasman. First light was usually the best time to visit the lake, when everything was flat calm and there was not so much as a ripple on the water.

A couple of years back, Bob Hannigan and I had got up real early one morning, after spending the night in the old pioneer's cottage,

*The old pioneer's cottage at Clearwater River Fox Glacier
(photo Bob Hannigan)*

with every intention of getting round the back of the lake before
the breeze got up and spoiled the surface of the black waters. Kim
the dog was with us, and I had Shep and Tip, dogs that had been
trained to rip pigs and goats apart on culling blocks in Marlborough.
Shep was a good old dog from my own pack, but Tip, a massive bull
terrier-Labrador-goodness knows what type of a cross, was a bit of
an unknown entity. One of my culling mates who had thrown in the
hills for city life had given him to me just before we sailed from the
North Island. He reckoned the dog was a regular killer and too good
to be tied up round town. Bob parked the Chev near the beginning
of the track and we took off at a run down through the bush towards
the lake, Shep and Tip ranging out ahead. A few minutes down the
track somewhere way up ahead of us the dogs started to perform.
They had something bailed. I had never heard of wild pigs around
Lake Matheson so I could only imagine they must have gotten on to
a straggling deer. Anyway whatever it was, they had it bailed, because
their barking wasn't going anywhere.

"Get hold of it, Tip! Go get 'im Shep!" I started hollering at the
top of my voice. And the two of us took off in the direction full tit,
yelling wild encouragement to the dogs to get stuck in and not let the
so-and-so get away.

We belted round a portion of the track hollering and shouting for
the dogs to rip it apart, and there they were. Tip was frothing round
the jowls, hackles up and Shep alongside, barking furiously. It was a

perfect bail. Backed up against a big old tree was one very terrified looking tourist.

"Oops! Sorry!" I said. "Get away you bunch of dumb idiots." I yelled at the dogs. And turning on our heels we took off back up the track about three times the speed we had just run down it, into the Chev and gone.

I guess the dogs had got as big a fright as the tourist, suddenly coming upon him like that on the track, and that was why they had bailed him. But I never did figure out how that tourist had got there. There was no vehicle other than Bob's Chev in the parking lot. Not even a bicycle.

Just a few miles from the old pioneer's cottage at Clearwater River there lived a couple of elderly gold fossickers, the Shaw brothers, of Gillespies Beach. During a previous visit they had told me how they had worked their way up the Coast from the goldfields of Otago. They had come looking for the legendry nuggets of gold that were said to be nestled in amongst the black ironsands of Westland just waiting for someone to come by and fill their pockets with them. They had worked their way past Knights Point, negotiating dangerous river mouths and tide washed bluffs, panning for colours as they went. Then one day with hardly a speck of gold to show for their efforts, they arrived at Gillespies. It was a peculiar tide running that day. One that occurred only once in a blue moon. Surf was pounding the coast sending foaming waters surging up the beach, and as the tide receded the black sands were being sluiced back into the sea leaving nuggets of gold glittering in the sunshine as far as the eye could see.

The Shaw brothers reckoned that was one heck of a day. They raced round like a couple of madmen, filling their pockets with pieces of gold, and from that day on they had stayed at Gillespies working the black sands and getting rich. According to the Shaws, it was not often that the tides sluiced the sands and exposed the gold, so at first they had spent a lot of time watching and waiting for the right conditions to occur. But eventually they had set up pumps and sluiced their claims at their leisure.

Rain was pelting down. Rivers were rising, and by the look of it there was not going to be much filming for a day or two. Nor was there going to be much sluicing of gold claims. The conditions were just right for visiting the Shaw brothers.

Ben and his wife immediately hit it off with the Shaws. The four of them laughed and joked, played cards and talked about everything and anything until I got bored with it all and decided there was more fun in hanging out with the housemaids and waitresses back at the Fox Hotel.

For as far back as history made mention, the housemaids and waitresses at the Fox Hotel had been a diversion and source of entertainment for hunters, shooters, and Haast Road construction workers alike. It was nothing driving seventy five miles or so from Lake Moeraki to Fox and back at the end of a day, for a jug of beer and a chance to perve at the "sheilas", as our friend Jim Barkle referred to it.

During the summer of 1965, with our meat shooting base just a few miles down the road at Karangarua, Bob and I were in and out of Fox for stores often, and as a result we got to know several of the housemaids and waitresses. But for Barkle, isolated down at Lake Moeraki with nothing but fellow bulldozer drivers to talk with, Fox was like Tinsel Town to a gold miner. With a few beers under his belt, Barkle had plucked up sufficient courage to want to be introduced to some of the girls we knew. Dinner was over and the waitresses had knocked off, the bar was bustling with drinkers, and the house maids were busily doing their rounds turning down beds and putting mint chocolates on the pillows for the house guests who would soon be retiring for the night. The three of us, Barkle, Bob and I, ducked away from the bar to go have a coffee in the staff quarters before starting on the return trip back to our camps. Then Barkle noticed a couple of housemaids entering one of the guest rooms doing their rounds. Thinking we were right behind him, he crept along the passageway, got down on his hands and knees and sticking his face full of whiskers close up to the door he began squinting through the keyhole and giving a running commentary on what the "sheilas" were doing inside the room.

"Come and get a load of these sheilas, you guys," says Barkle, in a slightly pitched tone.

Meanwhile Bob and I had noticed an elderly American tourist and his wife right behind us, and sensing that Barkle was about to do something embarrassing we had hung back and let them past us. In the excitement of the moment Barkle had failed to notice that we were hanging back at the far end of the passage almost out of sight and it was no longer us but the elderly tourists standing alongside him that he was now talking to.

"They're working on the bed," adds Barkle. "I should go in and give them a hand."

The old couple, who obviously could not believe what they were seeing, had stopped in their tracks.

"You guys go and look in the keyhole next door," says Barkle. And as he turns around to give us the extra needed encouragement to go get our own keyhole, for the first time realizes that he has been talking all along to a couple of shocked tourists. Barkle was a big bloke, and his face full of whiskers probably made him look even bigger than he really was, but I will say one thing for him: He could certainly move quite quickly when he wanted to. He was up on his feet and sprinting.

Bob and I took off the other way, just about wetting our pants with laughter.

By the time Barkle found Bob and me, we were back in the bar and still spluttering in our glasses with laughter.

"G'day! Where have you been?" said Bob as Barkle comes alongside. "You look all steamed up as if you've been for a run or something."

"Nope, haven't been anywhere," says Barkle. "Just been out the back to the men's."

"Are you ready for a cup of coffee with the housemaids?" I asked.

"Nah! I'm getting a bit tired. Think I'll call it a day and start heading for Moeraki."

It continued to rain for several more days and by now the Morris' had checked out of the Fox Hotel and moved in with the Shaws, who seemed to be really enjoying their company. And then it stopped raining and the sun came out and, as is typical on the Coast, in a very short while all the excess water had drained off the hills, everything was back to normal and we were piling on board the Shaw brothers' aluminium dinghy, powered by a small outboard jet motor, and negotiating blackwater creeks through pakihi swamplands and kahikatea forests and heading downstream to Gillespie Point, home of a large seal colony.

Ben was really taken with this opportunity of filming fur seals at such close quarters. Previously I had watched him filming glow worms and other forms of wild life of parallel intelligence hanging beneath waterlogged banks and so forth, but this was the first time I had witnessed him handling the camera on free thinking intelligent animals. I was also taken. Not with the seals, but with his filming technique. Walking boldly straight up to the seals he set his tripod in amongst the beach gravel and captured some first class shots of panicking seals disappearing into the surf. There was another cluster of them basking just a little further afield, so with the first lot gone, Ben headed straight for these and immediately panicked them also. This time, though, he was more fortunate with the result. One heavyweight old bull seal had been dozing and taking little notice as the rest of the colony dispersed. But when he suddenly realized that all his mates were gone and here he was on his own with Ben and his tripod standing between him and the sea.... Ben managed some exciting footage of a boldly advancing bull seal intent on forcing passage, before it suddenly dawned on Ben that if he didn't uplift his camera and make his own hasty retreat both he and camera were about to become history. After that little incident Ben decided he had sufficient footage of fur seals for the folks back home and it was time to retire to the boat.

Although it may be amusing thinking back on Ben being scattered by a bull seal, I was far from amused at the time. Purportedly he was a wildlife cameraman who was supposed to know what he was doing. I could hardly believe what I had just seen. Anyone with half a brain would already have known how wild creatures are going to react at the sight of a man charging in amongst them. I could only wonder how he might have faired if rather than a cut-off frightened bull seal the subject had been an enraged cornered rhinoceros.

Although somewhat disconcerting, the incident had also aroused my curiosity. I wondered just how close to a fur seal one might be able to get if they were approached sensibly. It seemed rather obvious to me that as long as you got down to their level and posed no apparent threat they would probably allow you to approach quite close. More seals were basking on rocks a hundred or so yards further on again and with Ben and the team heading back to the dinghy, I got down low and began working my way in amongst them. Getting on the inland side of them so they wouldn't feel cut off if they became disturbed by my presence, I slithered right in amongst them with no problem at all, and poked my imaginary camera in the face of a magnificent old bull seal as he rolled over and yawned nonchalantly into the imaginary lens. Just as quietly as I had slithered in amongst them I slithered back out, and not one of them showed the slightest concern at my presence.

I now knew that I wasn't even going to try and walk Ben and his darling up into the open tops to film mobs of chamois, deer and tahr. It would be quite pointless, because even if I did get them there, the best they would get on their film would be panicking animals hightailing it over the distant skyline.

By the time I got back to the dinghy, they were almost loaded and ready to go. Ben seemed quite happy with the footage he had secured, but as we putt-putted our way through the pakihi I remained somewhat pensive and withdrawn. While they were busily talking I was busily formulating a plan for getting them in amongst the animals and getting some exciting footage in the can. And I reckoned that before I was done I would give them something to write home about into the bargain. Rex Forrester had led them to believe that I was capable of giving them all that they hoped for. Somehow, I was going to have to do it.

As we drove south, past the Karangarua Valley, and Ben got to gazing on the enormity of the country — the huge bush faces rising from the river flats, and thousands of feet up the bush faces the alpine meadows shimmering gold beneath the steely grey bluffs of granite, and beyond the bluffs the hanging glaciers and fields of eternal snow dazzling white against the clear blue sky — it started to dawn on him that getting he and Mrs Morris up there amongst the clouds, and hanging valleys, and snow grass, and stuff might be a bit more demanding than it was back home driving the family wagon round Yellowstone Park with a camera dangling out the window.

An hour or so up the Karangarua River, there was a leading ridge with well defined deer tracks all the way to the tops that Bob Hannigan and I had gotten onto a couple of years previous to this. We had imagined it would take no more than three hours travel to break through into the open tops. Five hours of solid slogging later we eventually broke through the moss-encrusted upper-storey level of sub-alpine growth, into the golden glow of late afternoon sun drenched open snow grass tops. By then it was just about too late in the day to make it back down to the valley before dark, so we decided to camp out in the open tops and drop back down the following day. Fortunately the weather stayed fine overnight, but it was bitterly cold up in the tops with insufficient clothing and no adequate shelter. Then early the next morning the weather broke. Cloud poured into the valley from the Tasman Sea quickly enveloping everything from skyline to valley floor. Then came the rain. A deluge of it. Wet, cold and hungry we took off into the bush and headed back down the ridge we had climbed the previous afternoon. But in the confusion of rain and swirling cloud we got onto a spur and ended up in a mess of bluffs and rubbish in the McTaggart watershed. We eventually got back to our base near the Karangarua Bridge getting on dark at the end of an exhausting and pretty miserable sort of a day full of bush whacking and ploughing through mud and water and rubbish up to our eyeballs. The one consolation for our little excursion was that the open tops were just about virgin at the time and we had a fair sort of a bomb up on the deer while up there. But since then the choppers had shot those particular tops to hell and gone. Ben enjoyed the story, but it didn't do much towards building up his enthusiasm for trying it. I had hoped it wouldn't.

The trout were rising as we drove past Lake Paringa but we kept going until we got to Lake Moeraki where I knew the trout were big and often easy to secure if you cared to sneak through the bush a few yards up river from the bridge and lob a zeddy into the current. There was nothing wrong with the fishing but we could not stay too long. Mrs Morris' make-up was melting in the midday heat. Nor was she doing too good with the sandflies chewing bits out of her and the sun discolouring her pale and delicate skin. So we moved on to Knights Point and stopped there for a roadside picnic lunch with colourful gingham napkins and flasks of coffee that the Morris' had somehow managed to smuggle into the Land Rover back at the White Heron Lodge. And we enjoyed a lovely picnic, not vastly different to what all the other regular tourists do when they get to places like Knights Point; excepting that Mrs Morris looked a little strange, even for a regular tourist, sitting there with newspapers draped all over her head to protect her skin and face from the ravages of sunburn.

By now the Morris' had seen enough of Westland and the Southern Alps to have come to their own foregone conclusion that the average American cine photographer and cine photographer's wife were just not cut out for handling this sort of country. The time was right to implement my plan.

With only six more shopping days to Christmas, the chopper boys at Mussel Point, south of Haast, were tending more towards thoughts of booze, wild women and song, rather than all out efforts to boost the tally prior to their Christmas break. Our timing was spot on. A few days earlier and we would not have got a hearing, but so close to Christmas no one cared a hoot whether we hired their chopper for a couple of hours before sunset, or not. No one, that is, apart from their boofheaded Australian cook, who was harbouring some sort of a snitch against Rex Forrester and thought he would take it out on me instead. This caught my fancy somewhat, so I asked him what Forrester might have done to so upset him, to which he slurred, "Nothing, never met the bastard. But if I ever do I'm going to hang one on him anyway." Cookie didn't stay rattled for long. By all accounts he was already half fonged. Someone handed him another jug of beer and his conversation drifted away into blowing bubbles and slobbers and froth. I never did bother mentioning it to Rex.

There was room in the chopper for only three persons and Mrs Morris said she wasn't too keen on going anywhere anyway. Ben was asked to pay up front... I supposed in case the chopper did not make it back... and he and I piled in with the pilot who, I recall, was dressed in white bobby socks and was also named Ben Morris. Seeing we were packing only a camera, the shooters did not mind telling me that no one had worked the Landsborough tops for sometime, and that was where there were bound to be plenty of deer. And there were.

I nearly broke down and cried when I saw how easy it was zipping up to the tops in a nifty little Hiller 12E compared to the way I had always done it; following deer trails and ridges and stumbling over roots and plodding wearily on hour after hour after hour with a pack full of provisions busting your gut and whittling away your resolve. I pointed out to Ben Morris the pilot where I wanted him to hit the tops, on the east side of the Landsborough somewhere upriver from Fraser Hut and not too far removed from the Broderick Pass, and straight away there were deer.

Ben Morris, the pilot, had been based at Mussel Point long enough to know what he was doing. The deer, about a dozen of them, broke uphill, and Ben the pilot got in behind them, while Ben the cinematographer hung out the bubble reeling off film by the furlong just yards behind them. Then Ben Morris overshot them with the chopper and the deer turned and ran back down the hill while the other Ben Morris hung out the bubble again and shot furlongs more film as they ran all the way back down to where they had just come from. Then the first Ben Morris swung the chopper round and chased them across a plateau whilst the other Ben Morris continued to hang out the bubble and shoot off streets more 16mm film. By now most of the deer had their tongues hanging out and I reckoned if we chased them uphill one more time they would all expire of combustion or something and we would be able to get out and load them on the racks and deliver them back to Mussel Point as venison. But I didn't want to do that as I had told the boys we were only shooting with a camera and they weren't expecting us to go around shooting them dead with the camera and killing them into the bargain.

Then Ben Morris turned the chopper on its tail rotor and we screamed off across the plateau in the other direction and we were so close to the tussock I imagined I was travelling on the ground, and when he drove us right off the edge of a bluff with a sheer three thousand foot drop below us I nearly dropped dead of fright myself because I knew that when you do that sort of thing, like charging over sheer drop offs up in the tops of mountains, you normally don't come back. It took a bit of getting used to the idea that choppers are different. Ben Morris hung us all in mid air while I gripped the edges of my seat and braced myself for the inevitable drop, but when I next opened my eyes we were chasing another mob of deer up another slope while the other Ben Morris continued reeling off the footage. This was more fun than I could have imagined. And then the deer all bunched up and stopped running, and hunkered down amongst the alpine scrub and looked terrified while we hovered over the top of them and Ben Morris continued reeling off film, and I started feeling sorry for the deer because I had never seen deer react like that before. But I supposed if I had been out on the hill and something as alien as a space craft full of little green monsters or something other that I could not comprehend started chasing me all over the hills and hovering over the top of me I would have been hunkering down also, but even more so.

Ben Morris was so excited about all the deer he was filming while his name sake was chasing them with the helicopter, that he clean forgot to enquire about chasing tahr, which was just as well, because I didn't fancy clipping rock faces with the rotors while one Ben Morris got in behind a bunch of agile tahr bouncing from ledge to ledge with the other Ben Morris hanging out the bubble egging his fellow on.

So Ben Morris got to filming mobs of deer up in the open tops, and something to write home about. And Mrs Morris got to enjoying drinks with the boys down at Mussel Point, who all, with the exception of Aussie cook who was still busily engrossed in slobbering up to his ears in froth in his jug, and would not have known any better anyway, acted like perfect gentlemen in her presence.

We still had a few days to fill in before Christmas, so we fished and filmed our way down the Makarora Valley to Lake Wanaka and through the gap to Lake Hawea, until Mrs Morris decided she was fed up with her make-up melting beneath her sheets of newspaper draped all over her head, and we were instructed in no uncertain terms to abandon the safari and drive straight to Queenstown where Ben had booked rooms for the three of us at Eichardt's THC Hotel on the waterfront.

As far as I was concerned the safari was over. The Morris' had thoroughly enjoyed themselves and immediately after Christmas they were moving on to Erewhon where they expected to hunt and film chamois and tahr. But for now they wanted me to stay on with them at Eichardt's as their guest, because it was their custom to share their Christmas turkey and cranberry sauce, and steamed plum pudding topped with gallons of whipped cream with family, and this year there were not any of their family around to share it with.

However, according to Mrs Morris, from the time we drove out of Christchurch I had been growing upon them just like I was one of their own family, and if the number of times she had displayed photos of her youngest daughter for my approval was anything to go by, I was inclined to worrying that that just might have been an underlying thought she had been contemplating all along.

At their insistence I moved into the Eichhardt Manse, where I was able to enjoy fabulous views from my bedroom window of a coffee shop straight across the street, while they moved into the main hotel, where they too had fabulous views from their bedroom window, but of the "M.V. Earnslaw" docked across at the wharf, and of the harbour and a gorgeous panorama of mountain scenery and beautiful Lake Wakatipu. And we all hung around and waited for Christmas.

Somewhere around this time some of my friends and associates from the hunting fraternity arrived in town for a bit of celebrating and general Christmas booze, and they got to hearing about me living in regal splendour batched up in Eichhardt's Manse with the fabulous view of the coffee shop from my bedroom window while their lot was sleeping under the macrocarpa hedge outside the Forestry Office up on the hill, with dogs chained all around them and empty beer bottles. Being full of good cheer and happiness for me that I was doing so well, and they were not, I suppose it was inevitable that something had to transpire. So it was not entirely unexpected when Mrs M. came and woke me from my slumbers one morning around about morning tea time, sunk down deep in my Sleepyhead mattress and padded all around with soft pillows filled with finest down, and insisted that I come downstairs and pose alongside my Land Rover while she take photos of me and the Land Rover from various angles, because someone had plastered all the windows with "Danger Keep Out, 1080 Poison" and "Cyanide Poison" posters freshly perked from the Forestry Office, and it was raising quite a stir down there in the main shopping street, because no one was quite sure whether the signs were genuinely warning people to keep away from a vehicle full of toxic gases or it was all some sort of a joke. And while Mrs M. got me to stand this way and pose that way, and passersby gave Mrs M., me and the Land Rover a wide berth, I became increasingly aware that unusual amounts of mirth and merriment, and raucous jeering were issuing forth from the coffee shop across the street. And after awhile I got to realizing that it was no ordinary mob of tourists in the coffee shop having a good time — not with those whiskery faces peering out from behind the lacy curtains looking for all the world like Dale Hunter, Bob Hannigan, Freddy Langenegger and Doug Ford, all making fools of themselves laughing at my discomfort and embarrassment.

It didn't take a whole lot of guessing figuring out which one of them was responsible. We were all mates and there wasn't anything unusual about pulling pranks on one's mates whenever the opportunity arose. But more often than not the instigator of a practical joke ended up the subject of a reciprocal. And sometimes before it was all over the going got a little heavy. Dale knew that I would be looking for the opportunity, and he knew I'd be setting my sights on his Series One open top Land Rover.

When he flew out of Queenstown later that day heading for the North Island he took great pains to park his Land Rover well out of the way, tucked under the pines one end of the airport. But being a professional trapper and hunter, I was well used to tracking things down.

It was with great jubilation that I eventually found it, parked alongside meat shooter George Wyber's vehicle. With Dale gone there was really no need to rush, but I could hardly contain myself. I tore back into town, bought a pot of lolly-dolly pink paint and a paint brush, and inside of two hours Dale's rugged little army green shooting rig was the colour of Pink Sugar Dolly's lace panties. By the time Dale returned to Queenstown I was well and truly gone, hauling crayfish somewhere off the Fiordland Coast.

Meanwhile Dale arrived back in Queenstown, wandered down to the general area where he had hidden his vehicle, saw this ridiculously painted candy pink Land Rover tucked away beneath the pines and stood there chuckling to himself that anybody could be so stupid as to paint their Land Rover such an effeminate colour.... Only a la-la-pooftah would drive round in a vehicle with a colour scheme like that.... And suddenly it dawned on him, he was laughing at his own vehicle. That was where he had parked his Land Rover — right

Turning a green Land Rover pink (photo Doug Ford)

alongside George Wyber's rig.

Dale drove his Land Rover, just once, into town to stock up with provisions before flying back into his meat shooting block in the Pyke. Self consciously he drove through town, imagining all the tourists were laughing and pointing him out, which they probably were, and as quickly as he could do so he drove back to the airport and parked his vehicle, but this time well clear of George Wyber's vehicle in case George, if he had not already done so, got to seeing it too. He never drove it again.

He sold the vehicle, "as is, where is" to fellow meat shooter, Ray Finn, who promptly repainted it, pine needles and all, a more dignified shade of black.

(If he ever saw it, Dale's L/R was possibly the last great laugh that George Wyber had. Sad to say, not long after, George crashed his Auster aircraft in heavy fog while flying to Queenstown off the Alabaster strip and was killed.)

"Pinky Dink!" (photo Doug Ford)

CHAPTER 11

Craypots and Venison

Robbie Ballantyne braced himself at the helm of the "F.V. Tarawai" as the old wooden ship pitched off the crest of a towering wave and crashed heavily into the trough below. For a moment she seemed to sit there, juddering, buried deep in the trough, Then as the stem came up with the oncoming sea, a huge wall of water smashed heavily against the port beam. Foaming green water cascaded over the bow, surged round the deck and poured out the scuppers. Back aft, one of Ballantyne's young sons sprawled out the companionway, head lolling from side to side upon the deck with the lurch of the ship. Sick beyond caring, nothing left to vomit, green bile and saliva dribbling from his mouth, and we still hadn't gotten past Centre Island with sixty or more miles to go before land fall. A younger Ballantyne lad lay griping in a corner on the wheelhouse floor. He was beyond making a mess. He'd puked up all he had within the hour of leaving Bluff. Sixty more miles of Roaring Forties sou'westerly to Puysegur Point and already the two boys were looking sicker than a couple of dead chickens.

Back on the wharf at Bluff, I had followed closely behind Robbie and his first mate, Des, as they clambered onto the deck of a sturdy looking fishing vessel and I could not help but think what a pleasure it was going to be sailing out of port on such a fine looking ship. Big, beamy and solid. Working aboard a boat such as this was going to be great. But Robbie went neither to the wheelhouse, nor to the companionway. He carried on across the deck, climbed over the bulwark and lowered himself onto "something else" that was tied alongside — an old wooden hulled vessel that might have been a great old ship in her day. But that was then and this was now. She was long, about 60 feet from stem to stern, and narrow gutted. Somewhere along the way someone told me that she had once been a Bluff Harbour tug, until she was pensioned off. Someone else reckoned she had been an old dunger on the waters of Lake Manapouri, until she was pensioned off. Whatever! I think my first impression summed her up quite adequately.... She was "something else"! This was the fishing vessel "Tarawai"! And she probably should have been pensioned off!

She certainly wasn't the most beautiful ship I had ever seen, the old F.V."Tarawai", what with her weird looking wheelhouse up for'ard giving more the impression of a floating telephone box than a fishing boat. But she was still sound. She had been re-engined, painted green, fitted out for crayfishing and she was still going strong. Even if she was ugly as sin. The first vessel, the fine looking one we were tied alongside, wasn't even a cray boat; she was one of the Bluff oyster fleet.

Many long hours of punching and pitching later we hove to in the lee of Puysegar Point and Robbie's two young boys, looking greener than the waters we had just sailed through, gratefully disembarked to spend their school holidays with the Puysegar lighthouse keeper's family. That night we anchored the "Tarawai" in the calm waters of Otago Retreat alongside Coal Island and I slept like a log on a gently undulating sea.

Long before daybreak Des was up, stoking the coal range and cooking a batch of scrambled eggs. And in the grey chill of early dawn we weighed anchor and steamed out into the Tasman, a huge beam sea, all that remained of the previous day's storm, rolling in from the Antarctic.

Coal Island and Preservation Inlet were soon behind us and as we rounded Cape Providence at the northern head of Chalky Inlet the southerly swells got astern of us, and with a pleasant surging motion, helped us on our way as we pushed north past wild and rugged coast and untamed bush lands that would barely have changed a skerrick since the day Captain James Cook and his crew first laid eyes upon them back in the early part of 1770. And likely nor would there have been much change down through the several preceding millenniums either.

Endless new things for the eyes to feast upon now opened up before me. Great surging breakers smashing relentlessly against sheer seaward bluffs; mollymawks and gulls cresting foaming seas, sliding expertly through the troughs, wingtips skimming the surface while never making contact with the ocean beneath; stunted wind sculpted coastal forest rising like a mantle above the bluffs; tantalising glimpses into sheltered sounds and fiords; inlets fringed by massive cliffs and boundless tracts of impenetrable virgin forest; distant peaks and mountain ranges. Charts to check, reefs and rocky outcrops, bush clad islands big and small, mile upon mile of uninhabited rugged landscape. The wildest and most isolated corner of New Zealand; one huge section of virtually unexplored, very inhospitable and unforgiving piece of country. No one lived here. Fishermen came and went. Fur sealers had been and gone. The venison hunters were just getting to look at it. But they too would be just a passing phase; little more than a blink of an eye in an unbroken and untameable land. A few hardy souls had passed through, but no-one ever stayed; maybe for a year or two, or even a mite longer. But eventually the isolation and the wet would get them, or else the sandflies would drive them insane.

Moose had been liberated in Dusky Sound in 1910, but the country was so wild there was no way of knowing whether a remnant had survived. It was even believed possible that in some inaccessible pocket of Fiordland species of Moa could well still exist. After all, the Takahe had been believed extinct for years when it suddenly turned up alive and well in the Murchison Mountains above Lake Te Anau. Who would know. Much of Fiordland no one had ever set foot in, and much of it would likely stay that way for a long time to come.

By the time we reached Caswell Sound I had wore my binoculars thin. There was so much to look at, so much to take in. My first taste of the deep Sou'west was an experience that I would never forget. From punching a storm through one of the roughest stretches of water in the world to the thick of Wapiti country all in short order.

With all three of us on board double checking charts as well as references in "The New Zealand Pilot" all the way from Puysegur, I would have thought it was fairly obvious where we were, but the skipper had never been this way before and he wanted to make sure, and I suppose there wasn't nothing much wrong with that. A stone's throw south of Caswell a cray boat was hauling a pot. Robbie brought the "Tarawai" in close and hailed them and they told us once we rounded Styles Island lying over yonder, that was Caswell on the other side.

From out to sea, Styles Island and the huge rocky headland of Hansard Point block the view into Caswell Sound. But having rounded McKerr Point and cleared Styles and Hansard, Caswell opens up like a huge mill pond before you. Some ten miles of sheltered Fiord, barely a mile wide at its widest point, cliffs rising perpendicularly from the sea thousands of feet high, and sinking sheer below the surface who knows how many more. Fiordland is subjected to an annual average rainfall in excess of two hundred and fifty inches, and some years well over three hundred inches, most of which falls during the few short months of summer. As a result the waters of the Fiords are brackish dark brown, more fresh than salt and stained from run-off from the rain forests that cover much of the hinterland. Beneath these waters all manner of strange creatures thrive, including rare and delicate corals that one might feel hardly belonged so far removed from the tropical South Pacific. Here was an entirely different ecosystem all of its own.

About thirty minutes into the fiord we came to an anchorage where a couple of fishing boats, "Buccaneer" and "Gleniffer", were already moored for the night. The first ship to arrive would have set its anchor then reversed towards the shore and picked up a mooring rope. After that, others coming alongside would run springs, sturdy ropes crossed from stem to stern, between each ship. Several ships could tie up alongside one another in this manner with only one or two of them setting their anchors to hold everything steady. I quickly came to realize that tying the "Tarawai" with springs was much simpler than setting the anchor. I also quickly came to hate having anything to do with the "Tarawai's" anchor owing to two hazardous faults that I immediately became aware of. First, when that 200lb dreadnaught anchor left the cat head, the chain went whipping off the deck with a mind of its own and if you were not well clear it was just likely to pick you up and take you with it. Second, hauling the anchor in was fine for the skipper standing in the wheel house revving up the capstan winch. But the deck hand, with wet gloves and acting like an earthing-pin was treated to a powerful dose of continuous electrical shock as he hauled on the chain. I was never sure whether it was due to static electricity building up with the chain fairing round the capstan winch, or whether there was some sort of an electrical short in the system. Either way, I hated setting and I hated hauling the "Tarawai's" anchor. There was also a third fault, that I failed to attach much significance to. But a few years later it caused the death of a man. That dreadnaught anchor sometimes came in faster than the crew could safely handle it, and one day it came smashing in through the cat head and stove in the side a crewmember's head.

"Buccaneer" was a ship full of character. She had previously been owned by the commodore of the Royal Tasmanian Yacht Club, who had maintained her as the flag ship of the fleet and mounted a brass plaque in the wheelhouse proudly stating as much. Now owned by Jimmy Waitiri, who had converted her into a crayfishing boat, the "Buccaneer" was big and beamy, about 52 feet long by 17 feet across the deck. She rode well in big seas, with a pleasant motion about her, and was a lovely ship to work on. Her wheel house was aft, and for'ard of the wheelhouse there was a huge working deck, giving the skipper an unobstructed view of what was going on while his offsider was hauling in pots. To my way of looking at it, this made the "Buccaneer" a safer ship to work on than if the wheelhouse was up for'ard and the working deck aft, where the skipper had to keep looking back over his shoulder to see what was going on out on the deck. There were plenty of ships about with their working deck aft of the wheelhouse and there were seldom any problems, but I heard of at least one crew member who could count himself lucky that his skipper happened to be looking over his shoulder at the right time.

The ship was the "F.V. Caroline", a 46 foot steel boat that was owned and skippered by Peter Roderique, from Riverton.. They were working in heavy seas and Trevor Antill, his mate, was balancing

F.V.Buccaneer at anchor, Ruapuke
(photo courtesy Jimmy Ryan)

a cray pot on the gunnel in preparation for shying it back into the depths when he suddenly lost his balance and over the side he went. Naturally, water immediately began pouring into his thigh boots, and with the weight of his rain gear adding to it as the boat came up he went under. At that stage there was only one way left to go... straight down. Regardless of the fact that Trevor was not altogether lucky falling overboard in the first place, he was nevertheless just plain lucky that his skipper saw him doing so. Peter bolted out of the wheelhouse, managed to grab a handful of his mate by the scruff of his raincoat as he disappeared beneath the waves, and with one mighty heave hauled him bodily back onto the deck Neither man was what you would call small, each weighing probably somewhere in the vicinity of 15 stone, or more. Add to that the weight of water in Trevor's boots plus the weight of his wet weather gear, hauling him back onto deck like that with just one hand was nothing short of a Herculean effort. Fortunately it was not often that someone fell overboard.

I got the opportunity to work with Jimmy Waitiri on the "Buccanneer" a few weeks later. His mate, Charlie Fisher, put a grapnel through his wrist when the hook fouled on a float and then came springing back at him under pressure. Charlie was pretty tough and within a couple of days he took over once more. But in just that short time, I grew to wishing I could have stayed on, crewing for Jimmy on the "Buccaneer".

"Gleniffer" the other ship moored on the anchorage when we

arrived in Caswell Sound, was owned and skippered by Bill Davis. He and Jimmy Waitiri were mates and they usually hung out fairly close to one another. They were as nice a couple of blokes as I ever met, and I got to liking them straight off. I think you tend to catch on pretty quick what sort of men you have about you when your life might depend on it sometime. It is not that you like prejudging people. But in high risk jobs it tends to be a bit like that. You get a gut feeling, and somehow you just know you either can, or you feel that maybe you can't, depend on someone. Most hunters were probably that way inclined; taking note of their gut feelings. Maybe the fishermen of Fiordland were too. Anyway, because of the sort of blokes they were, it would have been hard not liking Bill Davis and Jimmy Waitiri.

F.V.Buccaneer *punching a bit of a breeze (photo Jimmy Ryan)*

As the day drew on more ships came in off the fishing grounds and tied up alongside. Sounds of generators blast freezing the day's catch, the smell of salt air and fishing boats, food cooking in the galley, hot coffee and cold beer. Evening shadows crept into the fiord as the sun slipped lower and lower towards the Tasman Sea and a few of us lounged about on the deck of "Buccaneer", eyed inquiringly by a couple of bludging gulls perching atop of the bulwark. We laughed and joked and spun yarns; semi true, slightly embellished, and highly unlikely, as hoards of pestering sandflies hovered about looking for chinks in the "Dimp". There was at least a trace of Maori in many of the men, and quite a few were related to one another. Some had descended down through generations of fishermen, sealers, whalers, muttonbirders, Mainlanders and Stewart Islanders. They were hardy, they were close knit, and they were hospitable. And from the very first I felt accepted by them. In many ways these men of the sea were no different to the men of the bush. They were rough, tough, and could be serious when they needed to be, but they were also full of camaraderie and good humour.

Nicknames were common amongst them and once you were dubbed with one it was yours for life. In the course of time proper names might be forgotten, but nicknames never were; names like "Skull", "Muck-a-luck", "Boong", "Spud", "Magilla Gorilla"... Even the crayfish were nicknamed; "crabs"! Much to his dismay, Robbie Ballantyne was nicknamed "The Taxi Driver'. Prior to buying his boat that was what he had been back in Invercargill, and they reckoned the way he used to drive his taxi was the same way he now drove his boat... whatever that might mean! Bill Davis soon noticed that I seemed to spend more time glassing the coastline for Wapiti than I spent searching the sea for cray pot floats so he called me "White Hunter". But Jimmy Ryan, noticing my fishing gear was old worn out hunting mocker, all chewed up and full of rips and tears, reckoned it looked like the moths had been having a go at me and from there on I was nicknamed, "Mothbite"! A few weeks later, just for fun, Bill Davis thought he would try a new tack and casually mention here and there that he believed I was on the run from the law and I had joined the Bluff fleet until the heat passed over. It was not the first time that I had had a story like that concocted about me, but the previous time, a couple of years earlier, Bob Hannigan and I thought we were going to end up in a shoot out with a loopy Taranaki farmer who had a similar unfounded notion planted in his head. Fortunately none of the other fishermen took it too seriously or I probably would have been dubbed with some unflattering sobriquet to suit.

The first streaks of dawn were barely tinting the morning sky, engines were being fired up, mooring ropes slipped and ships were edging out into the fiord to head for the open sea. And as the gathering light of day gradually replaced the shadows of night a new scene began to unfold. A bevy of bare backsides began to adorn the aft rails of the various ships; black ones, white ones and various hues of brown. Long streamers of toilet paper trailed in the breeze. Not many ships of the Bluff fleet enjoyed the luxury of flush toilets and that left little room for coyness. If you had to go, you had to go. It was simply a matter of down trou', point the aft section in the general direction of

Fiordland self flushing toilet system (photo Jimmy Ryan)

downwind and let rip. In actual fact, no one took much notice. It was just part and parcel of life deep in the depths of Fiordland. And cruising down the fiord doing it, at least you didn't get the bits and pieces chewed up by sandflies. However, from time to time downsides to all of this had been known to occur.

One of the fishermen, suffering the after effects of a hard session in the Milford Pub, was hanging his backside over the aft rail of his boat down Fresh Water Basin about mid morning one day, when he heard an ungodly scream of horror from the direction of the wharf. In his befuddled state, he had completely forgotten where he was. A Fiordlander boat loaded with tourists was backing away from the wharf and the first scenic wonder that had come into view was his bared hairy backside. Joe Murphy, who was chuckling away telling us the story reckoned: "Poor bloke didn't even have time to polish his flute. But I tell you, for a man hobbled round the ankles by his underpants, he made bloody good time disappearing into the wheelhouse."

Just inside the mouth of Caswell, in the lee of Styles Island, we hove to while Des hauled a couple of crates of bait up from the freezer; reject fish unfit for human consumption. We would tie two fish to a pot, hanging from the wire mesh on opposite sides of the cage by a strand of hemp laced through the eye sockets.

The crayfish pots probably should have been called cages rather than pots. They were 4 feet by 3 feet across the top and 18 inches deep, formed from welded half inch reinforcing rods with a couple of solid bars of steel welded into their base for ballast. They were enmeshed with a netting of Hurricane fencing wire, and each pot weighed about 60 pounds. One man could handle a pot on his own, but they were nevertheless quite big and bulky. The "Tarawai" was carrying 28 pots and they were all rigged for fishing into 40 fathoms, with about 250 feet of rope spliced onto each pot topped with a couple of floats bearing the ship's registration number.

Clear of the sound, we steamed slowly northwards, heading up the coast towards George Sound where we would shelter that night, with Robbie eyeing the depth sounder, searching for forty fathom foul, and Des and me on the starboard deck balancing a baited craypot on the railing, rope and floats neatly laid out and taking care to keep our feet well clear of the coils. Forty fathoms was a long way down when you were all dollied up in wet weather gear and thigh length fishing boots.

A short sharp blast on the foghorn was our cue to give the pot a shove, and over it would go, plummeting to the depths below, synthetic rope whipping over the side. At the last minute, the floats were manually heaved overboard to avoid their smashing against the bulwark, and we all stood by watching, making sure that Robbie had sounded the horn at the right instant. For if by chance he had not, and the pot happened to miss the foul, it would go plummeting down to murkier depths and never be seen again. This happened on rare occasions and that was the end of that.

With the loss of a pot, more so than the replacement cost of the lost gear, it was the loss of catching ability that mattered to the skipper. But from my way of looking at it there was also the fact that any pots lost like that might go on catching almost indefinitely. Crayfish would continue to crawl into them, but nothing would ever crawl back out.

I was absolutely absorbed in what we were doing that first day out; just soaking it all up. Apart from the occasional glance coastward, to take a bearing off some landmark or other, my eyes were barely raised from what was going on around the ship. The bottomless blue-green sea, sooty shearwaters and gulls gliding and wheeling across waves, an occasional fishing vessel hauling pots nearby, the endless motion of the mighty Tasman, the manhandling of pots that had been stacked on the aft deck while bracing against rolling ocean swells, baiting up, heaving pots into the brine, trying to memorise the sets as we progressed towards George Sound. Four miles to Two Thumb Bay, and three to Looking Glass. Then three more to Houseroof Rock and another five to George. Fifteen miles of rugged Fiordland coast with pinnacles of 40 fathom foul, said to be crawling with "red gold!", and "red gold", indeed, is what they were.

A lot of boats had their pots rigged for fishing into 60 fathoms, but Robbie reckoned the extra 20 fathoms of rigging made a lot of difference to the cost of a pot. It also opened up a heap more water in

Hauling "Red Gold" aboard Jimmy Ryan's Boat
(photo courtesy Jimmy Ryan)

which to lower your pots! I suppose I could afford to be critical, being brand new to the game and taking everything in with a fresh and open mind. But the way I calculated it, 60 fathom rigging increased the amount of fishable territory in the same length of coast to probably more than double what we were finding, and this had to convert into savings in running, and ultimately savings in fuel. Marine Diesel didn't cost a great deal, but a ship's tanks could hold only so much. And when you had to trek all the way up the coast to Milford for refuelling, with less than a freezer full of cray tails on board, and you added to that the loss of catch — anything from three to seven bags of tails per day, each one of which was worth some astronomical figure that left the mind boggling — because of downtime while off the fishing grounds.... I could hardly see that the cost of an extra 20 fathoms of rope was of great significance.

Had I owned a ship, or been skipper of one, I would have stowed a whole heap more than 28 pots on board before leaving port, and they all would have been rigged for plumbing sixty so I could fish both that and forty and everything else in between. But I didn't, and I wasn't. Nor was I even thinking about it during that first day out on the ocean setting pots. That sort of philosophying began to surface a week or two later when I started comparing what some of the other boats were hauling from the same stretch of sea. Right now though, I was on a learning curve, and mighty grateful for the privilege of finding myself in one of the most isolated, and beautiful spots this country had to offer; where very few had ever had the opportunity to venture.

At the time, Fiordland was literally crawling with crayfish. It did not seem to matter much where you set your pots, they nearly always came up loaded with "crabs". Sometimes when the weather was really foul and we were holed up on some sheltered mooring deep within some fiord, Jimmy Waitiri would get on the radio transmitter to check out how the boats down Breaksea and Dusky were doing, It was amusing listening to them spin their tales of woe about how few crayfish tails they were taking each day.

"Fishing's pretty bad down Dusky," Jimmy would tell us, with a chuckle in his eyes. "No one's catching anything down that way. But you notice how none of them are in a hurry to abandon the area and try their luck up here."

Hunters were no different. When you were onto a good thing you didn't go blowing your trumpet in case every other yahoo came rushing into your territory.

Next morning, long before the sun had crested the Glaisnock Tops, we were back out in the ocean hauling pots. It was normal starting early, men up and about, boats casting off in the cold grey chill of dawn, and finishing early, often before mid afternoon, which was fine from a socializing point of view, but eventually left me wondering whether a considerable amount of valuable fishing time might have gone begging during the latter part of the day because of it. Hauling pots in big ocean swells certainly was not light work, and there was nothing wrong with relaxing at the end of it. But because I had been used to working right through the daylight hours and on into the night on my possum block, I could not help but feel that lounging round on the deck of a snugly moored cray boat, though kind of restful, was also wasting productive time that could have been used putting tails in sacks. As third hand on the boat I was not expecting to make much money for my effort, but I still got to thinking about the system and how it could have been more productive.

Nevertheless, our pots were pulling in plenty of crays. We would come in close to a set of floats, Des would hurl a grapnel over the adjoining rope, the floats were then hauled on deck, the rope run over a block slung from a boom positioned midships above the starboard gunnel, a couple of turns taken around a capstan winch mounted behind the wheel house, and up would come the pot.

Watching the pots surface was always interesting. One never knew what might be inside. Usually there were plenty of crayfish, quite often one or two blue cod, and it wasn't nothing unusual finding huge conger eels slithering in amongst the catch. A few other weird and wonderful wogs and critters, such as occasional small sharks of indeterminate variety, sometimes ended up on the deck. But anything with no commercial value attached usually ended up back where it had just come from, strung up in the pot for bait.

The crayfish were emptied into bins for sorting, sizing and tailing. Anything obviously too small was thrown back straight away, and the borderline crays were measured and sorted as we steamed between pots. The blue cod were filleted and the fillets bagged and frozen. I was quick with a knife so this job was given to me. Later, the proceeds were to be split three ways... or so I was led to believe. The conger eels were a little different. They were loosed onto the deck to be taken care of once we had finished rebaiting the pot and firing it back over the side.

I never did like conger eels, and I was not the only one. They were mean and nasty critters. Jimmy Waitiri reckoned they were taniwha: "They give me the shivers," Jimmy told me. "I have seen them come up with horns on their heads down Te Waewae Bay. They're like demons lurking about in the sea. I chop them up as quick as I can and send them back down where they came from."

I didn't know about all that taniwha stuff, but they certainly were sinister critters. And nor did I like them slithering about the deck near my feet, even if my feet were well wrapped up inside good solid fishing boots.

I was bracing against the swell with a craypot balanced on the gunnel, Robbie on one side, me on the other and Des rebaiting for us. Two huge congers that had just been tipped out of the pot were slithering around my ankles snapping at everything they could see, and I was doing a dance trying to stay clear of them. Robbie took this as his cue to make himself look a big shot.

"What's up?" he started up. "I've never seen anybody jumping round frightened of a harmless little eel before. What do you think they're going to do? Eat you or something?"

I did not mind making fun of myself, but I wasn't very keen on Ballantyne doing it for me, skipper or no skipper. So my hackles raised a bit and I booted one of them along the deck at him, and told him I only needed one of them and he was quite welcome to the other one. It was a heavy weight brute, and it went slithering past the scuppers with its mouth opening and closing, and as it came up against Robbie's boot it clamped down hard on his toes. For a man, who just a minute before, had been trying to take the mickey out of me for being "frightened" of a harmless little eel, his reaction was priceless. He took off doing a jig, kicking and hopping, and hollering.

"Argh!" he shrieked in the brightest of blue language. "Leggo my flippin' foot, damn it! Flippin' bloody eel! Get the flippin' thing off!"

Naturally I hung on the other side of the pot roaring with laughter... which may or may not have done much towards good relations between the skipper and his third hand. Des was a bit more discreet. He simply looked the other way and tried to conceal his sniggers, while I egged Robbie on telling him, when he had finished playing with the eel to please pass it back so I could whack it with the hammer.

In actual fact, we did keep a hammer handy for thumping congers fair between the eyes, and while they were still quivering they were duly chopped into bait sized chunks and sent back down where they had just come from.

It was during one of our first days tending pots, as we were working our way south towards Caswell, that I first noticed the Wapiti in on the beach just south of Houseroof Rock. I had never seen anything like it before. He was massive! Creamy coloured, with a white rump patch and dark mane, and carrying a huge rack of velvet antlers. I had been glassing the waves between the ship and the distant shoreline with my 7 x 35's looking for craypot floats, and without giving it much thought, I took a sweep along the beach. First thing I noticed was a colony of seals basking in the sun, and then there was this massive beast just behind them, head down, browsing the coastal grasses. The first Wapiti I had ever seen! And even from where we were, perhaps a mile or more out to sea, it was clear that this was no mean critter. He was magnificent. Potentially an incredible trophy for someone's den. I was transfixed. My eyes riveted. My interest in searching for craypot floats suddenly all dried up. That night, when we tied up alongside "Buccaneer" I mentioned the Wapiti to Jimmy Waitiri, and asked how could you get in through the surf for a crack at him and how could you get back out again without swamping the dinghy and drowning yourself in the process.

Jimmy told me how he and his mates got ashore on the muttonbird islands: "Most of the time there are big swells running and it takes a fair bit of skill and muscle power handling the oars and keeping the boat under control." he said. "And sometimes it is easier getting off than it is getting on," he added.

He said they would load up, sit in their boat with the stem facing out to sea and wait for a big swell to lift them off the rocks. Then, rowing like the blazes, they would be dragged off the rocks with the outgoing surge, and still rowing like the blazes, they would clear the area before the next incoming wave picked them up and smashed the lot of them back against the rocks they had just been dragged clear of. Sounded pretty simple, but massive bull Wapiti or not, I realized that getting ashore through a pounding surf onto a beach running a horrendous undertow wasn't likely to be quite that simple. And not only that, even if you were fortunate enough to pick a time when there was little surf running, there would be no guarantee that there would still be no surf running by the time you had shot your beast, dressed it out, dragged it down to the boat (assuming you could even move such a massive chunk of meat), manhandled it into the boat and gotten yourself ready to get back out to the ship. And nor was it likely that anybody was going to be hanging around during their fishing hours while you were romping the shoreline entertaining yourself looking for some prize Wapiti to shoot. Jimmy was the first to point out that even if you did safely make it ashore, you might then be stuck there for two or three weeks waiting for the right conditions to get back off again. And when and if those conditions did arise, there probably wouldn't be any fishing boats nearby to pick you up anyway. So much for hunting coastal Wapiti! That was probably one very good reason why he was there, and why he was so big and magnificent. No one had likely ever been able to get in to have a go at him.

Sighting that Wapiti though, was the turning point. From that moment on my binoculars spent at least as much time again glassing the coast for Wapiti as they did glassing the sea for floats. Robbie tolerated it, but I think it got him a little brassed off nevertheless. He was right, of course. I was on the ship for the sake of crayfishing. But then I had only been a fisherman for a day or so, whereas I had been a hunter since I was a boy, and seeing bull Wapiti parading all over the place like that would have been enough to send any hunter's heart a-flutter. We were now running between George, Caswell and Charles Sounds each day, mooring in which ever we ended up in for the night. This was the thick of Wapiti country and more than anything I wanted to have a go at one.

I knew where we were heading before stepping aboard in Bluff, and the priority piece of gear stowed away with my kit was a hunting rifle; a reliable old S.M.L.E. Three O with the barrel securely wrapped with insulation tape and the working parts heavily coated with Vaseline as a protection against salt and sea. There were a few rusting rifles stowed away on various ships, but from what I could make out none of the fishermen appeared over interested in using them. I quickly came to realize that there were plenty of deer around and in some of the areas we tied up I doubted they had ever been bothered too much. Lounging round with a cup of coffee or a cold bottle of beer after a day's work hauling pots was more in vogue than scrambling through bush and bluffs. Therefore no one minded if I took the dinghy once the ship was moored with the deck hosed down and the catch blast freezing safely below, and headed for shore with the rifle and a pocket full of ammo. From time to time I would come back with a Red deer trussed up in the bottom of the dinghy, but I never did come face to face with a Wapiti.

Then one afternoon, a little more than six miles up the fiord on the northern side of George Sound, we tied up in Anchorage Cove at the mouth of the George River. My fixation with getting a Wapiti was well known amongst the fishermen by now, and some of them were starting to sit up and take notice. We dropped anchor and I immediately launched the dinghy, threw in my rifle, and climbed down over the gunnel. At the same time I noticed one or two other young blokes about the same age as me looking as if they were developing an interest in the proceedings. As I pulled away they also began lowering their dinghies. Rowing ashore to stretch the legs was nothing unusual, but I hardly needed a bunch of rowdy, thigh-booted fishermen yahooing up the river in my wake to blow it for me.

I rowed like crazy, dragged the dinghy onto the shingly hard, lashed the painter to a water logged stump, and charged off around the shoreline into the mouth of the George River. Over my shoulder I noticed three small boats full of fishermen rowing frantically for shore heading for the same spot I had left my dinghy. I took off at a gallop, rifle at the ready with a cartridge half up the spout. The river was running nice and low, and just a short way up from the mouth it opened out into clear grassy areas — an ideal spot for spooking a deer. And that was exactly what I had already done. The biggest set of deer prints I had ever seen lay freshly imbedded in the river sand — as big as a cattle beast's. A huge Wapiti that had been grazing way out in the open had heard all the noise... mine and my fishing mate's as they ran up the river behind me laughing and shouting out to one another in their eagerness to see me gunning down my first Wap'. In its fright, the Wapiti had crashed through the river, splashing water all over the river boulders, charged out the other side, up into the bush and gone.

Abbo Lovell, Boong Ryan and Doug Adams relaxing after a day on the sea (photo courtesy of Jimmy Ryan)

I was really disappointed. But there would be little gained by complaining. These guys were fishermen, not hunters. The reason they were hanging on my tail was because they counted me in as one of them and they were interested in what I was doing. If they had thought of me otherwise they probably would not have been interested in what I was doing in the first place. Besides, there was genuine concern amongst some of them for my welfare. I was new to the fiords and there were pitfalls that I knew little about. "Boong" Ryan yelled out to me that we only had minutes to get back to our dinghies unless we wanted to be swimming back to the boats. We turned and began running back down river and as we broke out of the bush near the river mouth I saw what he meant. The tide had turned and was racing across the flats towards the shoreline like a flash flood. We literally galloped through rising water to our dinghies that just moments earlier had been sitting on dry ground. A short while later we were back on the boats but the area where the dinghies had been tied was awash, the water already well above our depth.

I do not recall any of those Fiordland fishermen being terribly religious sorts of blokes. Superstitious — Yes! But religious — No! Anyway it was early Sunday morning, and we were anchored with several other ships in the head of Caswell sound, and we had been working solidly for a month or so without a day off, and someone said: "Hey, it's Sunday!" I was into the dinghy and sculling for the shore before you could blink an eye. Lake Marchant, the home of big Wap's

Caswell Sound Hut, a relic of the New Zealand-American Fiordland Expedition (photo Dave Richardson)

was barely a mile yonder.

A track, still in good order, leading from Caswell beachhead to the lake, had been cut by members of the New Zealand-American Fiordland Expedition that had carried out scientific studies of the New Zealand Wapiti herd back in 1949. I quickly beached the dinghy, hightailed it into the bush and was gone. From previous experience I had this feeling that somehow time was going to be against me in this little jaunt.

About fifteen minutes up the track I broke out of the bush onto a small clearing of wetland grasses and there before me was Lake Marchant; near enough to 150 feet above sea level, approximately two miles long, something more than half a mile wide, and more than likely very deep. Straight ahead of me, to the south east, below Mount Pluvius, the valley of the Large Burn could be seen disappearing behind the bush clad bluffs that rose abruptly out of the lake to the twin Mary Peaks above. Behind me, to the north, was the Stillwater River. The aforementioned team of New Zealand-American scientists had recorded that this huge body of water had risen about 16 feet in just 6 hours during one storm, and the Stillwater river that drained into it from behind my left shoulder had risen 24 feet during the same downpour. Standing there thinking about it was sort of frightening This was no small body of water, this lake. And the Stillwater was a fair sized catchment area. If Noah had been there at the time, I reckon he would have been hightailing it for the ark.

There really was not much time for standing round excogitating such matters. Deer had been milling about everywhere, and there must have been heaps of them in the vicinity. The muddy ground where the groves of horopito fringed the lake was a churned up mass of deer prints. But their size was more typically Red deer than Wapiti. I was frantically scouting round looking for something bigger to start tracking when a familiar noise broke out through the bush:

"White Hunter! Where are you mate? Don't shoot! It's only us, in case you're thinking on firing any shots this way." The thought had not really been in my mind prior to their suggesting it!

We were coming in off the sea, cruising up Charles Sound, one afternoon and I still had not got me a Wapiti, when Bill Davis called up on the radio:

""Tarawai", "Tarawai", "Gleniffer" calling "Tarawai"! Hey, Taxi! Tell the White Hunter we overtook a Wapiti having a swim in the Tasman. I think it was on its way to Australia when we came across it."

I was into the wheelhouse like a shot.

"Where are you? And where's the Wapiti?" I called back.

"We've got it on board," Bill replied. "It looked pretty tired, swimming about in the ocean. So I reached over and hit it on the head with a hammer and hauled it aboard."

"Are you serious, or just having me on?" I asked.

"I'm not having you on. When you get in, I want you to dress it down for me and truss it up, so I can put it down in the freezer."

Bill had previously watched me rolling deer carcasses up into a neat and tidy ball by cramming their haunches up into their rib cages and threading the front leg joints through the stomach flaps. This way they took up a minimum of valuable space down in the freezer. But I still had my reservations as to whether he was having me on or not. I could hardly wait to get to the anchorage to find out.

Bill was trying hard to look blasé as we came alongside, but as I climbed over the bulwark with my eyes popping he could no longer stifle the smersh on his face. There lying on the deck of his ship was the Wapiti he had found swimming out in the Tasman! A young cow, as it turned out. I looked it all over for a bullet hole but found none, and I was pretty well puzzled as to how Bill had gotten the Wapiti until I started gutting it. Then it all fell into place. The animal's veins were full of blood, so it had obviously died without being bled and its lungs were full of water. It also had a dislocated shoulder. And now I twigged as to what must have happened.

It had been deluging rain during the previous few days. The rivers were in full flood and everywhere you looked there were massive waterfalls plummeting from the cliffs. The country was so precipitous that it was not uncommon for animals to suffer serious injuries, and more so during such inclement weather. This one must have stumbled somewhere, dislocated her shoulder, got swept into a stream and drowned. Quite possibly she had gone over a waterfall before ending up floating round in Charles Sound where Bill Davis had come across her.

"Aw, heck!" said Bill, as I laid my theory before him. "Who went and told you all that? I thought you'd believe it when I told you we found her swimming out in the Tasman."

Despite the fact she had not been bled, the meat was in perfectly good order. I finished cleaning her up, trussed her into a ball and she was lowered into the freezer.

Not so many days later, some fortunate American tourists, dining on the finest of fare at the high class Milford Hotel would no doubt have been delighted with their dainty dish of wild New Zealand elk, marinated in sauces and semi fresh from the depths of Fiordland. While not too far away, the lads off the boats lounged about in the Milford pub, revelling away the proceeds as they laughed and joked and spoke of many things, of sailing ships and sealing wax and cabbages and kings.

CHAPTER 12

Life on the Ocean Wave

We were off George Sound, plying back and forth amidst huge swells that were rolling up the coast from somewhere down south, Des standing by with the grapnel. We had criss-crossed the area searching for floats where we knew we had lowered a couple of pots, and then we saw them, taught on the end of their rigging, vibrating in the current a couple of fathoms beneath the surface, held under by a strong set coming from the direction of Puysegur.

Somewhere towards Looking Glass Bay the coastline faded from view behind a thick mantle of spray, while high above the foam washed jagged coastal rocks dense black gloom swaddled the bush, obliterating the tops with thunderous rain. There was a tempest brewing. To the south of us several ships could already be seen running for shelter before the imminent storm. Everywhere, all around, pillars and shrouds of thick black murk loomed from the sea, and it could only be a matter of time before we too would be engulfed in pelting rain. Awarua Radio had indicated there was a deep trough bearing in from the south and we could expect bad weather for several days. Floats down, seas running, visibility rapidly diminishing. Locating and retrieving pots under these conditions was nigh impossible. I knew we too would soon be calling it a day and running for shelter back inside George.

"Okay! Stow the grapnel," Robbie yelled back to us from the wheelhouse. "We're heading for Milford."

No-one wanted to be stuck inside a cabin holed up in the far reaches of George Sound for the next week or so. Boats had been communicating and the general consensus was to run before the storm. Some of the crews were looking for a chance to go visit their wives, others were looking for a chance to hit the booze. For me it was my first chance to see Milford Sound, and although I was eagerly looking forward to it, I was also a little disappointed. It had always been my hope that if we ever headed that way it would be on a bright and sunny day with the skyline shimmering and Mitre Peak standing clear and bold against a dazzling blue sky. But then, I had never imagined what Milford had to offer in storm mode.

We ploughed up the coast, surfing on the downside of massive green waves, slipped into the depths of huge troughs, then as the seas overtook us, laboured up the backs of the very waves that just moments before we had been surfing down the front of, fell back into the next trough as the seas surged ahead of us again, got picked up then pulled back down the face of the following sea, and so it went. Sliding, surfing, juddering, labouring, for something akin three, maybe four hours; running before the storm until gradually it caught up with us, and then it overtook us. But the seas were hardly any the rougher because of it. Just a bit more froth and slop on top of the swells as the wind began to howl and now the rain came pelting down.

Long before we got to Milford Sound the foul weather had sucked along the mountains ahead of us, lashing Fiordland with torrential rains and howling winds. Huge updraughts funnelled up the fiords from out in the Tasman and by the time we arrived off the mouth of Milford the land was spilling water by the billions of tons.

We turned into the sound to a scene like I could never have pictured. The other fiords where we had been working were magnificent. But Milford in storm mode was absolutely spectacular, awesome beyond belief. Sheltered by the close proximity of the adjacent walls of the sound, the seas rapidly levelled off to little more than a short sharp chop. Sheer bluffs, shrouded in bush and swirling cloud, rose perpendicularly from the water, and every few hundred yards massive waterfalls thundered through the mists and plummeted to the fiord below. But time and again, great updraughts of wind would turn these massive foaming waterfalls clear about, hurling them, driving them, blasting them, back whence they had come. Huge thundering waterfalls picked up bodily and thrown back up the mountain sides, the fall of water completely dispersed and rendered into mere sheets of mist and fine spray. Then as the gusts subsided the water would once more come thundering down into the brackish fiord below, only to again be turned back as the next great updraught billowed in off the sea. And as we churned our way along the sound, this incredible scene kept repeating itself, mile after mile along much of the sheer walls of the fiord.

Our entrance to Fresh Water Basin, at the head of the Sound, did not have the same magnificence as our entrance to the Sound at the seaward end. Taxi drivers in general probably have little difficulty understanding the traffic signs and signals one finds cluttering up cities and roadsides. But not so the ones cluttering up the sea. "Red to red, and green to green" meant nothing to this taxi driver. Hesitating just long enough to decide that the green marker he had suddenly noticed was probably of no consequence anyway, we veered off to starboard and promptly ran aground. I think that right to the last "Taxi' had imagined that the various fishermen who were standing on the decks of their boats waving and indicating for us to go to port, were some sort of a wildly waving welcoming committee! Fortunately the tide was not receding at the time or we may well have had the added embarrassment of being stuck on the mud for the rest of the day. Feeling somewhat abashed we came alongside the wharf just long enough to unload the catch, then took our position on the end of the long line of fishing vessels moored in the Basin, dropped anchor, lashed a spring between us and the boat we had come alongside and shut the engine down. Robbie and Des called up a cab and promptly took off for Invercargill, leaving me to work the rest out for myself.

Hanging round Milford with a bunch of thirsty fishermen, there was really not a great deal to work out. You were either in the pub, or else you were on the way there, or else you were just about to be on the way there, or else you were on one of the boats having a feed and as soon as that was done then you would be on the way there. Other than that, the pub was probably closed for the night and you were getting a bit of sleep in order to regain your equilibrium ready for the next day of being there.

Getting back to the boats at the end of such a day was not always quite so straight forward as it had been getting away from the boats

F.V.Solander off Caswell Sound (photo Jimmy Ryan)

earlier in the day. If Porky the tour bus driver was in Milford, we would all pile into his bus and refuse to get out again until he had driven us down to our boats. He always seemed quite happy doing it, but then I suppose it was the quickest way he knew of getting all those drunken sots out of his bus. Peace and sobriety failed to exist on such a trip. If someone was not banging out songs on a guitar with everyone singing off key, then Jimmy Ryan would be giving a running commentary over the public address of what was supposedly occurring on the outside while we was all laughing hysterically at what at least seemed very funny under the circumstances. Several blokes didn't quite make it. They were helped off the bus, pointed in the general direction of the wharf, and having reached the other end, went straight in the tide around about the place where they imagined their boats were meant to be. One such fellow took off swimming for safety in the wrong direction after landing in the tide and having come to the last boat on the mooring, which so happened to be "Tarawai", decided there was no future in going any further. He pulled him self out, stripped off his outer garments and left them on the "Tarawai" to drip dry, then made his way home through a tangle of springs and craypots in his underwear, never to return. In reality, by the next morning he probably never even knew where he had been and I never knew who had left the outer garments.

I am pleased to be able to say that Government hunters and meat shooters were not like that. Whereas it was not unknown for them to drink themselves silly, it would nevertheless have been a rare occasion indeed for one of them to come wandering out of the pub and walk straight off the end of a wharf into the sea. The mere fact that the bush pubs where they drank usually did not have a wharf and sea nearby could have had some bearing on the matter. But hunters had their own peculiar hazards to surmount if and when they drank too much. One fellow, for example, was once seen lying prone along the floor of the Hampden Hotel in Murchison with his arms outstretched above his head, clinging desperately to the stem of a potted palm, as he pleaded pathetically for his mates, who callously drank on regardless, to come and help him before he lost his grip and fell to his death. Then there was the time when Alan "The Guide' Hunter, Johnny McSquirter, an Awatere Valley musterer's greasy, and a couple of other cullers from Marlborough got tired of sitting on the same bar stools in their Blenheim pub during the Christmas break. So they all piled into a taxi and headed West. When they had got as far as Motueka they decided they had travelled far enough and it was time for another drink. They left The Guide out in the taxi to sort matters out with the driver while they wandered into the hotel and checked themselves in. The receptionist noticing that they had entered without their luggage, asked if she should send a porter out to the cab to assist the other member of the party with the bags, to which they all agreed that this would be a good idea. A short while later the porter re-entered the hotel carrying "The Guide's" toothbrush. This, they tried to explain to a not too tolerant receptionist, was all the luggage they had between them. Back in Blenheim, seated once again on the same bar stools, they were still trying to figure out what they had said or done that warranted their being ushered back to their taxi from the hotel in Mot'.

After a couple of days of wild carousing, most deer cullers tended to split company and take off to their respective towns and homes to visit their families until the time came to head back into the bush. But that was not quite the way with the fishermen of Milford. I guess there just was not much else to do. You could hang around on your boat and get bored; or you could hang around the pub and get plastered. Most settled for the latter. For me the novelty soon wore thin. But for my crayfishing buddies, that was never the case. They simply revelled in it. But for all the earnestness off it, this soaking up booze while endeavouring to drink the pub dry in as brief a time as possible, they were, generally speaking, a well behaved lot and only once did I ever witness what might have passed for an altercation:

Spud Murphy got into a bear hug with one of his mates. No one threw any punches or anything like that, so when it happened no one was really sure whether they were mad at one another, or merely doing an Irish jig. Anyway, the outcome was the two of them tumbled through the glass doors of the pub and quicker than Murphy could say, "Polish yer flute!" they was both lying in a pool of blood with shards and splinters and enough cut ligaments to justify an emergency flight to the nearest hospital in a Cessna 180. The situation was actually quite serious. By the time they were admitted they were both suffering from a serious loss of alcohol through their arteries, but the upside of the matter was, there was little likelihood of infection. The wounds were already thoroughly sterilized owing to their not being a great deal of blood mixed in with their alcohol systems. They were stitched up, wheeled off down the corridor and admitted. Spud was stuck up one end of the ward and his mate isolated down the other, with the chief matron's strict instructions to all orderlies and nursing staff, to make sure neither one got near the other.

When they got strong enough to raise their heads and observe one another, strapped down in their individual beds, one at this end of the ward and the other at that end of it with a row of dead and dying patients lying in between, they began pleading with the matron to move their beds close up to one another, because as they said, "they were fishermen and they were good mates and they wanted to talk with one another. And neither were they too keen on all these cow cockies full of rye grass staggers and hay fever coming between them."

At first the matron was not too keen on the idea, but eventually she reasoned that if they really were the best of mates, and yet they had gone and slashed one another up the way they had, it might be better to put them back alongside one another rather than risk having them break free and work their way down through the ward slashing and slicing all the other patients in the middle of the night. Because if that was the way they did it to each other whom they claimed they liked, what might they do to some poor coot who got in between them whom they more than likely didn't!

The weather had settled and been good for a few days by the time Robbie and Des got back into Milford. But the next day was a Friday, and none of the fishermen were prepared to leave port on a Friday, and nor would they allow us to. Hauling pots on a Friday was okay if you were already on the fishing grounds. But starting out on a journey on a Friday was bad luck and no one was allowed to do it. In the mouth of Milford Sound, at Anita Bay, you could pick up greenstone pebbles off the beach, but that was bad luck too. Bill Davis told me that one fellow once tried it on the "Gleniffer".

"So I told him to bring his pebbles into the wheelhouse," said Bill. "And each time he wasn't looking, I'd throw another one back in the sea. By the time we were off Bligh the whole lot had gone back where they came from."

Keeping coral was also bad luck. We often pulled pieces of it up on our pots. The time Charlie injured his wrist and I was helping Jimmy out, I unhooked some off the mesh and just for a joke, laid it carefully alongside the scuppers. From back in the wheel house, Jimmy wasn't missing a thing. He was just waiting to catch my eye and the minute I looked back in his direction he was indicating with his thumb to heave it back over the side.

"I don't believe in pushing my luck," Jimmy told me. "It came from the sea, it goes back in the sea."

Being superstitious did not bother me too much, but it bothered me a bit the way my mates talked about alcohol taking the lining off one's stomach. Even old, hardened sailors threw up heading back down the coast after a bash on the booze, so they said.

We sailed out of Fresh Water Basin, past Bowen Falls, and down the fiord with clear blue skies and the lightest of breezes. Out on the ocean there was a very light swell running, and something like 30 miles to go from Anita Bay to George Sound. I resigned myself to believing that my stomach lining was gone and before long I would be hanging over the side puking my innards out.

About an hour down the coast and I was beginning to feel that way. The continual riding and lurching of the boat was starting to turn my stomach inside out. Judging by outward appearances, Des wasn't feeling too good neither. He was sitting on the cray bins splicing rigging on a pot in an effort to keep his mind off his discomfort. My warped sense of humour suddenly found this rather intriguing. Des was turning shades of green and looking like he was about to puke.

"What's up Des?" I prompted. "Not feeling too good?"

"Actually, no," he replied. "In fact......, I'm about to........," Des made a grab for his false teeth and took off for the rails.

I suppose it was hardly an amusing situation from Des' point of view. But watching him grab for his teeth like that before he shied them over the side; I just saw the funny side of it. And that was all I needed to bring me right. Suddenly I felt great. Those hard case mates of mine had led me to believe that getting seasick was part and parcel with a bash on the booze. And I had fallen for it. The power of autosuggestion!

That was the first and last time I ever felt queasy on a boat. I suddenly felt very, very hungry instead.

With big freezer space to store it in and the general attitude that life on the ocean wave demanded good eating habits, there was all manner of goodies stowed down below. Pot roasts, legs of lamb, export quality beef steak, sides of bacon, pork chops, steamed puddings, rich fruit cake, prime quality muttonbirds.... Now there was something new that I had never eaten before... muttonbirds. I had often seen them back in Wellington, all fat and greasy looking, hanging in bundles from butchers' hooks in the window of Jury's fish shop in Courtney Place. But no one that I had ever met knew anything about how to prepare them. Who better than the mutton-birders themselves. One night, Bill Davis invited me aboard for a meal of muttonbird stew... actually, several muttonbirds, stew.

First the birds were boiled in fresh water long enough to remove most of the preserving salt that had been rubbed into them, then with the galley busting open with mouth watering aromas, they were transferred to a second large pot of unsalted fresh water. A few whole onions, some halved potatoes, a large cabbage chopped into quarters thrown in, and the whole lot was brought to the boil then simmered to finger lickin' perfection. The end result was a mouth wateringly succulent dish.

I tried to be innovative when it came to my turn in the galley. Nevertheless it was hardly surprising that Robbie and Des were not over enthused when I told them I was going to cook a batch of crayfish for dinner one night. The only way they knew about preparing crayfish was plain unadulterated boiled tails... and men who worked with crayfish day after day until they got to dreaming nightmares about them at night were not usually over keen on having them served up shortly before bedtime, plain and fancy free for dinner. But there were other ways and means: You start by precooking a pot of tails. Let them cool then remove them from their shells. Melt a dob of butter in a frying pan, add a chopped onion and flake in the meat. Stir in a packet of frozen mixed vegetables to add some sustenance and colouring. Reheat the lot in a spicy hot, curried white sauce. Add a little salt to taste, and serve on a bed of flaky white rice decorated with sliced hard-boiled eggs. Compliment that lot with sprinklings of malt vinegar for the curried crayfish, a smattering of Soy sauce for the rice, and a side plate of hot buttered toast. And after dining on that lot, no one on board the "Tarawai" ever again said crayfish tails are not edible.

I always saved the livers from the blue cod that came up in our pots. Rolled in flour, fried in butter, served with lightly done fried eggs... they were rich, highly nutritious and scrumptious!

Not only were the ships' freezers stocked with food; the entire region abounded with delicacies... whitebait, oysters, paua, mussels, octopus, kina, muttonbirds....

"You ever eaten a kiwi, Mothbite?" one old fellow asked me one day. Sort of knocked me back a bit. Eating something as rare as a kiwi would have been the last thing to have entered my mind. "They're not bad, but nowhere near as nice as a moa," he added.

Now I knew he was joking.

"Since when did you eat a moa?" I laughed.

"Only ever tried it once," he said. "It was a long time back. She was a big blue bird and I've never seen drumsticks like it in my life. We came across her sitting in amongst the flax on the sand dunes, not far from the bush along the south end of Martins Bay. Had a heck of a struggle lashing her down with a mooring rope while my mate wrung her neck. Her egg tasted pretty good too!"

Well I hope he was joking. Alice McKenzie claimed to have seen a blue bird, bigger than she was, somewhere in that same locality when she was just a little pioneer girl living at Martins Bay. She believed it to have been a moa.

Surely one of the Bluff fishermen would never have eaten the last breeding moa!?! I was not altogether sure. There were the odd way out things that happened.

We were about three miles into Charles Sound late one afternoon, coming in off the fishing grounds, when a Southern Scenic float plane came flying in off the sea at about 500 feet elevation. As it overshot us I noticed that its navigation lights were flashing, which seemed a bit out of the ordinary for up here in the sounds in broad daylight. A mile further up the sound, several fishing boats were already moored for the night. The plane flew low over the top of them, then swung in over Eleanor Island and carried on up Emelius Arm. A short while later back into view comes the float plane, navigation lights still blinking, and now flying at about 1000 feet. Way back down the fiord it went, heading towards the coast, but short of flying out into the Tasman, it banked steeply and this time it made a long gradual descent back up the fiord once more over the top of us and gently came in to land several hundred metres beyond the moored boats.

Meanwhile a scurrying had broken out on deck of one of the cray boats about the same time they had been first buzzed by the plane, and within minutes black smoke was billowing out of the stack, and the said boat was ploughing back down the fiord towards the open sea. Taking its time and moving very slowly, the plane taxied up alongside the remaining boats and I could see someone on one of the boats fastening a mooring line to the plane.

Now all of these goings on piqued my curiosity somewhat, so eventually I popped the question, "What's going on?"

"There's a fisheries inspector on board the float plane," I was informed. "We look after the pilots and the pilots look after us. That's what they do if there is an inspector on board. They take their time coming in to land with their lights flashing so anyone with undersized crayfish on board has time to up anchor and away."

"So those guys must have undersized crays on board?"

"Nope! They've got a load of seal meat in their freezer. That's what they're using for bait."

It would have been a good job if they had gone and gotten themselves nabbed!

Untold thousands of fur seals were clubbed to death for their skins during the early days round the Fiordland Coast, almost to the point of extinction.

"They look harmless, but they're not altogether defenceless," Jimmy Waitiri told me. "I had a fox terrier dog that was killed by one once."

"Yeah? What happened?" I asked.

"That dog used to follow me everywhere," he said. "I couldn't leave port without him. He always knew when I was getting ready to sail and he would be down on the ship waiting for me before I ever got there. I used to take him ashore up the coast to stretch his legs, but he was bad news when it came to annoying the seals. He would duck in yapping and nipping at them, until he had driven them into the sea. One day, one old bull seal just lay there, making out he was ignoring the dog as the little devil kept nipping at his sides. Then quick as a flash the seal suddenly grabbed a mouthful of the dog by his back. He held him above his head while the dog yelped and howled, and then he started spinning him around and around. Next thing he gave a sudden powerful flick of his head and the dog went flying. Poor little blighter crashed into the rocks and lay there whimpering."

"Did crashing onto the rocks kill the dog?" I asked.

"No. I had to thump him with a stick to finish him off myself," Jimmy replied. "You see the seal never let go of the dog's back. He came down about thirty feet away from the seal with the skin and flesh completely ripped off his back. The seal was still holding onto that part of him clamped between its teeth."

Made me think back to those seals at Gillespies when I had slithered right in amongst them and poked my imaginary camera in the face of a magnificent old bull seal as he rolled over to look at me and yawn nonchalantly into the imaginary lens. It seemed pretty clever at the time but maybe it had not been such a bright idea after all.

CHAPTER 13

Time 'n' Tide

Depending on the prevailing winds decided which place we tied up in a storm. So one day we found ourselves tucked in behind Eleanor Island, sheltering from a bit of bad weather that had been driving in from the nor'west.

F.V.Mijay running before the wind (photo courtesy Jimmy Ryan)

The "Tarawai" was not a particularly accommodating ship. Her living quarters were below deck and somewhat cramped, and her deck was past due for a recaulking; which if it had been done might have directed the water out through the scuppers rather than trickling all over my bunk which was tucked in behind the companionway in the aft section of the boat. We visited other ships a lot, but no one ever visited the "Tarawai", which probably said plenty for the general comfort and living conditions on board.

Anyway, Magilla Gorilla didn't mind us spending the day sitting in the galley of his ship the "Duncan", playing cards and drinking hot rum toddies. In fact he probably would have considered us an unsociable bunch if we had not come on over, seeing he had everyone else from round about also crammed on board whiling away the storm.

I had not been this far up Charles Sound before and I was just itching to get ashore for a shot. Throughout the day I had been keeping one weather-eye out the cabin, then fairly late in the afternoon everything started to come right. The rain eased up, the wind suddenly dropped off, the low lying misty clouds began to disperse. That was my cue. I was off the "Duncan", scrambling on board "Tarawai", gathering my rifle and spotlighting gear, into the dinghy and gone. It was about three miles rowing up Emelius Arm to where the Irene River spilled out of the bush.

Although the Irene was of reasonable size it was not what you would call a big river. Nor was it turbulent and fast flowing. But like all these black water rivers, just by looking there was no way of telling how deep it was, nor what sort of ugly monsters lurked beneath the surface. Beyond the bush, it channelled out through a series of moraine tidal flats, scattered with coastal grasses, that stretched almost a mile down the fiord... ideal locations for catching something out with the spotlight.

Going on what I could gather, it seemed likely that the deer of Emelius Arm would not even know what a spotlight was. At least, none of the fishermen whom I asked had ever heard of anyone spotlighting the area before, and they were the ones most likely to know. Had meat shooters been working the area most certainly the deer would have been educated. But Charles Sound was Wapiti country. The so called exclusive domain of private shooters and their ilk; hand picked members of the Deer Stalkers Association and their chosen few, who won ballots by fair means or foul to shoot the area for sport and jolly good fun. And blinding deer in the dead of night with 60,000 candle power of spotlight, before bowling them with a bullet, was considered by such worthies, unethical and unsportsmanlike to the extreme.... All well and good from the sportsman's point of view. But looking at it from the defenceless deer's point of view, I doubt that collecting a high powered bullet in the dead of night whilst blinded by a spotlight would have been regarded any less sporting than collecting the same high powered bullet in the light of day. Neither way could really be considered sport and jolly good fun for the unfortunate beast collecting the bullet.

Besides if someone did not start educating them now, think how it was going to be for the poor creatures when the meat shooters finally did arrive with their spotlights, jet boats, helicopters and all. I'm sure could they have commented on the matter, any deer of the day would have said how grateful he was that I had turned up doing my little bit to enlighten them.

With an hour or more of daylight up my sleeve, I rowed as far as I could up the Irene through black and foreboding beech stained waters; the air humming with mosquitoes and ravenous sandflies, the river overhung with impenetrable thick jungle foliage and tangled roots. Then about two miles upstream the way was blocked by a fallen tree semi-submerged across the river, and I had to turn back. It was an interesting little exercise that achieved nothing of great value other than fill in a bit of time to last light when I knew the deer would most likely be venturing out, and by the time I got back to the river mouth daylight was all but gone.

With the passing of the storm everything had gone calm, but now there was the slightest of downstream drift in the air. Realizing it could carry my scent across the flats and spook anything that was out, I hung in close to the southern side of the fiord, staying in the main channel of the river for a way before cutting back in to the top end of one of the flats. With just enough light left to see what I was doing, I lashed the dinghy to a half buried log, eased myself into shin deep water and climbed onto dry ground. From there, there was a thigh deep channel to wade before climbing up onto the next island, from where I could get a good view to the bush edge.

Straight away I picked up two deer in the spot and dropped them both. And then another set of eyes popped up over to the right and that one went down too. Nothing else showed up under the sweep of the light, but I reckoned that would do me for awhile anyway; until I had that lot gutted and dragged to the dinghy. Already the night was blacker than pitch and more by feel than sight I worked my way through the carcasses, bleeding and gutting and dragging them over to the channel. And that was when I realized that the tide had turned.

Where I had waded just thigh deep awhile back, the sea was now lapping close to the top of the bank that I had climbed to get up onto the flat. The river was backing up with the tide rising fast. Suddenly I felt scared. I should have realized that the entire area was tidal, but I had not even given it a thought until now. In a very short time everything, right back to the main bush and beyond, would be completely submerged. My deer no longer seemed very important. I left them in a heap and pushed into the channel, but barely a step from the shore the water was already lapping over the top of my thigh boots. To go any further would be to risk falling into a hole and getting dragged down by the weight of my boots. The only way back to the dinghy now would be to strip off and swim. But there was another problem. There had been very little slack in the painter when I tied the dinghy, and with the amount of water flowing upstream, it was probably already pulled under and sunk. For just a short while, I stood there deliberating, wondering what to do. Huge amounts of water were moving through the fiord. Really, there was only one choice. Head for the bush and hope to keep above the rising tide. Without any further delay I turned and started for the bush edge, but already it was too late for that too. Streams of water had formed between me and the bush effectively stranding me on a fast disappearing tidal flat way out in the middle of Emelius Arm. Desperately I swept the spotlight around me, but everyway I looked all I could see was fast rising water.

And then in the still of the night I heard someone hollering from down the fiord. Then it came again; someone calling my name. Then the beam of a powerful torch piercing the sky from somewhere out in the main channel beyond where I had tied the dinghy.

I replied with a tonsil rattling roar: "Over here!" I yelled, as I raked the sky with my spotlight. A couple of minutes went by, punctuated with a fair exchange of hollering back and forth, then "Buccaneer's" dinghy lit up in the spot from the bottom end of the channel. It was Charlie Fisher and Des come looking for me.

They had rowed up the main channel, come across my dinghy as it was about to go under and managed to cut it loose. That was when they got really concerned and started hollering out.

Earlier, Jimmy Waitiri had learned that I had taken the dinghy and gone hunting, and he started to worry about me. He told Charlie and Des to launch the dinghy off "Buccaneer" and get looking for me. For once I was more than a little grateful that he had. You could be battling a hurricane out on the ocean and they probably would not even raise an eyelid of concern. That was the sea, and although they respected it, these fishermen did not fear the sea. But mountains and bush!? That was something else. Whenever I hopped in a dinghy with my rifle, Jimmy, or Bill, or some other fishing mate who cared, started getting concerned — and that was the underlying reason why they had followed me up the George River and to Lake Marchant, when they blew my chances of getting a Wapiti.

Although I got a bit of a fright in the head of Emelius Arm, the consequences would not very likely have been serious. Just a mite uncomfortable until someone came and rescued me. At the worst I may have had to abandon a bit of gear and swim to safety where the bush rose out of the sea. But a few days later something else happened that could well have ended with far more disastrous consequences.

The weather was fine with blue skies, light breezes and gentle seas, and we were entering George Sound with another day of hauling pots behind us. Des and I were sifting through the catch, sorting, tailing, and throwing the undersized crays back in the sea. But as usual, I had only one eye in the fish bin. The other was scanning the coast for anything of interest, which of course consisted mainly of deer.

In most places the bush came right to the sea, but just inside George Sound, along the southern headland, there was a patch of coastal grasses and stunted scrub, scattered with large blocks of rock that had at some stage either tumbled off the mountain above or, over the millenniums, been eroded away by rain and sea. And there, about 100 feet up the slope and not much more than 150 yards distance from the ship was a fine looking venison, busily munching on his last supper.

Robbie hove the "Tarawai" to, while I worked on trying to line up the sights as the ship gently pitched fore and aft, port and starboard, and with a couple of misplaced shots to my credit and the deer obliviously munching on, I finally managed to place a bullet just behind its shoulder and down it went. We lowered the boat and while Des and Robbie carried on with the tailing, I rowed ashore to retrieve the carcass.

Huge blocks of stone littered the edge of the fiord, but beaching the dinghy was not difficult. The tide was full and there was just the slightest of swells running. I slipped easily onto the top of a massive piece of stone, hopped out and dragged the dinghy up onto the hard. One thing that could be said for these little Praam dinghies; because there was nothing much to them, they were easily manhandled.

I would have thought that hardly thirty minutes had elapsed from when I had left the dinghy to when I got back again with the carcass, but in just that short time the sea had changed. Actually it was not really the sea, but the tide that had changed. Perhaps it was due to the long narrow nature of the fiords that such rapid change in the levels of the sea occurred. Anyway, the tide was now on the way out. Already it had dropped by more than a foot and I realized immediately that getting the dinghy back off the rock was going to be nowhere near as easy as it had been getting it up onto it.

With the receding tide the sea no longer flowed gently onto the shoreline. Quite large swells had begun rolling into the headland, hitting the rocks with force; surging up over the top of them, then sucking back down into the fiord. Even holding the dinghy steady on top of the rock while trying to get aboard was proving tricky. I knew exactly what I had to do to get off the rock. The same way the muttonbirders did it, I needed to get into the boat with the prow facing in to the oncoming sea, oars firmly placed in their rowlocks, and as soon as an incoming wave lifted me off the hard I was to row like mad. The outgoing wave would then take me with it and away I would go. Problem was it didn't quite work that way. Each time a wave came crashing over the rock the boat slewed side on and got pushed back up against the shoreline and this left me in a precarious out of control situation that would see me either tipped into the sea as my dinghy was dragged off into the fiord, or else, if I was fortunate enough not to be tipped out, the dinghy at best would be broached to the next incoming wave which would then pick me up and smash me back onto the rocks from where I had just come.

A couple of times I managed to position the boat head on, pile in and grab the oars. But each time the dinghy got slewed side on by the incoming sea, and just as quickly I had to pile out again and hold the boat with all my strength to stop it being sucked off the rock with me not in it. Once or twice I looked over towards the "Tarawai", drifting not more than 100 yards away, to see if my mates were aware of my plight, but no one was taking any notice. Both men had their backs to me, tailing on regardless.

You can't fight the sea. Its power is too great. It is better to conserve your energy by going with it. Already I was in a proper lather trying to figure it all out. But by now I could see that the only way that I was likely to get clear of the rock would be to stand alongside, holding the dinghy in position until after an incoming wave had lifted the boat, and then in the brief seconds prior to the water being sucked back off again I would have to clamber in, grab the oars, and row like mad. Hopefully I would still be afloat and rowing after hitting the fiord, now some two or three feet below.

Time and tide wait for no man. The longer I dallied the worse my situation became. With the tide receding, each consecutive wave rolling in off the sea appeared bigger and each drop-off as the seas poured back into the fiord greater. But conversely, by now most of the incoming waves no longer spilled as much water onto the rock as they had done just a short while earlier. Soon I would be left high and dry. I knew I had little time remaining, and once I was in the boat and committed to a wave there would be no turning back. Almost in desperation, I elected an incoming sea, struggling to keep the prow pointing forward as the froth and bubbles swirled round my thigh boots, I watched and waited until the wave was just starting to turn back. Hurriedly I clambered aboard, took up the oars and pulled as hard as I could. Now the sea began to suck back off the huge slab. Over the edge and down I went, splashing into the fiord, water frothing and spilling all around me, oars whipping wildly as I desperately endeavoured to drag myself clear, and then the right hand rowlock bounced out of its block. The dinghy slew hard about, broaching me to the next sea. Franticly I tucked the left oar under my arm and wrestled the loose rowlock back into its block. About 25 yards out a new wave was beginning to form. I had to get well clear before it came racing in, picking me up and taking me with it. Again I pulled wildly on the oars, and I could feel the sea starting to draw me into the wave, but somehow I had made it. I must have been just clear enough of the rocks for the dinghy to ride over the top. Immediately astern of me the wave started to crest and hiss towards the waiting rocks. More waves would follow. I pulled hard on the oars and kept going without let up until I was a good fifty yards out into the fiord. I was so heated up from the exertion and fright, steam was rising from my shirt.

Des took the painter as I came alongside "Tarawai" and together we hoisted the deer onto the deck, then stowed the dinghy. Neither of them had seen what nearly happened, nor did I bother telling them.

About six miles into the sound we came to our mooring alongside Bill Davis' ship the "Gleniffer". I was still overheated, ruddy faced and steaming. Bill took one look at me and laughingly said: "What have you been up to, White Hunter? You been for a run or something?"

When I told him where I had been and what happened, he just about hit the roof. Bill was an easy going sort of a bloke who didn't get ruffled too often. But now he was furious. He was furious that the skipper of my ship could be so foolish as to let me venture onto the headland in a small six foot Praam dinghy in the first place. Then he was furious at me, for thinking I could do single handed in a flat bottomed skiff what several highly experienced muttonbirders do as a team in large ocean going rowing boats. And then he noticed my thigh boots, looped to the belt of my pants. I had never seen a brown skinned Maori turn so white so quick.

"Come over here!" he said. And grabbing a fish knife he took hold of first one loop, and then the other, and sliced them clean off the top

Lou Moses tempting fate, recovering a set of floats
(photo Jimmy Ryan)

of my boots. "Don't you ever let me see you wearing a pair of boots tied on like that again. What chance do you think you would have had if you had tipped into the sea? You would have gone down quicker than a lead weight."

Yes, I had been dead fortunate I hadn't tipped the dinghy. The cards had been quite literally stacked against me and it was more by good luck than good management that I was still around to talk about it. I picked up a few valuable lessons that day, and one that I never forgot was: Fishing boots should always be at least two sizes too big for your feet, so that if you should fall into the sea they can be easily kicked off, and second and most important, no matter how many sizes too big they are, if they are looped to your belt you're not going to kick them off anyway. I was grateful to be still alive, and grateful to Bill for helping drive home a few much needed truths.

Once I got to thinking about it, after that wearing thigh boots in the dinghy lost much of its appeal. Weighed down with heavy clothing and wet weather gear to protect yourself against the roaring forties weather, there was no guarantee you would ever get your boots kicked off in time even if they were two sizes too big. Thigh boots weren't the best for hunting in anyway, and going ashore for a spot of hunting was after all, the main reason for my being in the dinghy in the first place. Unlaced hunting boots made more sense, even if they did mean wet feet getting ashore.

Finding ourselves anchored for the night in some out of the way

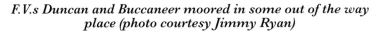

F.V.s Duncan and Buccaneer moored in some out of the way place (photo courtesy Jimmy Ryan)

sort of place, hemmed in by impossible bluffs or impenetrable bush, rain hosing down and keeping us ship bound was nothing out of the ordinary. So whenever we tied up in some likely looking spot and the weather was reasonable, I would grab the rifle and head for shore.

Late one afternoon we were anchored in one of those out of the way sort of places, hemmed in by impossible bluffs close to Green Point, about seven miles into Caswell Sound, but it was not raining. Ships all around were kicking up a din blasting down fresh caught bags of crayfish tails, and I was lounging on the deck of "Tarawai", cradling a hot mug of coffee. I wasn't entertaining thoughts on doing anything much other than sitting back and enjoying the scenery, when my eye suddenly caught sight of first one, and then a second Wapiti across the sound a mile to the southwest, browsing their way out of the bush several hundred feet up a grassy slip directly beneath Lake Shirley. It looked pretty steep going but quite straight forward none the less, and getting the carcasses back to the dinghy would be easy as pie with down hill dragging all the way. Robbie said to take the dinghy and I was gone with my boots and a handful of ammo for the opposite shore. It wasn't long and I was up on the slip, sneaking in amongst massive boulders right where I had seen the Wapiti from down on the boat.

Later, when I was back on board, Des told me that he and a couple of the other fishermen had watched both animals moving back into the bush the same time as I beached the dinghy, and they had tried yelling to me that they were gone but the distance was too great to carry their voices. I realized soon enough that they were gone, but thinking they would not have gone far and I might still be able to cut them off I climbed higher and began sidling into the bush with the intention of edging down onto them. It turned out to be fairly tight foliage in there and the further I went the tighter it got. I soon realized that I had made a mistake, trying to force my way through this impenetrable jungle. Animals the size of Wapiti would have to have been using well formed tracks or they would never have got through it. By now I was pushing and pulling, squeezing and dragging, trying not to make any noise. I had already edged in quite some distance and there was no point in losing all the ground I had gained by backtracking out of the bush and starting all over. I decided to begin working my way down to the level where I hoped to intercept the deer and if nothing else I should come across their tracks and have easier going getting back out of this mess. But dropping down proved worse than edging in. The face was near vertical and climbing down into the tightly packed undergrowth was more difficult than sidling round through it. Eventually the going became too tough to continue. There was only one sensible thing left to do; sidle back out to the slip and give the whole thing a miss. So again I changed my tack and began forcing my way out and immediately got tangled up in a series of tight ledges, tree roots, and nasty little bluffs. Hanging on by the eyebrows, rifle slung about my neck, I somehow worked my way into an even tighter mess on a very precarious ledge.

I was properly bluffed and could not see any way out, when all of a sudden there was a loud hissing and squawking and some furiously wild little critter came charging out at me from beneath a bit of an overhang. I got such a fright I all but fell off the bluff. Adrenalin surging, heart pounding, I shot back the way I had just come, quickly extricated myself from the tangle of ledges, roots and bluffs that just minutes before had had me completely bamboozled, quickly lowered myself onto easier going and in no time at all I was safely back onto the grassy slip; bits of foliage tangled in my hair and heart still thumping wildly.

Actually, it was only a yellow crested penguin frightening the living daylights out of me for coming too close to her nest. But it was the last thing I was expecting way up there. And she certainly helped drive home the point that for some, being attacked by little black and yellow demons is much more to be dreaded than dying a slow and lingering death on some lonely and inextricable bluff.

Experiencing Fiordland from the relative comfort of a cray boat was a fantastic experience. The scenery, the sheer rugged magnificence of it; the unruly Tasman Sea with its wild and unpredictable moods; the excitement of hauling bulky pots from murky depths and watching that red gold pouring out on the decks. Wapiti roaming wild and free just beyond reach; dolphins leaping and cavorting about the ship. Mirror calm seas and mollymawks gobbling hand held scraps while hove-to off Looking Glass Bay. Racing for'ard to watch humpback whales almost as long as our ship plying out of Caswell, so close in front of us that the skipper had to throttle back for fear of hitting one. The rain; that incessant deluging rain. And those incredible men who lived, and occasionally died, on the sea.

I was sitting having a beer with Jimmy Waitiri on the deck of "Buccaneer" one evening, when he noticed a young fisherman on a nearby boat pick up a guitar and wander off on his own to the stern of the ship. He sat on the railing, eyes closed, quietly strumming a tune. Jimmy nodded in the direction and said: "See that young fellow. He's finding it hard being separated from his girlfriend."

"How do you know?" I asked.

"When a young fellow draws away on his own like that you can count on it that his thoughts are drifting back home."

I guess that might have been a major reason why we steamed into Milford for the second time that season. The skipper was missing his wife and kids. Although, we did need to unload a freezer full of tails and refuel the ship with Diesel, and take on a fresh supply of bait for

Hauling pots on the F.V.Mijay (photo courtesy Jimmy Ryan)

the pots.

Robbie had come up with a new thought regarding bait... sheep heads! A whole truck load of them. The idea was quite a good one as they would hang in the pots for ages attracting crays while emitting the smell of rotting flesh, with the smelly bits tucked away inside the bone cavities where they could not be easily got at. We loaded them down into the freezer, blast froze them and Robbie and Des took off for Invercargill.

I think I already mentioned somewhere along the way that the good ship " Tarawai" was not one of the finest looking vessels in the fleet. And with all those good looking waitresses and housemaids pottering about the Milford Hotel and occasionally venturing as far as the wharf, I found the appearance embarrassing to say the least and preferred their not connecting me with it. I had plenty of mates hanging round Fresh Water Basin, owning, skippering and crewing fine looking ships. And besides all that, I did not really enjoy having to sleep in a damp and musty bunk beneath a leaking deck in the rear of the ship any more than I had to... stuck in the "after berth", as I called it. With Des and Robbie gone, I too abandoned ship and moved into more respectable looking quarters with some of my mates.

There was a storm lashing Milford one day and I was sitting in the cabin of Boong Ryan's boat, the "Solander", enjoying a cup of coffee with him and Jimmy, when a couple of meat shooters whom I knew, along with a young bloke who had been working for them as camp cook and rousie, came in off the coast in their little 15 foot jet boats. Whatever induced them to risk their necks out in the Tasman in such atrocious conditions I would not even like to hazard a guess. But they nearly didn't make it. They had come from Martins Bay, through the treacherous McKerrow Bar, no radios, no one advised they were going anywhere, a spare 12 gallon drum of fuel between them as a contingency measure. Neither boat had a compass on board, huge seas were running, visibility was down to a few hundred yards and their bearing was off the southerly wind, which they believed would get them where they wanted to go as long as they maintained their course directly into it.

They had been ploughing into the waves for some considerable time when the boat carrying the rousie and spare fuel, came thumping off the top of a huge wave with such force, the drum broke loose. The next wave saw the drum airborne, and as it came crashing back down, it took a bite out of the heel of my mate and smashed through the floor boards. The rousie went into a panic and was promptly flattened by my mate to quieten him down, and while all this was going on one of them happened to glance back over his shoulder and in a rare break in the mist caught a glimpse of the coastline lying dead astern. It was an incredibly lucky thing that he did, because unbeknown to them, the wind had shifted to the west and for some time they had been heading straight out into the Tasman. They immediately changed course and doubled back for the coast, but their blunder, apart from nearly costing them their lives, had cost them a lot of burned fuel and they only just made the shelter of Milford Sound before both boats ran dry. Worried now that if they refuelled both boats they might again run dry before reaching the head of the Sound, they emptied the drum into just one of their boats and arrived in Fresh Water Basin with the second boat in tow.

I remember at least one fisherman getting really angry when he heard about it: "It is because of foolish people doing stupid things in small boats, that we fishermen end up getting penalized," he told me. "When something goes wrong and lives are lost, we are the ones who have to live with new sets of regulations that encroach on our activity."

Robbie and Des had been gone about ten days, while I had been living on other boats, and having not been back on board the "Tarawai" since they left, I was unaware that things on board were not quite right.

As the skipper climbed on board his good ship he reeled backwards, gasping and gagging, just about throwing up all over the deck... probably something to do with the smell of rotting flesh oozing up from down below.

Unless one had all the facts, one might at first, mistakenly, conclude that I had been neglectful and delinquent not freezing down the bait every couple of days. But in truth I hadn't even given it a thought. Not to mention the fact that neither had the skipper before taking off for Invercargill. Right from the time I began crewing on board his ship I had been left out of anything bordering on "technical". I had never been shown, nor entrusted with operating the freezer, firing up the engine, even taking the helm for a few minutes. I was always willing, but never welcome. I was merely the third hand... on board to haul pots, tail crayfish and fillet cod. Now with the return of the skipper from his 10 day furlough, I was promptly relegated ex-third hand and ordered off the ship.

I thought that was pretty ungrateful. Everybody knows crayfish are carrion eaters, and he would never have thought of turning the bait into putrid carrion without my assistance. In reality, if the two of them could stomach living with the smell for a few weeks, they probably had on board the finest load of cray bait they were ever likely to latch onto.

They didn't even bother to thank me... and they never bothered to write. Amazing!

Stranded in Milford, with my Land Rover 180 miles away in Invercargill, no share in the cod fillets and hardly enough wages to raise the bus fare, I sat on my duffel bag nursing my rifle on the end of the wharf, and as the sun set slowly over the horizon and the sandflies started homing in, I got to wondering what does a normal person do in a situation such as this.

But then, I guessed, normal persons probably don't usually get theirselves into situations such as this.

CHAPTER 14

Dabbling in the Dobson

By the time I had extricated myself from the mess that I had gotten myself into it was about that time of year when fur trappers should already be back on their winter blocks. But I had heard that my old mate Bob Hannigan, was back in the Dobson once more, shooting tahr for the Forestry. And seeing the Dobson was more or less en route to the North Island I decided to go pay him a visit. Johnny Reardon issued me with a hunting permit and told me that the last he had seen Bob, he was at Ohau Base.

***Looking up the Dobson from above Irishmans Creek
(photo Bob Hannigan)***

A blustering gale was whipping up Lake Ohau from the freezing south, and anyone of right mind would have been hut bound and staying that way. But who said anything about Hannigan and me being of right mind? Here I was, layered up against the chill factor in a thick black bush singlet, Moose Lodge hunting shirt, woollen pullover, two pairs of thick woollen socks, long johns, shearing longs, nailed Anson boots, swannie, balaclava, nylon parka, all held together with my hunting belt; gasping for breath and close to vomiting with the exertion, endeavouring to keep pace with Bob Hannigan as the two of us raced up near vertical slopes about two miles up river from Ohau Base.

From way back down on the flats we had picked out a mob of deer just below the cloud level. Ten of them, contentedly feeding. Secure in the knowledge that no one of right mind would be out hunting on a day like this.

Totally unfit from weeks of virtual inactivity standing about on the deck of a crayfishing boat, we reached their level and I collapsed in a steaming heap behind a hummock while Bob pushed on to cut around above them and get them in a cross fire.

I could no longer see Bob, but that hardly mattered. The deer were in clear view, and as soon as he opened fire so did I. Utterly confused at the shots coming from different directions they milled about waiting to be reduced to $3.50 tails with a strip of skin and a couple of ears threaded on. The high country leaseholder, if he ever got wind of it, could now justify his banging another ten tussock denuding, cattle onto the block; totally negating any good we might have just accomplished in the process, and I led our merry way back down the slopes to the Hopkins valley below reassuring Bob Hannigan as we went that weeks of working on a fishing boat had not diminished my level of fitness one iota.

Bob had been hanging round Ohau Base because he no longer had a block mate. There was a little flexibility in it, but Forestry rules required two shooters to a block for safety reasons. They were meant to work in fairly close proximity so that if one got injured the other could raise the alarm. In actual practice it did not always work that way. A lot of shooters preferred their own company when out on the hills. Sometimes they worked as a team, such as Bob and I had just done with the mob of ten deer. In this case, Bob got the tails anyway. But when you were working on bonus, it was usually more productive going it alone. Reardon had told Bob not to go far until he sent in a new mate.

Men had come and men had gone. One bloke, who later made a name for himself as a writer of numerous hunting books, arrived fresh from the North Island, took one look at the enormity of the landscape with its massive rock faces, shingle screes and cloud piercing mountain peaks and promptly opted out. I had heard that prior to Bob's arrival, Johnny Reardon had gotten through some 67 "Dobson hopefuls' in just twelve months, with an average stay of three days per man. The country was simply too tough for them. Climbing to 5,000 feet every day just to get started looking for the animals you were meant to shoot didn't suit everybody. But that was the general pattern if you were planning on hunting mobs of tahr.

Bob would have been quite happy plodding on in the Dobson on his own, but I was a welcome arrival on the block nevertheless. He could now return to the Dobson with Reardon's blessing. The Land Rover was stocked with fresh bread, cabbages, and a large

Tahr Country. Glen Mary Glacier from above Irishmans (photo Bob Hannigan)

sack of Rabbit Board carrots that I had found lying in the middle of the road skirting the lake, and with two guns firing and only one man collecting the bounty here was a great opportunity for Bob to boost his tally. Bob also wanted me tagging along behind him on a tahr hunt, shooting footage through his 8mm cine camera. We both realized that charging up and down bluffs and mountain peaks with a gun and a dog, bowling animals left, right and centre, would one day be a thing of the past. While we had the chance, it was worth canning for posterity. We checked out of Ohau and took off for the Dobson

Seven miles beyond Glen Lyon Station, at the four bunk Kershaw Hut, we off-loaded the Land Rover of anything unrelated to tahr shooting, meat hunting and functionality, and then moved on to Kennedy Hut, 12 miles further again up the valley on the right hand side.

Perhaps it is worth mentioning at this juncture that purists and such, would most likely here insist that I was referring to the left of the valley, the "true left' that is, and not the right hand side at

**We off-loaded all the superfluous gear at Kershaw
(photo Bob Hannigan)**

all. However, most Government shooters never cared too much for purists and their technicalities. We all knew which side of valleys and rivers we were referring to by qualifying our discussions for the sake of the uncomprehending with the simple expression: "travelling up" or

Kershaw Hut (photo Bob Hannigan)

"travelling down" the left or right side. In this case we were travelling up!

So we moved on to Kennedy Hut which was, at the time, about 19 miles up the right hand side of the Dobson Valley from Glen Lyon Station. But, just to confuse the purists a little further, Kennedy Hut has since been relocated and is now shown on maps as being up the left hand side.

Snared from Kershaw Lagoon 'going up' the right hand side (photo Bob Hannigan)

The road from Kershaw did not extend right the way to Kennedy, and what there was of it was more tractor track than road. In places it was not even much of a tractor track. Hence, rather than knock the stuffing out of his truck, Bob parked it at Kershaw and then walked. Driving along tractor tracks was no problem for the Land Rover though, and being decidedly easier than walking, drive was what we did.

Max Kershaw, the field officer after whom the Kershaw Hut had been named, was commonly known as "Macaroni Max", owing to his custom of throwing open the food cupboard door and pointing to the ever present packet of macaroni sitting lonely on the shelf whenever some shooter complained that there wasn't enough food in the hut.

"Not enough food!" he would exclaim. "What do you mean, not enough food? What the hell do you call that if it's not food?"

Freddy Langenegger at Ohau Base (photo Bob Hannigan)

Macaroni Max's reputation for being a hard man had gone before him and he was well known, even to shooters who had never met him. Few were the men who relished the idea of dining on macaroni day in and day out. But according to Bob Hannigan, Max Kershaw may

Freddy with a young bull tahr (photo Bob Hannigan)

well have known something about macaroni that the average shooter wasn't prepared to start learning. Anyway, something in the diet was giving Bob enough energy to get up about daybreak everyday, climb almost vertically to 5,000 feet and more, spend the day scrambling about in bluffs and blizzards and howling gales searching out chamois and tahr, often getting back to the hut after dark, and Bob reckoned it was macaroni. Each day he packed a leg of tahr meat back to the hut off of the hill, boned it out, diced it into small cubes, browned the cubes in the camp oven along with a handful of chopped onion, boiled a billy full of macaroni elbows, melted in a tin of cheese along with a dob of butter, salt and pepper to taste, stirred in the browned cubes of tahr meat and onion, added some cornflour for thickening and sloshed the resultant gooey mess heaped high on his old enamel plate. "Hannigan's scroggin', I called it. Bob thrived on it, and with a big plate full of it tucked under his belt he was able to do what many others, before and after him were not able to do.

One bloke who had hung in a little longer than most of the other recruits was Freddie Langenegger, Bob's block mate until recently. He had been an exception to the "three day' rule, sticking with the job for about a year or so. Freddie was a German-Swiss who had been raised in the Swiss Alps. But it was the Dobson that nearly took him out. Like the time he took off down the slopes, up above Kennedy Hut, on a chunk of windslab snow and only just managed to save himself by rolling over onto his belly and using his ice axe tucked

Tahr with nowhere to go (photo Bob Hannigan)

under his armpit for a brake. He was teetering on the edge of a sheer drop-off when he finally came to a stop. Took him weeks to get over it according to Bob. Mind you, it was a crazy place for him to have been in mid winter anyway.

It was in that same area, up above the Kennedy Hut, where we now found ourselves, Bob with a rifle, me with the 8mm cine camera and Kim the dog tagging along. It was a blustery day, grey, cold and miserable and we probably would not have even known there were any tahr in the area if Kim had not put his nose in the air and gotten all excited. They were hiding in amongst the rocks with nowhere to go and Bob dropped five or six of them one after the other with his Remmington .222 Carbine when they panicked and broke. And I got the lot... stalking, shooting and tailing... on film. Then we cut back across and down a huge broad scree ending up on the edge of a sheer drop-off, with me balancing on a large overhanging rock with hundreds of feet of space below me, taking in the scenery.

Bob got the wind up seeing me hanging there over nothing, and he more or less ordered me back to safer ground. But not without good reason. It was one of those places where your feet go tingly just thinking about it, and he had nearly been blown off similar type outcrops in similar blustery conditions on previous occasions and was well aware of the danger. I was not altogether blind to it. We had all had our share of frights, but I didn't really think anything like that could happen to me. Hunters never do. In snowless conditions the area was as safe as anywhere else in the Southern Alps, but we knew this same spot had nearly claimed Freddie's life and we strongly suspected that this was where James Kennedy, the field officer whom the Kennedy Hut was named after, had gone over, either on windslab or with an avalanche, and died. Kennedy's Memorial plaque near the hut below spoke of his being swept away in an avalanche. We understood he had been caught out on a windslab that broke free and took him with it. Either way, you could sense something not quite right about the place. There was an ominous aura hanging over it that gave you a sort of a creepy feeling just being there, and it was not difficult picturing James Kennedy going over the edge in this spot, right here. When you know that an area is hazardous and you get that sort of feeling along with it, you normally do not hang round for long.

The quickest way down off the tops — other than falling off a precipice that is — the one most favoured by shooters racing home before the failing light, was to jump on a shingle scree and take off running, glissading and skiing with the stones you had set loose. But this too had its hidden dangers. Boulders often got loosed up behind you and came crashing down in your wake cutting a swathe through foliage and trees as they plummeted into the bush below. The wise thing then, was to take off at a tangent before reaching the bottom

**Kim the dog sitting on the Kennedy Memorial
(photo Bob Hannigan)**

of the scree, and let any following boulders take off past you lest they smashed your head to pulp as they caught up with you. We were doing this, glissading down through the beech trees above Kennedy, when we overtook three Red deer, probably wondering what all the noise was about. Bob took the tails and I took the carcasses. Taking hold of the front leg of a deer in each hand, and sharing the middle one between us, we took off at a downhill run and managed to drag all three carcasses to the valley in one haul.

Gruff Hut was four miles downstream from Kennedy, on the opposite bank, and according to Bob, the Neumann Range up above Gruff had not been worked for some time. Most likely there would be a few relatively quiet animals living up there.

Fairly late one afternoon, we were picking our way across the Dobson on the way to Gruff Hut, when I bottomed out the Land Rover in a patch of quicksand. In fast flowing water, it is not always easy to see. In fact it does not necessarily look much different to any other patch of sandy riverbed. But it is a trap for the unwary; dense particles of sand free floating in water and just waiting to bog something down.

South Island high country rivers are notoriously prone to flash flooding. And sitting out in the middle of one, bogged to the floor boards is not a good feeling. Especially when it is already late in the afternoon and the nearest help is 16 miles away at Glen Lyon Station. My Land Rover was well equipped for getting out of difficulties. It was not fitted with a winch, but with the use of a crowbar, wire

***Looking back towards Kennedy from near Gruff Hut
(photo Bob Hannigan)***

strainers and a good length of chain, I could usually work my way out
of most problems. But quick sand was different to anything I had ever
encountered before. We tried every trick we knew but she was locked
firmly in a vacuum that refused to break its grip. Digging, shovelling,
winching, straining, bouncing, rocking, up and down the gears, in and
out of low reduction, forward, reverse, she wouldn't budge an inch,
and eventually I had to concede defeat.

The remaining hours of daylight were slipping away and by
now there were not many of them left. All that was needed was a
good dumping of rain up in the headwaters during the night and by
morning my land Rover could well be gone; tumbled down the river
and buried beneath a bank of gravel. Bob reckoned it was about five
hours from Gruff to Glen Lyon. Even if we left straight away, it would
be well into the night by the time we got there. We decided there was
nothing for it but to unload everything out of the vehicle, stack it out
of harm's reach up on the banks of the river and get moving. As a
last resort against the worst happening, we sank the crowbar into the
riverbed as deep and firm as possible to act as an anchor, stropped a
length of chain back on to the tow bar and tensioned it up with the
wire strainers. With everything we could do done, we took off flat
tack for Glen Lyon, carrying nothing but our rifles and sleeping bags,
down the boulder strewn farm track that skirted the river flats at the
foot of the Ben Ohau Range.

As we strode off down the track, there was little on my mind other
than how I would be affected if my Land Rover got washed away

during the night. The vehicle was uninsured, I was still trying to pay it off, and there was not much money in the bank. The February fur sale in London had not been a good one with a large portion of my skins being turned in unsold. These would now have to wait until May before coming up for offer again. I had barely made wages on the "Tarawai" after Ballantyne had deducted board and keep, and although I had been promised a share in the cod fillets, I never saw it. I still had to find and finance the provisioning and setting up of a new camp before I could get underway with the forthcoming trapping season. If a flash flood should happen along right now all would be lost and there would not be a forthcoming trapping season.

Head full of worry, mind set on reaching Glen Lyon in the shortest possible time, Bob sharing in my fears, we were some twenty minutes south of Kershaw, eyes set firmly on the road watching for potholes and boulders beneath our feet and frightening ourselves with the sparks from our horseshoe nails, when it suddenly dawned on Bob that we had walked right past his Chev truck, parked alongside the hut back there in the dark, and we had not even given it a thought. There wasn't much point in walking when we could ride, but nor was I giving up any of the ground I had gained. I let Bob go back for the truck and I pressed on into the night. By the time he finally caught up with me there was less than four more miles to Glen Lyon and I was more than happy to thumb a ride for the last stretch. Coming up twelve miles of dusty, boulder strewn, farm track between the Land Rover and me, all on an empty stomach and a mind heavily weighed with worry in a little over three hours of solid slog.

It was worry more than common sense driving me on through the night, and if I was imagining that John Moya, the station manager, would promptly don his hat and boots, mount the Glen Lyon tractor and drive off into the darkness, I was wrong.

His dogs heralding our approach, had him waiting outside the homestead for our arrival well before we drove in the gate. But considering the seriousness of the situation that had brought us here in the dead of night, he was nowhere near as concerned about my Land Rover sitting out there, fifteen or so miles up the valley in the middle of the Dobson River, as I would have liked him to have been. Glancing casually about the skyline he observed: "It probably won't rain before morning. Come in for a feed, then you can bunk down in the musterer's quarters. We'll go take a look after breakfast."

To my way of looking at it, "Probably won't rain!" was little different to saying, "Possibly will rain!" The observation from John Moya was obviously not supposed to be ambiguous, but in my frame of mind, his kind assurance did little for my peace of mind, and much of the night I spent tossing about in my sleeping bag, looking out the window at the star filled sky, worrying myself frantic that it might have already closed in up in the headwaters with the rain thundering down.

Worrying does not usually alter much, and neither did it rain. Soon after breakfast one of the station workers took off on the tractor followed by John and me in the Glen Lyon Land Rover, and Bob returning his Chev to where he normally parked it, at Kershaw Hut. Way out in the river near Gruff, nothing had changed from the way we had left things the night before, and considering all the drama and panic of the previous few hours, unbogging her from the quicksand was almost a non event. All it took was a wire strop between the tractor and the Land Rover tow bar, and just like that my vehicle was pulled free.

I was really grateful to John for his willing assistance, but then that was what one comes to expect from back country folks. It would be most unusual for them not to lend a hand when someone is in a bit of strife. As soon as they knew I was okay they turned around and headed back to Glen Lyon, while I parked up on the grass and drained the diffs, the sump and the gear box in case any water had gotten in, and replaced the drained oils with new clean stuff.

And then back into the river we went, all loaded up with gear and on our way to Gruff Hut once more. Only this time I trailed a few yards behind Bob, while he waded ahead probing the sandy spots with his boots. Country folks are pretty obliging, but one would not want to push one's luck too far by getting stuck in the same place twice in the same day.

CHAPTER 15

Out For a Duck

We were just thinking what we were going to have for dinner that first night at Gruff, when three honking Canadian geese came flying low over the tussie flats and landed on a large tarn just north of the hut. I immediately started conjuring up all the different means I knew of how to catch a wild poultry.

My old mate Hank, said catching turkeys was easier than falling off a log. Mind you he was not talking about wild ones. The ones he was referring to were the domestic kind... the kind that lived on his old man's next door neighbour's farm when he was a boy.

"You have to be careful you don't get them too excited and start them all gobbling all over the place," said Hank. "Otherwise everyone gets to know what you're up to. The first time I had a go at them I was only about seven years old and I didn't have much experience to fall back on. I waited 'til I thought no one was around and I went charging in and grabbed a young one by its neck. The rest of the turkeys took off in all directions making a heck of a ruckus, gobbling and squawking and hissing and snorting, while I struggled to get the one I was near strangling to death under control.

"Then all of a sudden this big old grand daddy of a gobbler turned around and noticed what I was doing to his little mokopuna. He stuck his neck out near horizontal to the ground, all the red bits round his head went crimson, he started flapping his wings and then he launched himself at me.

"I saw him coming and I tried to take off, dragging my turkey behind me, but I was only a little fellow and I was weighed down with this scrawching female that was bent on dragging me back to where I was coming from. I couldn't get up enough steam. I never have had much luck with females and this one was probably where it all started. I only made a few yards before the old gobbler overtook me.

"My old man used to give me some pretty good hidings from time to time, but I'm telling you, that old gobbler gave me the worst hiding I had ever had in my life. I got such a fright I let go of the turkey I was hanging onto and fell flat on my face in the dust. That was all the old gobbler needed. He jumped straight on my back and got stuck into me, spurs, claws, teeth and all. My shirt was all torn and there were bits of skin missing off my back and ribs, and I probably would have gone down in history as the first human ever killed by a turkey if the farmer's wife hadn't heard all the commotion and come running out of her kitchen and seen me lying there being attacked by their prize gobbler. Dear old thing was most upset by what had happened. She bashed up the gobbler with a yard broom and took me into her kitchen and sat me down, and gave me a big glass of milk and a buttered scone and told her husband to go and chop the gobbler's head off immediately.

"'Stupid bird! It must have got a bit too much sun and gone mad,' she said.

"Then she hand cranks the phone on the kitchen wall and calls up my mum and tells her that one of their turkeys had gone mad, but she didn't think it had rabies, and her husband was chopping off its head right now, and then she was going to stuff it and roast it in the oven. And when that was done she was going to send it over to our house for us to eat, and she knew we were all good neighbours and she hoped my mum wouldn't take her and her husband to court for having dangerous turkeys on their property that attacked little children."

"Do you call that 'easier than falling off a log'?" I asked.

"No, I call that gaining experience," said Hank. "Never had another go using that method. It was a bit too painful, although it seemed to work okay and get results.

"It was about a year later when I finally came up with the foolproof method. The old man was down at the local football club playing darts with some of his mates and my mum was away playing bridge. I had been left at home to keep an eye on the place, and I was getting bored with just hanging around. Then I decided to check out my old man's home brew just to see how it was getting on. He had popped the top off one of the bottles and left a silver teaspoon standing in it so it wouldn't go flat. I never could figure out how he managed to drink the stuff. Just smelling it was enough to make me feel dizzy.

"Then I started thinking about them turkey gobblers once again. If only there was some way of making them smell the old man's home brew they would all get dizzy and I would be able to catch one of them and wring its neck without getting myself scragged. Then I could drag it down the back into the bush, and cut off its drumsticks and roast them over an open fire just like I'd seen them do it in the Western Movies. So I raced inside and grabbed a loaf of stale bread and broke it up into little bits and soaked the pieces in some of the old man's home brew. Then I started throwing bits and pieces of sloshy beer soaked bread over the fence for the neighbour's turkeys to come and have a sniff.

"For awhile I thought it wasn't going to work, because instead of sniffing the bread they rushed round grabbing it up and eating it. I was getting really mad because I had already wasted the first loaf and not one of them had taken time to sniff it before they had swallowed it down. So I raced back home to get another stale loaf and try again, and by the time I got back there was a whole heap of them getting up and falling down. And some were lying paralytic with their eyes rolled back and their tongues lolling out, and I realized they must have been sniffing the old man's home brew after all, probably same time as they were picking it up and swallowing it down."

Hank said the same principal applied to catching most poultry... although I could not see how I was going to apply it to catching one of these Canadian geese, seeing we had no home brew, and we had already eaten all the stale bread.

Hank said home brew wasn't the only method that worked. Possum traps were also pretty good, but from his experience these seemed to work better on ducks than geese and gobblers.

"I was passing through Wanganui one year," said Hank. "Heading up country for a spot of duck shooting. Anyway, I was feeling like a break, so I stopped the old truck at Lake Victoria, right on the edge of town.

"I couldn't believe how many ducks there were waddling about. The cunning sods must have known the duck shooting season had just opened, and they had all flocked into town where they knew they was safe and there was plenty of free handouts. It didn't seem right to me, all those ducks hanging round town being hand fed bread and cakes, while the duck shooters were sitting out in their maimai's wet, cold and miserable with probably not a duck anywhere to be seen. There didn't seem much point in heading off out into the swamps looking for ducks if they were all here, in town, hanging around Lake Victoria.

"So I wandered back to the truck and fetched me a possum trap. Then I tied a piece of bread on the plate, loaded it and wandered back down to the edge of the lake.

"They were cunning little sods alright, those ducks. They seemed to know I was up to something. When they saw me coming they all waddled into the lake and started swimming about. So I thought, "I'll show you bunch of so-'n'-so's who's the cunning sod round here!"

"I ducked back to the truck for another length of string and a tack out board and tied the trap onto the board. Then I tied the rest of the string onto the end of my board and gave it a gentle push out into the lake. Straight away one of them swims up to the board for a look, sees the bread, makes a grab and "Bang!" the trap goes off on his neck. Right at the same moment this little old lady from the local duck lovers club comes walking round the lake edge and immediately sees all the splashing going on a few yards out in the lake. So I sits there holding onto my ol' piece of string while at the same time trying to hide it under my trouser leg and looking the other way as if I hadn't noticed anything of particular interest. Then she stops alongside me and says: 'Look at that dear little duck. Isn't he lovely. I think he's trying to catch little fish or something from underneath that piece of timber floating on the lake.'

"I wasn't game to let on that I could hear her, so I keeps looking the other way, but then I takes a sneaky little look just to see what the duck's up to.

"The weight of the trap had turned the board upside down and the duck was kicking its feet in the air with its head held under by the trap. So I quietly lets go of the string, slowly gets to my feet and still looking the other direction I wander off in a big circuit, down around the lake until I'm out of sight, then I doubles back as quick as I could, hops in the truck and takes off. It cost me a trap and a board, and I never did get my duck, but the method works alright," Hank added.

I made a mental note to try it sometime when I was back in Taupo. There were usually plenty of ducks waddling up and down the footpath above the Lake waiting for free handouts. You could probably sit right there in your vehicle dangling a loaded trap out the window.

Hank's means of catching poultry may have been effective when applied in the appropriate setting, but for Canadian geese up the middle of the Dobson I had a different method.

In the failing light of day, we snuck down from the hut and tweaked over the top of a large hump of moraine gravel to plan our course of attack. Already the birds had waddled out of the tarn and settled themselves down in the tussock, preening their feathers and preparing to tuck their heads beneath their wings for the night. All we needed at this stage was a bearing on their roosting quarters, and an hour or so after dark we would be back.

Back in the hut, Bob got a nice fire going, building up a decent bed of coals, while I figured out a dainty stuffing of crumbed camp oven loaf, diced potato, chopped onions and mixed herbs. And while all the preparation was getting done I got to reminiscing back a few years to when I was a teenager and I was spending a few weeks on D'Urville Island and I was out hunting deer with Fred Leov on his old man's property at Greville Harbour. That was when Fred showed me how to catch Canadian geese in the middle of the night, except Fred and I were not hunting geese; we were actually hunting deer.

Len Leov didn't mind me hanging round with his son, because I was always willing to chip in and give him and Fred a hand with the farm work. One day Fred and I took off on a couple of horses to go grub thistles up in the gullies above the track to Port Hardy, and that was the time I stuck my first wild boar. Fred's dogs got a bail and our horses were hobbled across the other side of the creek and our rifles were over there too, stuck in our saddle scabbards, and I was the only one wearing a knife. Some nights we went hunting eels with a spot light and a slasher round the edge of the lagoon. There were heaps of them but we only took the silver bellies. Fred reckoned the yellow bellies tasted like mud, but his mum would jelly the silver bellies, and when they were ready we would get stuck into them for our lunch with chunks of fresh baked farm bread and heaps of freshly churned butter. But it was while out hunting deer with a spotlight that Fred showed me how you could catch Canadian geese in the middle of the night.

We had skirted the lagoon and were heading round the edge of the swamp when two deer showed up in the middle of the road. Fred switched off the engine, grabbed his spotlight and jumped out of the Land Rover. I was right behind him, toting the hardware — Fred's battered old Winchester .44-40. Suddenly Fred switched off the spot leaving us in total darkness. I had never been spotlighting before so I didn't have a clue what Fred was doing. About five seconds later Fred switches on the spot once more and we ran several yards closer to the two deer which were still standing dazzled in the same place. Fred kept this up, switching the light off and on as we kept moving in, until we were within a few yards of them and then suddenly they broke. One took off up into the bush above the road and the other one ran straight down the road towards us, while Fred continued dazzling the oncoming deer with light and blinding it with darkness. At the last minute, still utterly blinded by alternating light and dark, it veered off the road in front of us, jumped into the swamp and immediately sank up to its belly in a drainage ditch. By now Fred was yelling for a knife, but all I had was the old Forty-four. Fred's knife was back in the Land Rover, sitting on the floor, and I was not wearing one. We pithed the deer at point blank range with the Forty-four, but what Fred had really wanted to do was jump on its back and cut its throat with his knife, just so that he could say he had done it. That night I learned the principles of closing in on game with a spotlight.

There were no Canadian Geese on D'Urville so as I said, Fred was not really showing me how to catch Canadian geese, but the principles are the same. Canadian geese cannot fly when they are dazzled with a light, nor when they are blinded with darkness. And if they do take off, as soon as you switch from light to dark, or vice versa, they crash.

Most all breeds of poultry take pleasure in socializing and chatting with one another until darkness overtakes them. Then they take a bit more time testing their security before settling down. When they are quite satisfied there are no intruders hanging around, that is when they tuck their heads beneath their wings and doze off. Even then, geese are real skittery critters, and it does not take much movement in the vicinity to have a gaggle of geese wide awake and planning their escape. But the advantage we had was the spotlight. We only wanted one bird for the pot, and in a short while we had him; young and fat, plucked, gutted and sizzling in the camp oven, hot coals piled on the lid as it hung above a glowing fire. Occasionally the lid was gently eased, the legs and breast basted with sizzling fat and more fresh glowing coals piled on top.

It was a long mouth watering wait while that fat and juicy piece of poultry simmered to perfection, but eventually it was done. The cabbage was lightly steamed with a little bit of salt and a big blob of butter, the carrots and potatoes were baked crisp and brown, the stuffing was filling the hut with appetizing aromas, the gravy was thickened rich and moorish. Bob forked the poultry out of the camp oven onto a large enamel plate and sliced it clean down the middle; half for him and half for me. And before we crawled into our sleeping bags for the night there was nothing left to show for it but a couple of dirty dishes and a few chewed up bones. And if come breakfast we were feeling peckish once more, we would just have to go look for a trout, because the two remaining geese were not likely to be flying back into Gruff tarns for a long, long time to come after the hurry-up they had just experienced.

Even though the Dobson and the Hopkins Rivers were right side by side, separated only by the Neumann Range, they were vastly different in composition and appearance. For example, there was nowhere near as much beech forest in the Dobson watershed as in the Hopkins. But there was a reasonable stretch of bush covering the slopes either side of Gruff Hut. And I reckoned that under the cover of night, there were bound to be a few deer wandering out of the lower bush edge onto the great rolling stretches of tussock that lay between the forest and the river. If we worked our way along the bush edge with the spotlight a few hours before daybreak one morning, I believed there was every likelihood that we would nab one or two easy deer for our effort.

It was 4.30am going on 5.00 and the night had been black as pitch with barely a trace of cloud in the sky and the merest hint of air flow sifting downriver from the north. We were quietly working our way upstream into the drift, searching for anything that might be foraging the flats. But there was no need for us to have gotten up so early. Nor was there a need for us to have taken precautions against spooking anything with our scent.... There had not been anything out to spook.

We had waded through three miles of cold, dew drenched tussock, to beyond where the beech forest ran out. Saturated and frigid from the waist down, boots squitching icy water, traces of dawn breaking over the skyline, and the chances of catching anything out at this stage

Looking up the Dobson from near Gruff Hut
(photo Bob Hannigan)

just about nil. And that was when I wished I was still back at the hut, snug and warm in my sleeping bag, a crackling fire heating the hut, the billy brewing and a nice hot cup of tea in the offing to be followed closely by breakfast and the start to another beautiful day. But rather than back at the hut, here we were miles upriver, out in the middle of the cold wet tussock with nothing to show for it except a good hour's return journey between us and breakfast. There was no point going any further so we turned around and started backtracking to Gruff.

Meat shooting was like that. Sometimes you caught something out, sometimes you didn't. But the waste of time was annoying. And if I was annoyed by it, Bob was probably more so because he was bounty hunting, or bonus shooting as we called it, and he needed to maintain his tally. Just before daybreak was the time of day when we should have been leaving the hut for the early morning shoot, and here we were heading the opposite direction with nothing to show for it.

I suppose it was playing pretty heavily on our minds, because we had only gone a short way when Bob suggested that if we gained a little elevation we might still fluke something. So we stashed the spotlighting gear beneath a prominent piece of scrub, and started following the bush edge up a mountain stream towards the open tops, hoping we just might get on to something. But that was another waste of time. Broad daylight found us up in the alpine meadows just so much more removed from breakfast and wondering: "What now?".

For awhile we sat there, soaking up the early morning sun,

deliberating. We could return the way we had just come, but we knew the area was devoid of game, so there was not much future in that. We could also shelve breakfast, cut around the tops, hunt our way into Don Creek then drop back down to Gruff Hut and be back there in time for lunch. We chose to do the latter.

It is interesting observing the survival mechanisms of various wild animals. Rabbits and hares usually keep one weather eye to the heavens in case a bird of prey should suddenly swoop on them. But alpine critters tend to give more caution to being sneaked up on from below than being dropped down on from above. Tahr, for example, generally station themselves on bluffy ledges during much of the day, positioning themselves in such a manner that, between the various members of the mob, they are able to take in the entire surrounding landscape leaving virtually no way of approach without the intruder being observed. Often perched hundreds of feet above their feeding grounds, backed up against impossible crags and surrounded by sheer drop-offs, they spend much of the daylight hours just hanging out, secure in the knowledge that no one can get anywhere near them, their defences all but impregnable. Chewing their cuds, taking in everything below them, not missing a beat, seldom ever looking up. If you can see a way to sneak round behind them and drop down from above, that's the way to go. Chamois though, are different. They have an uncanny knack of seemingly being able to pick things out with almost global 360 degree vision. Up, down, round and around.

Chamois (Photo Dave Richardson)

Still working our way towards Don Creek, we were pushing passage through stunted alpine scrub, wondering where all the animals had gone, when we came out on a ledge of rock overlooking a scrubby mountain stream. Instantly, a shrill whistle rent the air from about 50 yards almost directly beneath us. Two treble-two rifle shots exploded simultaneously and one chunky little buck chamois collapsed under the combined shock of some two thousand foot-pounds of kinetic energy. Almost one ton of hitting power! If he had not whistled he might have got away. There was plenty of cover for him if he had taken off running, and we had not seen him first. So what made him look up above his head? We were not making any noise. Actually, a chamois' eyes protrude well out of his skull and maybe this does offer almost 360 degree vision. Anyway, they are certainly good at picking things out. Nevertheless, despite their incredible all round vision, it is not impossible sneaking in real close to them. All that is needed is care and patience.

On one occasion I stalked in so close to a chamois doe and her joey in the headwaters of the Karangarua River, that I could have quite literally whacked her with a big stick. Had it been a rifle I was hunting with I probably would have started shooting from anything up to a hundred yards distance. But this time I was hunting with a 16mm camera and I really wanted to try and get in as close as possible. They were several hundred yards out when I first noticed them, sitting in amongst some broken rocks on approximately the same level as me. But much of the country between us was quite open with only a smattering of rock for cover. It was a long and painful stalk, utilizing whatever cover I could. At one stage I was able to use the cover of a gut to gain some quick elevation and from there I was able to work my way in behind them. From here I had the advantage of the broken rocks they were sheltering in and when I next saw them I had come out so close that the joey stood looking up into the lens at point blank range while the doe sat chewing her cud with me filming over the top of her head. Suddenly the whirring of the camera registered and with a shrill whistle she sprang to her feet, hightailing it with innocent little joey hanging hot on her heels. That was all back in the days before high magnification video cameras took most of the fun out of close stalking.

Bob recovered the tail and ears off the buck we had just dropped and we pressed on to Don Creek.

It was mid morning by the time we got to overlooking Don Creek watershed. From an elevated vantage point we sat on a bed of scabweed and lichens in amongst huge boulders and glassed the surrounding countryside. Way below us the creek cascaded through broken rocks to disappear into the beech forest, while all around shingle screes spewed down the slopes, interspersed with sharp ridges and vicious looking stone outcrops. And where there wasn't shingle and rock there were steep faces covered with an assortment of alpine herbs and grasses. Here and there scattered patches of sweet tasting aromatic pink and white snowberries crawled upwards over the screes trying to bond things back together. Walls of granite and rugged peaks capped the watershed, interposed with bits of glacier and fields of ancient ice. Cold, stark, and beautiful. And there, high on an impossible ledge of mountain stone, blending in almost perfectly with the colour of the mountain walls, positioned in classic sentinel formation and unapproachable from no matter what direction, were four big old bull tahr surveying the entire watershed laid out before them. They were a long way distant from us, high up in the headwaters, and it was unlikely that we had been noticed. But even if we had, they were not indicating any apparent concern about it.

Now had those tahr been browsing herbs in amongst the sharp ridges and vicious looking stone outcrops, we could have snuck right in, bombed the lot of them and headed home for lunch. But laying about as they were, high up on their lofty perch, I just knew that not only breakfast, but now lunch also was about to go out the door. Tahr reclining in high resting places do not usually bother getting up to dine until the shadows have already gotten long down in the valley.

They are quite incredible animals; the way they scramble about on near vertical walls of rock. Immensely powerful, with a live weight often well in excess of 200 pounds, their long shaggy coats adding emphasis to their bulk, they are quite rightfully categorized as "big game". Yet somehow they seem to be able to hurl themselves up into the crags, managing to find footholds in impossible places with barely enough ledge for their hooves to grip. Springing from foothold to foothold with so little tolerance that if they paused to catch their breath they would tumble to their death, up the side of seemingly sheer bluffs they go until they reach the resting ledge they're aiming for. There were a lot of places tahr went that cullers were not silly enough to even try. And seeing cullers got paid only for the tails they produced neither was there much point in shooting at them perched in the middle of some impossible bluff. It looked like it was going to be a long day, waiting for them to come down to our level. At least some of that long day would be spent closing the gap and getting ourselves into a better attacking position. But to do that, we were going to have to back track from our vantage point, work our way down through Don Creek, then climb high through the other side of the watershed while at all times keeping ourselves concealed from their ever watchful gaze.

By now I was feeling decidedly peckish. A good drink of fresh mountain water always helps when you are tired and hungry, but not for long. Down in the creek we stoked up with water and then started slowly up the other side, maintaining cover by positioning a razorback ridge between us and the tahr, and as we climbed ever higher out of the creek bed, the day got progressively hotter, and hotter, and drier, and drier, and now there was no more water to be had.

Bob reckoned we would need to climb to almost 6,000 feet to get an advantage over the tahr. There was virtually no cover through which to stalk in the basin into which they would be coming down to feed, so unless we were up at their level when they scrambled off their ledge we would have no show of getting them. I fully appreciated all of that, but climbing to 6,000 feet on an empty stomach on a hot and thirsty day with a bubbling mountain stream in broad tormenting view several thousand feet below was not the makings of an easy day on the hill.

In reality though, it was not all that bad. With fingernails worn down to the quick from digging and scratching holes to bedrock through gravel slides and mud, there was sufficient gritty water to be found seeping down the mountainside to wet the inside lining of your mouth. And there were the odd scattered patches of snowberries to be found... even if it did take a couple of hours searching to find half a handful of berries, which was somewhat less than the amount required to replace the energy burned in trying to find them in the first place. No, it wasn't really much worse than any other typical day slogging round the hills.

In time, scratching out water pools and searching for snowberries as we went, we worked our way up to a vantage point on the razorback, and somewhere about mid-afternoon found us propped up against rocks, sitting in the dust out of sight behind the razorback, one eye on the tahr, waiting for them to make the first move, and the other on the sun as it slowly, very slowly, worked its way towards the western skyline. We sat and we sat and we sat. Semi-dozing, stomachs rumbling, gazing longingly at the creek and yearning for a long, cool draught of water. Same time we were surveying the four tahr, while they took their time and pleasure surveying the watershed. And late in the afternoon, as the shadows were lengthening and a coolness was settling over the ranges, our four tahr slowly got off their butts and after a fair bit of deliberating first one, then another, then all four of them began the downward descent from ledge to ledge, crevice to crevice, until they were off the bluffs and now slowly feeding their way in the general direction of us; still lying in the dust patiently waiting for them up on the razorback ridge. Apart from wait, there was not much else we could do. The ground between us and the tahr was quite open offering no cover if we tried to close the gap, and after patiently waiting for them all day, it was not going to make much sense suddenly getting impatient now and losing them as a result. So we just lay there, waiting. Bob, me and Kim, rifles sighted and one half up the spout. And after an endless eternity, as the valley emptied of sunlight and a cold nip set in, we could at last see the whites of their eyes, and we let rip and bowled the lot.

We quickly removed the tokens, hacked the back legs from the youngest bull in the bunch and took off down the creek and into the forest. Now it was going to be a race against time getting off the hill and back to camp before dark; which of course we failed to do. Sometime well into the night, we stumbled into Gruff Hut worn out and exhausted, and near famished to death, and wondering why some people choose such difficult ways to earn a living. Tomorrow, somewhere about the first streak of dawn would begin our next day on the hill. Little wonder the average bloke had only lasted three days on the Dobson Block!

Archaeologists say that one of the most exciting things they can find is old rubbish pits, because from the refuse in a rubbish pit they can quickly learn much about how earlier civilizations lived. I found a loosely covered rubbish pit just behind Gruff Hut, but not being an archaeologist, I was not terribly excited about it. And not only that,

Bob Hannigan with his 12 point head shot high in the Watson watershed

it took me the rest of the morning trying to jack the front end of my Land Rover up, with nothing to support the jack on, other than a heap of empty space and old rusty tin cans, so as I could get my vehicle back onto solid ground.

Meanwhile, while I was busily entertaining myself with the rubbish pit, Bob was blowing holes through a 12 point Red stag high up in the Watson watershed that he and Kim had come across. And although he had shot it high up in the bush, just in case I fancied recovering the carcass, he had gutted it and laid it open with a stick propped in the ribcage to help cool it down. Bob said it was a monstrous beast and one man would never handle it on his own, so we swung the billy, and after stoking up with a slab of camp oven loaf and a hot mug of tea we took off up Watson Stream, Kim leading the way.

Dragging deer downhill is not necessarily quite as easy as one might imagine. It is certainly easier than trying to drag them uphill, but that is not the point of what I am trying to say. Once a handhold has been cut between the hamstring and the bone, it is easier gripping the carcass by a back leg than it is gripping it by a front leg. But dragging a deer by the back leg is against the lay of the hair and this creates a certain amount of natural resistance. Dragging by the front leg, the carcass slides easier, but the neck tends to get in the way, and if there are two men dragging, hanging onto a front leg each, one of them is going to be forever getting that neck caught up beneath his boots. A heavyweight sliding carcass also tends to build up a momentum of its own, getting hung up round tree trunks and sliding sideways into guts and hollows and ruts and watercourses. If you are sidling above a stream, almost always it will eventually work its way into the stream, and dragging down a rough mountain stream is even harder than dragging through the bush. By the time we had it all sorted out and had gotten it down to where I could load it on the front rack of the Land Rover, about two hours solid exasperation and brightly coloured adjectives had been left in a thick trail that could be traced out through the stream bed and leaf mould right the way back up to about where we had gotten started. As Bob had said, it was a monstrous beast, and I would never have handled it on my own. Actually it was as big as any Red stag I had ever seen, and not far removed from being more than the two of us put together could handle.

Now it so transpired that this particular deer also happened to be the heaviest carcass that had yet been weighed in by the local venison agent down at Omarama, and being duly impressed with it's enormity, I had barely cleared town and headed back to the Dobson, when our venison buying friend takes off knocking on Johnny Reardon's door to come and have a geek at this huge hunk of meat hanging in his freezer. Johnny was most impressed... a whole rack of deer carcasses, all neatly gutted and all neatly tailed!

Loaded up with Bob's big stag and a regular sized deer on the roof rack (photo Bob Hannigan)

We had moved camp back across the river to Station Hut, and were quietly enjoying some of the fresh bread and goodies I had fetched back from Omarama, when in bowls Johnny Reardon, spitting sparks and tacks. He wasn't sure whether Bob had been tailing my carcasses or I had been carcassing his tails, but either way, something didn't tally quite right according to the NZFS "book of rules".

I argued that it wasn't none of the Forestry's business. My hunting permit gave me licence to do what I liked with the animals I shot, and that included selling them in Omarama with or without their tails attached, or if it suited me, leaving them to rot on the hill with or without their tails attached, whatever the case may be. And what was more, if I happened across some carcass that had been abandoned on the hill and decided to lug that out also I could not see that that was anybody else's business either, other than my own.

Johnny reminded me that all animals shot by Forestry employees remained the property of the New Zealand Forest Service and could not be taken off the block.

I reminded him that I was not a Forestry employee, and beyond that it would take an awful lot of proving establishing whether or not any of these animals had been shot by one of his employees. And anyway, what about the legs of venison the Forestry bosses were forever perking off the shooters whenever the opportunity arose... didn't they end up being taken off the block?

I would have thought that would have ended our little altercation and nothing more would have been said. But no! It seemed that as long as I remained in the district there was always the likelihood that the New Zealand Forest Service would be further embarrassed in front of the local town folks with more tailless carcasses turning up in the Omarama venison depot. So to ensure that this was not likely to occur, Bob was told to pack his gear. He was going to be docked ten tails off his pay, with the prospect of perhaps having them returned if he behaved himself, and as a further disciplinary measure he would be transferred forthwith to the Dingle Burn, where he would be kept conveniently out sight until this whole embarrassing episode had blown over. And, it was added, notice was hereby posted that no further hunting permits would be issued to the other member of the party, that might in any way enable Hannigan and his troublesome mate the possibility of being within a hundred miles of one another.

I didn't mind too much. I had been dabbling in the Dobson long enough. It was, as it happened, long gone time when trappers 'n' co. should already have been back on their possum blocks.

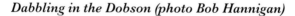

Dabbling in the Dobson (photo Bob Hannigan)

CHAPTER 16

Odey Country

Some four years had slipped by since Bob Hannigan and I had first stumbled upon Dave Odey and his possum trapping camp down the Middle Road at Horopito, and by then he had already spent fourteen consecutive winters catching possums out of the same vast block of bush. Now eighteen years gone, still working the same territory, nobody could lay claim to knowing Odey country a patch better than how Dave Odey knew it. From Horopito north to National Park by way of the Erua State Forest taking in all the adjoining land west of Highway 4. And to the east, everything from Waikune to Ohakune, from Highway 4 back to the nigh impenetrable Wilderness Area verging the slopes of snow capped Mount Ruapehu; this was Odey country.

Dave Odey, outside his camp (photo courtesy Anne Odey)

Dave was hospitable, and ever ready to share his extensive knowledge of bush lore and trapping skills with any one wishing to learn. But just like any other possum hunter, he was never very keen on sharing what he liked to think of as his piece of bush. From previous experience I knew there would be no point dropping in to ask Dave Odey which blocks were taken and which blocks were free. He would more than likely make out everything had been allocated; that there was not anything anywhere in the district. So prior to stopping off at his camp to say "G'day!", I had already been to both the Ohakune Forestry Office and Tongariro National Park Headquarters and claimed some blocks for myself. And with all that officially taken care of, there wasn't much more he could do other than act nice and welcome me into his territory. Armed with the necessary permits to trap Moturoa Bush and Mount Hauhangatahi in the Tongariro National Park, and a large slice of Erua State Forest from where it bordered the Park to somewhere south of Pokaka village, I fronted up to Dave's camp to let him know, here I was.

Securing land was one thing, finding somewhere to call camp was something else. I hoped that Dave Odey might be able to help. He and his brother, Ernie, were pottering about in Dave's camp when I called in.

Trappers camp at Sue Joe's, Pokaka (photo Bob Hannigan)

"Nope! I doubt that there is anything anywhere in the district," said Dave. "Certainly can't think of anything."

Then Ernie up's and says he knows a place and not all that far away: "Three quarters of a mile before you get to Pokaka, not far from the Mangaturuturu River. Right alongside the main road," said Ernie. "You know the place, Dave. It's that old blue house of Sue Joe's."

I could fully appreciate how Dave might have overlooked it, lying there empty and waiting for someone to come along and set up camp. There was something like five and a half miles of road between Dave Odey's camp and Sue Joe's little old blue house, with every bit of half a dozen houses scattered between the two. Six houses... that was a lot of houses to remember, and if some new bloke had been looking to set up camp in the middle of my piece of bush, I daresay I would have most likely suffered a memory lapse, too.

The Sue Joe family were market gardeners from Ohakune, but they had originated from Pokaka where the old blue house was situated. When approached, Ken Sue Joe never so much as hesitated. It was mine, he said, rent free and for as long as I wished to stay there. I moved in right away, very grateful for his warm and generous hospitality.

In many parts of the country the nights were just starting to get cold enough for getting underway. Depending on where you were, it was either late summer or early autumn. But in the shadow of Mount Ruapehu, even by early March, there was a decidedly cool nip in the air and the possums would already be stacking on fur in preparation for the chill of winter to come. This allowed for early trap lines producing good quality fur and ultimately, a longer trapping season. Dave had already accumulated a reasonable stack of new season furs in his camp and I was particularly interested in looking them over.

When we first ran into Dave Odey, Bob and I knew very little about trapping possums, although we thought we knew it all. But in just a few days of following him around one of his trap lines we realized just how little we did know. It was a humbling experience and in the book, "Trappers Dogs 'n' Deer (and other critters)" I devoted a chapter to our meeting up with Dave Odey and being instructed in "The Art of Trapping". Dave introduced Bob and me to the rudiments, but to become proficient in the skills we had to build on those rudiments over the course of several seasons, gaining knowledge with experience while sharing noteworthy observations. I put my heart and soul into it and developed considerable skill in the art of trapping, but the prices I was realizing for my furs confirmed that there was still much to be desired with regard to my fur presentation.

The obvious objective for a fur trapper, is to produce good quality fur. Strangely enough, out of the countless numbers of men who have had a go at possum hunting, very few have ever learned the secret of how it is done. Admittedly, the end result depended to a large degree on the type of possum as well as the colour of the fur and the environment in which they found themselves. But even the most beautiful skin can easily be ruined if handled in such a way that the fur is not evenly distributed throughout the finished product. I had never seen a possum waddling through the bush with its coat over stretched, or conversely, looking all "ass and pockets". But that was the way most dried possum skins ended up. Over stretching was not one of my sins, but I was aware that my finished furs never looked entirely even. They always tended towards thick around the haunches and sparse about the shoulders and up until now I had never figured out how to overcome this problem.

Whenever Dave Odey's skins were presented for auction his returns topped the sale. If there were new world record prices realized he would have been the trapper who achieved them. Based on those simple facts, regardless of how highly other possum hunters around the country might have fancied their selves, nowhere were you going to find a better yardstick for measuring yourself by than right there in amongst Dave Odey's pile of skins. It was not only the clear colours that set his furs apart, making them so outstandingly beautiful, but more so the full and even density of the fur, from nape of neck to base of tail.. Dave had a knack for doing something to distribute that fur real nice and even, and I was determined to find it out. Considering I had just edged in on his territory and would henceforth likely be pulling the same high quality animals into my camp he was pulling into his, it seemed hardly likely that he would be in too much of a hurry parting with the information.

For Dave Odey "the proof was in the pudding". He knew that his consistently breaking and retaining world record prices also distinguished him as one of the world's top fur trappers. Most certainly it made him the world's top "possum" fur trapper. The less I knew, the less likelihood there would be of my equalling his achievements. But whether or not he was willing to tell me, I aimed on finding out anyway. So I hung around watching while he and Ernie skinned a few possums. But there was not anything new they were doing in that department that I was not also doing.

Nor was there anything noticeably different about Dave's tack out method. We both used four by one, or five by one inch boards, depending on the size of animal being tacked out. He used one and a half inch clout head nails for fastening the skins to the boards and so did I, and the number of nails used, the points of fastening and the sequence followed was virtually the same. So nor was it in the tack out department where the difference lay.

So what was Dave Odey doing that I was not?

Up to this point everything seemed much the same. But there was one notable difference that did catch my eye. The possum skins, hanging from the wire mesh, drying on Dave's boards, already looked thick about the shoulders even when viewed from the flesh side. And it was while pondering upon this observation that I twigged to what it was that made the difference and kept his furs apart.

When a green skin is hanging fresh on a board, the weight of fur around the haunches tends to drag on it and make it sag a little. This

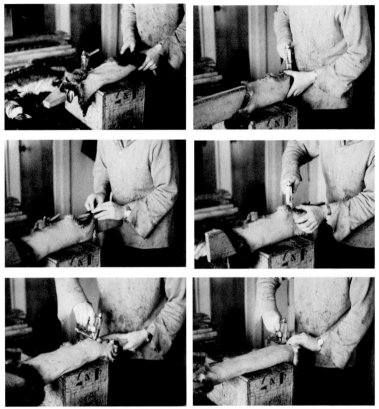

Tack out sequence, there are 14 tack out points to a skin

may not appear too noticeable to the untrained eye, but the sag is there and it is enough to drag fur from around the shoulders. Somehow you have to get that fur back to where it belongs. Dave did it, consciously or not, by lightly gripping the tacked out pelt a wee bit higher than the middle of the back and just below the shoulders while hooking the board onto the mesh for drying. Handling the pelt in this manner tended to allow the weight of the board to slip through his fingers beneath the fur just a little, effectively reshaping the pelt and pulling the sagging skin back up to where it belonged. By this stage there was just enough drying in the pelt for it to stay there. I never did get to know whether or not Dave was aware of what he was doing that made the difference. He was no fool so I assume he knew. And quite likely he consciously did it with deliberate subtlety so that onlookers would not even realize what he was doing. Anyway, he wasn't letting on and I never asked him. I simply applied to my own furs what I had observed; physically hoisting the fur back into place when hanging up each board. And the difference to the finished article was stunning. Suddenly I was producing furs that were up there in the same calibre as the ones coming out of Dave Odey's camp. I was jubilant. After more than four years striving for it, not only was I finally handling top quality possums, but my furs were also looking like it.

Pushing through the Pokaka bush was not the easiest at the best of times, overgrown as it was with thick coprosma and regenerating undergrowth. And loaded down with a pikau full of traps didn't help any. But the biggest problem, I was soon to learn, was the wetness of it all. Being pumice land it should have drained quickly, but in the country adjacent to Sue Joe's house it wasn't that way at all. Across the main trunk line, on the mountain side of the road, there was more than four miles of dense beech forest, sprinkled with Dacrydiums, Podocarps and what-have-you, gently rising from the rail track to where the beech clad slopes of Ruapehu climbed more steeply through scattered alpine scrub and scoria to jagged volcanic rocks and eternal snow. And in that gently rising four miles of bench land forest the 200 or more inches of rain that fell annually gathered in huge wet areas and stayed there for much of the winter, and for all I knew on into the summer too. The pools were cold and deep, and wading through them was far from pleasurable. I quickly realized that there was a limit as to how far one could force passage towards the mountain before, quite literally, getting into deep water. Plodding through the bush wearing heavy duty hooded rain wear and rubber thigh boots did not make manoeuvring any the easier, but dressing that way was necessary in order to keep warm and dry. While getting used to it I found it more exhausting from wearing the clothing I was wearing than from trapping the possums I was trapping. And for all that there were not all that many possums in the wet Pokaka bush to be caught. I pulled my first lot of traps out after little more than a week had gone by. There was nowhere I could extend to without water spilling over the top of my thigh boots and my tallies were no longer good enough to sustain the line. Dave Odey's current blocks were all to the west of the main highway. I suspected he had not worked these wetlands to the east for years and I could well imagine why. With lakes and tarns whichever way I looked, the country was not productive enough and the going was just too difficult.

I was working hard and struggling to maintain a tally. If I came home at night with 20 skins for my effort I was doing well. But even if the numbers were not there, the quality was. Mainly they were large, clear grey animals with clean white belly fur, and hardly a blemish was to be found on any of them. There was a small number of dark furred possums scattered amongst them, but they too were superb; good size animals clothed in a thick pile of deep brown fur with just slightly lighter colour along the belly. Night times would find me working in my skin room by the light of a Coleman pressure lamp, wood-range out in the kitchen simmering up a stew and firewood glowing in the hearth, scraping fat and gently combing out tails and brushing and fluffing up furs, and gloating over the sheer beauty of those hard won genuine furrier grade pelts that were slowly accumulating on finishing wires in a warm dry room set aside for them. This was the sort of stuff that would have the Italian fur buyers scrambling for their share.

To boost my tallies I needed to run longer lines into the bush, and the only way I could see of doing that would be to locate the old bush tram tracks. It was years since the forest had been worked for its timber, and the entrances to the tracks were getting lost in amongst the regeneration. A little bit of local knowledge would go a long way, and it soon turned up in the form of Pokaka Joe.

Old Joe had lived around Pokaka for an awful long time. Perhaps from as far back as the time they drove the final spike into the main trunk line back in the year 1908. Well, maybe not quite so far back. But anyway, he was well up in years and he had been working bush in the district for an awful long time. It was not long after I moved into Sue Joe's that Pokaka Joe dropped in for a visit — wobbling down the highway on his old vintage pushbike, chainsaw wrapped up in a gunny sack slung over his shoulder, coughing and wheezing like his lungs were on their last legs. Just wanted to say, "Hello!" — which was the normal thing for bush folks to do to one another under the circumstances.

Joe Leslie was his real name and he lived out back of the old hand crank petrol bowser, right next to the rail siding at Pokaka Station just three quarters of a mile up the road from where I was batched up. He was far from well with all his coughing and wheezing and emphysema and stuff, but he still pottered about in the bush cutting silver pine posts as he came across them. I never had any trouble finding the tracks where Joe was working. All I had to do was stand still awhile and listen for the wheezing and coughing. Once he knew he was welcome, Joe Leslie called in for a brew and a chat as often as he was peddling by, whenever he thought I was at home. And even if I wasn't he was still welcome to drop in and make himself a brew. His lungs were in such bad shape I think he was real grateful for the chance to wobble through the gate and sit down awhile.

Joe Leslie knew where all the snig tracks started and finished, and with his local knowledge assisting I was soon pushing my way through bush behind Sue Joe's house, laying out lines in slightly better conditions than I had found on the mountain side of the highway, first one side of the Mangaturuturu River then the other. But still the tallies were slow coming and hard won when they did. None of the old tram tracks went far before running into dense overgrown regeneration. And although there were no longer eel ponds rising over my depth, there was still the bothersome problem of trying to contend with the wet and marshy conditions that seemed to be part and parcel of it all. Working for decades in this sort of damp and boggy country, as he had, I could well appreciate how it was Joe could be heard barking his way through the bush long before he could be seen.

By now I had been working day and night without let up for more than a month and all I had to show for it was about 400 skins hanging in the camp. Perhaps it was a wetter than normal winter causing the ground to be so boggy. I did not have anything to gauge it by so I did not know. But everywhere I went the bush was waterlogged, making trapping very, very difficult. I needed to find drier ground and the most obvious place to start looking for that was behind Erua up on the steep sides of Mount Hauhangatahi.

Packing fifty traps and a light Thermos of tea, I headed off up the Hauhangatahi Mountain Track, setting traps as I went. About four in the afternoon I was finished and well pleased with the sets I had found and the effort I had put in to them. I was resting up against a tawhero having a short break before starting on the hike back down to Erua, when a bunch of trampers came charging down off the top of the mountain, not one of them showing manners enough to even acknowledge my presence as they ploughed by. And as I watched, one after another their thunking great hobnailed boots found and trampled upon the sets I had just so carefully completed, springing traps and buckling jaws as they went. I knew that what I had just witnessed on the last two sets of the day would be happening all the way back down the track. I was brassed off beyond words. Unpouching my tomahawk, I followed in their wake knocking out staples and packing out the traps I had just spent the best part of a day carefully getting into place.

It was not long after this, late one afternoon as evening shadows were gathering, I arrived back at camp from a trap line above the Makatote Gorge, and even before I stepped inside the house I sensed something was wrong. Someone had called in to my camp while I was out working my traps. The imprint of his tyre marks were clear as day in the gravel driveway alongside the house. He had entered the gate from the south and headed north when he left. It was the normal thing to do leaving your camp open so that if any of your mates called in they could help themselves to a brew in your absence. But whoever it was paid me a visit on this day was no mate. He had gone straight to my skin room and stripped it bare. Just under four hundred of my finest grade furs gone! Weeks of back breaking toil, wading through water half way up my thighs, in rain and sleet and icy conditions, and some dirty low down pig had come and stolen just about every last skin I had in the camp.

As far as I knew, there were only four skin merchants operating in the North Island at the time; Smith Brothers Trading of Hawera, a fellow by the name of Woodcraft from Mount Maunganui, Bob Gibbs from Upper Hutt, and Mooney's travelling skin buyer. At the prompting of the Ohakune and Raetihi police officers, I immediately contacted all of them with a description of the skins that had been stolen. From the description I gave they would have been unmistakeable and easily identified. No two men ever tacked out their skins absolutely identically. Everyone had their own individual technique. When you were working with piles of skins every day you got into a regular routine of placing every nail in exactly the same spot on every skin you handled. For example, I always placed the nails that tacked the ears to the board directly beneath the lobe. There would not have been another trapper in the country that placed all his nails exactly the way I placed all mine. And apart from Dave Odey and Bill Broadfoot, whose camp was tucked in beneath Mount Kakaramea, I doubted very much that there was another trapper in the country with skins that matched the quality of mine. Any skin buyer with half an eye, and half a heart for it, could easily have recognised my skins based on the description I gave. I think it spoke volumes that not one of these skin merchants wanted to involve himself in the matter. "They handled thousands of skins', they told me. 'How could they ever identify mine in amongst so many?" The mere fact that they handled thousands would have made it just so much the easier, had they wanted to!

A mile and a half along the road from my camp, a car packed with Ohakune teenagers had gone out of control on a bend and plunged into the Manganui o te Ao Gorge, killing all the occupants. They had been missing for several days and it was early morning the day after my camp had been burgled someone noticed their vehicle all smashed up in the bottom of the gorge. About mid morning, a patrol car full of police officers fresh from the accident scene, pulled into my camp. It was a wonder they did, because to all outward appearances there was no one at home. The back door was open inviting free entry. But my Land Rover was parked out of sight behind some scrub across the road. There was no fire lit, and the cottage was quiet and cold.

I think Bill Feasey, the policeman from Raetihi, immediately realized what I was up to. In his spare time, of which I think he had plenty, he did possuming to keep himself occupied. The Raetihi Police

Station doubled up as his skin shelter with drying skins hanging from the ceiling and his desk pressed into service as a tack out bench. So being somewhat involved in the industry himself, he probably fully appreciated my little ploy. He and his mates didn't stay long. Just long enough to look the camp over and jot down a few details. But as they were going, Bill looked back at me and said: "Don't go doing anything stupid, Wayne!"

I deliberately wanted to give the impression that no one was around the camp, with the hope that who ever had got stuck into my skins might start thinking about the few he had left behind and would drop in for another visit. I was sitting quietly in the skin room surrounded by the empty wires where my beautiful export skins had so recently been stacked, patiently waiting for him. It was freezing cold with no fire to warm the camp, and as time ticked by I was getting more and more bitter by the minute. My carbine was lying handy with a chopped off bullet half up the spout, and I had every intention of putting it to good use if he returned and dared to step inside my camp. Bill Feasey knew, and so did I, that if it so happened, at the end of it all it would be very difficult indeed for any investigating officers to establish that I had not acted in self defence. There had been times, in my hot-headed past, when I had loosely threatened to gut shoot the odd irritating coot who had crossed my path, but this individual... someone who could sink so low as to do what he had done to a fellow hunter, if indeed he was a fellow hunter...!!

Would I really have gone and shot him given the chance? In retrospect, I cannot say I really know. One would like to think not. But at the time I was exceedingly angry, and in my fury, it is just possible he may not have seen another day had he ventured back for the rest of my skins. But seeing he never came back I guess we will never know, will we?

After a couple of days hanging low inside a freezing cold camp without a fire burning to draw the chill out of my bones, and no smoke drifting out the chimney to reveal my presence, it became fairly obvious that whoever it was had broken in was not likely to return. I unloaded the carbine and put it back in the rack and started a new trap line in the Moturoa Bush north of Waikune Prison.

From that time on I stamped all my skins very clearly right across the brisket "WAYNE BLAKE", in big bold indelible letters, and securely locked the camp and chained the door whenever I was away.

The loss of my skins had devastating effects. There was no such thing as a fortnightly or monthly salary when you were exporting to London. At the most you received payment two or three times a year. Auctions took place in February, May and September, and your bank account was not normally credited with any proceeds until several weeks after the sale. Winter trapping was my bread and butter, and whatever I earned during the summer was usually only just enough to offset expenses. This year, working for Robbie Ballantyne, I had not even done that. The May auction was pending, but in the meantime I had been struggling to survive. I had fallen behind with my Land Rover repayments and unless I made some quick deposits it was quite likely that it would be repossessed. It had been my intention to hold onto the best of my furs for the London market and skim off the rest and sell them locally to keep the wolves at bay. With the camp stripped of just about everything I had caught there was nothing left to meet the crisis. Appreciating how I had been affected, it is hardly surprising that Bill Feasey was concerned I might "do something stupid!" to this scumbag of a person if he returned to my camp.

Moturoa Bush was big enough to house at least eighty good trap sets, all on dry ground, and with a sense of urgency I quickly went about getting in as many traps as I could. Now, for the first time since

From here on I stamped my name on every skin in indelible ink

moving into the district I began bringing home good tallies, averaging about 30 to 35 skins a day, and the quality was every bit as good as the ones I had been picking out of the bush around Pokaka. Within a few days they were starting to pile up back in my camp — more than 250 the first week. And then Colin Campbell turned up; sent by Cable Price to repossess my vehicle.

Colin knew I was in the Ruapehu District but just where, he did not know. To find out he had called into the Raetihi Police Station and run into Bill Feasey, who told him what had happened to my furs. I think that Bill had this mental picture of me still sitting in an empty skin room inside a blacked out camp, cradling my sawn-off Jungle Carbine, chopped off bullet half up the spout, listening for vehicles pulling into the drive. As Colin was leaving the police station he warned him: "Take it easy mate, and don't go doing anything stupid!"

I was not really likely to start taking shots at one of my mates, but at the same time I made it quite clear to Colin that it would be over my dead body that he would be towing my Land Rover away in the night. Colin was in a quandary. He knew that without the Land Rover I would not be able to continue trapping, but he also had a job to do. I told him so did I!

We sat around Sue Joe's, drinking brews of tea, with Colin wondering what his employers were going to say to him when he returned without my vehicle in tow. I later learned that he told them I was away in the bush somewhere and could not be located, but he had got a glimpse into the camp and it was chock-a-block with furs, so they would no doubt be getting a cheque from me in the very near future.

I had hoped that Cable Price would delay taking action until after I received my returns from the May sale, but that was obviously not going to happen and I was now forced into temporarily closing down my line and selling every last fur that I had in the camp, including my beautiful export quality furs from Moturoa Bush.

Rodney Smith, of Smith Brothers Trading, had never seen possum furs anything like the ones I turned up with a few days later. He had been used to buying rubbish off Taranaki farmers and schoolboys, along with the odd fly by night individuals that ran poison lines around pockets of cow cocky bush and up the sides of Mount Egmont. His eyes fair boggled at the sight of them. But if he thought he was going to get my hard won export furs without a tussle he was sadly mistaken. I knew he wanted those skins come hell or high water and I had no option but to sell. But he did not know that, and something else he did not know... I hated selling to local skin buyers as a matter of principle.

So it looked like the stage was set for a fight.

Rodney began by inspecting each pelt topside and bottom. Then he slid his fingers through the pile... almost drooling over the density and silkiness of what he was fingering. Then he gave them a flick and held them up to the light, looking for windows... none of which he could find. Then he threw them into piles as he fancied was his idea of first, second and third grade skins... greys over here and darks over there.

I was fully aware of what he was doing, but just to keep things on an even keel, I asked, "What's that pile over there for?"

"That's your third grades," he replied.

"And that one?"

"Second grades."

Striding over to heap number two, I bundled up what he had graded seconds and dumped them on top of what were obviously the firsts.

"Seconds do not come that clean, so that means they are all firsts," I advised, "And the other heap over there are seconds. As I do not process thirds I doubt very much you are going to find any."

"Hang on a minute. You can't do that," he protested.

"Yes I can. And I just did. And if you want my skins that's the way they're going to stay. How much are you paying for the firsts?"

Smith looked like he was going to cry.

"A dollar fifty for first grade greys, and a dollar for seconds. A dollar thirty for first darks, and seventy five cents for seconds."

"Are you serious?" I asked. "There's no way you're going to get these skins for that! These are not Taranaki trash you're looking at. These are the finest grade furs you're ever likely to see. Two fifty across the board for the firsts and two dollars for the seconds, or nothing at all."

Beads of sweat began to show on Rodney's top lip. He had probably never had to contend with anything quite like this before. He obviously wanted my furs and he obviously did not want to pay too much. On the other hand, if he played his cards right, he might be able to persuade me that I would be better off selling all my furs to him for an immediate cash return, rather than having the hassle of exporting and waiting for months for my cheque.

"I can't do that," he countered. "I could never get that much back for them. But if you will agree to continue supplying me I'll make it $1.50 average for the lot."

"Like to help me load them back into my Land Rover?"

"Make it $1.75... final offer!"

And so we haggled until Smith was a gibbering wreck and I had walked out the door with $2.00 across the board, cash cheque in my hand, and Rodney had extracted the hint of a promise from me that if all went accordingly I would continue to supply him as the occasion arose, or something to that effect... which didn't amount to very much of a promise at all, all things considered. It wasn't that I had anything against Rodney in particular. It was just that I had this thing against local buyers, full stop.

Even before leaving my camp with my Moturoa skins in my Land Rover, I had determined that this was going to be a once only affair, my parting with my top grade export furs to some local buyer. True to my word though, I did continue supplying Rodney... but only with what I considered the rubbish and inferior stuff that was not good enough for export. We continued to haggle over prices and grades, me arguing that Rodney's interpretation of thirds looked more like seconds to me, and his seconds were right there on the borderline of being firsts. With Rodney, almost reduced to tears pointing out that the quality seemed to have dropped somewhat from that first consignment I had brought in, but never-the-less paying me much more than he thought they were worth, and living on the hope of a suggestion that the quality of the next consignment might be back up there with the first.

Those SF90 furs of mine that had been sitting unsold in London finally cleared in the May sale. I received settlement in June and with a huge feeling of relief I wrote out a cheque and cleared the debt on my Land Rover. Twice, in about as many months, I had nearly lost my vehicle and it had taught me that stacking up liabilities against ones security can be a risky business.

If ever there was a turning point in my career, it was there in that little old blue house of Sue Joe's. I had edged my way into top possum country, weathered the storm and cleared myself of debt, and had discovered the secret of producing world class furs. From here on there was nothing to stop me establishing a name for myself in London, and possibly even challenging Dave Odey for those world record prices.

Well anyway, that was what I had thought.

I got a letter from Bob Hannigan early July. A few weeks after his being banished to the Dingle Burn by Ranger Reardon he once more found himself back in the Dobson. He had swapped his Chev 15 cwt for a big old Chev ex army 4 x 4 to do away with the pain of wading through icy rivers. But now shooting had come to a standstill. Southern Lakes Conservancy was all iced up with most of the blocks completely snowed in. He knew that I had set up camp in the thick of Odey country and he asked if he could come and join me for the remainder of the winter.

I was keen to have Bob join me, but owing to the waterlogged nature of my blocks I had hardly enough territory for myself let alone for two of us working from the same camp. And to complicate matters even more, it would not be practical for Bob to bring his 4 x 4 all that

Much better than getting the feet wet (photo Bob Hannigan)

way so we would be working with just one vehicle between us... my Land Rover.

I spent the next couple of weeks scouting out new country. I ran poison lines through the bush off the Turoa Ski Field road behind Ohakune, and behind farms down in the Kaitieke Valley, and then someone told me about the Whangapeki... a huge expanse of cut-over bush between the Wanganui River and the Pungapunga Road, south east of Taumarunui. Matt Frew was managing the farmlands fringing the block. He was also custodian for the Whangapeki. I was told to go have a chat with him.

Matt Frew said it should not be a problem. As far as he was concerned, Bob and I would be more than welcome to have access through the farmlands to trap the Whangapeki. However, as he was about to be transferred to Oraukura Station, some miles away, he no longer had much say in it. The Bennett brothers, Ray and Maurice, would be taking over after him, so he supposed I would have to talk it over with them.

"But," said Matt, "Just tell them I said you are a couple of good young blokes and everything should be fine."

Matt Frew said the Bennett brothers were a couple of good blokes too, and they were. With a key to the Whangapeki gate and everything arranged, I drove down to Wellington with my trailer hitched on behind the Land Rover to go get Bob and his trapping gear. There was more land in the Whangapeki than we were likely to get through in the remainder of the season. But I just knew the possums in the

Whangapeki weren't going to be as good as the possums I was leaving behind back in Odey country.

CHAPTER 17

Horoeka Tent Camp

There was no shortage of possums in the new block, but they were, as I had surmised, a very different breed of animal to my Pokaka possums. Predominantly greys, which was good, a shade smaller in body size, which was not so good, and nowhere near as densely furred, which was not at all good. We had edged into territory too far removed from the central mountains for really top quality stuff. But the main thing was we had gotten hold of a sizeable block of bush to see us through the winter.

Some 45 miles of road stretched between Sue Joe's old blue house at Pokaka and our Whangapeki block. But regardless of the travel, I had no intention of giving up my Sue Joe base camp too quickly. A warm dry base for tacking out and drying skins and somewhere to fall back on when the weather turned bad was essential, and we had all that at Sue Joe's. And it looked like we were going to need it. A quick reconnoitre and a few discreet enquiries had failed to turn up any abandoned bush huts or empty mill houses in the vicinity of the Whangapeki. So we opted for building an advance base tent camp right on the block. We would run lines for about a week or so, accumulating green skins, and then head back to Pokaka where we would do our tacking out and dressing of furs. Neither of us had ever trapped this way before, working from an advance base, and just how long the skins would keep before either slipping or starting to dry out we had no idea. The first run would be a bit of trial and error, but the critical factor would be careful storage. Each individual fur would need to be rolled up tightly, taking care that the flesh side was not exposed to the air whereby premature drying might occur. The other potential problem to guard against would be slipping fur, caused by overheating in storage or maggots hatching and sending everything rotten. Location and construction of the camp would also be important. Living out the depths of winter in a tent camp could prove rather unpleasant if it was not done right.

Tucked away in a sheltered valley, well protected from the icy winds that sometimes howled off the snow capped central mountains but open to a bit of sun when it was around, we sorted out a suitable piece of level ground, ideally located alongside an old logging road. The area had been heavily denuded of millable trees, but there was a lot of small stuff poking through — groves of tree ferns, pate and five finger, fuschia, rangiora, wineberry, and here and there a smattering of juvenile podocarps — rimu, matai, miro and totara — that given a chance might be millable come a half thousand years or so. There was also a sparkling little stream of potable water meandered by our chosen site, and a fair sized stand of mature lancewoods, tall straight and ideal for tent poles. It said plenty for the self healing properties inherent in New Zealand's beautiful subtropical rain forests, that despite the raping the area had suffered the campsite area we chose, with its variety of tree ferns, hardwoods, clumps of endemic grasses and a multitude of other flora, was still park like and pleasant in appearance.

Not so far away from all this, in an adjacent valley that was accessible from the Pungapunga Road, timber fellers were still lobbing down ancient trees and hauling logs from virgin forest just as fast as they could go. Giant podocarps that tended to clutter up the countryside in an appalling manner and were much better eradicated; matai, miro, rimu, and totara; a sheltering blanket of protection towering high above the forest floor, seasonally laden with lush drupes that were of little value to anything other than the native birds that depended on them. But so what! Who needed native birds, anyway?

Framing up Horoeka Tent Camp (photo Bob Hannigan)

Between us we had the necessary tentage for constructing a typical culler's type tent camp. Bob had a large sheet of canvas for the fly and I had a sizeable two-man pup tent for the sleeping quarters. The surrounding bush had all the necessary extras.

Making good use of some of the sturdier lancewood for posts, while using several of the longer pieces for diagonals and a ridgepole, we erected the main frame to support the fly, which acted as roof over the galley and a second skin over the pup tent. In the back half of the structure we slung a smaller ridge pole beneath the main ridge, and from this we pitched the pup tent. With the pup tent and fly firmly pegged down Bob turned his attention to constructing a chimney and fireplace — "a job that only the qualified should attempt," I was advised.

"It takes considerable skill designing a chimney that is not only pleasing to the eye, but also works well," he added.

"You know, I had never looked at it that way before," I replied. "Up until now I had just sort of taken them for granted. Where did you learn about them?"

"Mainly in the Ruahines. I made a study of them while I was culling there."

"So how do you ensure the chimney will draw properly and won't belch smoke back into the galley?" I asked, genuinely interested.

"No two chimneys are the same. Now if you really want to do something useful, why not go and occupy yourself chopping a huge heap of firewood in readiness for the finished article."

Having never actually built a cullers tent camp before, although I had certainly spent enough time living in them, I decided to leave this part of it to the expert. Bob obviously knew what he was doing.

Sighting up off the broken face of a nearby bluff, he began by erecting a couple of upright poles about hearth distance from the end of the fly. They weren't too perpendicular, but Bob said that was because they were meant to conform to their surroundings.

"You mean you want them looking natural like a couple of leaning trees?" I asked.

"Actually, I was tending more towards the erosion over on the bluff," he replied. "How's your firewood heap coming along?"

Next, a rough frame of lancewood was nailed onto the unperpendicular poles and joined to the front of the galley followed by some old sheets of corrugated iron that were bent into place and nailed to the framework to form the outside sheathing. This was followed by an inner skin of corrugated iron which was positioned inside all of the foregoing. The space thus formed between the inner and outer bent sections of corrugated iron was then filled with pumice dirt to form an insulated section for keeping the heat in while protecting the wooden frame from igniting with the heat of the fire.

Bob's chimney taking shap (photo Bob Hannigan)

More lengths of corrugated iron were nailed in place to form the chimney stack. A length of 1 inch water pipe was poked through the fire surround for swinging the camp oven and billies, and Bob's masterpiece was complete.

On observing the finished article, I had to admit it didn't look at all out of place, set as it was deep in the heart of a badly eroding block of totally demolished native bush with hill sides battered and scarred and roads slipping away. It did not quite line up with the rest of the construction, but still, it looked at one with the surroundings, and I just hoped it didn't smoke as bad as it looked.

"That's amazing!" I said, when the job was complete. "Have you built many tent camp chimneys, before?"

"Not really. Actually this is my first," said Bob. "Although you would hardly know it by looking!"

Next job was to block and draught-proof all the remaining open spaces of the tentage. First the galley sides were closed in with horizontally stacked ponga stems. And following that the gap between pup tent roof and underside of the fly was blocked off with thick strips of sacking tacked firmly into place.

Then came the beds and mattresses.

It is not good for the bones, sleeping in cold damp places. At first, when you are young and fit you do not seem to notice the discomfort. But later on in life the joints start to creak. Aches and pains set in, along with lumbago and arthritis. Or anyway, that was what one or two old bushmen had led us to believe, and we could well believe it to be true. The minimum allowable space, for satisfactory ventilation, between timber and earth in the foundation of a house is 12 inches, and I believed a man's back should be at least the same distance from the cold damp ground in a tent camp. Building beds was entirely up to the individual who was doing it. But what you made you had to sleep on. The base of mine was built from juvenile lancewoods elevated on thick ponga logs. A thick padding of fern fronds, mingimingi, tussock, whatever could be found that gave padding and comfort, was piled on top and covered with a ground sheet. It made for a comfortable night of rest and if at some stage the spring went out of it, all I had to do was go gather a fresh lot of mingimingi.

To add the finishing touches, we scavenged enough rough sawn timber to deck the galley floor, a door was hung on the entrance and fitted with a sturdy chain and padlock, and our tent camp was complete. The Maori name for lancewood is horoeka, and seeing that was what it was largely constructed from, that was what we called it

Horoeka Tent Camp (photo Bob Hannigan)

— "Horoeka Tent Camp". It had taken very little time to construct and now, with a nice warm galley for cooking in and comfortable beds for sleeping on, we were ready to go.

Whenever we worked from the same camp, we always split our territory in two. This time Bob had everything to the east of Horoeka; a vast expanse of cut over bush that extended far beyond what he was likely to be able to work in what was left of the winter. I had everything to the west, which included one or two long bush ridges and all the frontal country verging onto the Maori Affairs farmlands. Both of us had country beyond what we could cover in the three months or so remaining to the spring moult, so everything was shaping up well.

One of the first days out on the block I caught a big old billy goat in one of my traps, and just to make sure he wasn't going to go charging off down the line springing traps as he went, I finished him off with my tomahawk. I had never tried killing a tough old goat with a tomahawk before, and before I was finished I wished I had never started. There are quick and humane ways of putting animals down and this was not one of them. I felt really bad about it and vowed I would rather have my traps trampled on than employ such grisly methods again. Then I sprung Gladdy.

Gladdy was a little golden brown nanny, with black stockings, a black stripe down her back and a white patch on her right shoulder. I doubt she was more than a couple of weeks old when she got caught. She was not hurt by the trap, but standing there abandoned by her mum, bleating pitifully for someone to come along and set her free.... I felt real sorry for her, and without giving it a great deal of thought, bundled her up in the front pocket of my pikau with just her head sticking out the flap, and continued on along my line. She seemed hardly old enough to survive without her mother's milk, but even if she could have got by on solids I still doubted that she would make it alone without her mum's protection.

She had a soft furry coat that would make a lovely little mat for a dressing table and I resolved to knock her on the head somewhere along the way. But as the day progressed with me working my way along the line and Gladdy sitting on my back, little head poking out the flap of my pikau and me chatting to her and stroking behind her ears between killing possums and resetting traps, I got to realizing that she was enjoying the company as much as I was. And as the hours slipped by the resolve started to weaken.

Deliberating for extended periods on hitting a cute little baby animal on the head and whipping off its skin isn't wise. It's the same as tucking a furry little joey possum inside your shirt to keep it warm straight after you have just bopped its mum on the head. Next thing you know you have bonded with it and it has become too cute to kill. And now you do have a problem... a darned nuisance little animal around the camp to waste your time and drip feed milk through an eye dropper.

So Gladdy never did become that lovely little mat for a dressing table. That evening found her perched on my knee back at Horoeka Tent Camp, soaking up some warmth from the fire, nibbling bits of hand fed bread, while our dinner was simmering over the coals. And that night, quite oblivious to the fact that I had spent half the day

A cute little critter

A darned nuisance. An absolute pain

deliberating on smashing her head in with the back of my tomahawk, she slept curled up on the end of my bunk, happy and content to have found someone fool enough to care for her needs and offer her a comfortable foster home.

Obviously, there was no way I could lug a baby goat round the block tucked in the pocket of my pikau each day, so I simply left her roaming free at Horoeka. Each morning, as I pulled away in the Land Rover, Gladdy would stand by the roadside, dolefully bleating her little heart out as she watched me go, and in the afternoon when I returned she would still be hanging round in pretty much the same spot awaiting my return. After a week or two she plucked up a bit more courage and while I was out on the block she would wander off into the bluffs up above the camp. But she always had an ear to the ground for my returning Land Rover, and the minute she picked up the sound of it she would come recklessly bounding down the bluffs, pumice and scoria flying from beneath her hooves as she hit level ground at the bottom, then out through the scrub, tussock and toetoe she would come, little blur of golden brown hurtling past the tent camp. If I was quick enough pulling on the handbrake and getting out of the vehicle, she would take a flying leap and launch herself off the bank landing in my arms. If I wasn't, she would launch herself off the bank anyway, but would end up making dents in the aluminium door panel from her sharp little hoofs as she clambered to get in on top of me. So usually it was a mad race between me and Gladdy for the sake of the panels on the Land Rover. I was still in the process of adjusting to having a pet goat called Gladdy hanging round camp when I sprung Pork Chop.

Carrying Pork Chop around my trap line, jammed in the front pocket of my pikau was a slightly different proposition to what it had been packing Gladdy. He and Gladdy were probably about the same age but the similarities went no further than that. She was a soft lovable little nanny goat; Pork Chop was a beady eyed, cantankerous little wild boar. Gladdy enjoyed being petted; Pork Chop was not too partial to over familiarity. He gave the impression he was enjoying having his whiskers stroked, but his beady little eyes weren't missing a thing. The instant your fingers came close enough, Porky would lash out with his chompers and try and nip one of them off. Had it not been that I was used to moving fast, protecting fingers from springing traps, Porky Chop would have been digesting bits of digits. I think Pork Chop would have loved to have been the meanest little piggy in the Whangapeki, but he was a striped little piggy with alternating black and dark brown stripes along either flank; and who ever took a little piggy wearing black striped pyjamas seriously!?!

For the first couple of days, until he had learned a few necessary camp manners, such as refraining from screaming and biting whenever one of us Horoeka residents came too close, I kept Pork Chop restrained in a box with a lid on top. But in a very short while he had settled into camp life and he became just about the sweetest natured little piggy one could ever imagine... not withstanding his ongoing tendency of attempting to remove finger joints when-so-ever they got near enough to his chompers. But once he came to appreciate we had no plans for putting him in the camp oven, he began applying what he was being taught and in no time at all night time would find him queuing up with Gladdy, looking for someone's knee to climb onto close up before the warming glow of our tent camp fire.

Then came Myrtle. Myrtle could well have been Pork Chop's sister, although I sprung her on a different ridge about a mile from where

I had sprung him. But she still could have been his sister. They were almost identical size, but Myrtle was clothed in gingery-brown striped pyjamas and a site more irascible than her piggy bro'. She never did settle down to being petted. She would tolerate just so much familiarity before having a go at you. But for all that, she soon adapted to being one of the camp residents. Most times she, Pork Chop, Gladdy and Kim all got on very well together... except for during the heat of the moment when they heard the Land Rover returning from out in the bush, and Pork Chop would attack Gladdy as she came hurtling past the tent camp, and then Myrtle would get all fired up and attack Pork Chop, and Gladdy in her confusion would start thumping Kim, and poor docile Kim would just sit there looking tweeky, tolerating all the thumping because he was a Border Collie possum trapper's dog and far too well bred to get upset over a young lady like Gladdy giving him a hiding.

Horoeka tent camp was meant to be a possum trappers' camp, but things were getting a little out of hand. It had gotten to the stage where one never knew what was going to turn up next. Most every day there were goats in at least one or two of my traps. They were in their full winter coats and most of them were attractively marked. So I killed all the females as well as the young males that had not yet started smelling like billy goats, and packed their skins back to the camp. After rubbing in a bit of raw salt, they were left rolled up and pickling until such time as they could be forwarded to Dunedin for tanning. Apart from their usefulness as gifts for friends, goat skins had little commercial value, and the goats themselves, forever getting tangled up in my traps, were an utter nuisance to me as they were interfering with my possum catching ability. One day I ended up with a total of nine of them scattered along my line. This, in effect, meant nine traps out of commission, or nine possums valued at two or more dollars a skin that I might have got but did not. The upshot though was we were never short of good quality roast leg of goat for the camp oven. Nor was there much fault to be found in a camp oven full of curried goat meat stewed up with chopped onions, diced potatoes, and a couple of tins of mixed vegetables thrown in for good measure. And if you felt like something simple for tea, the meat from a boned-out back leg, sliced across the grain as steaks, rubbed with garlic, rolled in flour and done medium-rare to medium in a hot pan made a very tasty dish.

Several weeks had slipped by since we had moved in to Horoeka and I had long given up on carrying any more living critters back to camp. Then, one evening, Bob arrived back at camp with Drumsticks.

Possum trapping had been our winter jobs for the past five years and during that time, between the two of us, we had logged many hundreds of nights of trapping, with well in excess of a hundred thousand traps having been set during those accumulated nights. Out of all of that, prior to Drumsticks, we had only ever trapped one kiwi between us. It was my doing, and I was devastated when I saw that its leg was badly damaged. I promptly dropped everything and took off into town with the injured bird comfortably nestled on a bed of fern fronds in a large cardboard box. I was quite expecting a bit of a rough time from the local ranger for trapping it in the first place, but the ranger was not so much mad at me for accidentally trapping it as for bringing it in to him.

"Why the hell didn't you whip off its damaged leg and liberate it back into the bush right where you got it?" he said. "Kiwis have a very high metabolism so it would almost certainly have survived. Now, because you have removed it from its environment, it may not."

I was told in no uncertain terms to never ever, under any circumstances, remove a kiwi from its local bush environment again, injured or not.

Fortunately Drumsticks was not badly injured. All he had suffered was a bruised and swollen foot. But for all the mollycoddling he got from Bob and me, he might just as well have been a dedicated cot case. After the traumatic experience with that first kiwi, Bob had no

Drumsticks

intention of taking this one anywhere. He just wanted to hold it in the camp for a few days while he kept it under observation as the swelling subsided and ensure that it had sufficient food while it was recuperating. We both felt responsible for the bird and wanted to be sure everything was okay before it was returned to where it had come from. And rather than risk catching him a second time, Bob could not do that until after he had closed down his trap line in that particular part of the bush. We immediately made up a comfortable nest of grasses and ferns in a well ventilated box and settled him down for a bit of rest and recuperation.

Finding enough food for Drumsticks was no problem. But ensuring he received it was something else again. Just a few yards up the road from Horoeka there were several rotting logs lying alongside the road and these were riddled with fat and juicy huhu grubs. Trouble was, just like Drumsticks, I too had a hankering for succulent wriggling huhu grubs. They were rich and creamy with a taste similar to peanut butter, and as I dug them from the wood, I would dig one for Drumsticks, one for me. Usually I got the biggest, fattest, juiciest ones, which was a bit tough on Drumsticks. I ate mine straight off. Gave them a tap to remove any wood dust that might be adhering to their skin, nipped off their heads and munched them there and then. However, it was not all one sided. One nipped me on the tongue once when I was in the process of nipping its head off, which slowed me down a bit and gave me something to ponder.

Drumsticks, being nocturnal, slept in his box inside the tent camp all day. Then when all was dark and quiet, after we had bedded down for the night, he would come venturing out, probing about the tent with his long beak, sniffing for edibles and things of interest with his sensitive nostrils as he wandered about the camp. Every other bird I ever knew has its nostrils situated somewhere near its eyeballs. But not so the kiwi. He's got his planted right at the tip of his beak, well positioned for close quarters sniffing of grubs and goodies as he pokes his beak into rotting logs and leaf mould. There were times when I awoke in the middle of the night with the weight of Drumsticks hopping onto my sleeping bag and walking up my legs and along my body. I would lie dead still so as not to alarm him as he probed his way towards my shoulders, then he would climb on top of my head with his big powerful legs and poke his beak deep into my thick mop of hair, sniffing and snorting for grubs and kutu's. I don't think he ever found any. But it was quite an experience having a kiwi do that to you in the middle of the night.

Having Drumsticks resident in the camp was a great experience. Somewhere further up the valley there lived another kiwi, and occasionally, in the dead of night Drumsticks would almost fire us out the tent as he initiated an exchange of "kiwi" communication with his mate. We would be dead to the world when suddenly a shrill and reverberating: "Ki-wee, ki-wee!" would just about pierce your eardrums from alongside your pillow. Then his mate would answer from up the valley: "Ki-wee, ki-wee!" By now all dreams would be shattered and sleep gone out the door as you lay there electrified, heart pounding, recuperating from the shock of it all.

Drumsticks was a wild critter that belonged in the next valley over, and as soon as he was a hundred per cent fit Bob aimed on returning him to his location and re-liberating him. The bird wasn't over chuffed about our getting too friendly and familiar with him and we weren't making any effort to tame him. When you picked him up, he would sit there in your grip, touch hairs round his face twitching, growling just like a dog, and it was going to be too bad for you if you weren't hanging on tight to those super-powerful legs of his. Suddenly he would lash out with a kick designed for ripping logs apart, and adequately capable of disembowelling some lesser creature like a ferret or a cat. He got his name "Drumsticks" because basically that was exactly what he appeared to be; a set of oversized drumsticks with a beak on the end. One morning we woke up and Drumsticks was gone. He had found his way out of the tent during the night and returned to the wild. We missed Drumstick's company, but we were not unhappy about it. He was already perfectly fit and well and we were considerably richer for the experience. Maybe Drumsticks was too!

Drumsticks was the only critter we ever had whose freedom was curtailed while resident at Horoeka Tent camp. All the rest were free to come and go and roam as they pleased, but they never went far from the camp unless it was because we had loaded them onto the trailer and taken them.

About once a week we did just that when we drove back to Pokaka to work on our skins. Kim was quite at home sitting out back on the trailer, and Gladdy seemed to think it was quite a lot of fun. But Pork Chop wasn't over fussed on the idea, and Myrtle's screams of anger at being bodily picked up and anchored to the deck with a dog collar fixed behind her ears and a chain tethered to the floorboards amply testified to the fact that she never had trusted trailers and even less so the persons who owned them. To add to Pork Chop and Myrtle's discomfort, neither of them were good travellers. Kim was no problem and Gladdy stayed on her feet, bracing herself then going with the roll as we careered down the highway humping rises and swinging round corners. But Pork Chop and Myrtle would fight the motion all the way, rolling back and forth across the deck of the trailer until eventually both of them would throw up all over the deck. And once they started there was no stopping them until they had completely emptied themselves, creating a disgusting mess of half digested possum's entrails, galley scraps, beetles, hair and general slush for me to bucket down at journey's end.

Pork Chop's main consolation for the discomforts of travelling 45 miles to Pokaka was the pleasure of having his very own kapok

Preparing to load the trailer. Coming to grips with Myrtle (photo Bob Hannigan)

pillow tucked away beneath Sue Joe's house. It was Porky's pillow and he possessively guarded it from Myrtle. She was not even allowed to come close to it. Porky was very much enamoured to that pillow. He would nose it into shape, and snuggle up to it, and generally treat it with the love and devotion that only a Pork Chop could lavish upon something so precious as a kapok pillow. It was about as dirty and grime covered as any pillow could ever possibly get, and I suppose from Porky Chop's point of view it was near enough to perfect. But love affairs like that seldom last!

We arrived at Pokaka early one afternoon with the trailer typically full of dog, goat, pigs and vomit. These weekly trips were rather taxing on our little piggies. But this time there was a special treat awaiting them. A bottle of beer had been opened during our previous visit then forgotten. Naturally, with no cap on it, it had gone flat. But our two little piggies loved it. They slurped and slopped and frothed. They guzzled and they blew bubbles. I couldn't help but think how they altogether reminded me of Aussie cook back at Mussel Point in South Westland. Not unlike him at all in fact. Then they got drunk. I suppose that the best part of a bottle of beer was quite a lot for two little pigs on an empty stomach. It hit them pretty fast. They didn't even make it away from the trough. First Myrtles' legs went wobbly, then she collapsed in a heap with her snout still in the empty trough. Pork Chop crashed on top of her. We retired to the house, leaving them where they had fallen, snoring peacefully.

About an hour later I went out to check on them and they were still lying in exactly the same place. But something did not look quite right with Myrtle. She was lying dead still, not a movement showing. Suddenly I got concerned. She looked as if she was dead. I bent down over the top of her, put my ear close to her nose to feel and listen for breath, and placed my hand on her brisket to feel for pulse.

Suddenly she woke up. She saw me and my ear pressed up real close to her nose and she let rip with one hellishingly loud, wild pig scream. If she had just got a fright, it was nothing to what I had just got. She near catapulted me into the bush. Pork Chop too. He shot to his drunken little feet giving Myrtle a good tusking as he went. Then he took off, squealing with rage, to beneath the house. Myrtle was right behind him. Pork Chop threw himself at his pillow and spun around and gave Myrtle another thumping for being too close. Myrtle disappeared into the shadows beneath the house, still screaming, and Pork Chop flopped onto his pillow, beady little eyes all blood shot and sulking, and refused to budge.

My biggest concern was that with the foul moods and hangovers they were suffering they might wander out onto the main highway and get bowled by a car. No manner of coaxing or enticing could encourage them out, so there was nothing I could do but let them sober up and come out in their own good time.

Just on dusk, Pork Chop emerged. He must have blamed his beloved kapok pillow for his thumping headache. The pillow was in shreds beneath the house and there was kapok everywhere. He was almost drowned in the stuff. It was stuck to his whiskers, hanging off his little tusks, embedded through his coarse hair, adorning his long piggy eyelashes. But apparently his headache was gone. So was his foul mood. So perhaps it had been all the fault of his kapok pillow.

Next time we drove down from Horoeka, we decided to leave Pork Chop and Myrtle behind. All this travelling back and forth each week was too much for them. I picked out a real dandy of a spot not far from the tent camp, with a trickle of water running through it and several beautiful clumps of mature toetoe for them to nestle under. Around this we constructed a nice little pen of sturdy chicken mesh for their security. It had to be the prettiest most picturesque little piggy pen in the whole of the King Country. We threw in a dead goat for sustenance, told them to make themselves comfortable and we would be back in a few days.

We couldn't believe our eyes when we got back. We had only been gone for the weekend but the pen looked like a tornado had passed through it. The clumps of toetoe were completely demolished, bits of goat carcass and entrails were hanging off the mesh and scattered into every corner, and the blowflies were having a ball. The contrast between inside and outside the mesh was unbelievable. Outside, the setting was pretty and parklike. Inside, was a disgusting fly blown bog.

It was obvious Pork Chop and Myrtle had no hankering for aesthetic values. They also had no hankering for being couped up in a pen. They were wild little piggies and were letting us know in no uncertain terms they expected to be free to come and go exactly as they pleased.

The unexpected critters that kept popping out of the woodwork made Horoeka Tent Camp a little out of the normal. We had actually said: "No more!" But then Gags turned up.

Gags was a 14 year old schoolboy, bent on learning the ways and means of trappers 'n' dogs, with firmly entrenched ideas of becoming one his self, a trapper that is, once he was sprung out of school. The lad seemed to have his priorities right, but his old man thought differently. Somewhere along the way the old man had acquired this quaint idea that scholastic abilities were much more important; and a couple of weeks roughing it might get the boy sorted out. So when he asked if Bob and I would look after the lad for the school holidays, I said: "Yeah, I suppose we could put up with him." Actually, although I was not exactly advertising the fact, I would have loved to have had a little brother of my own tagging along behind me on my trap lines, so I was in reality quite happy with the idea.

First thing Gags was commissioned to do was head off at an angle, well away from the camp, with a shovel and a spade and dig himself a pit toilet. We each had our own private hole in the ground, and there was no way either one of us intended sharing holes with young Gags. Camp hygiene was important, and there was nothing more important than keeping human excrement buried beneath turf. There was no shortage of blowflies out in the bush, and anything left lying around was quickly trampled upon and blown by the filthy little brutes. There had been more than one occasion when the lid had been left slightly askew and whole camp ovens of food had been ruined by blowflies. And on more than one occasion we had found out too late... after the meal was over and a dead blowfly turned up floating in the gravy. Chewing on blowflies and their little offspring was bad enough, but who wanted to eat goat stew floating with dead blowflies that had stopped off to sample a bit of human excrement on their way to the pot!

One morning I had a nasty turn in regard to all this when I noticed a huge fat maggot crawling around my hole in the ground just as I was about to cover the doings with turf. Everything from the previous days had been neatly buried and the smug look in this maggot's eye gave me the sickening dread that he was a new arrival along with the most recent deposit. I had no idea whether it was possible to eat a batch of fly blown stew and then hatch a batch of maggots in your innards. But I was convinced I could feel them oozing round inside my gut as I thought about it.

Next thing Gags needed to understand was: "What you put on your plate you eat. If you are not sure whether you can eat it then don't put it on your plate in the first place." We were not exactly short on food, but like most ex cullers we had graduated from a hard school. I doubt there was ever a South Island deer culler had not learned to not waste. When a man has to carry his next few weeks' provisions on his back, he does not normally go throwing away plates of uneaten food come dinner time. Working your way through the mountains with your food on your back, everything was rationed and there were times when there was hardly enough to keep you going, let alone waste!

Then Gags was shown how to make himself a bunk. The boy needed to learn self sufficiency. It was bad enough cosseting a bunch of pigs and goats without having to do the same for fourteen year old school boys as well.

First day out on the hill with Gags, he and I took off bright and early straight after breakfast. Gags was bubbling over with enthusiasm. At some stage his old man had had a go at laying poison lines and somewhere along the way Gags had followed along behind him, but the old man was just another fly by night and he had not the faintest idea about trapping. The line I was working was producing well and already there were large heaps of rotting carcasses scattered throughout the bush. The odd traps that were no longer catching I was pulling up as I went to be placed on new sets at the end of the line, and meanwhile I was killing possums, resetting and covering traps, skinning out caches and enjoying myself explaining to Gags the finer points of trapping. Gags was taking it all in.

Working a full length trap line meant a long day out in the bush, so before leaving camp, I had packed a thermos of tea, along with some bread and butter and a few cooked possum legs for our lunch. Around midday we topped a bit of a rise and I plonked myself down alongside a festering mound of humming carcasses and started pouring myself and Gags a nice hot cup of tea. I was ready for a break but Gags wanted to keep going.

"Aren't you hungry enough yet?" I asked

"Yes, I am," he replied, "but couldn't we go on a bit further before we stop to eat?"

I was impressed with his enthusiasm, but explained that that would not work. Straight after we had eaten I had a large cache of yesterday's possums to skin right here which was going to take at least half an hour to complete, and by then we would be near dead from hunger, so that was why I wanted to have the break here, now.

Gags said, well I could eat, but he couldn't. The smell coming off the rotting carcasses was turning his stomach. Actually, I hadn't even noticed it. I was so used to working through the bush with rotting carcasses heaped here and there I had never stopped to think the smell of it might turn someone off their food. And here was me

It was enough to put Gags off his lunch

thinking Gags just wanted to keep working. Out of deference for young Gags we moved a few yards into the bush, out of sight, out of smell, plonked down on a log and there Gags got tucked in, eating like a hungry horse.

Within a couple of days Gags was into the thick of it. Practicing his skinning techniques on the rejects, pithing goats and carting legs of meat back for the camp oven and come lunch time, plonking down in amongst the rotting carcasses and getting stuck into his legs of possum meat between skinning and caching as if he'd always done it that way. Gags was getting the hang of it.

There was a solid mill gate barring entrance to the Whangapeki that quite effectively deterred private shooters accessing the block. So with little likelihood of being shot at there was not much point humping a rifle round the line.

In fact it had become so unusual for me to be packing a rifle, that one day when I did happen to take the Sako Vixen along, I had worked my way half an hour down the bush before I started feeling a bit naked and it suddenly dawned on me that I no longer had my rifle with me. I could vaguely remember propping it up against a tree near a cache, but I had to sit down and think hard in order to remember just which cache. There were deer in the block and occasionally I would stumble onto one, but trapping possums was one job, carcassing deer was another, and there wasn't time enough for doing both. Nevertheless, I always kept the Sako handy in the Land Rover just in case an easy deer showed up while I was driving to and from the line.

We were heading up the hill from Horoeka straight after breakfast one morning when we got tucked in behind a mob of goats. Normally I would not have cared, but this particular day we had Gags along. I screeched to a halt. Gags was bundled out the door and piled up front in the spare wheel. Bob told him to anchor his feet up against the crash rack and my rifle was plonked on his knee.

"Try not to fall out of the wheel Gags!" I yelled over the roar of the engine as we took off in pursuit. "I want all eight of them, so as soon as you line up let 'em have it," Gags nodded in grim agreement... he apparently didn't realize a Sako mag only holds five shots

The goats had gained a bit of an advantage while we were getting Gags organized, and by the time we got started they were already disappearing around the first bend. The Land Rover was roaring as we came belting up the hill behind them. Round the first bend, bouncing through ruts, Gags holding on like grim death, bobbing up and down all over the place in front of the windscreen.

"Try and hold him down Bob," I said. "I wouldn't want to see my rifle get bent if he goes flying off the bonnet!"

By now the goats were racing in top gear, chips of pumice flying from their hooves as they pelted up the road and disappeared round the next bend. Bob was hanging out one window holding Gags down by his shirt tails, and I was hanging out the other trying to see past Gags and keep the road in view while at the same time manoeuvring the Land Rover at high speed round corners and trying to catch up on the goats. We would come flying round one corner just as the goats would be hightailing it round the one ahead with Gags getting all excited and firing off shots and shooting up pumice and leaves, and me still trying to get glimpses of where I was driving through Gags back which was violently bumping up and down, and Bob still hanging out the opposite window "Yahooing!" and "Yodelling!" and roaring with laughter and egging Gags on while anchoring him from hurtling into space, and the goats just about succumbing of fright but relatively safe as long as it was only Gags doing the shooting.

It was about half a mile of frantic action before the goats came to realizing that if they plied off of the road they would find their selves a lot less chased about than what was happening while they stayed on it. Meanwhile Gags had emptied the mag without creating any casualties and we all knew there wasn't any point in stopping to reload, because the goats were not going to wait round while we did. So we just kept going, charging up the hill hard on their hammer until they all took off into the bush.

Gags was shaking all over with excitement. Bob and I were shaking all over with laughter.

"That was pretty good shooting Gags. How many do you reckon you hit?" Bob asked as we bundled him back into the front of the

Land Rover.

"Don't know," said Gags. "The Land Rover was bouncing too much for me to be able to tell. But I don't think I hit all eight of them!"

Catching big old billy goats in my traps was nothing unusual, but on one occasion I had hopped on the back of one of them just for the heck of it, and tried riding him through the bush. The poor old fellow wasn't up to it. His legs buckled beneath my weight and after collapsing in a heap with me on top I think he thought he had died and gone to heaven. For quite some time he just lay there with his eyes rolled back and it took quite a lot of coaxing getting him back on his feet and sending him on his way with a boot in the backside. Gags was just a light little fellow though, and I believed it would be a different story altogether if I could talk him into getting on the back of some old billy. I was interested to see just how far an angry billy goat travelling fast in a downhill direction would get with someone about the size of Gags onboard. Under the circumstances, I didn't think it was necessary explaining to Gags that I was planning on using him as the object of an experiment.

The ideal goat turned up anchored by a rear hoof and running round in circles on the end of the chain on the downhill side of an eroded knoll that headed off towards the farmlands. Gags was always keen to lend a hand so he did not mind when I asked him to come and help while I released the goat.

"We're going to need a bit of ballast to anchor this one while I release the trap. Come and give us a hand Gags."

"Okay. What should I do?"

"We've got to stop the stroppy devil from jumping about so I can set him loose before he knocks my trap to pieces. I'll get a hold of him and you straddle his back and grab a hold on his horns to put a bit of weight on him while I release the trap. Okay?"

Gags was keen enough, but it wasn't that easy. Each time I tried to move in the billy would lower his head and brace himself for a charge. He was a proper smart ass, but there was no way I was going to let some smart ass goat get the better of me!

"Gags! You stand out front a couple of yards and hold his attention while I snuck round behind and grab him by the horns."

Gags was good at this. He came up just beyond the stretch limit of the chain and stood there eyeballing the goat while I crept in from the rear. But the minute I grabbed his horns he went berko. First he tried a backward flip, followed by a cartwheel, then he tried to take off in a circle. And when he realized I was still holding on he just stood there angrily stamping his front feet while at the same time violently trying to shake me loose. Gradually I started pointing him in a downhill direction.

"Okay Gags. Get round here and sling your leg over his back and weigh him down while I manoeuvre round and release the trap. Get a good grip on those horns to steady yourself. You right there?"

"Yep!" said Gags.

I grabbed down low on his back leg, eased off the trap, and was still holding on when he suddenly got it into his head to make his dash for freedom. With a sudden lurch, Gags shot backwards, I was dragged forwards, the goat slipped out of my grip and Gags came down on top of me. The two of us lay in the dust and droppings watching the other party to my experiment disappearing down through the trees.

"You know what Gags," I said, as I slowly got to my feet. "If I had thought that smart ass goat was going to get the better of me like that, I reckon I would have whacked him fair between the eyes and been done with it."

Living at Horoeka tent camp must have been a bit tough on Gags. I guess it sorted him out though. At the end of his school holidays we returned him to his family with his priorities back where they ought to be for a young lad of his age. The boy was now more fully convinced than ever that hunting possums and beating up wild billy goats was definitely the only thing worth doing in life.

After that, it did not make much difference what unexpected critters came popping out of the woodwork round Horoeka. Once Gags was gone we said, "Definitely no more!"

CHAPTER 18

Sweet Apples 'n' Sour Pork

Horoeka Tent Camp was about as cosy as a tent camp could get; but it did not compare with our iron roofed, weatherboard house at Pokaka with its big open fireplace for keeping everything warm and dry and its solid old wood range for heating up the kitchen and cooking decent meals on. We would always stock up with plenty of fresh supplies on our way back to base; meat, bread, eggs, vegetables, fruit....

I remember my old mate Hank telling me about fruit. He reckoned he'd had his fair share of trouble because of fruit. And because of that he never had much to do with it any more..

"You got to watch out for fruit," Hank said. "It can get you into an awful lot of difficulty if you're not careful. An armful of apples nearly killed me once when I was about eleven years old."

"C'mon, Hank," I countered. "I have never heard of anyone being attacked by apples before!"

"Well, I wasn't actually attacked by the apples, but they nearly killed me all the same." Hank replied....

"We was having a break off the farm, visiting my mum's sister in Wellington, and they was all sitting up prim and proper in the living room drinking cups of tea and talking a load of crap with their crumpets. I was getting sick of listening because there wasn't nothing being said that interested me very much and they looked stupid anyway sitting inside wearing hats with funny bits of net dangling down round the edges hanging there in front of their faces. So I thought I'd go for a wander up the road because I had never been to Wellington before and I wanted to check out whether the neighbours had any turkeys.

"About a half a mile from my aunty's there was this house perched up on a bit of a rise. Actually there were lots of houses perched up on bits of rises round where my aunty lived, but this one was different because between me and the house, there was a steep bank covered in scrub that dropped away from the footpath, then at the bottom of the bank there was a hedge been planted along a number 8 wire fence, and right behind the hedge there was a fairly big garden with potatoes and a few rows of peas and carrots and stuff, and then there was this house up on the rise on the other side of the garden. But what caught my eye was these apple trees loaded with big juicy looking apples not far from the hedge. Right where I was standing the road went round a fairly sharp bend with a high bank rising above it on the opposite side. So it looked like no one, apart from this one house, would be able to see me if I raided the apples. I couldn't see any sign of life up at the house, so I scrambled down the bank and poked my way through the hedge. There wasn't any cover once you were in the garden, but I didn't plan on being there long.

"The nearest tree had the best looking apples, so I went straight for that one. I had already grabbed an armful and stuffed them inside my shirt when I glanced up to check on the house and suddenly noticed there was a man standing on the back porch. I wasn't sure whether he was looking straight at me or somewhere up on the road above me. But nor was I waiting to find out. All I knew was, if someone caught you raiding orchards back where I came from you was likely to cop a charge of saltpetre up your gungah. I scrambled back through the hedge and took off running with my head down. But what I didn't know was some stupid townie idiot had gone and stayed back a corner post with a length of barbed wire. I ran straight into the wire, and one of the barbs spragged me right through the top of my head.

"I bounced backwards and sprawled in a heap of apples with blood dripping all over the place. It felt good lying there under the hedge with my eyes rolled back in their sockets, but I couldn't stay long, because for all I knew that fellow in the doorway might be charging down on me with his loaded shotgun. I was going to be in enough trouble trying to explain how I'd nearly been killed with a barbed wire spoke through my head, without stopping a load of saltpetre as well and having to explain that I had just been shot dead because of an armful of apples."

"Hang on Hank!" I interrupted. "You wouldn't have had to explain anything if you had been shot dead."

"Well I wasn't shot dead that particular time and I never said the armful of apples killed me. I said they nearly killed me. Anyway, I got up from where I was lying and took off. I must have been a bit dazed because in my rush to get away I didn't even think about picking up any of the apples that were lying all over the ground, and so after all that I ended up with nothing."

"If you ended up with nothing, Hank," I said, "then I would not have said you was nearly killed for an armful of apples. I would have said you was nearly killed for nothing!"

"Yeah! I suppose you're right." Hank agreed. "I hadn't thought of it that way before. But it doesn't alter the fact that fruit can get you into an awful lot of trouble. There was another time," he added. "I was nearly mauled by a police dog and got a criminal charge against me just because of one lousy apple."

"I was camping in a tent out the back of a friend's property up at Russell one summer, and for some unknown reason this apple tree in the front yard of one of the neighbours' houses had caught my eye. There was just one big apple hanging on the tree and it was a huge apple and from down on the street I couldn't tell what variety it was. But I knew being that big it had to be something special.

"Anyway, I was lying in my tent one night, and it was some time after midnight, and it was stinking hot, and I couldn't get to sleep. And you know how it is, when you are trying to get to sleep and you can't, silly things keep coming up in your mind. Well I started thinking about that stupid apple, and the next thing you know I had got up off my camp stretcher, pulled on a pair of jeans and I was heading off up the road to go check it out.

"I didn't want to wake anyone up so I crept quietly up the front path towards the tree, came round from behind a boat parked on the lawn, and was just about to walk over to the apple tree for a look when a voice from almost right above me at the house called out: 'What do you think you're doing? Get away from that boat?'

"I almost jumped out of my skin. I shot off down the path, out the gate, tore across the road and disappeared into a thick hillside of gorse. I knew there was a dirt road that followed round the side of the hill somewhere up above the gorse. But it was thicker in there than I had thought. I was stuck in the middle of it near punctured to death with sharp bits and pieces sticking out of me everywhere. I was still trying to make it to the road when I hears the local constable arrive on the scene in his old Hillman car. And as I tweeks out through a bit of gorse I see he's got his German Shepherd police dog on a leash.

"I think it was my lucky day I was skewered on a gorse bush halfway up the slope. Because if I had made it to the road I probably would have been overtaken by the constable and his dog.

"'He took off straight across the road and into the gorse,' says the man with the apple tree. 'He must know his way around. There's probably a track up through the gorse that he knows about!'

"'Did you see what he looked like?' asked the constable.

"'No, I think he'd disguised himself with some sort of a spiky looking woollen cap on his head. I'm pretty sure he was trying to steal something off my boat!'

"'Okay. I'll drive up the road and see if I can put the dog onto him!'

"There wasn't no track up through that gorse," Hank said, "other than the one I was in the throes of making, and that wasn't no woollen cap on my head neither. It was my hair standing on end from the fright he'd given me when he yelled at me from up at his window!

"I lay flat in the gorse not daring to move while the constable and his dog drove up the road just a few feet above me. Then about twenty minutes later back they come to report to the neighbour that the 'boat thief' had somehow eluded them, but they would hang around awhile longer in the hope of catching him. So I continues lying there punctured all over with prickles while the constable drives up and down the dirt road a few more times and after about two or three hours of agonising pain I assumed that he and his dog had finally got sick of it all and taken off home for the night. Which was just as well. Because by now the dawn was nearly breaking, and once that happened there would have been no show of getting out of the mess I was already in.

"I pushed my way out of the prickles onto the dirt road and took off in a westerly direction. It was a long way in a big circle back down to the bay, around some jagged coastal rocks, and back to the safety of my tent. By now it was just cracking daylight and I was terrified that someone would be up and about and see me sneaking home. I shot into the tent, dove onto my camp stretcher and pulled a blanket over my head.

"I only just made it when there was a crunching of footsteps in the gravel outside the tent. I lay there beneath the blanket, breathing heavy making out I was in a deep sleep. I sensed the tent flap being eased open but I didn't dare look. To this day I'm not sure whether it was the constable still snooping round and just checking to see if I was in. But the next day when I saw him walking through town, I gave him a big smile and said, 'G'day!' He nodded back politely, so I guess he hadn't found any reason to press charges.

"You know what?" Hank added. "I'll tell you something else I learned about fruit that summer at Russell. It's bad luck to take bananas on a fishing boat. There was one bloke I heard of got his head thumped by his mates because he took along some banana sandwiches in his lunch and everyone reckoned that was the reason none of them caught any fish."

"That's way out Hank," I replied. "How could the fish know that someone had banana sandwiches on the boat?"

"Yeah! That was what I wondered," said Hank. "But you got to admit that bananas were unlucky for the bloke who took them out on the boat. He was the only one out of the whole bunch who got his head thumped! Anyway, I don't like pushing it so I usually keep well clear of fruit these days!"

I was not particularly superstitious about fruit, and apart from the odd sore stomach from eating too much at one sitting, I do not think that I had ever suffered any truly traumatic experiences, in the manner of Hank, that could be attributed to fruit. So stocking up with a bit of fruit on our way back to base opened the way for some nice desserts to compliment the diet.

I like stewed apples with custard and whipped cream on top. And even more so do I like stewed tree tomatoes with liberal quantities of whipped cream on top. Stewed fruit is easy enough to prepare. Peel the fruit, slice it fairly small, sprinkle with a liberal amount of sugar, cover with water, and simmer until you reckon it is cooked. Whipping up the cream is no problem either. If there is no egg beater in the camp, pour the cream into a clean glass jar with a lid and shake the living daylights out of it until it is whipped just right. If you prefer custard; again that is not difficult. All you need to do is follow the instructions on the packet.

Despite the convenience of a few more home comforts at Sue Joe's, we still preferred the environment back at Horoeka. Nights were never as restful hanging out at Pokaka Base. Not only was the house situated right alongside State Highway 4 with its Diesel belching freight trucks and semi-trailers thundering up and down the highway right outside the bedroom windows throughout the night. But right opposite the house, on the other side of the highway, was the main trunk line. And regular as clockwork, every night about 2300 hours a huge lumbering goods train would come belting down the tracks heading south. Then an hour or so later the Wellington to Auckland Express would come rattling past... and another express heading the opposite way, from Auckland to Wellington... plus railcars and other rolling stock at odd hours of the night. In time one did tend to become accustomed to all the traffic round Pokaka but it didn't seem natural living in a possum camp with all that nonsense going on all around you all the time.

In comparison, the tranquillity around Horoeka was like balm to the bones... the faintest whisper of a breeze gently caressing the surrounding foliage, the comforting crackle of a log lighting up the hearth, the call of a kiwi sounding through the gully, a morepork high on the ridge... the soothing sounds of peace and sanity.

One might think that creatures as timid as deer would never get accustomed to the noise and disturbance of Diesel locomotives hauling freight cars through the night, but they do. Plenty of grass grew along the rail sidings and deer sometimes browsed it. I knew that across the track from Sue Joe's, deer were coming out of the bush some nights because I had seen their droppings scattered about. Several times I wandered over with the rifle and a spotlight in the dead of night but I had never caught them out.

Then one night I got there just on 2300 hours and there they were, two of them standing up against the bush edge back towards the Pokaka rail siding. They were so used to the penetrating beam of railcars and Diesel locomotives that my spotlight barely had them raise an eyebrow. They were a fair distance away and I needed to get across the track to close the gap. Trouble was, a mile or so down the track I could hear the freight train already lumbering over the

Manganui o te Ao Viaduct and any minute it would be swinging round the bend and thundering down the home straight. I scrambled over the barbed wire and got as far as the middle of the track when round the bend she came. It was a long way between me and that train, and I would hardly have thought the driver would have seen me at that distance, but there was no other accounting for why he chose that very moment to blast his horn. I leapt off the track, dove into the long grass and lay there out of sight and muttering uncomplimentary adjectives pertaining to the stupidity of railroading men in general. What with the blasting of the horn shattering the night and me all lit up in the middle of the tracks, it was highly likely the deer had already disappeared back into the bush. All I could do was lie low and wait for the train to pass.

There wasn't long to wait. A goods train hurtling down that straight at full pelt gets there in slightly more than one minute flat. But that is one awesome sort of a minute when you are lying hard up against the sleepers, listening to the clattering and chunking in the tracks, feeling the ground rumbling and shaking, the night lit like day, that huge steel beast bearing down on you in a rising crescendo of cacophonous noise. Closer and closer, louder and louder, then suddenly this massive chunk of thundering Diesel is upon you, roaring over the top of you, ground shaking violently, steel wheels clacking over the joints, exhaust blaring into the still night air, so close, so unexpectedly huge. And right then at that very moment, the engine thundering over the top of me, adrenalin surging through my veins, that damned stupid engine driver blasted off his horn once more. Danged fool of a man! I all but suffered a seizure!

So much for spotlighting deer for that night. If they had not already taken off with the first blast, they certainly would have with the second one. Anyway, my heart was palpitating so erratically after what that blithering idiot had just gone and done to me, there was no way I could have held a rifle steady even had I tried. Maybe there were some timid critters, such as deer, that got accustomed to the noise and disturbance of Diesel locomotives hauling freight cars through the night, but that was not likely to be the case with a certain possum trapper I knew. I never went back looking for those two deer. Any wild creature game enough to venture out in the thick of night and front up to that lunatic railroading man and his rowdy goods train deserved a pat on the back, not a bullet.

It was not often that I went looking for deer in the middle of the night. Usually, I was either too busy working in the skin room or else I was too tired to worry about them. Standing up against a workbench all day tacking out skins was much more tiring than a day of slogging through heavy bush working a trap line. I think it was all to do with circulation of the blood. Out on the line I would be forever on the go, moving about, oxygen pumping through my veins. But in the skin room I was more or less anchored to one spot for hours on end. And this system of stockpiling skins for up to a week at a time and then having to tack them all out in one go made particularly heavy going of it. It made for easier days out in the bush when all you had to do was tend your traps, eat and sleep. But once back at Pokaka with a load of skins, some of them already on the verge of drying out and spoiling it all caught up on you. Out of necessity you had to get stuck in and work hard and fast. I would try to keep going for three or four hours solid, but by then I would be feeling groggy and more than ready for a break Once you stopped it was often hard getting started again, but there would still be several hours tacking out to be done, as well as a couple of hundred dried skins waiting to be scraped of fat, rubbed clean and stripped off their boards to make room for those still waiting to be tacked out.

Stripping boards. Remove staples with long nosed pliers.
Scraping fat off the skin.
Rubbing dry with old sacking.
Cutting open the belly.
Removing the skin from the board.
Cutting open the tail.
A clean, first grade skin. Skin will now be hung over ropes to allow the ears to dry properly.

Most of the techniques we employed in both trapping possums and handling skins had initially stemmed from Dave Odey's camp, and this included our method of tacking out. There were fourteen anchor points on a skin, which meant fourteen 1½ inch flat head nails were tacked into every skin to hold it in shape while it dried. Obviously, all those nails had to be pulled out again before the dried skins could be stripped off their boards. If there were 200 boards to strip that added up to 2,800 nails to be removed, and the only way of doing so was to grip each individual nail in turn between thumb and index finger and wiggle it free. As the skins dried they tended to shrink slightly and often they would bind tightly around the nails making some of them very difficult to pull free. This not only made stripping boards time consuming, but also wrecked havoc on the fingers and thumbs, causing painful splits and cuts in the joints.

When tacking out, I used a light weight upholstery hammer, which was great to use from the weight point of view. But with a face not much broader than the head of the nails I was trying to hit and things oftentimes slippery with possum fat, there were many misses and resultant bruised thumbs. So what with feeling groggy from standing too long in one place, legs going numb from lack of circulation, cracked and bleeding finger joints from sharp nail heads, and bruised thumbs from misplaced hammer blows, long days spent tacking out skins and stripping boards was never one of my favourite pastimes.

I was chatting with Bill Broadfoot one day, and he told me that he had thrown Odey's cumbersome method of hammer and nails out the door ages ago. He had come up with the idea of using an adjustable staple tacker, and not only was it highly efficient, it trimmed considerable time off both the tacking out and stripping procedures. I could immediately see the advantages and took off for the stationery

We began using a staple machine and never looked back

store in Taumarunui and bought myself a Primo Automatic Tacker and several bulk packets of 5/16" staples. There were several staple guns on the market, but the critical, deciding factor, when choosing the Primo Automatic Tacker above all others was that it could be easily and positively adjusted so the heads of the staples were left protruding far enough above the skin to allow for a pair of long nosed pliers to get in and quickly whip them back out again when it came to stripping boards. It was a sturdy, well constructed piece of equipment, manufactured in England and built for long, heavy duty service. It was also the model that Bill used and recommended.

Bill's method was certainly a jump up on Odey's. No more damaged fingers and thumbs, it was faster and easier and a huge saving in time. Stripping boards was likewise just so much faster and easier. What was more, the holes left in the dried skins from the staples were almost non existent and far less detracting than those left by nails. Dave knew that Bill had come up with a new method for fastening skins to boards, but there was no way that he could bring himself to accepting that the method might not only be "new" but also "improved". Dave was the one who had initially shown us how to go about it, and Dave being Dave, there was not much likelihood that he would be quickly switching over to some other procedure that had been conceived by one of his protégé. Once enlightened, Bob and I never looked back. Dave, however, plodded resolutely on with his hammer and nails.

Dave plodded on with hammer and nails

Five or six days possuming in the Whangapeki usually produced anything from 130 to 200 skins each, and by then, regardless of how well we had been caring for them, at least some of the first day's catch would be starting to show signs of drying round the edges. There was not a great deal you could do with a skin that had begun to dry before you got it tacked onto a board. So at the very first indication we would spring our traps and make a dash for Pokaka.

The other situation we had to watch out for was maggots hatching in amongst the furs. Once this occurred, in no time at all there would be a seething mass of them crawling through your pack, the whole mess would be stinking like an old man's urinal, and next thing the fur would start to slip. If you were quick enough getting them tacked out — before they started to slip — you would more than likely be okay. The maggots would dry up and drop off the skins and the smell would eventually disappear. But working against time, frantically trying to salvage a pack full of stinking possum skins, blowflies buzzing round your ears and thousands of revolting little maggots crawling all over your hands and arms was not one of the more delectable aspects of fur trapping.

Having to travel back and forth to Pokaka each week meant quite a lot of down time from our trap lines, but the numbers were piling up in our skin rooms nevertheless. Anything of merit we were hanging on to for export and the rubbish we were dumping on Rodney's table. But having now mastered the art of spreading the density of fur evenly throughout the pelt, even our rejects looked pretty good, and being none the wiser concerning what he never saw, Rodney settled for the fact that despite not being Pokaka furs our lines were still a site better presented than the skins he was getting from anybody else.

Trapping possums in the Central North Island bush and shooting tahr in the Southern Alps were probably just about as far removed from one another as modes of hunting could get. So I guess it was nothing unnatural that Bob got this hankering every now and again for climbing hills and plastering even-toed ungulates. There were mornings that I would be buckling on my tomahawk and preparing to take off for my trap line while Bob would be fingering his rifle and considering his chances of nailing a deer up on the back ridge.

The season had moved along. Gladdy goat was considerably bigger now than when I had first brought her in. She was quite content hanging round in the bluffs up above the tent camp while we were away in the bush. In fact unbeknown to us, she had enticed a couple of amorous young billy goats into the area and while we were away she and the billy goats did play. It was not at first apparent, but later it became obvious that the rotten devils had gone and duffed the poor little lass. I suppose it was all part of the over all plan of things. But I was quite shocked when I came to realize that little Gladdy was pregnant, and at such a tender young age. In due season the billies did get their due reward.

I noticed Bob counting out bullets one morning while I was still preparing some roast goat sandwiches for my lunch. Grabbing his rifle and a handful of ammo, he took off out the door of the tent camp. Kim, immediately noticed Bob on his way with a rifle and he promptly fell in behind. Gladdy, realizing that I would soon be taking off in the opposite direction in the Land Rover, promptly fell in behind Kim. Pork Chop and Myrtle, noticing Kim following Bob, and Gladdy following Kim, immediately stopped whatever they were doing and promptly fell in behind Gladdy, Kim and Bob. And with Bob leading the procession, rifle to hand, he, Kim, Gladdy, Porky and Myrtle all took off towards the bluffs en route to the back ridge to go looking for a deer.

The first ones to tire out were Porky and Myrtle. Little piggies do not do too well in bluffs. They decided to turn back and look after the tent camp instead. But Gladdy was quite keen on the idea of hunting so she hung in close behind Bob and Kim. Bob was setting a good pace by now and Gladdy was running along behind giving little, "Me-e-e's!" every couple of steps.

On reaching the top of the bluffs, Bob stopped for a look around in case there was anything handy, and Gladdy decided to take advantage of the situation to call up her boy friends just to let them know that she and Bob and Kim were passing through on their way to the back ridge looking for a deer.

Bob told me later that Gladdy gave a loud bleat and stood there waiting and listening. Then this billy goat bleated back at her from not far away. So she called again. Bob closed on a round and waited. There were one or two more exchanges between Gladdy and the billy with Gladdy standing there alongside Bob and Kim, and the billy — actually two billies — working their way through the scrub toward them. It is hard to categorically say that Gladdy knew what she was doing calling up those billies, but Bob could hardly believe his eyes that as he lined up on the first billy, Gladdy lowered her head and looked the other way. Nor did she look up until after he had dropped both of them. Bob felt a bit guilty about using Gladdy like that. But I'm not altogether convinced that it wasn't Gladdy using Bob. I was real proud of my little goat. I knew plenty of blokes who owned hunting dogs, but I had never before heard of anyone who owned a hunting goat.

On another occasion, during a bitterly cold and blustery spell of weather, Bob was mooching about with Kim and his treble two on top of a ridge well back in the block. The wind was whipping off the tops of the Central Plateau mountains and burling over the high ridges of the Whangapeki, and there was little likelihood of catching a deer out in those conditions, but Bob was up there looking anyway. And he happened to peek over the side of a drop-off and there below were a couple of big fat deer sheltering from the elements. He bowled the two of them and toddled off back to camp to fetch me and the Land Rover.

Generally speaking most of the roads in the Whangapeki were still in relatively good condition considering there was no one interested in maintaining them and how long it was since the logging gangs had been gone. But some of the roads were getting a little weather worn through general lack of repair, and in one or two places it was a shade tricky negotiating the Land Rover past the slip-outs. This was the case with the road I now had to take to go get Bob's deer. Water had washed down a gully, spilled across the road and taken the downhill side with it. You could just squeeze through, with a pinch, but if you happened to miscalculate or perhaps make a wrong move... winching the Land Rover back up to the road again from the bottom of the gully was going to be quite a problem. Once the big trees were gone and the ground cover removed there was not much stopping the erosion taking hold and tearing the place apart.

We were aware that way back in history, before time began, worse things had happened in these parts than a gang of logging contractors let on the loose. There were places where water courses had scoured deep into the cuts made by the bulldozers and log haulers, and there, some twenty feet beneath the present surface, the charcoal remnants of the original ancient forest that had been obliterated by the Taupo eruption some two thousand years previous lay freshly exposed to the elements. It was interesting to note that in the absence of man's interference it had taken two thousand years for the land to heal and a new forest to mature. Then along comes this handful of men with chainsaws, bulldozer and a length of wire strop, and in the twinkling of an eye, there goes two thousand years of healing, stripped bare just like that! And just to ensure that this time around the healing process was not likely to get started, let alone happen come two thousand years, they then stocked the place with wild goats, deer, pigs and possums, as well as a few wild cats, stoats, rabbits and hares. Says heaps for man's ingenuity!

Up on the back ridge, we had run into a wee spot of bother figuring out how to haul out Bob's two deer. They were too far down the bush to hook up to the Land Rover and drag them. And the going was too steep to climb down and lug them back up. Eventually we managed to winch the both of them up to the road, working from tree to tree, inch by inch with the aid of my wire strainers and length of chain.

Back at Horoeka, handy to the camp there were pockets, scattered in amongst the bush, where the winter sun never reached and frost lingered for days; ideal places for hanging deer carcasses between trips into town. It was not always convenient dropping what we were doing and taking off to town just for the sake of a couple of deer.

One day, soon after this, Bob had heard some distant rifle shots when he was well back in the block working his trap line. Then a day or so later he came across this huge old boar lying boots up in a clearing. Someone had gut shot it and the pig had run until it had dropped. Bob could hardly believe his good fortune. He gutted it, finished working his traps, and once more toddled off back to camp to fetch me and the Land Rover.

"Do you think it's still okay?" I asked, as we worked it into the back of the Land Rover. "I reckon it looks a bit suspect."

"Nah! It's just about perfect." said Bob. "Rich, strong, gamey! This is exactly how the Germans like their meat. I'm sure some wog will be wrapped getting his teeth stuck into this beautiful piece of pork. "

Well I was not so sure, so I told Bob we had better throw the pig and his two deer on the trailer and rush them into Charlie Jone's meat depot straight away. Blowflies were an ongoing problem in the bush, and they were not wasting any time homing in on Bob's wild pork.

There was no one around when we arrived at Charlie's depot, but that was nothing unusual, there hardly ever was. It was quite the normal thing to telephone Charlie from the depot and tell him you had just dropped off a carcass or leave a note somewhere letting him know it was yours. Bob's deer would have been alright hanging out on the rails but I was more than just a little concerned about the condition of the pig. Hoards of blowflies were starting to mill about outside the depot, queuing to get in the door. I felt that if he did not get it into the chiller immediately he would likely lose it.

"I think you had better give Charlie a call on the phone and ask him to get down here straight away and get this stuff into the chiller,"

I suggested.

"Yeah, I think you're right," Bob replied. "If Charlie's blowflies get in here they're going to ruin this meat. We should have given it a good squirt with the fly spray before we left the bush; that would have slowed them down a bit. Don't open that door until after I get off the blower. We'll let Charlie sort it out when he gets here."

It was a few days later, on our way to Pokaka, that we dropped back into town and called up Charlie about Bob's meat cheque. I couldn't hear what Charlie was saying, but I could tell that things were not going too good on the other end of the phone. Bob's first reaction was defensive. Putting his hand over the mouthpiece he turned to me and said: "What the hell's Charlie coming at! There's no way that pig could have climbed down off the hook and crawled out the door on its own. It was already dead for at least a couple of days when I found it. Besides, I'd gutted it." Then, in reply to Charlie: "Okay, okay. So I got delayed in the Whangapeki.... No, it wasn't a couple of weeks... No, just a few days... It looked pretty fresh to me. Can't understand what could have happened. I shot the two deer a couple of days before I got the pig and the deer were okay, weren't they? Yep! Gutted it straight after I got it..."

By now I was near doubled up with laughter. By the sound of things Charlie wasn't too happy having a rotten pig hung up in his venison depot. If he heard me laughing in the background that would only make matters worse. I wandered quietly out the door and left Bob still talking on the phone. Wasn't long before he'd hung up and joined me out by the Land Rover.

"I think I caught Charlie in a bit of a bad mood," said Bob. "Went and blamed my pig for filling his scungy old meat depot with flies. Don't know what he's on about. They're his flies not mine. Then he started moaning about the back of his truck getting all messed up carting it down to the river where he dumped it. He reckoned it wouldn't even sink it was so rotten. Said he had never heard about Germans preferring ripe pork before. He said it was so ripe, even Hone Heke wouldn't have eaten it along with his rotten corn and huhu grubs.... Fellow's got no sense of humour at all... Almost threw a wobbly when I asked him if he was interested in buying any huhu grubs."

We left Charlie to calm down a little before picking up Bob's venison cheque on the return to Horoeka from Pokaka. After all the effort entailed in lugging it out of the bush and into Charlie's, Bob was quite disappointed about his pork. He still reckoned it was just about perfect for the German market. Besides he was trying to accumulate as much funds as he could to buy himself a Land Rover and, as he said: "Every little helps!"

CHAPTER 19

Waipakihi – Spring 1967

Easy access to the Waipakihi River had recently been opened up by way of a hydro road that had been pushed back towards the Kaimanawas from close to the summit of the Desert Road. Somehow Bob and I had got wind of it but we were trying to keep it quiet. From what we could make out the various blokes who we knew who might have been interested, were so preoccupied rushing round looking for deer in their favourite spots handy to town that they had not twigged to it, and that was the way we wanted to keep it. So here was a piece of virgin country just waiting to be shot. Spring growth was shooting up everywhere and there were bound to be some easy pickings for the taking.

A bulldozer track of sorts, laced with ruts and chasms deep enough to swallow a bus, dropped down off the plateau at a steep angle to the river below. Some parts looked a bit scary, but I reckoned there was just about enough room, most of the way down, for the wheels to straddle the crevices. And with Bob down on his hands and knees on the down hill side and me following his index finger slightly to the left and slightly to the right, I somehow made it safely to the river's edge. Half way down the track, somewhere beyond the point of no return, where the pumice tended to slip and all four wheels began to slide at once, a loud shrieking noise, which frightened the living daylights out of me, developed in the Land Rover somewhere between the front and rear transmission. But once I was safely at the bottom, I regained my usual composure and the shrieking noise slowly subsided to intense heavy breathing. In later times, as the hydro development activity in the area hotted up, the access track I had just descended was realigned and much better maintained taking much of the hilarity out of it, and no longer was it accessible only to fools, idiots and Wayne Blake.

From immediately beyond the bottom of the track there was a wide river crossing to negotiate, then a bit more bulldozer track, followed by about a mile and a half of open river flats, liberally scattered with Sika droppings. At the end of Sika Flat, there was a sharp bend in the river and a brief gorgy bit where it came out of the bush and from here on it was all back packing.

At the bottom of the track there was a wide river crossing to negotiate

That night we pitched a pup tent alongside the Land Rover on the far end of Sika Flat, and began sorting out gear for packing upstream.

Maintaining the bulldozer track of sorts

Our plan was to shoot our way quickly up the river, creaming whatever might be out on the river flats, and then float the carcasses on inflated tractor tubes downstream to the Land Rover and out.

I did not wish to spend too much time in the Waipakihi as I intended heading south as soon as the ears on our possum furs had dried enough for baling. Although it would be a little late in the season by the time I got there, and most of the crews would already be sorted out, I thought I might still have a chance of landing a job on a Bluff crayfishing boat to see out the summer. Bob was going to head for the Wairarapa where he intended spending a bit of time checking out the Haurangi Mountains. There was a good breed of Red deer in the Haurangi's if you could work your way in with the run holders, and possibly some good possum trapping blocks to try and secure for the next season as well. So this trip up the Waipakihi was really just a fill in while we were otherwise killing a bit of time. However, things never work out quite the way you expect.

The following morning, packing just our treble two's and a pocket full of ammo, we did a bit of a recce upstream to suss out the lay of the land and try and figure out what would be the best approach. For close to two miles beyond Sika Flat, the Waipakihi meandered through its valley with beech forest verging in on either side. But then it opened out onto what was the first of a string of river flats and with that much knowledge gained we decided to backtrack to Sika Flat and kill time until we were ready to head out for the evening shot. It would

Waipakihi River flats

have been rather pointless pressing on and leaving our scent wafting about to spook the area before we were ready to shoot it.

Late in the afternoon, travelling light with just our sleeping bags and a brew billy tucked away in our pikaus, we took off upstream once more. Back at the Land Rover, we had spent considerable time pouring over a map and planning our hunt. The best approach, it seemed, would be to race from river flat to river flat, knocking anything down that might be out. If there was nothing out on one flat then we would move quickly to the next, and then the next, covering as much territory as possible. Out of all this we hoped to catch out at least one or two deer for our effort. But as previously mentioned, things never work out quite the way you expect.

Travelling fast, we made good time to the first clearing with plenty of time remaining to last light, and straight away we were on to deer. Three of them, all with their heads down and picking away unconcernedly at something that had taken their fancy. Two of them lay kicking in the grit before they had time to swallow their mouthful, and their buddy got such a fright with the first volley of shots that he made the foolish mistake of leaping away from the cover of bush instead of back into it. All three were quickly gutted, dragged under the trees and left to air out with sticks propping open their rib cages.

Time, now, was everything. We took off again, at a fair sort of a pace. There was a bit of river crossing between here and the next clearing, but the river was running low and the crossings were easy. By

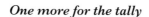

One more for the tally

Packing the tractor tube back up river

now the shadows of late afternoon were gone and the hint of evening was beginning to settle over the valley; just the right time of day for hungry deer to be getting serious about mooching out onto the flats for a bit of that spring growth.

Prior to coming onto our next clearing we left the river's edge and poked our way through the cover of bush. And it was from just inside the bush, with nice comfortable moss coated logs to bench rest our rifles over that we dropped two more unsuspecting deer. These too, we gutted, dragged into the bush, and propped open with sticks.

There was still a bit of daylight to spare and the next river flat produced one more for the tally, and the flat after that, two more. By now daylight was slipping away and it was taking too much time dragging the deer to the bush, so we gutted them where they dropped and quickly moved on.

Now there was a string of river flats almost one after the other, and we just kept on travelling fast and shooting deer until darkness overtook us and there was no longer enough light left to pick anything out through our scopes.

We had hardly expected anything quite like this. Close to the last deer that had been shot, we pulled our sleeping bags out of our pikaus, sorted out a comfortable spot for bedding down, boiled up a brew, sat in close to the warming fire and started discussing what we had done. We had moved so fast and come on deer so quickly that we were not even sure how many we had actually shot. Bob thought we had dropped about thirteen and I thought it was fourteen. But when we went over it, clearing by clearing, I agreed with Bob that his tally was correct. The interesting thing though, when we got to thinking about it, was the size of the deer. They were the runtiest lot of Red deer either of us had ever come across. It was not that they were sickly looking. They were just very small weedy little animals. And come to think of it, what little spring growth there was on the river flats was hardly enough to feed a decent sized deer. Probably there would not have been one amongst them that would have topped the scales at more than eighty pounds dressed out weight.. Picking one of these gutted carcasses up in your arms and carrying it bodily down to the river's edge would be no problem.

We were up at first light next morning and heading back downstream, dragging carcasses into the shade and propping open ribcages as we went. Six or seven carcasses was going to be load enough for a tractor tube, so the day's activity ahead of us, trekking back down to Sika Flat, putting away a breakfast solid enough to work on for the rest of the day, packing the tractor tubes back to where we had bedded down the previous night, and floating the carcasses down to the Land Rover was already mapped out.

Having always been weight conscious of anything I loaded on my back, I had a small little pump that I reckoned was a sensible size for packing miles up a river. And so it was. But as for when it came to pumping up a tractor tube…. Have you ever stopped to think how much air it takes to solidly inflate a full grown tractor tube? Well just try doing it sometime with a pump that was better designed for slow filling a kiddie's rubber ducky. For some unknown reason, I had always been in the habit of counting as I performed various tasks — two and a bit hefty whacks with a hammer to drive a flooring brad into a piece of tongue and groove as an apprentice carpenter; six of builder's mix, two of cement and then six more of builder's mix for the concrete mixer; four hundred steps up the side of a sheer bluff with a bag of cement under your arm just to get started on the average Wellington building site — no wonder I hated being a carpenter - fourteen tack out points to a possum board; three hundred skins to a bale; two spoons of sugar in the brew, one handful of tea for the billy — that was all easy enough to keep track of. But counting the pump strokes for one of those tractor tubes was sheer depressing. I get confused after counting about ten thousand and I have to stop for a rest. Then I forget what number I was up to and I have to start all over again. We took it in turns. I would go for about twenty minutes, pumping franticly all the way, until the tube looked as if it was about to start inflating, then Bob would borrow the pump and work on his tube for about the same. Then it would be my turn again, and then Bob's. Finally both tubes were inflated, but the thought of doing this every time we had another load of deer to transport was not very encouraging. And pity help anyone who might crack a smile if someone got a snag and punctured his tube on the way back downstream.

Nor was it all easy going floating those carcasses back down the river. Some places the river bed fanned out, and with the water spread out across the width of the river bed there was not enough depth to float the rafts. We would drag and pull and strain to move the load, painter ropes digging deep into our hands as we tried to get them going. In other places it was nice and deep and fast flowing, but just when everything seemed to be progressing well the raft would hang up in a log jam. The pressure of water would start forcing everything down into the branches. Then the ropes slinging the load would get snagged way down deep inside the jam. You could fight and struggle and pull and heave to your hearts desire, but once they were hooked up like that there was nothing left for it but to start unloading and carrying the carcasses ashore one by one. Then half way through this operation the load would suddenly become buoyant enough to spring back out from the log jamb... just as you were walking away from it with a soggy wet deer in your arms. And away it would go, racing off downstream with you charging after it with your soggy wet carcass still in your arms, and the rest of the load left behind half a mile back upstream still sitting on the river's edge where you had just off loaded it.

By the end of a very full and tiring day, we made it back down to Sika Flat with our loads of waterlogged venison carcasses and after a good solid meal we crawled into our sleeping bags and absolutely crashed for the night.

A couple of days later we were back in the Waipakihi once more, brimming over with enthusiasm and rearing to go. Miserable runty sized deer aside, neither of us had ever before seen anything quite like this for easy meat shooting.

Now that we had a much better idea of what the valley was like, we were able to plan things more efficiently. It seemed highly unlikely that we would reap much off the flats we had so recently shot, although we believed that there could still be the odd deer coming out onto them. The map indicated there were still quite a few open flats between where we had left off and Thunderbolt Creek, which was some ten miles upstream from our Sika Flat base camp. So to work it to the best advantage, we decided to get away from Sika Flat early enough to cruise the lower reaches in the late hours of the afternoon and by the time we reached unshot country it should be just about right timing for the evening shot. There was some eight miles of country to cover from the river flat where we had shot the first three deer to Thunderbolt Creek. To allow for possible mess ups and for the gutting of carcasses as we went, we would need to be moving through the first flat a good three hours before last light. We stoked up on a good solid midday meal and got away from Sika Flat nice and early. We hit the first clearing in the late afternoon shadows and were all set to charge through it at a great pace and make tracks for virgin territory. But that didn't quite happen. We had imagined that what with the smell of fresh kills and human scent still hanging round there would not likely be anything out on the first few flats and that was why we were hitting them so early. But here already, a runty little Red was out and browsing the far end of the flat. The only way to get at it without being seen was to stalk through the bush and this meant loss of time. I hung back to reduce the possibility of noise factor spooking it at the last minute, and left it for Bob to close in to where he could get a clear shot away. And with that little task taken care of, away we went once more. Now onto the next clearing, and again another deer.

Our treble-two rifles were brilliant for this sort of shooting. They were light, quiet and deadly accurate. Anything bigger would have had everything spooked off the flats for miles to come with the first

You can run but you won't escape

Thunderbolt Flats (photo by Bob Hannigan)

shot fired. But the muzzle blast from those deadly little .222 bullets hardly carried at all, and this was a major reason why they were such a favoured calibre with cullers and meat shooters alike. You could go from clearing to clearing, popping off animals as you went and the

Thunderbolt Creek (photo by Bob Hannigan)

shooting that had just taken place on one clearing hardly seemed to disturb the animals on the next.

Now we were into the string of river flats and again most every one of them seemed to have anything from one to three deer out browsing. We went like mad, working our way up river into the fading daylight, shooting and gutting as we went, and between us we proved deadly efficient. Nothing seemed to go wrong for us. If there was more than one deer out we would nominate our beast and fire in unison and not one animal escaped back into the bush. Then we ran out of clearings. With hardly any more daylight to our credit we pressed on upstream and in the last vestige of light we came round a final bend in the river and there before us stretched the largest flats of all — Thunderbolt Flats. But already the night was upon us. Last light was gone and if anything happened to be out on Thunderbolt we couldn't even see it. We had shot our way up ten miles of river and bowled 15 deer for the effort.

That night we camped in the monoao and tussock on the lower reaches of Thunderbolt Flats, and early the next morning we were up as first light was just tinting the Kaimanawa skyline, hoping we might catch something out, but there was nothing. Quite likely our scent had been drifting about in the night and spooked the area, but it did not really matter. We already had two full loads of deer awaiting recovery further downstream and, although we had not yet come to fully appreciating it, getting what we had out from the upper reaches of where we had left off the previous night was going to be work enough.

Perhaps the most striking thing we had noticed about Thunderbolt Flats was the potential for putting in an airstrip and freezer. All you needed was 300 yards for the strip and clearance either end for approach and take-off. Thunderbolt seemed to have all that and more. With such easy shooting and so many deer about the thought of it got me all worked up and the more we talked about it the more interested I became. The Waipakihi had more the features of a South Island river than any I had ever before hunted in the North Island... the beech forest rising to tussock tops, the open river flats, the numbers of deer, the hunt-ability of it. Hauling our way downstream, dragging our tractor tubes loaded with venison, I kept dwelling on the thought of it. The sun had still not left the morning sky before I had determined to pursue the matter further.

One of our acquaintances, Tom Sunnex from Raurimu, was taking flying lessons. He would more than likely jump at the chance to get in a few extra hours flying us into the Waipakihi. I would get him to take us over the Umukarikari Range from Rangipo, drop down through the head of the Waipakihi to Thunderbolt Flat, buzz the area a few times to check it out, and if all looked good I would then telephone

Rex Giles to see if Consolidated Traders would be interested in putting in a freezer if we levelled a strip.

Although we had travelled and hunted about ten miles of river from Sika Flat to Thunderbolt Flats, because we had shot nothing off Thunderbolt, nor within a mile or so prior to it, we did not have carcasses to drag all that distance on the return. But we probably had about eight miles to drag. And those eight miles eventually translated into two days of hand blistering hard yakker. The idea of the tractor tubes was to make light work of it by floating the carcasses back to the Land Rover. But where we were starting from there simply was not enough water in the river for getting underway.

The first couple of miles were the worst, with long shallow stretches of water spread across wide expanses of gravel and stone river bed, and not enough water flowing over the stones to float the rafts. We dragged, and hauled, and burned our hands with the ropes, and wore raw blisters into our fingers trying to make ground.

While it is true there was not much weight on our rafts to begin with, that is not much consolation when you are trying to drag what you've got over protruding stones. And as we made headway down the river, adding carcasses to our loads as we went, they got progressively heavier while at the same time the volume in the river was not increasing in proportion to the increasing displacement of the loads. We were adding deer quicker than the side creeks were adding water, and for the first few hours the going seemed to be getting tougher as

We were adding deer to our rafts quicker than the side creeks were adding water

the day drew on.

We were well aware that we could have made it easier for ourselves weight-wise if we had split our loads and recovered the carcasses in two goes, but really that was not an option. The mere thought of having to laboriously pump up those tractor tubes even one more time with that piddly little hand pump crushed that idea like a rotten egg well before it hatched. Instead, we struggled on, slipping and sliding on slippery river boulders, dragging and hauling our way slowly downstream, forever searching out deeper channels in which to float the rafts.

Easier going

The long painters we had attached to our rafts served two purposes: For dragging the rafts over the shallows, and for maintaining some semblance of control when they got moving in the current. Generally speaking however, once a loaded raft got picked up in a turbulent channel of water there was no stopping it. For awhile there you could run alongside whooping and hollering in the shallower water, having lots of fun bouncing over boulders while hanging onto the rope. But when it really started to pick up speed and take you with it you were left with two choices. First, you could hang on to the rope and maybe break your ankle before getting dragged into the current with it, or else you could simply let go and let it work its own way out. If you are ever doing this sort of river work and you decide to take the first option of hanging on to the rope, I would strongly recommend that first you tie the rope firmly around your neck. With a broken ankle you will need both hands free for flailing the water as you get dragged under. The second option probably made more sense from a survival point of view. Trouble was that often as not these fast channels ended up in a log jamb and that was where the next set of problems got their beginning.

Actually, there was a third option, and this one was by far and away more fun than all the others put together. While manoeuvring the raft into the channel and before things got out of control with the raft taking off with a mind of its own, you jumped aboard and went with the load. Once again, a recommendation… check for log jambs down the far end before hopping aboard. Having to make a split second life or death decision whether to abandon ship in mid stream while bouncing violently over big slippery goolies, or get strained through the jagged branches of a log jamb at fifty miles an hour takes much of the fun out of it.

Riding the raft through a deep pool

An hour before last light that first day of recovery, we still had a long way to go and it was obvious we were not going to make it. Bruised, battered and torn, we dragged our rafts out onto the side of the river, tethered them to branches and took off downstream for base. It was a strange and peculiarly light feeling, running unencumbered over river boulders without our 500 to 600 pound rafts dragging along behind us. The next day we would be back to further punish our already agonizing hands and bodies as we dragged and fought our way through the last few miles of alternating shallows, log jambs and deep swirling pools.

Even if they were not very impressive with regard to size, it looked good driving into town with a trailer stacked full of deer carcasses. A few questions were tossed in our direction as to where we were getting them and a bit of guess work was bandied about, but with all that water still sloshing about in our brains, neither of us could remember a single thing. The facts would leak out soon enough, but first we hoped to tie the area up and get Rex Giles to agree to giving us a freezer.

The airstrip idea on Thunderbolt Flat looked promising. After buzzing it a few times Tom Sunnex reckoned it was marginal, but he thought it might possibly work, although he was not over confident about the clearance on the down stream end of the flat. That all sounded pretty positive to us. Compared to some of the strips I had seen down south, there was heaps of room with ample clearance to spare. I could see that a good downdraft just as you were getting airborne with a load up might create its moments. But I did not think a little thing like that was worth getting all het up about. Too much worry never was conducive to floating good ideas.

Rex Giles sounded quite accommodating when I phoned him. He said I had rung at an opportune time and invited me down to Wellington to join him and one of his German venison buyers for lunch at his Thorndon residence the following day. Things were starting to shape up.

Business dinners with Giles were a formal affair of ties, suits and cufflinks, waited on by courteous members of the household. His residence was a fine old Victorian era home a mere stone's throw from Parliament Buildings, where he expended much of his time and energy (eventually with resounding success) lobbying the government of the day to legalize deer farming. Original oil paintings hung on the walls and the Giles' family tartan carpeted the floors. One, so fresh from the hills, tended to speak in hushed tones in such surroundings.

Rex, always the man of many words, soon directed the conversation away from hunting, shooting and venison recovery, and for about 30 minutes flat, expounded his hypothesis regarding the harvesting of a brand new untapped product for New Zealand — Paua meat. This was the spring of 1967, and no one had ever done it before. Rex had landed a French contract to supply something like 15 tonnes of meat and he was looking for someone whom he could finance into organising it. He had determined that the place to establish the fledgling industry was the Chatham Islands. According to Rex, the community at Waitangi would welcome the industry as a source of employment, and the waters there were simply teeming with the shell fish just waiting to be scooped up and shipped away. "There's millions of dollars, just sitting on the rocks, waiting for someone to go and pick them up!" Rex stated. I drove back out to my mother's home in Raumati, and stayed awake half the night thinking about it.

First thing next morning I was on the telephone to Giles, asking him if he could tell me more.

"I was expecting your call," he said when he heard my voice. "My secretary, Mrs Mouton, has already pencilled you in for morning tea at the office."

Things, once more, were not working out quite as expected!

CHAPTER 20

Deep South

Rex Giles had quite categorically stated that he was not prepared to drop a freezer into the Waipakihi. Some years back he had passed through the area with one of his mates and even then the deer were noticeably stunted. He believed we had struck it at just the right time for catching the deer out on the flats and as a result gained a false impression of the area. Beneath the beech forest that clad the valley slopes, the feed was of poor quality and there was not much of it. With the first signs of spring growth on the valley floor the deer were out in force.

"In a very short time," he said, "the spring growth will be gone and so will the deer."

Quite likely what Giles said was correct, but all that aside he was not willing to drop in a freezer because simply put, he did not want me in the Waipakihi He wanted me in the Chatham Islands.

Bob was somewhat philosophical about this new turn of events. He had scraped together enough money from the sale of unexportable furs to Rodney, supplemented with the deer carcasses he had sold to Charlie, to sufficiently raise his capital to where he could buy that Land Rover he had so eagerly pursued. And he still had enough good skins left over to make up a consignment for London thus assuring himself of some working capital to be gained from the February auction to get himself started on the next season's traps. We shot through to Hamilton and at Moller Motors he found just what he was looking for — a 1963 LWB cab and well-side Land Rover truck with a solid canopy built over the back that would be ideal for both sleeping in and carting his hunting and trapping gear around the country.

So from Bob's point of view it was merely a matter of reverting to Plan number One. We dismantled the tent camp in the Whangapeki and I bundled Gladdy, Myrtle and Pork Chop onto the back of the trailer and took off to Atiamuri where Ken Dunham, one of my old deer culling mates was now living on his old man's farm. Unfortunately, Pork Chop was due to become just that. I guessed Myrtle would probably end up as "Roast Myrtle". As for Gladdy; there were wild goats over the back of the farm, and I didn't think the Dunhams would mind if I liberated her amongst them. As long as she kept her head down she had even chances of not becoming a dog tucker.

Back at Pokaka, Bob loaded up his Land Rover and headed off down country in the general direction of Whiterock Station and the Haurangi Mountains.

I hung around Pokaka only long enough to finish drying off the ears on my skins, and then I too abandoned the camp and headed for Wellington. Sorting out the shipping arrangements for the furs was the first thing on my list and after that I was ready to head south. Rex Giles was still negotiating with his French buyers and he doubted things would be underway prior to autumn. That gave me plenty of time to check out a few things for myself.

For some reason beknown only to himself, Rex was set on the idea that this new industry could be launched from no other place than the Chathams. From what I had heard, the shell of Chatham Islands paua was not thick and heavy enough for crafting into quality jewellery and therefore it was not in demand. The shell from Fiordland and Stewart Island, though, was. I already knew that it grew to an excellent size and was thick heavy shell with deep rich colour. Giles had no interest in harvesting shell. Nor did he have any interest in my harvesting it; a moot point which I considered somewhat short sighted on his behalf. Giles was a venison man, and in that industry everything was taken; meat, skins, velvet, sinews, tails, pizzles, bladders, embryo, slinks, the lot. So I could not quite understand where he was coming from harbouring an aversion to capitalizing on something as valuable as the shell, along with the meat. Possibly he may have reasoned that my interest would tend to focus on the shell rather than the meat and this would detract from his objective. Be that as it may, if I was going to involve myself in harvesting meat I would also be involving myself in harvesting shell. And with that thought firmly in mind I booked passage on the Cook Strait ferry and made tracks for the deep south.

Mrs Joey D ran a bed and breakfast men's boarding house in Bluff which catered for a broad spectrum of passing traffic; freezing workers coming and going, fishermen waiting for boats, seamen missed their ship, salesmen selling goods, flotsam and jetsam doing little or nothing and the occasional alky drying out.

It was Milford "The Skull" Waitiri, who was temporarily back in Bluff from up the Fiordland Coast because his ship had slipped its shaft off the entrance to Caswell Sound, who suggested the only place in Bluff worth staying was booked into Mrs Joey D's fine establishment. And coming up forty years down the track, I still remember the place with the sort of memories for which I should be forever grateful to Milford for having suggested it.

Breakfast was served between six and eight — porridge in a huge black pot simmering on the wood range, going "Plop! Plop! Plop!" sort of like a Rotorua mud pool. It was the type of porridge that stuck to your ribs, once you got it unstuck from your teeth And if you ate all your porridge then you could have a choice of fried black sausage and hard cooked eggs swimming in dripping, or fried pink sausage and hard cooked eggs swimming in dripping. Toast just kept coming. Bread was cheap at four cents a loaf and butter was subsidised by the Government so it didn't matter. Coffee was Gregg's Coffee and Chicory Essence stewing on the range in a king sized jug. And tea was a couple of hefty handfuls of Broken Orange Pekoe tea leaves stewing alongside in a king sized kettle. "Good morning, luv. Sleep well last night? Help yourself to the porridge. And don't forget to say your grace!" Actually the breakfasts were nowhere near as bad as they may sound, they were in fact considerably worse.

Perhaps my fondest memory was of a particular alky who never seemed to work out just where the toilet was. One morning I was greeted with a disgusting explosion of bowel motion all over the floor of the bathroom, another time he completely missed the toilet bowl and managed to deposit the doings between the skirting and the bowl. But even Mrs Joey D had enough the morning her maid went in to tidy his room and found the proverbial doings neatly deposited in a drawer of his dresser. I think she felt bad about evicting the man, because as she put it, "He must be a very sick man, luv! But one can take only so much when one is catering for others in the house." And just so as I would not judge our good landlady harshly for evicting the fine gentleman, Mrs Joey D had me accompany her down the hall to the said bedroom and without forewarning me what I was about to see ushered me into the room and there was the doings, smelling like nothing on earth and looking resplendent in their drawer, which all but had me throwing up to add to the mess. So much for staying in men's boarding houses. And may the good Lord bless Milford "The Skull" Waitiri for suggesting it!

Clifford Skeggs was in the throes of building an oyster factory on the wharf at Bluff, and when he heard that I was looking for a job on a cray fishing boat, and I was also a qualified carpenter, he wasted no time making contact. Carpenters were few and far between and the oyster factory had to be finished in time for the opening of the next oyster season somewhere round March. I did not really want work as a carpenter, but agreed to help him out on the basis of a promise. He was expecting the arrival of some cray fishing boats within the next couple of weeks. They were then going to be sent to the Chatham Islands and he promised to give me a job crewing on one of them.

There were only four of us working on the factory at the time. Skeggsy was a good bloke and he offered us a good flat rate for our efforts. Three of us were freelancers and had never belonged to a union in our lives. The fourth bloke was the local labour union rep, and his sole objective in life was to sit on his chuff and do nothing while stirring up mud and encouraging everyone to go on strike and demand more pay. I could not hack this bloke and his despicable attitude. When he learned that I was not a union member and what was more nor did I have any intention of ever becoming one, he started reading the riot act: The job would be blacklisted! Skeggs would be closed down for employing non union carpenters! He would see that the other blokes downed their tools! And even the wharfies would be called out on strike! Then he learned that the other two blokes were the same as me. Next day Mr Union was gone and we never heard from him again. Clifford Skeggs thanked all three of us and shook us all heartily by the hand.

There wasn't much to do in Bluff at the end of a good day's work other than go hang out at the pub over a jug of beer. They was a good bunch used to hang out in the pub. One occasion some bloke hove-to alongside me and my drinking mate of the moment and next thing I hear him saying that he was going to subpoena my mate into court. Worked out my mate was in trouble. He and someone else had scuttled a ship after stealing the catch and selling it privately. Divers had checked the wreck and found the freezer, which was meant to be full of fish, was empty. This other bloke, who had been one of the crew, had somehow ended up taking the rap regarding the loss of the ship and he was now planning retribution.

Bluff was full of crooks. Freezing workers meant to lock up the wagons and chillers at Ocean Beach tended to forget this little triviality and more meat went out the back door than went to London by sea. There was always cheap meat could be picked up round town, and the butchers and chain men slept with the fishermen's wives while the fishermen were away at sea. The place was a den of thieves and it amazed me it was only sheep got their throats cut round town.

After about two weeks of this sort of carry on three clapped out looking fishing boats turned up alongside the wharf, and just where Clifford Skeggs managed to scrape them up from I have no idea. They were pretty ratchety looking ships. It was only some 300 or so miles out into the Roaring Forties where the Chatham Islands lay. Skeggs was short of a skipper for one of the boats and on the basis that I had spent part of the previous summer as third hand on Robbie Ballantyne's floating telephone booth, the "Tarawai", I was now asked to be it.

"You've never used a sextant! Doesn't make much difference. You can read a compass, can't you? Weather looks good and anyway you'll be in sight of one another all the time. All you have to do is stick with the other two boats, and before you know it you will be there."

Crayfishing was absolutely booming in the Chathams. Someone

had done a trawl across the bay at Waitangi and he somehow managed to get his net fouled up on something. When he finally got it winched in he found it had not been fouled at all, but it was jam packed with migrating crayfish. And so the gold rush began. Skeggsy was buying up anything that would stay afloat and packing it off to where the red gold was being hauled in by the ton.

I still was not over fussed about going to the Chathams but here was a chance to get in on the act and check out just what it was that so impressed Giles about the place. I was packing my bags to go when a phone call came through for me from Milford Sound. Chasey Edwards was holed up in Freshwater Basin without a crew. Word had got around that I was sitting it out in Bluff looking for a job and Chasey asked if I could come and join him straight away. Chasey was working pots down Dusky Sound. So here was my big chance to check out the quality of real Fiordland paua along with their shell. Skeggsy did not want to see me leave. Finding good chippies who were willing to work on oyster factories was hard enough. It was even harder finding inexperienced men foolish enough to sign on as skippers on dunger fishing boats and skippering them across 300 miles of open storm tossed sea to the Chatham Islands. Apparently I was one of a rare breed.

Fiordland had been in storm mode for about two weeks. Gale force winds and lashing rains were whipping up tumultuous seas from a huge depression lying deep to the south and ships were battened down and securely fastened to their moorings. No one was going anywhere. Half way down the Cleddau Valley a side creek had taken out a small bridge and then cut a huge swathe through the road making it completely impassable. Thick cloud swaddled the bush just a few hundred feet above sea level eliminating any possibility of access in or out by air. Tourists stranded in Milford with cruise ships to catch in Auckland were offering fistfuls of money to anyone who could get them out of this godforsaken hole. The pub was out of beer and for the past week Chasey and his mates had been sitting on the top shelf, getting more belligerent by the hour. When the road was eventually reopened, it was because the army had been called in to lay a Bailey bridge across the chasm and defuse the situation amongst a snarling bunch of red eyed fishermen who were on the verge of tearing one another apart. The first emergency rations rushed across the Bailey bridge was a load of beer destined for the Milford Pub. I followed in my Land Rover soon after.

Chasey was very pleased to see me.

"We'll be heading off down the Coast first thing in the morning," he announced to his mates sitting round a large table freshly sploshed with beer.

"You're crazy, Chasey," I remember one of them saying. "You can't go out there in this weather."

"I can, and I will," replied Chasey. "Now my mate's turned up there is no reason why I should hang out any longer with you bunch of piss-heads."

In even the worst of storms there are sheltered anchorages to be found deep in the fiords of South Westland; small islands to hide behind, jutting points, hidden coves and sheltered bays nestled in amongst the cliffs. Storms never last, so there is not a great deal of reason to go charging out into the thick of one. Freshwater Basin, tucked away as it is in the very head of Milford Sound, is a well sheltered harbour that has the added attraction of being a roadhead where boats can be re-provisioned, and a pub where fishermen can

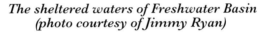

The sheltered waters of Freshwater Basin
(photo courtesy of Jimmy Ryan)

get sloshed. There was not much question as to whether my skipper liked getting sloshed. Just about every painting that was ever done and every postcard and calendar photo that was ever took featuring Freshwater Basin with Mitre Peak shimmering in the background, also featured Chasey Edwards' ship, the "Victor Hugo", riding at anchor close to Cemetery Point. While everyone else was gone fishing, my good skipper was still in the pub, getting sloshed. So why he chose the thick of a violent storm to up anchor and away can only be attributed to a foul mood from drinking too much whisky and not enough beer. Once we were out in the thick of it, Chasey actually admitted as much to me, but to his mates he said: "By the time the weather clears I will already be down Dusky lifting my pots, and you bunch will still be sitting here in the pub wondering what day it is."

Gusts of wind were swirling through the fiord as we made our way towards open waters. Much of Milford Sound, with its relatively narrow passage and sheer cliff faces rising abruptly from the brackish waters, is well protected from winds, but as we neared Dale Point just prior to turning out into more open water, the wind started to pick up and with it the sea. Visibility, which had been far from good from the word "Go!" now started to close in on us. Rounding the point and heading past Anita Bay towards Saint Anne Point and the open sea, there wasn't much left to see other than rain lashing the wheel house glass and spray crashing over the foredeck as the rising seas thumped into the port bow. By now our ship was heading nor'west and we were still in sheltered waters with a fair sized headland protecting us off to our port beam. Just up ahead though, all hell would break loose when we cleared Saint Anne Point and turned sou'west directly into the storm.

I had gotten to know Chasey, a little bit, my previous summer while cray fishing with Ballantyne. It was said that he was a hard little man and I had heard that he was not that easy to get along with. But he also had a reputation for being a very capable skipper who knew what his ship could handle, and a good fisherman who knew how to catch crayfish. He was short, irascible, and he chain smoked foul smelling hand rolled soagies that had the wheel house smelling worse than a Chinese brothel. Every finished cigarette must have held fond memories for Chasey, because he kept an old rusting tin close by on the instrument panel overflowing with maturing dribble stained butts that he seemed loathe to tip over the side. So we not only had a foul storm to plug into; we also had a foul wheel house to ride it out in. We were heading for Deep Cove at the head of Doubtful Sound some hours away, and under these conditions quite some hours away.

Chasey was pressed hard up against the helm, holding on firmly with two hands. The "Victor Hugo" had a fairly large wooden wheel and its brass rim was highly polished from the continual rubbing against his woollen clothing. The wheel house was asphyxiating and we had been plugging slowly sou'west for about three hours. There was nothing to see but foam, green water, huge seas and white out conditions all around us. No coast line, no birds; nothing but a compass veering about 10 degrees either side of sou'west or thereabouts, as we pitched and tossed and Chasey Edwards pressed up against the helm holding the ship into the storm with another dribble doused soagie hanging off his nicotine stained lip. There wasn't much for me to do other than feel crook from the bad air, but I knew Chasey would welcome a hot cup of tea if I went below and made one.

"Yeah, that's a good idea," he said. "Make a few sandwiches too. And you might as well stay down below until it's ready."

Without realizing that Chasey had his reasons for wanting me out of the wheelhouse, I took off down below glad to be out of it.

An hour or so later, with the sandwiches all gone, Chasey said there wasn't much reason why I should hang out in the wheelhouse, and I might as well go back down below and lie down for awhile. It was still some way to go so I might as well go have a sleep.

I do not know how long I was down in the cabin, but when I came back up, nothing much had changed. We were still plugging into the same violent storm, the cabin still reeked of tobacco smoke and Chasey said: "We'll be turning into Thompson Sound in twenty minutes from now."

"How can he know that?" I wondered to myself. Actually, as the day had progressed and the weather had not improved, and the white-out conditions had continued, and there was no landmarks or anything to bear from, I had wondered whether Chasey was able to work out where we were from the use of a watch, a compass and dead reckoning. It was a bit disconcerting thinking about it, but I preferred not to broach the subject.

Exactly twenty minutes later, Chasey altered course from sou'west to sou'east, and with the seas now pounding our starboard beam we ploughed on across the waves. Then slowly the dark shape of looming cliffs started to appear through the murk, and then foam crashing on huge coastal rocks, and without altering a whisker on the compass suddenly the "Victor Hugo" was in the narrow confines of Thompson Sound. Just like that the waves dropped away to nothing. The wind was shrieking down the sound between Secretary Island and the mainland creating streaks of froth in long lines on the surface of the water but, with no more open sea in which to build themselves up, the waves were completely gone. So after so many hours of plugging head on into such a violent storm, with nothing but a compass to work by, how did Chasey know that "in exactly twenty minutes" he would be turning smack into the narrow opening of Thompson Sound? I wished I had never asked him.

The reason he wanted me down below was he didn't want me freaking out while he was probing in amongst the coastal surf and rocks trying to find a land mark that he recognized. Three times he had gone and gotten in amongst the white water trying to figure it all out. The "Victor Hugo" was 49 feet long, with 14 feet of beam and 8 feet of draught so she was quite a cumbersome piece of equipment to be poking round in amongst the white water in those sort of conditions. With me down below, I would not have had much of a chance if he had clipped a rock. I would never have even gotten out of the cabin before the ship went down. But then I suppose that if the ship had clipped a rock and tipped over, even if I had been up top in the wheelhouse with Chasey, neither of us would have survived being dashed on the jagged coastal rocks anyway. And the other alternative to all of this was not finding our landfall before dark and maybe ending up on the rocks anyway. Now I fully understood why his mates back in Milford had told him he was crazy for leaving the refuge of Freshwater Basin and heading out into this storm.

With sheets of rain still pelting down and the wind shrieking in our rigging, cruising the twenty or so miles up Thompson, into Doubtful and then on to the head of Malaspina Reach in dead flat seas seemed a little unreal after the pounding we had just endured out there in that cold, green Tasman Sea.

We tied up in Deep Cove, opposite the "MV Wanganella," the old Huddart Parker Trans Tasman passenger liner that was seeing out its final days as a floating hostel for the Italian contractors working on the Lake Manapouri tail race project. As a little fellow, growing up in Wellington, I could remember sitting on the hillside with my great aunt and uncle, along with crowds of other sightseers, overlooking Breaker Bay and out into Cook Strait, eating pickled cucumber sandwiches, while salvagers worked around the clock trying to free this same old ship off Barrett Reef. I was just a little wee bloke at the time. The year was 1947 and I was only five years old. But I clearly remember it was well understood that if the weather turned bad the ship was lost. After about a week of unprecedented calm seas and frantic effort they eventually pulled her free on a high tide and dragged her up the Wellington harbour to safety, and almost as they were doing it, the weather broke and a violent storm burled through Cook Strait lashing the southern coastline with ferocious winds that would certainly have put paid to that lovely old ship. The "Wanganella" had been part and parcel of my growing up. From childhood to teens, from where I lived up above the harbour on the Miramar Heights, I had watched this fine old lady plying back and forth as she came and went between Wellington and Sydney. She had brought my grandfather to visit, and she had returned him to his home in Bondi, Now, in her dying days, almost as if in a parting gesture, she offered us a final kindness. At the end of a punishing trip down the Coast, coated with salt and stinking from Chasey's revolting second hand tobacco smoke, we were able to go aboard the "Wanganella" and enjoy the luxury of a steaming hot shower. I never saw the old "Wanganella" again. From Deep Cove, she sailed to Hong Kong where she was broken down for scrap.

Chasey was in a surly mood when he awoke the next morning. The storm was almost done and, Chasey said, so was he.

"I've had a guts full," he said. "This storm and the trip down the Coast were the last straw as far as I am concerned. All my gear will be gone. My pots were out in the sea off Dusky and after this battering there won't be anything left of them. I'm going to head back to Bluff and pull the boat out for the rest of the season. You can get a ride out on the works bus over the Wilmot Pass."

"Are you serious?" I asked. "Do you mean to tell me that you had me drive all the way from Bluff to Milford, and chuck in my only chance of getting to the Chathams, just to drag me down the Coast in this stinking storm and then tell me that you are signing me off before we have even got started?"

"I can't help that," said Chasey. "I've had enough and that's all there is to it. I'll pay your sea time for the trip down the Coast, and your bus fare back into Milford to where I signed you on."

The bus trip over the Wilmot Pass through swirling cloud, windows all steamed up and nothing to see, jamb packed with excitable gesturing Italians all smoking their disgusting cigarillos and cheroots was even worse than being enclosed in Chasey's wheelhouse on a storm tossed sea with him and his foul smelling soagies for company. But now I was moving on and at this stage I probably would not have gone back to work for Chasey even had he asked me. I was hopping mad at this new turn of events. And after the way he had just mucked me up I did not really care if I never saw him again; which I didn't.

The boat trip down Lake Manapouri to the Te Anau highway in a closed-in Fiordlander type of launch, packed to overflowing with a new contingent of tobacco puffing Italians who joined us at the head of the lake, was even more claustrophobic than the bus ride over the Wilmot Pass. I could only imagine that these bunch of Dago's were so used to breathing grit and dust and fumes tucked away in their tunnels under the ground, they simply did not like fresh air. Where they were all going, I had no idea. But I was glad to get off the ferry and see the end of them My maternal grandmother was an Italian. She was a very short little lady. As children, we were warned that smoking stunts your growth. I do not remember my grandmother smoking, but if all Italians smoked like this bunch, I could well understand why my grandmother was barely 5 foot tall.

I was not really sure what I was going to do now that I had blown my chance with the Chathams, and Chasey had screwed-up for me with regards to Dusky. There was still the better part of the summer ahead of me and I had nowhere in particular to go. Then I ran into Dale Hunter and Kevin Hallett in Te Anau.

Kevin had taken over George Wyber's meat shooting block in the Lower Pyke after George had killed himself when he crashed his plane in the Harris Saddle, flying between the Alabaster strip and Queenstown. Then Kevin had nearly killed himself when he flipped his jet boat trying to negotiate the McKerrow Bar at Martins Bay. Kevin had little experience with jet boats and none at all with the treacherous McKerrow Bar that is formed where the Lower Hollyford River pours out of Lake McKerrow into the Tasman Sea. Dale had previously crossed the bar several times and he knew that you had to tuck in between the waves racing towards the shore and at the same time prepare to meet the rip that comes tumbling out from the Hollyford estuary. Once committed to a trough between two breaking waves there was no turning back and no second shot if you goofed. Dale led the way with his jet boat and got safely through, but Kevin did not make it.

There were two "unfortunates" and two "fortunates" that resulted from all of this. Kevin could not swim, so he was very fortunate that he somehow got caught up in a large wave and got smashed onto the rocks where he clung like a limpet while the now receding wave, unable to drag him back into the rip sucked his socks off his feet. Unfortunately the socks got lost in the surf. The second, and I suppose greater, "unfortunate" was that his brand new Hamilton jet boat and all his hunting gear were never seen again. But everything was insured and so fortunately he was able to re-established himself with a another brand new Hamilton jet and an all new outfit of hunting equipment from his insurance claim. I happened to arrive in Te Anau just as Dale and Kevin were preparing to leave for their next attempt at the McKerrow Bar, reprovisioned with Kevin's new hunting equipment.

Before taking off, Dale mentioned that Ray "Huck" Finn was in town getting his jet boat fixed up. He had cracked the engine block and was having it stitched up. And while he was in town waiting for the repairs to be done, he was looking for a hunting mate to go work the Hollyford with him.

"Why don't you look him up?" Dale suggested. "He's staying with his mate Retford, out at Te Anau Downs Station."

CHAPTER 21

The Meat Shooters

Ray "Huckleberry" Finn was one of the few really good meat shooters of the day who had never worked as a Government deer culler. Just about every other top man in the industry had, at some time or other, been employed as a shooter either with the 'Old Firm' of Department of Internal Affairs Deer Cullers, or with the N.Z. Forest Service where, because of the broader variety of hunting they were employed in, they were often referred to as Government Shooters. Some of the best known names in the industry had gotten started as North Island bush hunters and then worked their way south, where they quickly became top tally men once they were let loose in the vast valleys and open tops of the South Island. Huck had been neither a North Island bush hunter nor a South Island deer culler, but he was good, regardless. He used to drive me to distraction with it. We would both pile into my Land Rover and drop into the Upper Hollyford from the Eglinton for an afternoon's bush stalking.

"Drop me off here," Huck would say. "I'll be waiting back here on the side of the road for you in about an hour from now. But there's no need to rush. Just take your time."

Huck would disappear into the forest, heading in the general direction of a fuschia grove he had spotted from the Land Rover, and I would take off down the valley going like mad to find my own fuschia grove before the inevitable shot from Huck's rifle got everything for miles around on edge and effectively eliminated any further chances of an easy deer for that afternoon. I would site my block of fuschia, come to a screaming halt in a shower of gravel and dust, grab my treble two, take off into the bush in the general direction, and just as the first strong smell of deer reached my nostrils, there would be one, maybe two, concussing thumps from up the valley, followed by echoes rolling and ricocheting off the valley walls. Pigeons would take off in alarm, kakas and keas would start screeching abuse, and anything that might have had its head down nibbling herbage would now be fully alert and already heading for higher ground. Huck always had a head start on me, getting to his patch, and that may have had some bearing on it. But working in the same close area with a bush hunter who is a darned site better than you are is frustrating to the extreme. That was Huck and me!

Up until about the time we teamed up, Ray had been the proud owner of a "tricky" Trekka, as he called it; a harebrained sort of a vehicle that someone in their wildest dreams had proposed as New Zealand's affordable answer to Jeeps and Land Rovers. Anyway, it only took one decent load of carcasses off Te Anau Downs Station to turn the transverse springs of Ray's "tricky' Trekka inside out and break its back. The "tricky" Trekka ended up on the scrap heap out the back of the Fiordland Venison factory and Ray and I were in business together, me driving us to the hunting grounds and him shooting all the deer.

I was not over keen getting myself into these demoralizing sort of situations, taking on joint ventures such as this, but Huck had no transport and I was helping him out until such time as his jet boat was ready to go. After that, we would tow his boat through the Homer tunnel to Milford Sound and head off round the coast to work his block, in another 'joint venture', in the Lower Hollyford.

Ray 'Huck' Finn's meat shooting block took in the Hollyford Valley from Martins Bay to the Hollyford Rapids, or thereabouts. In reality, National Parks Board hunting block boundaries were not of the utmost importance in this business, unless you happened to be poaching someone else's block, or worse still, someone else happened to be poaching yours. Accessibility was more of a delineating factor than comments written on hunting permits and lines drawn on maps. When you were working from a jet boat, your block ended somewhere about the limit of negotiable water plus a reasonable margin beyond. The 'reasonable margin beyond' being the extremities of your deer dragging capabilities, regardless of whether the permit said so or not. So from that point of view, if not the Park Board's more official boundaries, that was about the extent of Ray Finn's block.

There was a lot of weight in Ray's jet boat the morning we launched it into Fresh Water Basin. All his and all my hunting equipment to last out the rest of the summer; clothes, rifles, ammunition, sacks of potatoes and onions, fresh vegetables, a huge roll of bacon, a few dozen eggs, cartons of tinned and dry goods, powdered milk, sugar, salt, tea, coffee, spare fuel for the boat, white spirits for the hut lamps. There was enough food and supplies to keep us going until Southern Scenic's meat plane was called in to uplift our first load of meat, and more to spare in case of an emergency or extended bad weather closing in on us.

Just ten months or so earlier, I had watched a couple of my meat shooting mates doing this trip in reverse, arriving in Fresh Water Basin from the Hollyford, and I reckoned they were incredibly foolish risking their lives out there in the open Tasman Sea in such small and vulnerable little boats. Nothing had really changed in the interim. But there was only one way to get a jet boat into the Lower Hollyford, and this was it. We took off down Milford Sound, straining to get up on the plane with the weight inside the hull pulling us back. Riding so low on the water, somewhat lower than the Plimsoll line of a regular ship, the waters of the fiord somehow looked deeper and darker, the surrounding cliffs loomed menacingly taller than when viewed from up on the deck of a sturdy 50 foot fishing vessel.

The weather was fairly settled, but only a couple of weeks earlier Chasey Edwards and I had ventured out through these same waters into an incredibly violent storm in the fishing vessel, "Victor Hugo", and I well knew just what the open waters beyond the shelter of the fiords could dish up. From Dale Point, at the mouth of Milford Sound, to the McKerrow Bar, at the northern end of Martins Bay, a little more than twenty miles of open sea stretched before us with nowhere to run to if something went wrong along the way.

That was food enough for thought in itself. But there was something else that got me thinking once we were well out to sea. Actually we were about a mile off the coast a little north of the Kaipo River with huge ocean swells following us, then overtaking us. We were ploughing along at about 18 knots with the throttle just about full open, and the ocean swells were racing to shore faster than we were. One minute we would be riding up the back of a swell and the next minute that one would be gone and we would be surfing down the face of the following one. We were both hollering and yahooing and having a ball... until a sobering thought suddenly crossed my mind.

"Hey, Ray! How fast do you reckon these waves are travelling?" I yelled, above the roar of the engine

"About 27 knots," he replied.

"How fast can this jet boat go?" I asked.

"About 21 flat out... when she's not loaded down."

"That's what I thought. So how are we going to get in between two of these waves and stay there without one of them overtaking us and swamping us as we go in through the bar?"

"Don't worry," said Ray. "The waves slow down when they get closer to the shore."

"I never knew that," I replied. "I hope you're right."

"Yeah, you'll see!"

With the treacherous McKerrow bar looming ever closer and the ocean swells taking on great curling surfing proportions as they thundered towards the coastline, I could hardly wait "to see".

Now, a long line of spray and foam was whipping off the crest of huge waves just up ahead. Even over the roar of the engine, you could hear the waves hissing and thundering their way into Martins Bay, sucking sand off the spit in their undertow and dumping it back in the following sea. This was not a good time for wearing heavy boots. Quickly we pulled the laces and stowed our boots up for'ard beneath the foredeck.

And the next minute we were in the thick of it. One minute we were out in the open sea with waves overtaking us, the next Ray was yelling over the roar of the engine:

"Here we go!"

Green water suddenly turned to froth beneath the hull and everything seemed to be happening at once. Waves and foam hissed all around us. Now we were deep in a trough, towering seas racing in behind us. At this stage there was no possible turning back. Once committed to a wave you either keep going or you drown. Ray's eyes were fixed dead ahead, holding the boat a steady distance behind the preceding wave. Just astern of us the following sea was now foaming all along its crest and starting to curl as it too became surf. Way in ahead of us a huge cresting wave hurled in against the jagged rocks of Long Reef where Kevin Hallett had clung on for dear life. We would be okay only so long as we maintained our distance between the two waves. Time seemed meaningless as we hung between the crests, edging ever closer towards the coast. Then suddenly the wave ahead seemed to flatten out. There was a sudden cross current of sea and the nose buried deep in an oncoming wave. For a minute we seemed to stand still, engine screaming, boat juddering. Now we were fighting against a rip tide of fresh water burling out from the Hollyford estuary. Water foamed over the prow as we met this new rush of waves head on. This was the treacherous McKerrow Bar proper, where things sometimes went horribly wrong. Ray was holding on tight to the steering, I was white knuckled to the windshield railing as we bumped and bounced violently in the current. But this too lasted but a moment of time. Suddenly we were over the bar and porpoising safely across a series of smaller waves and next thing we were inside the fast flowing waters of the Hollyford estuary.

Well, it had been a bit of anxious moments, a bit of an adrenalin rush, and now that we had made it safely, quite a bit of fun.

There is always an element of risk attached to crossing bars in small craft. Later that same year, another meat shooter, Brian Wysanowski, had a remarkable brush with death when his jet boat overturned on the McKerrow Bar and he ended up clinging to the upturned hull miles out into the Tasman Sea. His mate, Dave Richardson, whose 22 foot double ender boat "Solvick" was also swamped, managed to reach shore and raise the alarm. But to do so he had to run through miles and miles of bush all the way to Gunn's Motor camp some distance beyond the road end in the Upper Hollyford Valley. By now Wysanowski should have been drowned, but through sheer grit and guts he managed to hang on to his upturned boat. For nearly three days he clung there until eventually, well over twenty miles out to sea and far beyond the limits of where it was felt he could have drifted, he was spotted by an Air Force Orion and ultimately rescued by a fishing trawler. Only fools, meat shooters and the sadly misinformed thus risk their lives for the sake of hunting a few deer.

Back in the year 1870, about 1½ miles beyond the Hollyford estuary, along the north eastern shore of Lake McKerrow, a different type of 'sadly misinformed', a small group of pioneers, began hacking the settlement of Jamestown out of dense Fiordland bush. It was supposed that Martins Bay and the Hollyford Valley would become the South Island gateway for trade and settlers arriving from Australia, and Jamestown would become a thriving metropolis. A poorer choice of locality for a township, it would be difficult to find and the project was doomed to disaster before it began. Supply ships failed to turn up with needed food, starvation threatened the pioneers, and eventually after accidents, sickness and tragedy claimed the lives of several of the early settlers and their children, the project was abandoned and the dense Fiordland rain forest rapidly claimed back what the pioneers had worked so hard to gain.

Nothing ever thrived in Jamestown other than the sandflies, and nearly 100 years down the track Jamestown had not changed a smidgen. It was still the same sandfly, mosquito ridden, inhospitable place that it always had been. It was a name on the map but, other

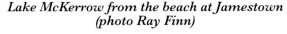

Lake McKerrow from the beach at Jamestown
(photo Ray Finn)

It was not as if we were in danger of starving. Huck alongside the estuary (photo Ray Finn)

than a solitary meat shooter's hut, it did not exist. And what was more, it was still prone to disasters. About a week after we moved into Jamestown, I noticed one or two big fat maggots crawling across the floor beneath the table. At first, I could not figure out where they were coming from. Then I remembered our roll of bacon, supposedly securely wrapped in muslin cloth, hanging from a rafter. Sure enough, a blowfly had found a chink in the muslin and deposited its stinking eggs deep inside the core. A green and putrid seething mass of the little blighters had worked its way right through the middle of our precious bacon completely ruining it. It was not as if we were now in danger of starving to death as those early settlers had been. But from our point of view, it was a disaster nevertheless. After all, what's the point of several cartons of eggs when you've got no bacon!

From a meat shooting point of view, there were better places to call base than Jamestown. But Ray favoured Jamestown as our base for at least two good reasons.

First and foremost, the lake edge adjacent to the hut was ideal for his preferred way of beaching his jet boat. He would come charging into the bay at full tit, engine roaring, foam flying, until he was more or less adjacent to the hut, then from about 50 yards out he would square off straight to the shore. Now came the exciting bit. Throttle full open, up on the plane and almost airborne, we would race straight towards the shore. Jet boats full of hunters and deer carcasses tend to pull up quite quickly when they are suddenly throttled off, so racing head on to shore like this and suddenly throttling off at the last minute would have been lots of fun. But Ray's way of doing it was even better. He just maintained full throttle, and kept it there. One minute we were skimming the waves, next minute we were careering up the beach over gravel and stones, pump turbine screaming as we hurtled into the bush. Ray would calmly flick off the engine as we came to a juddering halt in amongst the foliage, bits of broken branches and leaves all over the superstructure, and we would step out onto dry ground. I sort of gained the impression that Ray was a trifle hard on his gear, but it sure worked wonders for keeping the boots dry.

Ray "Huck" Finn with his jet boat at Jamestown (photo Ray Finn)

His second good reason for preferring Jamestown was to do with air strips. There wasn't one at Jamestown. Which meant we could call in the Southern Scenic float plane to uplift our carcasses and drop off some bread and fresh vegetables. And there wasn't nothing more exciting than watching a float plane sending foam flying as it came and went on the lake even if it was just about twice as expensive as chartering a Cessna 180 on a regular strip. If it was wet and wild and cowboyish, that was all it took to have Ray Huckleberry in his element.

When Bill Hamilton designed the jet boat, it was with charging up rivers in mind. And that is where they are at their best; there and in shallow water where the pump can force a bit of pressure through the

Loading a float plane at Jamestown (photo Ray Finn)

turbines to make them get up and fly. If you come charging out of a river into the deep still waters of a lake, the boat suddenly feels really sluggish in comparison. Ray was demonstrating this for my benefit and approval one day as we came charging out of the estuary into the lake. We burled in close to the shore, hurtled between a large semi submerged log and the lake edge almost exactly where we had hurtled a dozen times before. But this time we must have been just inches either to the left or to the right. There was a horrible crunch under the boat as we were both nearly knocked off our feet and suddenly there was water seeping up through the floor boards.

Ray held the throttle full open to keep the boat up on the plane as I rushed to the stern and whipped out the drainage bung. Now there was somewhere for the water to go other than filling the boat and swamping us. It was not uncommon cracking the underside of a jet boat on boulders and logs, and most blokes kept spare fibre glass cloth and a two pot mix of fibreglass resin for the occasion. In our case, charging round on the plane with the bung out seemed to work quite well, so Huck decided to settle for that. He never did get round to repairing the hull.

In bye-gone years, quite large areas of land around Martins Bay had been cleared of bush then grassed by the McKenzies and Gunns who had settled and grazed cattle there. The cattle were long gone, as were the McKenzies and the Gunns, and now deer ventured out around the bush edges first and last light. I quickly discovered that the deer were not exactly stupid round here. People had been shooting at them for a long time and they knew all about men and guns. As could be expected, they didn't hang around for long once they were spooked.

That was all well and good, but what was not good was the fact that I seemed to be spooking and missing out on more than my share of what should have been relatively easy deer. Somehow I had gotten myself into the thick of a bad run. And from here on nothing seemed to go right. I would be closing the gap on a couple of easy deer in open country when a sudden swirling wind would waft my scent fair up their chuffs. Humans must have a frightful bad odour to make wild animals put to flight the way they do with just the slightest whiff. No amount of regular washing makes the slightest difference. Humans smell bad and that is all there is to it. Okay, so perhaps the wind could be blamed for that one. But there were also the easy shots that I was throwing....

Ray and I came careering down the Hollyford one evening in his jet boat, charging in and out of huge submerged boulders and bouncing in and out of churning rapids at high speed, and as we hurled round a bend in the river, about eighty yards ahead of us two deer took off across a small river flat dodging in and out of the drift wood heading for the bush. Needless to say I clean missed the both of them. Okay, so that was not exactly an easy shot, but it probably looked like it to Ray who had just missed out on his fifty percent of the venison. It was a well known fact of the day, that Errol Brown, one of our mates who was shooting deer for Tim Wallace, maintained an average of about 96 clean head shots out of every 100 deer he shot. And this from a vibrating helicopter bouncing about in turbulent conditions up in the Fiordland tops with the deer on the run and making things difficult for him. In comparison, my record was not stacking up too well.

Once you got started on a bad run, it can quickly get the better of you. If you are missing shots the first thing you should do is set up a target and sight your rifle in to establish exactly where it is firing. Perhaps unbeknown to you it has taken a knock that has put the scope out of alignment. And travelling up and down rivers in a thumping, jarring jet boat is about as good a way as any of doing that to your scope. Once you re-sight your rifle and you know it is firing spot on, this can have the sort of calming effect that restores your confidence. But if you do not do it and you remain unsure whether it is you or the rifle that is out, you will more than likely continue screwing up simply because your confidence is likewise all screwed up. Seeing I knew all that, I do not know why I did not set right down and check out my rifle. Instead I just carried on, screwing up and as a result missing out on deer.

But other than that, things were not even going well with my bush stalking. Ray had been working the Hollyford for some time prior

**Ray knew were the deer were most likely to be hanging out
(photo Ray Finn)**

to my joining him and he knew his block fairly well. Hence he knew where the deer were most likely to be hanging out. Obviously this gave him a bit of an advantage. When we were working from our camp near the mouth of the Pyke River, Ray would usually drop me off for the evening shoot somewhere along the bank of the Hollyford and then he would take off in the boat to do a bit of hunting further upstream or downstream, as the case may be. Silver beech is the predominant species of the Lower Hollyford, and searching out deer in beech forest is quite different to searching out deer in podocarp-broadleaf forest. Like the fuschia groves of the Upper Hollyford, there are pockets of bush that provide good feed and naturally attract deer, but beneath a virtually unbroken canopy of silver beech, it is not always easy figuring out just where the deer ought be. With nothing but beech forest stretching in front of me for miles in every direction I was often at a loss as to where to begin. An hour or so later Ray would be back with a deer or two draped over the foredeck, and I would be back at the river's edge waiting for him, utterly depressed after sneaking fruitlessly up and down the slopes in what not only looked like, but also proved to be, totally barren country. There were odd deer scattered here and there throughout the bush but it was not easy finding them.

In difficult bush country such as this many were the times I would have gladly given my mate's right arm, his right leg too were it asked of me, for a decent eye dog that could quietly lead me right onto a deer. Kim was that type of a dog. When he was just a pup and I was working my first possum block in the Northern Tararuas, I trained Kim to stay close in, just ahead of me, working from hand signals. Ears erect and nose to the wind, he would stalk carefully and deliberately, stealthily leading me right onto deer. If he got a pace too far ahead, I would simply freeze in my tracks and when he looked back to see what was up, I would move my right index finger just enough to indicate that he was to come to heel. No words nor sounds were ever uttered. Then, with the dog back in position, we would start forward once again. Kim was a Border Collie/Kelpie cross, strong eye sheep dog, but he had never worked sheep. From an early age he had worked possum traps and deer with me, and later it was goats, and chamois, and tahr and pigs. He was brilliant and he was well written about in my book "Trappers Dogs 'n' Deer". At one stage I had left off hunting for a season owing to a stomach ailment, and rather than have Kim wasting around town, I gave him to Bob who at the time was culling deer in the Ruahine Ranges. Now, fruitlessly searching out deer in the vast beech forest of the Hollyford, if only I had the opportunity of getting hold of a dog like Kim by my side once more the thought passed through my mind that I might even be tempted to consider whether not only an arm and a leg but even my mate's head on a platter weren't too high a price to pay.

Back in the meat safe at Jamestown, we had accumulated a dozen hard won deer, and left them to cool their heels while we went off looking for a few more to make a couple of decent loads for the meat plane. Then the weather broke. First there was a bit of a cloud build up on Mount Tutoko, and in no time at all great banks of the stuff had rolled in off the sea thoroughly blanketing the tops, pushing swirling fingers of mist and vapour down through the bush and rolling out across the lake. Then came the rain. It don't come down in ordinary buckets down Fiordland. It begins with bathtubs, then fish ponds, progressing to swimming pools, and after that it really starts to rain. Cascading waterfalls suddenly erupt off dry cliff faces, docile streams become impassable raging torrents, rivers churn black as they surge over their banks. Old and weakened giants of the forest get ripped out by their roots and mercilessly dragged into the swirling mass. Piles of driftwood and log jams build up and get wrenched apart. And anyone in his right mind, battens down and holes up inside his hut, adds wood to the fire and mixes up a great camp oven full of venison stew, swings the billy then settles back on his bunk with a good book and waits for it to pass. Because there ain't nowhere that he's likely to be going nor anything other that he's likely to be doing until it does.

Usually it is but a day or two, perhaps three or four. But this time the weather wasn't letting up. The wind howled and shrieked through the forest, streaks of froth whipped off the lake and piled up along the beaches, branches snapped off trees, the hut shook and the windows rattled. And by the time it was all over, the rain had passed and the wind had settled down to what seemed like little more than a force ten hurricane, our deer in the meat safe were ripe and there wasn't nothing for it but to dump them in the lake.

It was sort of sad. I had grown quite attached to them while they had been hanging there in the meat safe. They were big animals in prime condition and I had already calculated their monetary value and decided how I was best going to spend my share of the proceeds. Ray was not overly concerned. As far as he was concerned it was just one of those things.

"We'll take them down to the estuary and throw them overboard, and then go get some more," said Ray.

There was nothing we could do about the loss of the meat. But I reckoned there was still some value in the skins and I could see no reason why we should not at least salvage these. Skinning deer is not all that difficult. If you do not want the meat hygiene does not come into it. Grass, sticks, stones and boots don't matter. You can roll them in the dirt, walk all over them, punch and kick the skins loose, and the whole procedure only takes a minute or two And with a couple of blokes working on them, one can swing on the legs while the other is tugging on the skin. It's all as easy as.

I was ripping into one old beast, punching the skin loose round the brisket, when a splinter of bone nicked my middle knuckle. It was the tiniest of nicks that whipped off a small shred of skin that didn't even have the decency to bleed. But within a day or two it was beginning to hurt. Infection had set into the knuckle.

Soon enough the Hollyford was back to normal, and with the bush fast drying out we decided to return to our camp near the mouth of the Pyke and work the upper reaches of our block once more. It was some time now since we had been up that way and the area had had plenty of time to settle down. Also we were running quite low on fuel for the boat by now and there was a cache of petrol waiting for us to pack through the bush down past the rapids. These rapids, created the geographical boundary between the Lower Hollyford and the Upper Hollyford hunting blocks. About 400 yards of huge jumbled boulders, submerged logs and crashing falls, they formed a barrier in the river that it was next to impossible for a jet boat to negotiate. Jacky Jordan, who was working the Upper Hollyford, had been pressed into service ferrying 20 drums of fuel down the river from the road end to the top side of the falls for us. All we had to do was lash them, one at a time, onto the frames of our packs and carry them down through the bush the 400 yards or so to the bottom end of the rapids where we could then load them into the jet boat. By doing this we were going to save ourselves a great deal of money that would have otherwise been spent

Jacky Jordan shooting the Hollyford Rapids (photo Ray Finn)

flying them in, 6 or 7 drums at a time, in the Cessna.

The all up weight of a full 12 gallon drum of fuel was somewhere around 140lbs. A fair sort of a load, but manageable nevertheless. First you lash a drum onto the frame of your pack, ease into the shoulder straps, slowly work your way off your backside into a standing position, while at the same time hoisting the load up off the ground. Immediately the fuel inside slops to one end of the drum all but throwing you off balance. Then as you counter the shift in weight, the point of balance suddenly changes and the fuel slops to the opposite end rolling you off balance the other way. If you stand there for a minute or two the fuel settles down and you are okay, but as soon as you start to move, so does the fuel. Once you get moving with that weight slopping about on your back and propelling you forward it is not that easy pulling up again. The two of us took off through the bush, crashing our way through undergrowth and pepper woods, reeling from side to side as we staggered and rolled under the weight of the fuel sloshing from side to side on our backs. Smashed and broken foliage littered the forest in our wake as we stumbled across roots and bounced off trees, ploughing our way towards the bottom end of the rapids.

"The first one is always the easiest one," said Ray, as we emerged from the bush near to where he had tied the boat, "From here on they get progressively heavier!"

With all that weight suddenly gone from off your back, you almost levitate as you drift effortlessly across the forest floor the first few yards of your return to go get another one.... A good time to run a few quick mental calculations through the head... before the feet once more make contact with the brain:

One ton equals 2,240 pounds. 20 x 140lbs equals 2,800lbs, which equals one and a quarter ton! Divide that by Ray and me: We each had more than ½ a ton of fuel to move!

One mile equals 1,760 yards. 20 drums x 400 yards equals 8,000 yards, which equals about 4½ miles! Divide that by Ray and me: We each had to move our ½ ton of fuel a total of 2¼ miles! And then there was a further 2¼ miles to add on going back to get another!

And none of that allowed for the fact that from here on the drums were going to feel heavier and the distance was going to seem longer with each consecutive load! By the time we were done with all twenty drums lying in a heap at the bottom end of the rapids, if at some stage I had ever thought that here was a good way of saving money, I was no longer deluded. The next lot were going to be delivered right to the door per fixed wing aircraft.

That evening, I decided to check out the country handy to the Pyke Hut, while Ray took off in the jet boat to hunt downstream. I was back at camp soon after dark but Ray had still not returned. Normally, with the river to negotiate, he would have been back by last light. Naturally I was a little concerned, but there was any of number of things that might have delayed him, and it was not impossible driving a jet boat in the dark, so there was no point getting too worked up just yet. I lit up the hut and got a meal going and went outside to see if I could catch sound of the boat coming up the river. An hour or so passed and I was starting to get really worried when there was a loud shout from back at the hut. It was Ray. He had walked back to camp from a few miles downstream, crossed the Pyke by way of the suspension bridge and while I was anxiously peering into the downstream darkness, he had arrived back at camp behind me.

He was okay, but it was more than could be said for the boat. He had been hurtling down the river when the engine began vibrating and making strange noises. There isn't much time for thinking in a jet boat. Almost instinctively, Ray swung hard towards the north bank and as the prow butted into the overhanging foliage the engine died on him. He just had time to grab the painter and vault over the windscreen and into the trees before the boat started to swing back out into the current. He managed to drag the boat back up against the current a short way and beach it on a gravel bank where he had left it, lashed to a sturdy branch.

Back in Te Anau the engineers had stitched up a crack in the engine block and Ray had been assured that the repairs 'would last a life time'. A fair enough assurance considering the conditions under which jet boats were worked. It seemed that the repair job had given out and the crack reopened. Anyway the sump was full of water and the engine oil had turned to thick white gunk. Had this happened way out in the Tasman, or crossing the McKerrow Bar, or in the middle of some churning rapids, it could well have been a job that lasted someone's lifetime. It was obvious the engine would have to be removed from the boat and air lifted back to Te Anau. In the meantime our meat shooting venture had come to a grinding halt. In this sort of country, without a jet boat, you were completely grounded. Our only means of flying deer carcasses out was either off Lake McKerrow or the Martins Bay strip. And with no means of getting the carcasses to either one of those places neither was there any point in shooting them.

The following day Kevin Hallett arrived in his jet boat from the adjoining Alabaster Block to help us lift out the engine and ferry it back to the Alabaster strip. But now another problem surfaced. A Cessna 180 can lift only so much off a 300 yard grass strip, and one jet boat engine plus Ray Finn was about it. With no carcasses to justify a second flight there would not be one so that meant I was not going anywhere. Most of my gear was at Jamestown, many miles away and without our jet boat there was no means of my getting to it. Meanwhile the infection that had got started in my knuckle had begun spreading up the back of my hand towards my wrist. My first thought was for my gear down at Jamestown, but Kevin's was for the infection that he could see was working it's way into my system. He told me to pile what gear I had into his boat. He and I were going to Dale Hunter's camp in the Upper Pyke where someone could keep an eye on me just in case the poison began spreading more quickly.

CHAPTER 22

The Alabaster Strip

Far to the northwest of Dale's camp, the distant 'thwack-thwack-thwack-thwack-thwack-thwack!" of a helicopter interspersed with rapid fire discharge from an FN 7.62mm SLR reverberated round the Mt McKenzie tops. It was the sound of death. And from the valley shooter's point of view it was a sound that could eventually be the death knell of his very livelihood.

As long as the open tops were left unshot, there would always be handy deer on the river flats. The alpine meadows up above the bush line was the valley shooter's meat safe from where the deer would spill down through the bush and work their way out into the river flats below. That was the way it had always been but times were changing. As far as the meat shooters were concerned, helicopter shooters were

George Wyber (left) and Dale Hunter (right) meat shooting the Pyke (photo Ray Finn)

plain bad news. "They sit on their asses in a chopper all day having it easy, creaming everything off the tops and screwing up the future for us meat shooters slogging our guts out in the valleys below," exclaimed one disgruntled hunter.

Whether it was really like that or not, with the "chopper shooters sitting on their asses all day and having it easy", there would not have been many helicopter crews around at the time that would have been foolish enough to take their chances flying back and forth at low altitude over a meat shooter's block.

Southern Scenic's meat plane was working flat out doing the rounds of the various meat shooting blocks, offloading venison into Te Anau and you just had to wait your turn. Both Dale's and Kevin's meat safes were close to full, but the Pyke and Alabaster Blocks were still a few days down the Southern Scenic list. The inconvenience of being dependent on a company plane coupled with the high cost of chartering it had already motivated some of the more intrepid to lash out and buy their own aircraft. George Wyber, who worked the Alabaster Block prior to Kevin Hallett, was said to be the first meat shooter to buy himself a plane. Although Goodwin McNutt, in the Central North Island might well have been in a position to challenge him to that distinction. George, though, became the first to kill himself in one when he crashed into the Humboldt Mountains flying out a load of venison in the thick of fog. In the early 70's, sometime after Kevin had vacated the block, Dave Saxton, a well known helicopter hunter, bought himself a fixed wing aircraft and also worked off the Alabaster strip. In between times and scattered about the country, several others were buying Piper Cubs and busily doing their own thing.

Meanwhile, everybody else had to wait their turn. So while we were killing time, waiting for the meat plane, and to get away from the irritating noise of that chopper that was shooting up the tops while keeping well out of .243 range, we decided to go visit Joe Driscoll down at Big Bay.

Joe was what you might call a hermit. He did a bit of white baiting when it suited him but other than that he seemed to get by quite well doing nothing much at all, and he was perfectly happy with his own company while doing it. Most hermits do not shun company. They just prefer it in small doses. Joe was happy to have us visit. He stoked up the fire, swung the billy and prepared himself for a good chat. During the course of conversation, Joe somehow got wind of it that I enjoyed writing for my own entertainment. Some time back, Joe told me, he had shared his own story with a fellow who had been staying with him, and that one had plagiarized Joe's story, and made a novel out of it. I believe Joe told me the title of the book was something to do with a "Moving" or "Running" Target or something similar. Joe and I got on well together, and he must have trusted me, because he asked me if I would take down his story and ghost write it for him. Not being a professional writer, I did not feel adequate to the task. But to compensate, rather than writing Joe a book, I will instead now endeavour to write him a brief paragraph:

During the Second World War, when all the young men of Joe's age were called up for military service, Joe lined up with the rest of them. At the recruiting office he was told to strip. A medical orderly looked up his backside, checked his tonsils and his testicles, told him he had passed his medical with flying honours and he was ushered into the fitting room. Next he was measured for width, breadth, height and depth, checked for distinguishing scars and birthmarks and issued with his uniform. For some reason that I can no longer recall, Joe took exception to the thick flannel khaki uniform that he was given and refused point blank to put it on. He grabbed his civvies, stormed out of the barracks and ran with whistles blowing, dogs barking and sergeant majors bellowing as he went. And so began a well documented manhunt for a military deserter who probably would have been court-martialled and possibly shot had he been caught. Joe worked his way down the Coast and into Big Bay with the military police hard on his hammer. He moved into his camp thinking he was safe, but the MP's discovered where he was and started to close in on him. The camp was in amongst the sand dunes and fairly well out in the open and Joe did not have time to run for it. He managed to crawl beneath the floor boards without being seen and conceal himself in amongst the junk that had accumulated over the years. Just inches above his face, the military moved in and took over his camp as their base. Joe lay there barely daring to breath way into the night listening to the plans being laid for the following day's search. Then when the candles were extinguished and all went quiet inside the camp, Joe wriggled out from beneath the floor boards and just to confuse everyone, he walked backwards along the beach a couple of times and disappeared into the bush. Joe's story had considerably more to it than what I have related but the short of it was, along with a heap of excitement and close calls, he was never caught by the army. About a year after the war ended he decided to set the record straight and turned himself in, and he was sentanced to 18 months in Paparua Prison.

Barry Crump had a much more interesting story concerning Joe that would have probably done better as a book than the one mentioned above.

Towards the end of 1979, Barry and his wife, Robin, spent a few months living just a couple of banana plots away from my home on the island of Aitutaki. They had spent the winter doing research for a forthcoming book while fossicking for gold in Otago, and Barry said he had never been so cold at any other time of his life. He said it was going to take several months of tropical heat to get the icicles out of their bones. I would sometimes take the two of them out on my boat and they would swim alongside in the warm lagoon waters as I was laying out fishing nets for the night. It was not unusual, about mid morning, to hear a little whistle from down the track and I would go out to see what was up and Barry would poke his head round from behind a coconut tree: "Where's the old dragon?" he'd ask in hushed tones. "Do you think she'll mind if we drop in for a brew?" The Crumps were Bahai's, my wife ("the old dragon", according to Crump) and I were not. Robin was fiery and my wife was intense. So while the two women got themselves all heated up and deeply entrenched in religious debate, Barry and I would extricate ourselves and go talk about hunting and news from back home, and relate stories about some of the many people we knew in common. One never knew with Barry whether it was news, a fabrication, or a down right lie. In retrospect I think it was generally the latter. "I suppose you heard what they did to poor old Joe Driscoll?" he said one day. "Couple of young fellows came down from the city and chopped the poor sod into little pieces with an axe!" I was utterly shocked. Joe was a harmless hospitable sort of a bloke. "Yeah!" Barry added. "Rotten young bastards had no motive. Did it just for the hell of it." A few years later Jules Tapper, who had taken over the Hollyford Tourist Track, was a guest in my Lodges. "That was terrible what happened to Joe Driscoll!" I mentioned.

"Joe? What happened to Joe?" replied Jules, apparently quite startled.

"How he got chopped up with an axe," I answered.

"Never heard anything about that," said Jules. "He was still in one piece and kicking last time I saw him, and that wasn't too long ago!"

The lightest of seas was running the day Dale and I were visiting with Joe Driscoll down Big Bay. In fact it was calm as a whisper. The tide was dead low with a thick mat of brown kelp spreading out into the bay, sunlight sparkling off its strands as the sea ever so gently stirred the surface. Everything was peaceful and quiet. Sand dunes and coastal grasses rolled away from the waters edge to as far back as the bank of the Awarua River and then there was swamp, and pakihi, and native forest. Mile upon mile of virtually impenetrable, water logged bush, all the way to the Pyke and beyond. Flax and coprosma, kamahi and kahikatea, inanga and whistling frogs, tawaki and koitareke, sandflies, mosquitoes, beetles and grubs. And out in the bay; greenbone, koura, kina and paua — lots and lots of paua! Summer was slipping by and soon I would be heading back to the North Island, and I still had not done anything about the paua.

Soon after Dale and I returned to the Pyke from Big Bay, Dale ferried me down to the Alabaster Hut to keep an eye on things there while Kevin returned with Dale to the Upper Pyke to assist with the loading of the meat plane which was now due. By now the poison that had started in my knuckle was getting in the way of my work and starting to bother me. The infection was picking up and had moved through my hand and into my wrist. So I was happy not to be doing anything more than I had to.

With a lot more meat to be flown out from the Upper Pyke than the Alabaster, the plan was to get that lot out first. The payload of a Cessna 180 flying off these short mountain strips was only 800lbs so that meant several loads had to be flown out during the course of the day. The meat shooter's responsibility was to weigh everything to make sure the loads were right and the pilot's responsibility was to do quick turnarounds to make sure he got everything out in one day. Kevin was going to pile in with the last load flown off the Pyke strip and wait for Dale and me out in the Upper Hollyford, where the carcasses were being off loaded for transfer by truck to Te Anau. As soon as Kevin was gone, Dale would come down to the Alabaster Hut in his jet boat, where I would have already been starting to drag carcasses from the meat safe onto the bottom end of the runway ready to be loaded into the plane for its final flight of the day.

Then it decided to rain once more. I was sitting in the Alabaster Hut with knife stabbing pains searing through my arm, admiring the streaks of green that had now moved well up towards my elbow and thinking about my paternal grandmother who had died of septicaemia, along with her new born infant, when my dad was a young child, and wondering whether I might not go the same way if this weather didn't hurry up and clear. Fortunately the rain only hung round for a night and a day, but that was all that was needed to see Huck's jet boat virtually disappear beneath a fresh bank of boulders and gravel.

Upon hearing about it, Huck never came back for his jet boat. He made a claim against his insurance and a few months later Dave Richardson was asked by the Insurance Company to salvage what was left of the hull and tow it around to Milford and then to Te Anau, which he did.

I had not slept too well with continual throbbing, interspersed with spasmodic pains, shooting through my arm and fever wracking my body, but it was a warm and sunny day that I awoke to. High above the beech forest, the drone of the meat plane sounded through the morning air. It was going to be a long and tedious day mainly just lazing about in the sun. It would be at least mid afternoon before I could start moving carcasses out to the strip, otherwise they would be fly blown before we got to loading them.

The day wore slowly on, occasionally punctuated by the comings and goings of the Cessna as it plied back and forth between the Upper

Hollyford and the Upper Pyke and then came the sound of Dale's jet boat. Now we had to move it. The day was well along and there was not going to be much time to spare getting this last load out to the Hollyford. We lashed the boat securely to its moorings, closed up the camp and got the last of the twelve carcasses piled up on the southern end of the strip. The Cessna came in from the south, turned round near the far end of the strip, taxied back down to us and immediately we began piling in carcasses. I was feeling slightly groggy and the pilot was anxiously looking into the lengthening shadows as the sun slipped further down the western sky.

"Come on you guys, move it," he encouraged, as we piled carcass on top of carcass back in the fuselage.

Next we pushed our frame packs in on top of the carcasses. Then Dale pushed his dog in on top of the packs. Next our rifles. Then Dale clambered in with his knees up round his ears. And that left just enough room for me to climb in alongside the pilot and shut the door. I was sitting on the rear end of a deer, hanging on to a hand

Dale Hunter at the Alabaster landing (photo Ray Finn)

strap, with Dale crouched behind me gripping onto the collar of my Swannee.

The pilot fired up the engine, built up the revs and gave it the gun. Slowly we started to lumber along the strip. You would think that it would only take seconds for a plane to charge down a 300 yard strip and fly off into the sky. But not so. Our little 180 lumbered slowly down the strip, single prop spinning frantically just in front of our noses, pilot cranking up the revs, easing back on the joy stick trying to lift the tail wheel off the grass. And on we lumbered. Halfway down the strip, rapidly running out of dirt. Two thirds down the strip and now the tail slowly begins to teeter off the grass into the slip stream. And that was when I realized we were not going to make it. Less than 50 yards to go and we would be sitting in the river with the prop wrapped round our teeth, buried beneath a pile of carcasses, packs, rifles and dog. We were going too fast to stop and not fast enough to get airborne. We shot off the end of the strip into the river boulders and as we started to bounce the pilot slammed the joy stick hard forward and immediately yanked it fully back. The plane bounced off the stones, ploughed into the air and barely skimming the water headed straight for the opposite bank of the river. I think between the three of us and the dog, we willed elevation into that little plane. Now we were moving. The bank shot underneath the fuselage quicker than one could blink an eye, bits of scrub getting tangled up in the tail wheel as it dragged through the foliage. We careered down the swamp barely gaining altitude. Now the trees down the far end of the swamp were starting to loom closer, and still the pilot clung on that joy stick just about pulling it right out of its fittings he was pulling so hard on it. He was a ruddy complexioned man, quite a well known bush pilot of his time, but it is expedient at the moment not to recall his name. What I do recall though was his ruddy complexion going bright scarlet. All of us sat there transfixed as the trees loomed ever closer and then slowly the plane started to respond and gain altitude. Gradually we eased into a slow climb and the pilot gently started to veer off to starboard as we turned back towards the Hollyford.

"That was too close for comfort!" I remember him exclaiming. "How much weight did you bloody idiots pile into this kite?"

I didn't know and Dale wasn't saying. Amazing how the pain had suddenly gone from my arm though. I was still hanging on like grim death to the hand strap but it didn't hurt anymore.

That night we stayed in Murray Gunn's motor camp, and next day I hitched a ride off a couple of tourists and fetched my Land Rover from where I had left it at the Milford motor camp. I then drove to Lumsden where I was thoroughly abused for leaving it so long before getting medical attention for my hand.

"Don't you know people have died from septicaemia with things like this?" the nurse scolded.

"Really!?!" I replied. "I would never have imagined such a thing."

I was told to come back in two days time for my second penicillin shot, but eventually talked the doctor into letting me take a needle and syringe and a shot of penicillin with me on the assurance that I would call into the district nurse at Te Anau to have it administered. I never did see the district nurse, feeling that here was a good opportunity to practice administering antibiotics to myself just in case the need ever arose someday. I actually botched it a little bit by not inserting the needle deep enough into my thigh. But after a fair bit of rubbing, pummelling and massaging I eventually dispersed the lump of antibiotic that was sitting not too far beneath the skin and within days the variegated network of red and green streaks that had decorated my arm had disappeared.

A few days later, Dale and Kevin were ready to return to their blocks and I flew back in with them. Kevin very kindly took me all the way back down to Jamestown in his jet boat to gather the rest of my gear and a day later I flew off the Martins Bay strip and once more I was back in Te Anau.

You could already feel the cool chill of autumn hanging in the air. The month of March was all but gone and in a short while the deer would be roaring. By now, my old mate Dave Odey would already have been about one month into the new trapping season. Once again, it was well gone time to be heading north. But I could not really go back without sorting out the paua situation first. I packed all my gear into the Land Rover and headed off down the Waiau Valley, in the general direction of south.

The cray fishing season was over and most of the Fiordland cray fishermen were back in their home ports by now. Some would be refitting their ships for a stint at cod fishing. Others had already slipped their ships for the annual repaint. A few would be on their way to the Mutton Bird Islands. And the rest were probably taking it easy and having a well earned rest.

Peter Roderique's boat the F.V. Caroline was up on the hard in Riverton and he and his mate, Trevor Antill, were getting ready to scrub her down and do a refit. Trevor was real pleased to see me. He had a "neat little day boat tied alongside the wharf that was exactly what I needed." It was a solid little wooden hulled ship, about 30 feet long, fitted out with ice boxes and licensed to day fish for crays out of Riverton. The asking price was "very reasonable."

I was not altogether sure that I needed a licence to fish out of Riverton and a boat to go with it, but Trevor rushed me down to the wharf fired up the ship and away we went, 'put-putting' out of the harbour into a beautifully calm Foveaux Strait. Being a lover of ships and the sea, I must admit I was impressed. We cruised around

Gary Hollows (left) and Ray Finn unloading at the Hollyford Road head (photo Dave Richardson)

for an hour or so, Trevor pointing out the navigation markers for the harbour channel so I would be quite at home once I got underway. We tied up at the wharf, closed up the ship and as we prepared to disembark, blue smoke began pouring out of the cabin behind us. For a big man, Trevor could move quite fast when he so pleased. "Just a minor problem, nothing very serious," he assured me. "Just a little bit of a melt down in the electrical system." He managed to stop the fire before it got a hold by yanking a fistful of smouldering wires out of the bulk head, and that afternoon I flew out of Invercargill on a Grumman Widgeon and a short while later I was on Stewart Island, sitting in the pub having a nice cool beer.

As evening approached, I strolled up the hill behind the hotel for a look over Paterson Inlet. From a vantage point, overlooking Paterson, the bush fringed green waters of the Inlet stretched far away into the distant south.

Looking down into the bays below, you could see just how beautifully clear the water was. Possibly the biggest, fattest, finest quality thick shelled paua that New Zealand produced, were sitting down there queuing and clamouring to be levered off their rocks.

In the valley behind me, as dusk slowly settled over the land, the odd little dwellings tucked away in the bush began firing up their single banger Lister generators. The clattering of Diesel engines echoed noisily through the bush. But to all accounts the clattering and banging was of little concern to the local deer fraternity. Here

**Ray Finn (left) and Gary Hollows with a load of venison
(photo Dave Richardson)**

and there, all the way up the hill I had noticed where Whitetail deer had been coming out of the scrub and moving about on the road. Not much point getting excited about it though. My rifle and spotlighting gear were a long way away, sitting in my land Rover at the airport in Invercargill.

Next morning I booked the Island's sole taxi, to check out an available property I had been told about on the far end of Horseshoe Bay. Everything about it seemed ideal for my requirements. There was a commercial wharf with a huge shed set up with walk in freezers, and a ramp leading up onto the wharf with a heavy duty winch and cradle for hauling out a fair sized boat. Across the road, set back in about 80 acres of land, a picturesque turn of the century villa homestead. The asking price was less than $10,000 for the lot!

I sailed on the "M.V. Wairoa" that afternoon back to Bluff. As was customary on those type of boats on those type of crossings, passengers lolled about, hanging over the rails puking into the wind, splattering themselves and everything around them with sour smelling puke. It was a pleasure being close by and in the immediate vicinity. Way out in the Strait, ships could be seen slowly dredging their way through the oyster beds. The oyster season was underway and Skeggsy's oyster factory was in full swing.

I bought a can of 15 dozen fresh oysters, got a taxi back to

Invercargill, picked up my Land Rover, and started on the long drive north to go talk with Rex Giles about Stewart Island and the paua industry.

CHAPTER 23

Taringamotu

I drove through the night arriving in Christchurch about dawn and after a hurried pie cart breakfast of sausages and eggs swirling in grease with bits of onion and charcoal, I drove through the Lyttleton Tunnel to book a daylight passage to Wellington on the "M.V. Wahine". Coming up Easter, with everyone wanting to get away for a break, it was as good a time as any, if not a little better than most, for the stewards to go out on strike.

"Sorry mate. Ships not sailing. Stewards are out on strike!.... No idea mate. Most likely they'll hang out 'til sometime after the long weekend.... Yeah mate, they sure know how to stuff up the works alright.... Hey, you'd better not go talking about the stewards like that round here mate. Someone might hear you and cut up nasty, like."

Picton was about 220 miles up the coast. If I left straight away and all went well I might get on the midday sailing of the "M.V. Aramoana".

A little north of Christchurch, with the old Land Rover humming along at a steady 55mph, early morning sun streaming in through the cab making me feel warm and cosy and suddenly I started to feel real drowsy. Just up ahead there was a major river cut across the Canterbury Plains with an access off the highway down under the bridge. I had not really stopped for a break since getting out of bed to go look at the property on Horseshoe Bay some 26 hours earlier. It was not the first time I had driven until I nearly dropped. I pulled off the highway down to the river, propped my sleeping bag behind my head, stretched out across the front bench seat of the cab, opened the drivers door, stuck my feet out in the sun and crashed. About an hour later I was up and on my way once more.

"Sorry mate. She's all booked up. It's a busy time mate, don't you know!.... Yeah, midday sailing, evening sailing, everything's booked.... If you hang around you might sneak in on the last sailing at ten o'clock tonight.... No, I don't think the stewards are planning to go out on strike before the last sailing, mate. Why'd you ask?"

In the autumn of 1968 Picton was a pokey little dump. It was also one very boring place to be sitting round watching Cook Strait ferries coming and going well into the cold of the night, while not knowing right up until just a few minutes before final muster whether you were going to get on or whether you were destined for another miserable night of sleeping in the cold confines of an uncomfortable cramped Land Rover cab

It was with quite some relief that I drove onto the "Aramoana" that night, the last vehicle squeezed into a packed vehicle deck and the doors of the ship were clanged shut behind me.

Rex Giles was not impressed with my find in Horseshoe Bay.

"I told you it was the Chathams or nothing!" said he. "Anyway, while you have been down Stewart Island wasting your time looking at properties that are no use to us, my French contacts have fallen through and there won't be anything doing now until later in the year at the earliest."

So, stuff the paua! I probably never really did want to be a business man sitting in an office with a bunch of other stuffed shirts. One week later, on the 10th of April, I was in Taumarunui sitting out a storm at my mate Kingsley Jones' home preparing to head into my new possum trapping block, while that same day the "M.V. Wahine" was getting wrecked in Wellington Harbour with the loss of many lives. And it was later that same year, during the winter of 1968, that someone other than Rex Giles and Wayne Blake got the paua industry up and running. And we all know about the millions of dollars involved, and the thieving and connivering, and the poaching and stripping of paua beds bare that still goes on to this very day.

There was about a thousand acres of farmland and good native bush backing onto the Pureora Forest up the Taringamotu River beyond Oruaiwi, that a nice old fellow who bred racehorses for a hobby just a little way down the road from Taumarunui, owned. Way up close to the top of a hill, in the very thick of the bush, he had cleared a paddock and planted it with turnips, and for some strange reason that he could not quite figure out it seemed to be attracting large numbers of possums which were doing considerable damage to the crop. He asked me if I would try and clean up a few of the possums before they cleaned up the last of the turnips.

I do not usually bother remembering names of people whom I do not much care for, and that could be why I do not remember the name of the bloke who looked after the farm for the old fellow. Anyway he did not care none too much for me either. In fact he was madder than a meat axe about the old fellow asking me to move into the shearer's cottage and make myself at home while I did justice to the local possum fraternity. I thought that was rather good, but seeing it was the old fellow who owned the property and this other bloke only worked for him, there was not much he could do about it.

It was a nice comfortable little cottage and I immediately went about hanging wire netting up in the living room for hanging my possum boards, and stringing ropes from wall to wall for airing my skins over. Looking out the kitchen window was like a big open-air movie theatre. Between me and the Taringamotu River there was a sloping plateau on top of a hill. And on this plateau there was an airstrip of a sorts with a Fletcher top dresser coming and going. He would come in from the south touching down on the low end of the strip, taxi up the hill to the super phosphate truck, get loaded to the gunnels, go charging off down the strip and literally drop off the end of the plateau into the Taringamotu valley below. I would sit there holding my breath waiting for the crash. But a few seconds later he would come labouring into view round the end of the hill giving his little Fletcher full tit. The top dresser would dump its load on the adjacent hills and back it would come for another load. This went on from dawn to dusk. Little wonder there were plenty of grey-haired top dressing pilots but not many of them were very old.

My block was on the opposite side of the Taringamotu River, which was quite an interesting little stream in its own right. A sturdy wooden bridge crossed the stream and a fat brown trout was sitting plumb in the middle of the stream right beneath the bridge. There was going to be trout for breakfast.

Soon across the stream the farm track wended its way into the bush and followed all the way up to the turnip patch… about 2½ miles in all of good trappable country with an abundance of mature canopy trees lining the road making life a lot less complicated. Most trap lines, you go pushing your way into the bush cutting tracks as you go with great pack loads of traps on your back. Here then was a trap line that could be worked in its entirety from the vehicle without ever having to step more than a pace from the side of the road, and there was not going to be any cutting tracks nor any packing traps.

I took off early next morning with a flask of tea and a packet of sandwiches, to get as many traps laid out as I could, and by late in the day I had 70 of them tucked in neat and tidy, all nicely covered with good rich humus soil, sharp sticks and bits of branches that could damage fur cleared well away from the sets. I had never before laid out so many new sets in one day. Usually you were doing well if you got 50 traps out the first day of a new line. I was just about had it, but I was pretty pleased with the effort, and now for the trout.

I still had a little setting up to do back at camp; getting everything ready to go. Gathering in and chopping more firewood, getting the tack-out area properly organised with the work table set up, boards stacked handy, staple gun oiled, wire spoke for turning tails, four gallon tin beneath the bench for scraps. Then the tools for stripping boards readied — long nosed pliers for removing staples, flat broad blade knife for scraping fat, empty milk powder tin for the oil, trimming knife for opening bellies and tails, old sacking for rubbing down oily skins, wire comb and brush. There wasn't going to be much time left for fishing, but there wasn't any reason why the fish could not go catch himself. All that needed to be done was to set a raisin on a hook in mid stream, and just after daybreak I was back down the stream hauling in breakfast.

My first set was on an old dying rata just outside the bush edge. Here was my first possum of the day, the first one off a new line, and over the next three weeks of trapping this set seldom failed to catch. Now there was a bit of a gap between this first set and the second one owing to a lack of suitable trees to work to. But from the second one on I was able to place traps relatively handy to one another all the way up the road. Trap after trap had been sprung with a possum sitting in each one. They were not startlingly good possums — a slightly smaller breed than I had been getting out of the Whangapeki. But they were almost 100% greys and that was the desirable colour of the day. Killing, caching and resetting as I went, by mid afternoon I had worked every trap and from the seventy I could only recall about three or four with nobody home. My work was going to be cut out on the morrow, not only tending traps, but also skinning this lot and after that tacking them out back at camp into the night.

I owned a total of 110 traps and I wanted to push the whole lot in. With plenty of road yet to go prior to the crop, I now needed to take advantage of what remaining daylight I had to extend the line. And before driving back to camp that night, I had managed to get a further 30 traps placed along the road. I now had 100 traps working for me out in the bush.

Back at camp, sitting over a brew, I got to thinking about the quality of these Pureora possums. They were typical greys. Quite nice in colour, but they did not have the clear white bellies of the finer grades. And they were only middling in size. Nor did they have the thick woolly appearance of my central country mountain possums. A line of furs like this would not enhance my reputation in London where the fur buyers associated one's name with the quality of the furs one produced. I decided that rather than detract from my name, this line might be better sold off as a cash crop to Rodney.

Waking up early was always a struggle during those cooler winter months. And nor was it helped any after a solid day of heavy manual labour out in the bush the preceding day. But I knew there was going to be heaps to do over the next few weeks and sleeping in in the mornings was not going to get me there. I was up early and away, and just as well for that. Once again, trap after trap had caught — this time a 90% catch rate!

Evening was approaching and I was feeling tired and ready to call it a day by the time I had tended my last set. But I still wanted to get those final ten traps into the bush. It was dark enough to have me driving with my lights on coming out of the bush that night, but all 110 traps were now out there, sitting pretty waiting for a catch.

That night, the first with all 110 traps set, I took 98 skinnable possums. Never before had I taken that many possums off a trap line in one night. The odd ones were less than full grown, but seeing I was not exporting them I had decided to take everything from ¾ grown and up. Nothing was rejected other than absolute rubbish. And the line just went on producing kills. By the end of the first week I had accumulated 500 skins back in the camp and I was running into difficulties clearing boards quickly enough to make room for the fresh ones that were coming in day by day. I only had 300 tack out boards, and the rate I was catching I needed 75 or more boards cleared and available for my incoming skins everyday.

Thick shearing longs were ideal clothing for holding down possums.
The first cut goes from foot to foot through the back legs.
Flip the possum and cut from foot to foot through the front legs.
Open through the bib to beneath the chin.
There's a bit of knife work clearing round the jowls.
Pull the skin off shoulders and front legs, cut base of ears so they remain attached to the skin. place foot across shoulders of carcass and pull clear of the brisket.
Cut the skin away from the back feet.
After clearing the backside remove skin from tail with a twisting motion.

314

To help the drying process the open fire was kept burning at full power. Even so, four days tacked on a board was marginal time for properly drying out a skin, and especially so when they were hanging from the mesh packed in close together with not much ventilation space between them.

The work went on. Each day I was up soon after daybreak, back at camp in the dark, barely time to get a meal started on the primus before I would be into whipping out staples and stripping boards in order to get the new lot tacked out and hanging from the mesh. There was no time to worry about brushing and combing dry furs. My work was completely cut out just doing what I was doing. Never once did I climb into my sleeping bag before about 1.30 in the morning, and it seemed like barely had I hit the sack before it was time to get started on the new day.

With so many traps set, there was not a great deal of time available to properly tend the sets, and within a week the catch rate began dropping off. I usually made time each day to uplift five to ten traps that were not doing too good and move them on to the end of the line, but with the large numbers of possums that had to be killed, cached, previous day's catch skinned, and the work accumulating back at camp, the trap line was not receiving the attention that it really needed to keep it going. Slowly the numbers tapered off until the tally for my second week had dropped to 350. There was nothing much wrong with averaging 50 skins a day, but still it was a big drop from what I had taken during the previous week.

It was early in the third week that I eventually arrived at the turnip plot, and straight away I could see that it was not going to produce many possums. Actually, I never did care too much for trapping crops. From early days, when I was first getting initiated into trapping back in the Wairarapa, I had learned that just a few possums make a lot of mess in a field of turnips. They take random bites out of everything going. Soon the rain and dew get into the bite marks and next thing the crop is spoiled. There are usually few decent places to be found around a crop for putting a trap and this crop was no exception. The odd pads could be seen leading under the fence and into the turnips, but I had no intention of putting traps down on pads beneath fence lines. Out of deference to the old fellow whose land I had been trapping, I laid out the odd traps where I could find a place worthwhile, but they produced nothing of great significance and by the end of the week my entire line had produced only 150 more skins. The line was more or less had it.

If I wanted to keep going I would need to pull up large numbers of worked out traps, more or less abandon the road and start pushing my way into bush. Doing this would then create huge gaps between traps in the early part of the line, and would entail so much territory being covered each day that it was hardly worthwhile. Three weeks was pretty good for any trap line. I decided to pull everything up and spend the next few days cleaning up the thousand skins I now had back in the camp.

A thousand possum skins is a lot of skins to clean up in one go. There is hours of work involved. In fact not just hours of work, but actually days of it. Long and tedious days. Standing up against a workbench in a stuffy room, possum fur floating about and cluttering up the air, settling on your whiskers and your nose, driving you crazy with the itch. Brush it off with your sleeve and leave twice as much behind where only a little had been previously. I have always maintained that standing in front of a workbench all day, stripping boards, scraping fat off possum skins, trimming, brushing and combing furs is heavier going than working a full day out in the bush on a trap line. Your body tends to bog up standing in one spot for several hours at a time. All that standing in one spot probably was not doing much good for the legs either. The circulation doesn't work properly and then you start feeling lethargic and groggy. Stopping for a brew might be relaxing, but it doesn't do anything for the circulation. Sometimes when I was feeling just about done I would go get out a Bullworker and do a 20 minute workout. That usually got the blood circulating through the veins once more and after that I would have a few more hours of go in me. There wasn't no escaping the tedium of the skin handling work though. You just plodded on and eventually it was done.

It had taken me exactly four weeks from the time I began setting up camp to the time I was finished packed up and ready to go with the Land Rover jamb packed with skins and the trailer loaded with all my gear. I once worked it out that there is approximately half an hour's work involved in every skin from the time one sets a trap to going through the process of killing, skinning, tacking out, stripping, scraping, combing, brushing and fluffing up a fur. A thousand skins equated to about 500 hours of effort. I had not really tried keeping track of it, but if the above figures were correct I had worked an average of 17 hours a day, non stop for 4 solid weeks gathering in and processing those 1000 skins. Interesting thing is, it doesn't matter whether they are top quality export furs or run of the mill middling skins like I had just been getting, there was still half an hour's effort goes into each one of them. So if you are putting that much effort into middling skins there has to be some compensation in it somewhere.

Rodney was always happy to see my Land Rover pull up outside his skin buying shed. Here at last might be the top line of export furs that he had once tasted and been living on a promise of ever since.

"What you got here?" asks Rodney, as he comes out to meet me with a happy smile plastered all over his face. "A nice line of Ruapehu possums?"

"Still working just a wee bit north of the Mountain." says I. "But straight after this I'm heading right back into the best of them. You'll like these furs though. Just about all greys with hardly a dark skin amongst them."

Rodney helped me carry them into his shed and dump them on the floor in a huge heap. I just knew he would be pleased once he got stuck into them. He picked up as many as he could fit in his arms and piled them onto his table. Now began the inspection. Skin side first, looking for blotches. Hold the pelt up to the light, looking for windows. Run the fingers through the fur, gauging the pile. It was all I could do to stifle a smile as I watched Rodney's face drop as it registered that this was a line far removed from the large, thickly furred 'Ruapehu Mountain' possums that he was still hanging out for.

"They're not very big possums, are they?" Rodney exclaims.

"I guess you might say they are up there somewhere about the middle of the road." replies me. "But they're a nice even line of greys, don't you think?"

"You've got a few kittens in amongst them." says Rodney.

"The odd one slipped in, but hardly any." says I. "Must make sure that I don't let that happen with the 'Mountain' possums I'll be trapping on my new block."

"If only these ones were a bit bigger.... They are quite a nice line of greys though." concedes Rodney.

"Yeah, they are. Look! Instead of wasting your time sorting them into firsts, seconds and thirds, why not just make me an offer for the entire line?" suggests me.

Rodney stops and thinks about that for awhile. I could almost see his brain ticking over as he tries to work out how he might gain the advantage out of such a deal.

"Alright," says he. "Fifty cents a skin!"

I step back a pace with a look of horror etched on my face.

"You've got to be joking, Rodney! There is no way that I could ever come back with all my top of the range 'Mountain' skins if I thought that this was the sort of deal I was going to get. I was considering giving it a go this season to see if it would be worthwhile supplying you rather than exporting to London."

"How about if I raise it to seventy five cents, then?" says Rodney with a rush.

"Rodney! I couldn't possibly let this line go for anything less than a dollar a skin. Otherwise I might as well take them back and just carry on exporting."

"But they're hardly worth a dollar each," says Rodney with a bit of a whine.

"I reckon they're probably worth a couple of dollars once I get them to London."

"Would you be prepared to export them, then?" asks Rodney.

"I'm thinking mighty hard about it," says me.

"Alright then. I'll give you a dollar. But I hope that next time you come it will be with a load of those really good furs."

'Thanks Rodney. Just make the cheque out to cash and I will take it round to the Bank on the way out of town.... No don't bother about deducting any Withholding Tax. I am self employed and that will all be taken care of when I do my accounts at the end of the year.... Well, I don't know anything about you're meant to take out Withholding Tax. All I know is I employ an accountant who does my tax for me.... Look Rodney, do you want these darned possums or not?.... Yeah, just make it out to cash.... No you don't have to spell 'cash' with a capital 'C" if you don't want to."

Rodney and me always had an enjoyable time once we got together over a pile of possum furs. For me, catching Rodney was almost as much fun as catching the possums in the first instance.

So was $1000 cash in the hand good earnings for four weeks work back in 1968? That I will let you figure out for yourself. But to help you along it could be useful comparing the cost of living at the time: A two year old SWB Safari Land Rover in excellent order would have cost $1,600 to $1,700. Everything else was more or less comparable. You could buy a house in National Park for $500, and there were plenty of 10 acre blocks of land selling close to Russell in the Bay of Islands for $5000 and less. Fully qualified tradesmen; carpenters, mechanics and the like, were earning about 90cents to $1 an hour before tax. Their weekly pay check was probably a little less than $40. And in general, the buying power of a dollar back in 1968 was some twenty to thirty times the buying power of a dollar today. So I guess $1000 back there equates to about $30,000 today! Not too bad for a month's effort, cash in the hand!

It was not long after this that I drove down to Wellington and bought myself a late model 2.4 litre Mark 11 Jaguar. I fancied something fast and luxurious for travelling up and down the country. After all these years of slogging it out, the money was starting to roll in and I could not see any reason why I should not start enjoying some of the benefits. Besides, the Land Rover was getting plenty of work in the bush and it was a bit too rattley for driving up to the Chateau. Oh! Yes! And seeing I was heading that way, I also bought a complete new ski outfit from my good friend, Scruffy Turner, at National Park. Skis, boots, poles, tailor made slacks, jacket, glasses, gloves, zinc ointment... the lot.

CHAPTER 24

Trapper's Camp at Ruamata

Matt Frew, who a year earlier, had opened the way for Bob and me to work the Whangapeki, was now Station Manager at Oraukura. Once again Matt opened the way for me onto his block of land and this time I was in the thick of top quality export grade furs. Matt was a sheep and cattle man and he wasn't interested in possums or deer, but he showed a lot of respect and kindness to me because he knew that was my way of making a living. He also went out of his way to try and make things easier for me.

You could gain access to Oraukura through Moerangi Station if you turned off the Pungapunga Road about halfway to Tokaanu. But you could not get in from the Tongariro end without a key to open the solid steel mill gate. Matt loaned me a key, told me to go get a good

Trappers camp at Ruamata

Ruamata Village consisted of five abandoned mill houses

heavy padlock and interlock it with his, and then he told me to go make myself at home in Ruamata Village.

Five abandoned houses belonging to Rex Smith, of the Marton Sash and Door Company made up what was left of Ruamata. But he was not very interested in what was going on at Ruamata, nor the houses that were sitting there. In fact a couple of years later, when I telephoned him to ask him if he would be willing to sell the lot of them for removal, he could not even remember that he owned them. However, having been reminded, he suddenly became interested, and on the basis that they just might be worth a bob or two, he decided that he would hang on to them.

In its heyday Ruamata must have been a busy little settlement. It was right in the hub of a thriving timber milling district. Some of the adjoining Tuwharetoa blocks had never been milled and if the beautiful native bush that was still standing in them was anything to go by, the logs that had been milled off Oraukura and the surrounding country must have been a lovely run of timber... tall, straight, magnificent podocarps that reached all the way to the sky. There was not much in the way of good millable timber left standing on Oraukura or around Ruamata by the time I moved in. But there was a lot of worked over bush that had not yet been broken in for farmland; large areas that were full of scattered trees, stumps, reject native and thriving second growth. Milling was not entirely finished in the area though. There were still one or two good stands of rewarewa that a couple of blokes were busily chopping down in the Waionenui Block. And dropping down off the Pungapunga Road into the heads of the Waione Stream, Whitecliffs Timber Company had the last of the big haulers, puffing Diesel and black smoke, pulling out what was remaining of the local giant rimu's.

Matt and his wife lived a mile and a bit to the north of Ruamata in the Oraukura homestead, and a couple of miles to the south, just about slap bang in the middle of nowhere, Yorky Paranihi and Edie Solomon lived in a shack with a bunch of snotty nosed little youngsters. I never did quite work out how many of them there were, but they were good tamariki and they always waved out whenever they went passing by. At first Yorky was not very happy about me moving into Ruamata. But Yorky was a good sort of a bloke and I got on pretty well with him, and in time he came round to thinking I was not such a bad sort of a bloke either and we became good mates.

But right at the beginning, just to help it along that I was here for a purpose, I laid out my first line of traps not too far from Yorky's backdoor. That may have appeared a little contentious, but rather than stir him up, I think it helped Yorky realize I was simply there to do a job and he soon settled down and accepted my presence. In no time at all Yorky and Edie were dropping in to say 'G'day!' and stop off for a brew and a bite to eat. He was a good bloke, old Yorky. So was Edie. And they were always welcome round my camp.

The house I chose to live in was the first building as you entered the village. All the houses were in good order, with flush toilets that worked, wood ranges for cooking on and coppers for boiling up the dirty washing in their laundries, and any one of them would have been worth living in. But why I chose the one I did was because it was closest to the Mangaparuparu Stream which flowed swiftly through a gully just below the house. It was from here that I would have to draw my water. A big solid McEwan Ram Pump that was still in good working order was set up on a small dam down at the stream, but the pipes and plumbing that fed the water up to a holding tank, from where it gravity fed back to the houses, was long gone. As I was not inclined to working on antique pipes and plumbing along with all its inherent headaches, I resigned myself to daily carting my water needs up to the house in weighty five gallon buckets.

Having a flush toilet in the camp was a lot of fun. It was also quite an interesting innovation that used up its fair share of carted water. What made it interesting though was, in the depths of winter, when everything turned to ice, so did the water sitting in the toilet bowl. That made things a little complicated when you did your business and after you had finished, there it was, sitting pretty on top of a block of ice. To flush it away, one had to boil up a pot of water and pour it down the bowl to first get rid of the ice. Now if you think the doings smelled bad enough in the first place, just try pouring a pot of boiling water over them in a confined space and see how bad it can really get. Shouldn't grumble though. Having a flush toilet in the camp was pretty nifty and not many trappers of the day had one. It was certainly an improvement on beating tracks through sleet and snow in the middle of a dark and violent night out to the long drop.

Like most wood ranges, mine smoked badly in certain winds. To work right they really need to be regularly maintained; the chimney swept once a year, good dry firewood for fuel and all the grills and grates cleaned and polished once in awhile. I doubt my wood range had ever seen any of that sort of nonsense and nor was I going to be the one to start doing it. So mine, like most of them, smoked rather badly.

The wood range smoked but I would not have wanted to be without it

I quickly settled into my new camp at Ruamata and in no time at all got to thinking it was a great sort of a place to be. The camp was warm and dry, it was not readily accessible to private shooters, it was in the thick of good possum country with plenty of territory to work and to top it off the neighbours either side were real nice people. The house was a roomy three bedroomed prefabricated building typical of the era. There were hundreds of them scattered round the country and you would find them wherever there were timber mills and works camps. I used one side of the house, which included the bathroom, laundry, kitchen and a bedroom, for living quarters, and the other side, which included another two bedrooms and the living room with its big open fireplace, for storage and skin handling. One spare bedroom was strung with ropes and benches for stacking dried skins and finishing their ears, the living room was my work space, with my tack out table set up one end and mesh slung from the ceiling

The dining area

The living room was used for skin drying with an area set aside for working skins

throughout for hanging the boards. The remaining bedroom was set aside for guests to use and a bit of storage space for things that needed getting out of the way. It was a nice, quiet and peaceful place to live with a pleasant view from the kitchen window that looked across part of Oraukura Station to the worked over Waipari hills in the distance.

I was standing at the sink boiling up a brew on the primus and taking in the view through the kitchen window late one afternoon when this pig dog comes trotting up the road from the general direction of Oraukura Station. I did not often get visits from pig dogs and without even thinking about it I picked up my treble two, poked it out the window and bowled the dog with one clean shot. Then it suddenly dawned on me that its owner could well be just around the corner and coming along behind it. Sudden panic! I rushed out the door, sprinted down to the dog that by this stage had just about stopped kicking, grabbed it by one of its hind legs and swung it round a couple of times and shied it down into the scrub growing along the banks of the Mangaparuparu.

It was a chunky little animal and it took a fair bit of swinging to get it airborne and lobbed out of sight and it's amazing how quick you get a sweat up when you're panicking. Any moment I was expecting to see its owner come wandering into view. I kicked some loose pumice over the pool of blood that was congealing in the middle of the road and bolted back to the camp. Now where had I left off? Oh yeah. I was making a cup of tea.

I stood looking through the window past the gate and down the road for about twenty minutes, but no one showed up. And eventually I hopped in the Land Rover and went for a drive down the road checking out whether anyone was around. Later I drove down to Oraukura and told Matt what I had done. He was delighted and told me if I saw any more pig dogs, shoot them even if their owners were walking right alongside them. No pig hunters had his permission to be on the property.

A couple of weeks later I was driving through the station and there were bloodied and mauled sheep scattered all the way down the road. I raced up to tell Matt but he already knew. Bill Broadfoot had been laying a poison line further over when he had heard dogs barking and sheep bleating. He managed to shoot both of the dogs involved; a large Alsation cross brute of a dog and a bully headed pig dog, that were having a marvellous time ripping Matt's sheep to shreds. They had chewed up about 25 sheep before Bill got to them and most of these were so mauled they had to be destroyed.

Bill's own dog, a Doberman pinscher, was a wild sort of a brute that you could never be too sure of. It had never taken out any sheep, but one night it nearly took me out. We were standing outside the National Park Pub having a chat, and somehow I must have moved round a little and got myself between Bill and his Volkswagon van. That was all the dog needed. Next minute this snarling gnashing brute of a thing was scrabbling at the window trying to get out and take my head off. Fortunately the window was not open wide enough for him to get through, but nevertheless it gave me quite a turn. Bill thought it was a great joke.

"You never want to come between me and the van when the dog's inside," said Bill.

"Yeah! Well I'll try and remember that for next time," I replied

Shooting pig hunter's dogs and comfortable living aside, it was the quality of the possums that really made Ruamata the highlight of my trapping career. Here at last were the top quality export furs that I had been striving for down though the years, and in good number. From the very first Ruamata possum that I took I knew that I had finally made it. Rodney would not be seeing very many of these woolly little critters, if any at all. They were the same breed of possum I had been getting at Pokaka, but here at Ruamata there were a lot more of them. Mostly they were greys — big, fluffy, clear grey animals with silver black tips to their fur and clean white fur lining their bellies. There was a smattering of dark possums in amongst them, but these too were incredibly beautiful — thick, densely furred dark chocolate brown animals, paling off very slightly beneath their bellies. Greys and darks alike, these were furrier grade possums of the highest order.

After running one or two lines around Yorky's patch, I packed my traps into the worked over bush between Ruamata Village and Maungakatote, the high knob that stands out prominently when looking into the sunset from Tongariro Village out on the main road. I was working about 80 traps to the line and from these I was averaging 30 to 35 skins a night over the two to three week life span of the line. Of course the first week you always took more than that, but the numbers gradually tapered off and allowing for good and bad nights — some nice, clear and frosty, some miserable, wet and cold — that is what I was averaging over the life of a trap line.

However, it would be wrong for me to imply that I was able to maintain such an average day in and day out right from the beginning to the end of the trapping season. There were dead days to be counted in, where there was no tally at all; times between trap lines when I spent a few days working in the skin room stripping boards and generally trying to catch up with dressing up the furs. And there were the odd times when I just wanted a break away from it all; for taking off in the Jag' to enjoy a bit of skiing, socialising, partying, visiting. Sometimes, after working solid for two or three weeks without a break, during which time you had not seen another soul to even say 'hello!' to, you got to feeling like that.

It was not long and Bill Broadfoot started to get the wind up about me being out there trapping possums and all. He knew the way I trapped and how I could keep a trap line going for up to three weeks or more, consistently taking good kills off of it night after night. And he reckoned that once I had been through a block of bush the place was ruined for other possumers for the next six years at least. I had never thought of it that way before Bill mentioned it, but come to think of it, I would not have bothered going back over any areas I had already worked through for a few years to come neither. So Bill started getting worried and early one morning he turned up at my camp and said we needed an agreement where the boundary between our territories should be. Well that stood to reason. Otherwise no one would know what was going on and we would probably end up shooting one another.

Bill's camp was down on the Tongariro Plains between Oraukura and Mount Kakaramea where Lake Otamangakau now sits. Therefore, he said, he thought the boundary should be the Ruamata Road coming in from Tongariro to Oraukura Station. Everything on the south side of the road would be mine and everything on the north side of the road would be his. At the time I thought that this was fair enough and I agreed to it. But later I got to thinking about it and I got to realizing that it would have been better if the boundary had been the Oraukura boundary fence that ran along the top of the plateau overlooking the plains.

There was no real reason why Bill should extend his territory up onto Oraukura so close to my camp. He already had a whole lot more country than he needed with all of Mount Kakaramea, plus a

Bill Broadfoot's camp was down on the Tongariro Plains (photo Bill Broadfoot)

huge slice of Rotoaira Forest, as well as bush land all the way back to the Pungapunga Road past Mangahouhou and across to Moerangi Station. Besides, from time to time I had been driving along the Ruamata Road and I had come across deer and shot them on the north side of the road, and what was I going to do now? Watch them wiggle their hips and walk away just because that was Bill's chosen piece of territory?

In time I had worked my way through just about all the easy Tuwharetoa country from Yorky's shack to Ruamata Village and back through the cutover almost as far as Maungakatote. As it was my custom to methodically work my way through my territory cleaning up whole sections as I went, the next most obvious place to start laying out traps was down the Ruamata Road and through the Oraukura cutover bush lying adjacent to it.

It was beautiful country to trap with endless good sets whichever way you looked. Huge old trees scattered everywhere, many of them dead or dying, but there was an abundance of good forage and cover to keep the possums fat and healthy. Working down just the one side of the road hardly made mush sense. Right alongside the road, on the northern side there were sets, smattered with possum droppings and all, that were just too good to pass up. Anyway, I could not see that it made much difference to the overall plan of things whether I put traps on them or not. After all here I was trapping my way along the road, and who was going to explain to the possums that they had to stay on one side of the road or the other, because all those to the north belonged to Bill Broadfoot and those to the south belonged to Wayne Blake, so it was okay for you guys on the south to step into a trap but all you fellers to the north were not allowed to do that sort of thing. It seemed pretty obvious that they were going to come and go as they pleased, so what difference did it make if I plonked traps on the odd tree sitting alongside the road.

I was finishing off breakfast one morning when Bill came charging into my camp madder than a pickled red herring, all set and ready to flatten me. He had been driving in to Oraukura and happened to spot one of my traps on his side of the road with a beautiful big black possum sitting in it. Bill was a bit of a wild man when he got worked up and not one you would want to trifle with. He had been a semi professional boxer and regimental champion during WW11. After the war ended, because Bill was the toughest, best, war hardened fighter still standing, his CO commissioned him as a body guard and they drove all over Italy in a personnel carrier while the CO and an officer mate went on a drinking binge and Bill provided personal protection for the two of them. It made sense not to ruffle Bill up the wrong way. He was a terrific sort of a bloke, but listening to him relate some of his war yarns, I knew that he could be dangerous if he felt so inclined. Charging into my camp in a fuming rage, I had every reason to believe that right now he was dangerous and he also felt so inclined.

"Trouble is if you have already crossed the road," fumed Bill, "I'm not sure how far you might have gone into my territory."

He was dancing round a bit on his toes as he spoke as if he was getting ready to start sparring and jabbing with his left. Meanwhile I was beginning to wonder whether it might not make good sense just to shoot the guy and get it over with. It probably was not a very good idea shooting your mate just for the sake of one possum, but the trouble was, and fortunately Bill apparently did not know this, I had traps scattered all through the north side of the road. It began with a fairly innocent trap on a set right alongside the road, and then I noticed another set too good to pass up a few yards further into the block, and then just a wee mite further in there would be another set that simply could not be ignored, then a teensy bit further a virtually perfect set literally calling out to me to put a trap on it. And so it went. Probably 50% of my traps were now scattered along the road in Bill's territory. If only he had known he would not have been wasting time with words.

"You're right Bill," I said. "It was a bit thoughtless of me putting that trap on your side of the road. First thing I'll do when I leave camp is go pull it up and you can rest assured that in the future I will keep all my traps on my side of the road."

Well, fortunately Bill calmed down over a hot cup of tea and on that occasion it was not necessary for me to take the drastic action of shooting him. I resented doing it, but owing to serious concerns for my health I promptly went and pulled up every trap on the north side of the road before Bill got to realizing the extent to which I had encroached into his territory and came charging back for more.

I did not normally go out of my way looking for trouble, but there were times when it seemed it came looking for me. I had just bunked down for the night somewhere after midnight one clear and frosty night, when the glare of a spotlight lit up the walls inside my bedroom. There was a vehicle approaching from Yorky's direction, but I knew it would not be him because Yorky did not go spotlighting deer. Besides he was a gentleman, and only persons lacking in manners would go lighting somebody's house up in the middle of the night. Whoever it was they had no right to be here, and how was I to know whether they might not be planning to start shooting up the village just for entertainment. By now they were almost right outside my camp and giving it a thorough going over with their light. Any moment I expected bullets to start thumping into the building. It is always a bit tricky standing up in the glare of a spotlight, because you never know what type of an idiot is on the other side of it. I yelled out to them as I stepped into view and told them to put down their light so I could see where I was going. Instead they held their spotlight right on my face. Obviously these blokes were idiots. But just how much so I was yet to find out.

I never did get a really clear look at either of them because they kept their light trained on my eyes. However, I could make out that there were two of them in a SWB Land Rover with the driver manipulating the light and his mate standing on the back with a rifle.

"Don't you know this is private land and you fellows are not supposed to be in here?" I asked as I came up to their vehicle.

"Hah! Who do you think you are?" said the fellow on the back, and spat as he added: "You're just a Pakeha!" Then he spat again and said: "This is Maori land and we will do what we want on it."

"Yeah, this is Maori land but you have no right to be on it. And neither will you be coming back a second time," I replied, and turned my back on them and walked away.

"We'll come back as often as we want," the same fellow snarled through another mouthful of spit.

"I don't think so, mate," I answered.

It feels a little creepy walking back through the night with a spotlight trained on your back, not knowing whether there is a rifle trained on it at the same time.

Next morning I followed their wheel marks back up through the scrub to see how they had managed to get into the block. The Ruamata Road into Oraukura Station was barred with a heavy steel padlocked forestry gate where it left the Tongariro Plains, and a bulldozer had long ago scoured deep ditches across the only other access road back in the cutover, and had also pushed a log across it eliminating any possible vehicle access. But these blokes must have been working on the Wanganui River Diversion Project, and they had brought a bulldozer up into the bush from the Italian works camp and cleared themselves an access.

I was still seething from the night before and there was no way I could let them walk all over me like that or life would no longer be worth living. I carefully picked out a narrow bit of downhill slope where they had opened a way through the scrub, and that was where I spiked the road. I gathered up some old 6" x 1" boards lying round the village, drove a heap of four inch nails through them, filed up the points, laid them the full width of the track and covered them with leaf mould. Then I went and told Yorky what I had done just in case he decided to go for a drive up in the bush.

Several days passed and there was no more sign of the spotlighters and I had almost forgotten about them. Then Yorky came gleefully into my camp one afternoon and told me: "You caught those blokes up in the bush". At first it did not register what he was talking about as it was no longer on my mind.

"Those same fellows," said Yorky. "You know, those couple of Maoris. The ones who came in spotlighting that night. They came in again about midnight and you took out all four of their tyres."

Yorky said they had been stuck up there in the bush in the freezing cold in their Land Rover all night. Then in the morning they had to walk out to the Italian camp for help.

It had been a freezing cold night that particular night and very, very dark as well. They could not have picked a better night for it.

I was a bit concerned at first that they might come in some time and torch my camp. But apparently they were not willing to tempt fate a second time as they would have had no idea whether I had laid more spikes in the road at various places. And even if they could have gained access through the Tonagariro forestry gate, coming in on the legitimate road would have been too risky if they intended committing a crime. They never did come back.

In the cold Central North Island country you can usually start taking good first grade skins quite early in the year, but by May they are mating and fighting and they tend to lose a fair bit of fur in the process. By July most of the fur has grown back again and from here on and right up to the end of September you are into prime quality winter furs. By August the camp should be busting at the seems with dry and drying skins piled in heaps on benches and stacked up on the ropes. And by now you should have a fairly good idea what your tally for the season is going to be. Come September and if you have not already got your tally you had better get your head down and your ass up and start working, because in no time at all that blue streak down the backbone is going to start showing up in the pelts and you are going to know that the summer moult is underway.

Throughout the year there were certain deadlines to be met if you wanted to catch the various London fur auctions. The first sale of the season was in May. But this was usually too early in the season for me to have a representation in it. Most of the furs offered in the May auction were leftovers that had been passed in in the February sale and the prices fetched were not necessarily an accurate indication of what the rest of the year might offer. The February auction was usually a big one with the bulk of the winter's catch coming on the floor. But there was one other sale, in September. This one had all the early winter furs in it and to keep the income flowing with a bit of regularity I always set a goal of having at least 1200 furs in London in time for this sale. To be represented I needed to have my consignment on the wharves in Wellington by July. It took about six weeks for the ship to arrive in London.

If fur was in fashion that year, the bidding would be keen and lively. Parcels of fur from trappers who were known for the quality of their product would be eagerly sort. I had been exporting for some years so I suppose that my furs and my name might have been recognized by a few, but suddenly that year, in the September sale, I hit the floor with a line of top quality furrier grade furs, beautifully presented, and equal to the very best New Zealand could offer. Ever since that scumbag had walked into my camp and stripped it bare back in Pokaka, I had made it a practice to stamp my name across the brisket of every fur as it came off the board. I was probably the only trapper who ever did, so the buyers could hardly fail to recognize the fact that a trapper by the name of 'Wayne Blake' was suddenly presenting an exceptionally good offering. When the returns came back through the Reserve Bank, I had averaged $3 a skin over the 1200 skins in the parcel and that was a lot of money suddenly showed up in my bank account.

It had taken about two months of trap lines to get them, not to mention the endless hours standing in front of the work bench fluffing them up just so. It was top dollars and the money was great, but I was not in it just for the money. First and foremost I was there because I loved fur trapping, and even more so I loved working with the fur. The appearance and the feel of it; the beautiful clear grey and rich dark brown colours, the silky feel of the fur, the depth of pile when I ran my fingers through the pelt. Then there was the satisfaction of knowing that I had finally arrived up there, counted in with the best trappers in the world. Not only had I developed the trapping skills, I was also producing the finest quality fur. Dave Odey was still achieving the top prices for individual furs from his offerings, and Bill Broadfoot was coming in with a very close second. But now I was right up there with them. And we all knew that the gloves were off and Odey was going to have to keep his head down and his bum up if he wanted to stay on top.

CHAPTER 25

Comings and Goings

Trapping was pretty much a solitary job. For days on end you might see no one. But not all that many trappers were solitary men. We could get along quite well without people around us, but we still enjoyed company when it was around.

Dave Odey was a family man. He used to spend a couple of weeks in the bush and then he would go home to his wife and children for a week. He reckoned that he probably spent more time with his children than the average wage worker did, and he was probably right.

Bill Broadfoot often used to have people staying with him in his camp. Two of his sisters would come and stay from time to time and thoroughly spoil him while they were at it. They would fuss around him, cleaning up the camp, boiling his washing and making sure he was well fed with plenty of home baked goodies. They were a close knit bunch and thought the world of one another.

There were also a couple of nephews that divided their time, somewhat lopsidedly, between coming and going round Bill's camp and propping up the bar of their home town pub. For awhile there, Bill also had a compo beneficiary coming and going — a fellow by the name of Graham.

Graham had been a linesman for the power board until he got zapped on a pylon by a high tension wire. He was thrown about fifty feet to the ground with his innards all fried. Just to keep things sweet the power board paid him off and sent him home to slowly wither away and die. Bill found Graham in the pub, drowning his sorrows in drink and trying to speed the process with an overdose of alcohol. He reckoned there was not much left worth living for. His body was wasted away to skin and bone and his wife had taken off with another man. All that kept him functioning was an overworked heart trying to do everything for him that his muscles once did. Bill took pity on him and brought him down to his camp to try and get his mind off his woes. Graham had bought himself a Vauxhall Velox car with some of his compensation money, and I was out at Tongariro one Friday night picking up my bread and a cabbage when a motorist pulled in and said there had been a head on smash a couple of miles back down the road. A Vauxhall Velox had piled head on into a truck and there was at least one dead guy pinned in behind the motor in the Velox. I knew Bill and Graham had gone to Waihi in Graham's car and they were due back that night. I took off out of there with my groceries still on the counter, but it was not Graham's Vauxhall. It was a car load of Italians from the works camp driving back from Turangi. They had wandered across the centre line and been taken out. One was dead and another ended up a paraplegic, virtually reduced to a vegetable. It was tough for the Italians, but I was relieved that my mates were not the victims.

Graham did not have all that much longer to go though. Bill was back in Waihi, and the two nephews and Graham were sitting up in their beds reading by candlelight late one night, when Graham gave a loud gasp and just sat there, propped up by his pillows, eyes popping out of his sallow cheeked head, dead as a dodo. Wally Broadfoot told me later that he and his brother absolutely freaked out. Neither of them had ever seen a corpse before and they were both terrified of the supernatural. They pulled their blankets over their heads and tried to shut the horror of it out of their minds, but every time they sneaked a look out of the blankets, there was Graham in the flickering candle light, sitting up staring at them through glazed and lifeless eyes. Neither of them slept a wink all night. Before the first light of dawn they were up and out of there. I never saw a great deal of them after that. Perhaps staying in Bill's camp had lost much of its appeal. Certainly, propping up the bar back home was a lot less scary.

At first I had a regular order of bread that I picked up from the petrol bowser at Tongariro every Friday night. Often I was in a rush to get back to camp because of the workload piling up. They did not have much in the way of groceries at the Tongariro bowser but it was the closest place to my camp so it was convenient shopping there. But in between trap lines I would often drive into Taumarunui and spend a night or two with Kingsley Jones. Kingsley had been a deer culler in the Ruahines for awhile. But when I first met him he was breaking down venison for River Ridge in Taupo. Now he owned the Taumarunui 'Pie Cart' which did not sell pies at all, but instead sold fish and chips.

Kingsley had a big, useless, shaggy haired mutt called Brannigan that used to make his house smell. One morning I was sitting in the kitchen eating a bowl of porridge when Kingsley pointed out that I was eating my porridge out of Brannigan's bowl.

"But, not to worry," said Kingsley. "Brannigan's a good natured sort of a dog and he probably wont take offence at it."

What the hell Brannigan's bowl was doing up on the kitchen sink in the first place I would not know. Anyway, I never cared too much for porridge, and I never cared too much for Brannigan neither. When Kinsley wasn't looking, I gave the dog a hefty boot up the backside and told him in the future to keep his filthy bowl on the floor where it belonged.

People also used to come and go at Kingsley's camp. Dave Saxton was poaching possums wherever there was a block of bush all the way from Ngaruawahia to Raetihi and beyond. He never had a block of his own. Reckoned he did not need one. While visiting his mother in Wadestown, Wellington, he ran poison lines through Wiltons Bush and ended up being chased through the flower gardens by a very irate caretaker. I was told he did the same thing in the Wellington Botanical Gardens. I do not really know about that, but it certainly would not have surprised me.

David 'Saxophone' would come and go and so would I. And often the two of us would be at Kingsley's at the same time. We all got on pretty well together except for just one time when I was sitting in Kingsley's lounge with an LP of Shirley Bassey playing on the Stereo. Dave Sax' came in from somewhere out in the rain and said he didn't care too much for Shirley Bassey.

"Tough!" said I. "Because unless you want to go back out in the rain where you just came from, you're going to have to listen to her."

Saxophone disappeared into the kitchen and made a cup of coffee and in a short while he was back, complaining once again about my choice of music. It must have irritated him that I was not caring too much about his moaning so he began looking for some other means of making me take notice.

Kingsley had a couple of Scottish swords propped up in a corner of the lounge. Dave was walking round with his coffee in his hand muttering unsavoury comments about Shirley Bassey when he noticed the swords. He stopped in his tracks. He looked at me, he looked back at the swords, and his face lit up. Next thing I felt this prick in my side and there was Saxton with a sword in his hand, laughing his head off and having a great time taking little jabs at me. He only did it a couple of times and I got mad. I bounced out of the chair grabbed up the other sword and took a swipe at him. The way Sax took off I think he realized I was not playing with him. He had not drawn blood, jabbing me in the side, but at the time I did not know that, and I was mad. He shot into the kitchen slamming the door behind him and I took off the other direction, into the hallway and into the kitchen from another door. We were still charging through the house swords in our hands, banging and shutting doors with Saxton on the run and me hot on his heels with thoughts of puncturing his hide when Kingsley happened to come home and managed to calm me down. That would have been the end of it, but Kingsley was terrified that once he returned to his pie cart, Saxton might do something to stir me up again and

I might end up impaling him. I was told to accompany him back to the pie cart and stay there until he closed up for the night. Later that night, just to be sure, Sax was made to sleep on the floor of Kingsley's room sandwiched between his bed and the wall, and I was banished to solitary confinement in the spare room.

Dave Saxton was a fairly big sort of a bloke and he had the strength of a young bull. When it came to possums he seemed to just rip their skins off their backs. He was as rough as guts, but he was also very fast. I never tried to rush the skins off my possums. The way I looked at it, they were worth too much to ruin just because you were in a hurry. I would rather plod on steadily and do the job nice and neat and tidy. But there were blokes could skin a possum in well under a minute and some of them just could not resist bragging about it. I do not think it was Saxophone's way to brag about how quick he was, but if ever he was challenged to a competition nor was he the sort of bloke to quickly back off.

He, Merv Templeton, Ron Hope and I had all been invited into the Cosmopolitan Club as guests of Sax's brother, who was an up and coming business man about town. As none of us were what you might call gentlemen, and the Cosmo was a gentleman's club, it probably was not a very wise move on Sax's brother's part to have extended the invitation in the first place. But nevertheless there we were, the four of us, all looking relatively respectable in our own little group that was set slightly apart from the rest of the gentlemen in the club, quietly sipping our beer and generally behaving ourselves. Until, that is, Templeton started bragging about how fast he could rip the skin off a possum's back The beer started flowing a little quicker and the conversation got a little more animated. The talk was not proving anything, but Merv reckoned he was the quickest and Saxophone reckoned he was not. While these two were getting all heated up, Ron and I kept out of it. Sax went out, we assumed to the men's room. But when he returned he had a couple of dead possums in his hand from the back of his Land Rover.

"Here you are, Templeton!" says Sax, tossing a possum at Merv. "Lets see if your hands are as quick as your mouth."

At this juncture I did not mind getting myself involved. I was appointed timekeeper, which meant I also told them when to 'Go!', and Ron was referee. Both participants stood there with a possum held between their legs and knife ready to go.

"Okay, you guys. Get ready. Go!"

Sax whipped the balls off his possum and hurled them over his shoulder. Templeton did the same. Already they were making their cuts from foot to foot through the back legs and now they had end for ended their possums and were starting on the front. The balls were just coming in for their landing on top of the bar.

There was a loud bellow from the barman as one set of balls landed on the sink next to the jug he was pouring and the other set splattered across the bar top and rolled onto the floor. We were not taking much notice of the barman. By now all four of us were caught up in the spirit of it all. I was closely watching the second hand on my watch, while at the same time keeping an eye on the competitors and shouting encouragement and it was only vaguely in the background that I noticed the barman vault over the bar. Now both men had their possums on the carpet with their foot across the shoulders. They were just about neck 'n' neck as they gripped the skin to pull it off with one last heave. And that was when the barman came charging into the back of Saxton.

Sax was already a little off balance as he leant into his possum. Caught completely off guard, he crashed into Templeton and the two of them went down. The barman was a surly sort of a bloke who did not seem to have much sense of humour. Merv and Dave just sat in a heap grinning up at the barman trying to explain to him that they were in the middle of a possum skinning competition. I do not know how surly blighters ever get jobs as barmen. Good PR is of prime importance for the welfare of the ongoing business. He just glared at the four of us. Told us to "Get those bloody possums off the carpet and get them out of here. And get your bloody selves out of here too, and don't ever come back!"

Jock Erceg, who was running a farm a few miles down the Wanganui River, had organised a possum block for Merv somewhere down that way. Next time I came into town I was told by Kingsley that Sax was now down that way too. I had bought a couple of brand new, good quality bath towels and gone back to the bush without them. Sax noticed them after I had gone, took a fancy to them and took them down the river with him when he went. I daresay he intended returning them at some later stage, but knowing how Sax lived I decided there was not much point in pursuing the matter. After a trip down the river with Sax they would never be new again.

Actually, I am not even sure that I ever saw Sax again. But about three years down the track, I once again caught up with Kingsley, who now had a fish and chip shop in Hamilton. Saxophone, he told me, had some time back left off possums and he was now down south hunting venison. He had bought himself a fixed wing plane and was working off the Alabaster strip. Apparently there were a few questions raised in Inland Revenue's mind about the previous owner of the aircraft, and during their audit they wanted to know who it was he had sold the aircraft to.

"Dave Saxton!?" the auditor returned. "We do not have any records or files at the Inland Revenue Department pertaining to any person by that name!"

According to Inland Revenue records, no one by the name of Dave Saxton even existed. It seemed he had somehow managed to get thus far in life without ever paying a dollar in tax.

Kingsley and I were sure Sax would eventually crash his plane and that would be the end of him. But he surprised us all by going on to become one of the country's most skilled helicopter operators and a living legend in the hunting fraternity.

Those mid winter months, keeping warm and dry was of utmost importance. You needed to keep well wrapped up and looking after yourself, because it can take it out of you working out in the wet and cold day after day. So when the cold months really set in I used to layer my clothing, starting with a pair of long johns beneath my thick woollen sharing trousers. The traditional bush singlet was indispensable for keeping the kidneys warm, and over that I wore a Moose Lodge bush shirt, a cotton shirt on top again to seal in the warm air, then a thick woollen jumper and on top of everything a dark navy boiler suit. This was a pretty warm get up, but occasionally, on the coldest of days I still found it necessary to wear my Swandri as well. And I always kept a nylon parka tied around my waist or tucked away in my pikau in case an icy wind got up and started boring into the bones.

If it was raining heavy, I might dispense with some of the layers and instead put on a rain hat, my old crayfishing thigh boots and a thoroughly waterproof knee length raincoat that hung down well over the boots. Thigh boots were good once you got used to walking in them. They certainly kept you warm and dry. Waterproof leggings tended to drag too much and they never felt right in the bush. The raincoat was not the pull over your head type. It was double domed up the front so that it could be opened up occasionally to air yourself out. The slip on types were no good because with no ventilation they got you sweating and you usually ended up sopping wet on the inside and the outside.

Once the rain really set in though there was not much point in carrying on until the weather cleared. Possums do not like rain. They stay at home and wait for it to clear before mooching about. But no matter how bad the weather, come rain or shine, I would always go out to skin my caches and make sure there were no possums sitting in any traps before I called it a day. After all, that was what the wet weather gear was for. If I had reason to believe the rain had set in for a day or two, I might spring all my traps and lay them to one side on the set out of the way until the weather came right. Heavy rain tended to wash the cover dirt off the plates, so they would all have to be redone before you could hope to catch anything in them again anyway.

Apart from dressing well, because the hours were long and the weather was cold it was also necessary to eat plenty of good solid food. Jimmy Forbes, the National Park butcher, was stocking export quality meat from the works at Patea, and once I realized just how good the quality of his meat was, I lodged a regular weekly order with him for a block of rump steak, a block of pork and a couple of pounds of mince.

From Ruamata to National Park and back was a good sixty miles, with about 32 miles of it pretty rough going. The Ruamata road was what you might call 'semi-metalled', that is, more mud than metalled. It was narrow, it twisted and wound its way through scrub and in places dropped off steeply into creek heads, and it was liberally dotted with potholes. But I knew every pothole, rut and bump on the road, and it did not take me long to get there and back in the Jag. For the sake of Jimmy Forbes meat and the good meals I could concoct from it, I considered it well worth the trip.

Trouble was though, that just as always in the past, I would often be so dog tired at the end of the night I would drop off to sleep sitting at the table with the food untouched. Many times I crawled into my sleeping bag exhausted and unfed. But when I got up in the morning there would be a king sized meal of steak and vegetables, or a huge bowl of Pork Chop Suey sitting on the table waiting to be eaten. All I had to do was heat it up and I would be working on high octane fuel for the rest of the day.

Having a regular order of meat with Jimmy Forbes, I got into a sort of routine with my meal preparation. The pork was the most likely to spoil so I would usually start off with a good solid roast. Once it had been roasted what was left of the pork was then good for two or three days at least, and apart from a few sandwiches filled with slabs of cold meat from the roast, the leftovers were set aside for the Chinese Chop Suey that would come later in the week.

This was an easy dish to prepare. First cut up the precooked cold pork however you prefer it — diced, sliced, it does not make much difference. Now chop up a big helping of cabbage, a bit on the chunky side, a heap of onions, carrots, capsicum, mushrooms, cauliflower, whatever you might have. If you do not have much in the way of fresh stuff, use frozen or tinned mixed vegetables in with the cabbage instead. While you are cutting up the vegetables, you can also be boiling a pot of egg noodles until they are nice and tender. Drain the water from the noodles but do not discard all of it as you will want to add a little to the Chop Suey towards the end of the cooking.

With all the vegetables cut up and ready to go, heat a small amount of cooking oil sizzling hot in the bottom of a deep frying pan, or better still a wok if you have one. The carrots take longer to cook so they go in first, then the precooked meat, the onions, and finally the leafy vegetables. Sprinkle in a little salt and some oyster sauce while you are tossing the food in the pan. Add in a small amount of the noodle juice and slightly thicken with a little cornflour. This meal does not take long to cook, and should be taken off the heat before the cabbage is soft and overcooked. Serve up a big helping of noodles onto your plate or into a bowl, cover the noodles with heaps of Chop Suey and sprinkle soy sauce over the top. If you prefer a different meat, substitute the pork with chicken or beef. On various occasions, I have been doing this same Chinese dish for friends and family for coming up 40 years now and still have not gotten sick of it. I do not think the family nor the friends have neither.

I usually served the mince on a bed of boiled spaghetti with cheese grated over the top. I still do this meal 40 odd years down the track and enjoy it just as much today as I did back there also. Mince may take a little longer to cook, and unless it is very lean you might want to drain off the juice and cool it to spoon off any fat. So start early with boiling the mince with a little salt and pepper to taste. Do not discard the juice when you drain it off. You are going to need it. All you are doing is cooling it so you can get rid of the fat that will settle on the top. Boil the spaghetti in a separate pot until it is tender, preferably following the instructions printed on the packet. When done stir in a wee bit of butter or cooking oil to stop it sticking. Now add the juice back to the mince and start adding in sliced carrots, chopped onions, a good shaking of Lea and Perrins Worcester Sauce, a few good smatterings of soy sauce, a dash or two of Tabasco if you like it spicy. As soon as the sliced carrots are tender pile in a whole lot of frozen, or tinned, mixed vegetables. Bring it back to the boil and immediately remove from the heat. Thicken slightly with cornflour, reheat but do not boil. That's it mate, its ready for eating. A side helping of lightly boiled cabbage sprinkled with malt vinegar after a good dob of butter has been melted into it makes the dish complete. Pile the mince up high on top of the spaghetti and grate a good helping of cheese on top.

What about the steak? Do I really need to tell you how to cook a steak?

Make sure you are cutting across the grain and not along it when slicing the steak! I cut mine slightly less than ¾ of an inch thick. Rump has a good taste to it but it can be a bit chewy if it is not tenderised. So give it a good thumping with a tenderiser both sides. Now smear crushed garlic on one side only and place it this side down on the plate you intend marinating it on. Next, on the top side sprinkle a little good quality dark soy sauce. Spread it evenly across the steak with a knife. Add a few drops of Tabasco if you like it spicy, splatter liberally with red wine. Old wine no longer good enough for drinking is okay. Give it a light dusting with barbecue or steak seasoning. Do you like pepper steak? Okay grind pepper to taste all over it from the pepper mill. Let it marinate for half an hour or longer. An hour or two is more than enough. Cook in a hot frying pan using a smear of good quality margarine to stop it sticking, and when you first put the steak in the pan it goes in garlic side down. I like my steak medium rare so it won't take long before you flip it over in the pan. When it is just about done pour in any surplus marinade. The heated marinade can be poured over your steak, or on top of your boiled rice if that is what you are complimenting it with. Cabbage, potatoes, onions, all go well with the steak and so do boiled carrots smeared with butter. If I was doing eggs with the steak I would go easy on the marinade but would fry up a heap of mushrooms and onions in butter to set it all off. Don't worry about the cholesterol. Just keep reminding yourself cholesterol doesn't exist. Anyway, if you're worth your salt as a hunter, you will be out there in the bush next day burning it all off. So, what the heck!?

That was the basic meals of the week. I suppose you are now going to say I was not living very well considering how much my possum skins were raking in. But I forgot to mention there was usually a bottle or two of red wine lying round the camp to go with the meal, and tins of Betty Crocker puddings and fruit cake to fill up the empty spaces. And there were plenty of variations over and beyond the foregoing. And if I really felt like something different and had the time to spare, I could always duck up to the Chateau in the Jag and get one of the waitresses to serve me something special. Then, if I felt inclined, I might just decide to share a glass of Champagne as well.

Fairly late in the season I was approached by a manufacturing furrier from Auckland, Mr Roy Maxwell, who asked if we could meet

Confrontation! Kim the dog and possum

at the Chateau to discuss furs. Roy advised that he was interested in buying top quality furs direct from my camp and thus cut out the middle man. After having them tanned, he would turn them into high fashion garments for retail through his Queen Street outlet. I took a bundle of furs with me for the meeting and Roy was somewhat taken aback by their quality. Previous to our meeting the only possum skins he had ever had anything to do with were what had been offered by local skin buyers. When I told him what I was now realizing in London for my furs, Roy realized that he was no longer in the running. Nevertheless he had roused my interest. We made a deal whereby I would send a parcel of furs to the tanners in Dunedin at my expense and Roy would sew them into garments for me to sell privately on consignment. I picked out about thirty of my finest grade dark furs, to be sewn into a premium quality hooded snow parka. I also picked out about sixty grey skins that I felt would be better left out of my export bale owing to their middling size. Their colour was nice and clear, but having come off animals that were not fully mature they were more or less in the reject category. Had Roy not turned up they would have been exported, but it improved my line by not including them in the overseas offering.

Fur prices were on a steady rise overseas and this year there did not seem to be much point in heading down south for the summer. I had made more money in just the first week of the trapping season with the inferior possums I had sold to Rodney than I had made during the entire previous summer chasing venison. I was keenly interested to see how a furrier transformed fur pelts into a finished garment and Roy had invited me to come to Auckland and be his guest while he did it.

Besides, there was something else on my mind.

CHAPTER 26

Summer Interlude

With regard to shooting deer, when you are onto a good thing you certainly do not go wandering about blowing your trumpet or in no time at all every Joe Hunt and his uncle will be walking all over the top of you trying to get themselves a piece of the pie. We had long abandoned any thoughts of putting a freezer in the Waipakihi and tying the valley up for a meat shooting block. But spring and early summer, there were still plenty of deer to be got out of it. Neither Bob Hannigan nor I had ever told anyone where we had been getting all our deer the previous spring and nor did we want anyone to know because we had further ideas for the place.

During the past winter, Bob had found himself back in the Northern Tararuas trapping possums on the same blocks where he and I first started out. But now, with the season all wrapped up, he headed north to join me at Ruamata.

Standing up against a work bench scraping fat and stripping boards is not exactly brain taxing work and the neurons and the synapses are left relatively free for expanding on thoughts and ideas far removed from possums. Many an empire was built and torn down again during the course of some of those endless hours of skin dressing, but one thought that had been niggling away for some time now was for Bob and me to go back into the Waipakihi and record a meat shooting, venison recovery sequence on 16mm film.

With the trapping season over and time on my hands while waiting for my skins to dry prior to baling, I sat down and drafted up a sequence of shots and scenes to be filmed. Professional Ektachrome EF 16mm film with magnetic sound strip down one edge was not cheap and to make something worth looking at was going to require quite a lot of it. I did not have endless finances to throw into such a project, so it was therefore necessary to carefully plan each scene and even the number of frames that were going to be used on each take. Commercial film is shot at 24 frames a second and with this in mind I needed to work out how many frames and seconds should be used in each instance to keep the action moving and the finished film worth looking at. Fade-ins, fade-outs and other types of scene transitions were worked out so that they could be done on location with the actual camera. Working with a generous budget, such careful planning would hardly be necessary, as the film editors would take care of all such trifling details in the editing room and ultimately, on the cutting room floor. But I could not afford such luxuries and therefore I was more or less editing before I had even loaded the film into the camera. Eventually I had it all worked out and making sense... scene plans, shooting sequences and finished script. One of the young typists up at the Chateau typed everything up for me and the cameras were ready to roll. Well, almost.

My camera was a Swiss made 16mm Paillard Bolex mounted with a three turret lens. It was a beautiful piece of machinery, made with the precision of a fine Swiss watch, but everything on it was manual. Even the motor worked on a wind up spring that had to be manually wound every so many frames. The lenses were swung into position according to whether you were shooting in wide angle, regular or telescopic mode. Fade ins and fade outs were done by slowly opening the shutter on a new scene or slowly closing the shutter on a completed scene. Dissolves were created in a somewhat similar way, but in this case after fading out, the film was back wound and the new scene double exposed over the preceding while at the same time being faded in to the correct aperture setting. Compared to modern video cameras that are programmed to do everything for you, it was

***Getting organised. Kim was told to keep his eyes off the rifle
and concentrate on the camera***

We set up our base camp in a little clearing just beyond Sika Flat

all rather complicated. It was not as if we did not know the theory behind doing all these things, but before we got into the Waipakihi and started using our valuable commercial film, we needed to get it right in practice. Bob was going to be the cameraman, while I would be directing and calling the shots, and at the same time handling the rifle and acting as meat shooter. So if the script called for a certain type of transition Bob would need to be able to do it. I bought a few rolls of regular Kodachrome film and we spent the next few days experimenting and practising until we had the feel of it. The results when they came back from the Kodak laboratory were quite pleasing and this time we really were ready to roll.

Shooting off a bit of 16mm film might sound like a pretty straight forward and simple affair. But in reality there was a good deal of thought and planning went into it. For a start off, we needed to buy in about a month's supply of food as we estimated that it could take all of that and longer shooting the scenes I had planned. While we were not restricted for time with regard to how long we could spend shooting the film, we knew the deer would be coming out on the river flats for only as long as there was spring growth about. So first off we needed to get the hunting and venison recovery scenes in the can. Everything else, the camp scenes, river crossings, travel, could be shot at our leisure. However, as the entire film was about a quick trip in and out of a river valley, shooting deer going in and dragging the carcasses out the following day, we would have to take care that the weather conditions, cloud mass, and even the elevation of the sun or the time of the day matched up with the various scenes for the sake of correct continuity. Little wonder film makers favoured California, where day in and day out the sun shone bright and skies were always blue. Not so in the Kaimanawa Mountains where Bob and I often waited patiently for half an hour or more for the sun to reappear from behind a cloud.

Wayne Blake with Bob Hannigan discussing a scene

Shooting several deer for the recovery footage did not take long, but shooting them with the camera took considerably longer. Stalking in quickly with a rifle to drop a deer is a relatively simple procedure, but stalking a deer with a cameraman stalking behind you and trying to cater to both is a little more tricky. It all took time.

We worked our way up through the valley, picking deer off flats and filming as we went over a period of two or three days. Meanwhile the carcasses had to be well cared for to protect them from flies until we were ready to start filming the recovery scenes.

We needed seven or eight deer to make a worthwhile load for the tractor tube, and as soon as the quota was filled we began the downriver haul. What had taken only a couple of days the previous year when we were simply recovering the carcasses, stretched into more than a week recording it on film.

After seven days of dragging and pushing the laden tube through

Recovering venison. Entering a pool backwards

shallows, pools, rapids and log jams, I was getting a little concerned at the deteriorating condition of the carcasses. Being in and under water most of that time, there was no problem with flies, but the colour of the meat had gone from a firm and healthy red to a pallid soggy pink. Eventually, I decided that they had done well enough and if we delayed any longer I would have to dump them in a deep pool and leave them there. We stowed the camera rushed them the final couple of miles down to our base camp on Sika Flat, piled them into the Land Rover, and delivered a very soggy, wet and waterlogged heap of venison to one of the local buyers.

They must have looked rather suspect. I recall him turning them over and poking at them and thoroughly inspecting them for some considerable time as he tried to draw it out of me where they had come from and how come they were so wet looking yet showing no signs of rigor mortis. Eventually greed must have got the better of him. He bought them anyway and I suppose the meat ultimately found its way onto the tables of some fortunate Germans; pre-tenderised, thoroughly bled, and blanched delicate pink.

With the hunting and recovery scenes safely in the can, we went back in and started work on all the other scenes that one dubs in for padding. River crossings with the Land Rover, camp and cooking, stalking, deer browsing and deer panicking, travelling and whatever else it takes.

We were ten miles upriver, holed up in a miserable little fly camp tent on Thunderbolt Flat, still working on sequences when Christmas

We went back to cover Land Rover scenes

Day overtook us. The rain was hosing down and we were stuck there. There was nothing left to eat except a billy full of sweetened boiled rice and some powdered milk. We lay around in our sleeping bags, damp, cold and hungry, thinking of the folks back home. They would be getting together over huge festive dinners of roast lamb and mint sauce, followed by Christmas pudding doused in brandy, coated with custard, plastered with dollops of whipped cream. There would be ice cream and candy, hundreds and thousands and lollipops, boxes of chocolate and glasses of wine, brandy snaps and cream cakes, good cheer, jovial company, bon-bons, and what the heck were we doing way up here in this miserable god forsaken place anyway? We should have been out there getting bloated, full and inebriated with them. So much for Christmas Dinner in the Waipakihi!

We were still working from Thunderbolt Flat when a film jammed in the camera. There was no way of fixing it without losing all the scenes that had already been so painstakingly shot on that particular reel. Most of them were irreplaceable, and the nearest camera technician was many hours and miles away in Wanganui. Bob stayed back at Thunderbolt and I began the long trek down stream, then the drive from Sika Flat to the Desert Road, and down the Parapara to Wanganui, and back.

Eventually, we had shot more than 2000 feet of film. I had spent a small fortune doing it, and I was still not even halfway there with regard to the finished film. Next step was to get the cans of film up to Auckland for processing. Then would come all the problems of how to edit, cut and splice, dub on sound, titles and credits. And after that I didn't even know.

Sticking with possums was probably a lot easier. It was certainly a lot cheaper. Anyway, my tanned furs had now returned from Dunedin. I also needed to get them up to Auckland for Roy Maxwell to begin fashioning into garments.

I parked the Land Rover back at Ruamata, packed everything into the Jaguar and took off for some northern sun, sand and saltwater.

Furrier Roy Maxwell dampens down the furs with clean water
They are then rolled and left overnight
The furs are now pliable and easy to work.
They are carefully colour matched
Damage is then removed

Furs are joined and sewn together
Then sewn into sheets
Patterns are laid over the furs and held in place with tacks
After scribing the pattern the fur is then cut out
Tape is hand sewn around the edges
Ready to be pieced together
Frances Probert models a garment made from "reject" furs.

CHAPTER 27

Waione (Winter 1969)

There was a vast area of cut over bush to the west of Oraukura and Moerangi Stations that took in the Waipari, Puketapu and Waione Blocks. And if you kept going you would eventually end up in the Whangapeki where Bob and I had worked from our Horoeka Tent Camp a couple of seasons earlier. The possums in the Whangapeki were not of very high quality but the Waipari, Puketapu and Waione possums were magnificent. I did not know where one type began and the other type finished. Nor did I really know why. But I supposed they were from two different liberations and the animals closer to Oraukura were still inside that zone of noticeably colder mountain climate. I know that some days when I was out working my trap lines in the Waipari the wind would come whipping off those mountains

After filming in the Waipakihi, Bob set up camp beneath Mount Kakaramea (photo Bob Hannigan)

He then moved on to Seven Mile Mill, behind Taurewa off SH47 where he saw out the trapping season

and bite right through to the bone it was so cold. Anyway the feed they were all on was no different, so it had to be a combination of climate and animal type. It was in this vast tract of cut over bush where I planned to spend most of my time this coming season.

Late February 1969 saw me back in my camp at Ruamata getting ready for what was to become, although I did not know it at the time, my final season of fur trapping. The results of Anning Chadwick and Kiver's February London Fur Auction had been cabled back to me and there had been a total clearance of my offering. The prices had again been incredibly good. The average realization was $3.50 per skin, with my finest greys reaching a little more than $12 each. Quality furrier grade furs were in strong demand and it looked as if prices were set to go even higher still.

I could hardly wait to get back into it, but February was just a bit too early to get started. It was never too early to start getting in the winter's supply of firewood though. Bill Broadfoot and I got together and cut a whole heap of logs into rounds and loaded them onto my trailer. You get through an awful lot of firewood in a possum camp during the course of a winter and I lost count of the number of trips I did back and forth to our camps carting that wood, but by the end of it both our woodsheds were piled high. Then came several days of chopping the rounds into pieces fit for a fire and splitting a huge heap of kindling. There is nothing worse than arriving home in the dark, wet, cold and tired from your trap line, and having to start cutting up kindling in order to get the fire started.

There was still a bit of warmth in the air and the deer were fat and healthy from browsing good summer grasses and fresh young leaves. Deer are naturally very lean animals, but prior to the roar both hinds and stags tone their bodies up in preparation for the rigours of the rut and gestation. Stags strip the velvet from their antlers on the trunks and lower branches of woody shrubs and small trees and polish and stain their tines on the tannin from the bark. They lie around in the sun, wallow in mud holes, eat and sleep. By late February most animals are fighting fit and in prime condition, and if ever they are going to carry fat on their back steaks it is now during these late months of summer. Wherever I went I kept a rifle close by.

Along the road from Ruamata heading towards Yorky Paranihi's, there were long sweeping open lahars that gently sloped away through monoao and sparse tussock to manuka and swampland. Deer tracks were thick through the manuka and often I had seen the same two deer out at a distance, sunning themselves in the morning sun on the warm pumice of the lahars. There was only one place they seemed to favour for this. A clear patch of ground about a chain out from the manuka. They were not altogether stupid though these deer. They positioned themselves in such a way that as you drove along the road you only got a momentary glimpse of them as you swept around a bend in the road and out of sight. I think they sat out there enjoying the sun with one ear to the road. They knew that the sound of a vehicle coming to a stop and backing up meant trouble. As long as you kept going they were not too concerned about you. But the minute you braked the Land Rover and sounded like you were about to pull up, they were on their feet and gone. The only time I had ever seen them was when I was driving through at speed, so apparently they were smart enough to connect a slow moving vehicle with trouble too.

The .222 was a handy little weapon, but on really big animals out at longer range, it sometimes paid to use a bigger calibre. I still owned and used my Savage 99F lever action .308 when the need arose. The lahars were way out in the middle of open country with no practical way of sneaking up on them under cover. The range was about 300 yards. Here was a typical situation where there was a need for a heavier long range calibre. The problem was, how to get onto them and take them by surprise. The only way I could see of doing it, was to come charging along the road, time it so that you braked and came to a halt in the exact spot from where you could get a clear shot and hope that on that particular occasion they were out and sunning themselves.

I picked a time when Yorky had gone to town and the road had been quiet for a few days. Everything had to be set up and ready and the timing had to be spot on. I loaded up the .308, propped it across my knee with the muzzle poking out the window and took off.

As I came into the bend I was travelling at a fair speed. Suddenly I slammed on the brakes and pulled hard on the hand brake. The Land Rover skidded to a halt with a clear view across the lahars, and the deer were taken completely by surprise. I was in such a hurry I clean forgot about pulling the Land Rover out of gear. It jerked to a stalling stop as I swung open the door, threw my feet out onto the road and steadied my rifle across the sill. Instantly the two deer were on their feet and running. I just had time to place the cross hairs behind the shoulder on one of them and squeeze off as they made it to the manuka. I heard the thwack as the bullet hit and saw the trailing deer stumble as it made cover. I found it lying just inside the manuka, and never again did I see any deer sitting out on those lahars.

Smart but not smart enough!

Pre season was a good time to go surveying your territory and planning out where and how you were going to lay your lines. Some blokes spent time during the summer cutting tracks, but I never found this necessary. Occasionally, while I was getting a new trap line into place, I would clear a way through a grove of pepperwood or a bit of tight scrub with my slasher. But if the undergrowth was that thick, I would try and find a way around it rather than through it. The area I had mapped out for this season was mainly cut over bush with numerous old logging roads scattered through it, so I doubted that the slasher would even get a look in.

I began the season in the Waipari, where an old timber road meandered through a valley making ideal conditions for working from the Land Rover. I would drive so far then pack bundles of ten traps and cut up into the hills either side of the road laying them out on the numerous big old trees that had been left behind as unsuitable for milling. The catch rate was quite good, but eventually the road came to nothing in amongst stands of rewarewa, hinau and other less favoured species. I managed to keep the line going for a couple of weeks then pulled up all my traps and moved on.

Bill turned up one day and asked me if I would like to share a poison line with him up on Mount Kakaramea. I never usually bothered with poison, much preferring to work with traps. Bill was the opposite. He did more with poison and he seemed to do very well with it. I was always eager to learn and seeing it was Bill's country we would be working I could not see that I had anything to lose by tagging along.

We took off early in the day packing a couple of tubes of Strong's liquid cyanide, a milk powder tin of flour spiked with eucalyptus oil and a flask of tea. We pushed and cut our way through bush and undergrowth, working up and down and around the mountain, Bill squirting little dobs of cyanide near the base of trees and on other likely looking spots and me sprinkling little bits of flour to encourage the possums to the bait. Early next morning we were back skinning out what had died on the line the night before. We shared the possums 50/50 with Bill picking up one possum and me picking up the next. Trouble was though, a lot of possums that I considered worth taking Bill regarded as rejects and wanted to leave behind. Some of them may have been just a little less than fully mature, or perhaps they may have been graded as seconds. However I knew that once I got working on them and tidying them up they would still fetch around $3 each. Bill did not mind me taking them to add to my tally, but doing so was slowing us down. We still had a lot of country to cover so in the end I had to leave them to waste. By the end of the day we had taken a total of 150 skins. In a couple of day's time Bill would have to go round the line once more to check for any stragglers that might yet take a bait.

I still could not see how the figures stacked up for a poison line. It had taken a day to lay and a day to pick up. Granted if Bill had been working on his own he would have got more skins, but then if he had been working on his own he probably would not have extended the line through so much country and therefore he would not have killed as many possums in the first place. In a couple of days he would have to go over the line once more and this time for a lot less possums. I do not know what he did with himself on the day in between, but he would not have been able to use it to lay another poison line, for if he did then he would no longer be free to go round the first line. If he picked up a total of 100 skins off the line, this would have to be divided by 3 or 4 days to find the average per night. There was nothing wrong with an average of twenty five to thirty possums a night. But the problem with poison was, that a good rain might wash out the line before it had a chance to kill and then you had nothing to show for all your work. Properly laid traps on the other hand just kept on catching.

When I was trapping at Pokaka, one of Dave Odey's mates talked me into sharing a poison line with him up on Mount Ruapehu in the native that slopes down from the Ohakune Mountain Road towards Karioi. It was exactly the same. We had a good kill off the first night and two nights later there was hardly anything to show for it. Still we needed to go round that second time just to make sure.

In both cases, apart from the experience gained, I would have been better off sticking with my traps.

Wherever I was working in the bush, I would fix large orange signs on gates or trees or other conspicuous places, painted upon with bold black letters, advising: "Possum Trapper Working, Danger, Cyanide Poison, Keep Out". In reality there was no poison laid, but the idea was to scare people off and provide me with a safer environment in which to work with less likelihood of being shot at in mistake for a deer. Some people either did not read signs or else they did not take them very seriously. And so one day I caught myself a tourist.

I was running a trap line that was doing quite well and producing good quality furs along the Te Ponanga Saddle Road, that lies between Lake Rotoaira and Lake Taupo. This was the northern extremity of my trapping territory, for as soon as you pass through the saddle and start descending towards Taupo you run into a different type of climate and a different type of possum. My two large, orange painted, warning signs were posted on prominent trees and there were traps stapled to giant podocarps all along either side of the road. But one day, one trap had been wrenched off its set and where it had been was a stick with a piece of notepaper attached just letting me know that somebody's little boy's fingers had been caught and my trap had been hurled down into the bush and what they would like to do to me if they had met up with me etc, etc. And what, might I ask, would a responsible adult be doing, allowing his little boy to be playing round trees where it had been clearly advertised that cyanide poison had been laid. The fellow was lucky it was only his little boy's fingers and not, as it could well have been, a crumpled little body choked to death on a cyanide bait.

It was a rare occurrence for me to lose a trap, but I lost that one.

Because I stacked my traps in bundles of ten, one up one down, nine of them threaded down the chain and handle of the first trap, it was quite easy to remember where the first and tenth traps were as I lay them out in the bush. Remembering where you began setting from a new bundle was not a very difficult thing to do. However, if there was ever any likelihood of confusion then it was okay making a tiny nick in the tree near the staple of the fifth trap and two tiny nicks near the staple of the tenth. If this procedure was followed, it was nigh on impossible misplacing any traps. However, soon after I began trapping the Waione Block I did lose one of my traps somewhere, within the short space of less than 200 yards, and I never could figure out where I had set it in the first place.

Off Ruamata Road, between Moerangi Station and State Highway 41, there was an abandoned logging road that followed a ridge up through the cut over bush, and off this road there were numerous side tracks that went short distances down the various spurs. I would park the Land Rover up on the logging road, grab a bundle of traps and jog down the spurs laying them out as close to the track as possible until all ten were set. In this case I was marking every fifth trap and on the very first spur that I worked I misplaced one of my traps between the first and fifth set. I went back and forth, up and down that track, checking and rechecking every possible place that I might have been likely to set a trap but I never did locate where it had been set. I worked the Waione Block for several weeks and many times I stopped at that spur while driving into the block to have another look for my trap, but all to no avail. I had definitely carried ten traps into the spur but only ever brought nine back out. I counted every last trap I owned just to make sure that I had not accidentally bundled nine instead of ten. All I could eventually conclude was that I must have initially put the missing trap in such a useless place that not only was no possum ever going to get caught in it, but it was in fact in such a useless place that even I could not go back to the same spot twice. I only ever did that once, and that is why to this day I have still never forgotten it.

There was, too, something else that happened in the Waione that I have never forgot. Late one afternoon I came out on a spur overlooking the Waipungapunga Stream at the end of my line and there down in the valley below was somebody's beat up old Vauxhall car. Now how somebody's old Vauxhall car got into my possum block beat me. There was a heavy steel mill gate blocking the road at the entrance to the block There was a bright orange sign stuck on the gate that read: "Possum Trapper Working, Danger, Cyanide Poison, Keep Out". There were also two interlocked padlocks securing the gate and the only persons supposed to have keys for them were the manager of Moerangi Station and myself. If it was deer stalkers, there was always the possibility that they might mistake me for a deer, and they should not have been in there in the first place. And if it was not deer stalkers then it was poachers helping themselves to my possums, and they should not have been in there, neither.

Naturally I was a little agitated and I wasted little time getting into my Land Rover and driving down to check out what was going on. When I arrived there was no one around to ask and being a little riled up and impatient by now I decided to get one jump ahead of them and take the liberty of checking out their vehicle for myself. I could see by their boot prints that two men had got out of the car. They had not left anything of great interest inside the car but in the boot there was a tin of flour, laced with oil of aniseed, and a fully loaded .303 rifle. Not only did we have a couple of poachers on our hands, we also had a couple of clowns with regard to rifle safety.

Under such circumstances you have a choice. You can either turn away and let them walk all over you. Or you can stick your neck out and make your stand. Naturally, I chose the latter. But having seen their cocked .303 in the boot I wasn't taking any chances. I parked my Land Rover sideways across the road a few yards behind their vehicle, got out my Sako Vixen, put one half up the spout and sat on a bank above the road and waited their return. It wasn't long and here they come, swinging a flour billy with a half empty tube of Strong's Sodium Cyanide, and so busy chatting away that they were almost back at their car before they suddenly noticed me sitting there on the bank with one half up the spout.

I was in no mood for pleasantries. I demanded what the hell they thought they were doing poaching my possum block, and illegally laying cyanide through the bush with no regulation warning notices having been posted. Naturally, being only one of me and being two of them, they started to get cheeky. So I told them to get into my Land Rover, I was taking them into Turangi to lay charges against them for trespassing and the illegal use of cyanide. They must have thought I was joking. But I wasn't. And nor were their smart replies doing much to help.

Now I started to get really mad. There might have been twice as many of them as there was of me, but the advantage I had was a rifle in my hands. I was not pointing it at anybody just yet, but my body language made it very clear that I was in no mood for their smart aleck replies and when I said, "get into my Land Rover!" I meant it. One of them started towards the boot of the car where I already knew there was a loaded 303. Suddenly it was all on! I knew that if he got hold of his rifle one of us was going to get badly hurt. And it was either him or me. How could I know he wasn't aiming on putting a bullet through me. With two of them to back up the story they could easily set it up to look as if I had fired the first shot and he had dropped me in self defence. I slammed the bolt shut on my rifle and ordered him away from the boot of his car. If he took one more step in that direction, I warned, I was about to gut shoot the two of them.

If they had thought I was joking a minute before, there was no mistaking my mood any longer. The one that had held back tried to calm me down, but I was far removed from that. The adrenalin was pumping and I was all worked up. I ordered them into the front of their car and told them to follow me out to the gate, and if they did anything stupid on the way I would be out of my Land Rover and putting my rifle to good use. Outside the block, with the gate locked behind us, I made them get into my Land Rover and I drove them into the police at Turangi.

It's a long way from up there on the Pungapunga to Turangi, so there was plenty of time for making things clear. Just in case I was not fully understood, I told them that if they came back into my block to try and pick up their poison line, it would be the last poison line they ever worked. I would mistake them for a deer. And they could figure out for themselves how they were going to get back out to Moerangi for their car.

The whole thing was more symbolic than anything else. They were probably mates of the local police anyway. And I daresay the police probably wondered how I had got two hefty blokes to leave their car behind way out in the bush and got them into my Land Rover in the first place.

If one of them had not gone for the boot of their car where I knew the loaded rifle was lying, things would probably have never gone as far as they did. It is not the done thing, poking one's loaded rifle in the belly of some individual out in the bush. However, the poachers were hardly acting within the law either, so they evidently did not consider it expedient to lay a complaint against me. It was unlawful for them to be laying cyanide without posting adequate signs that "Deadly Cyanide Poison for Possum Control" had been laid in the area. If this regulation was not adhered to their poisons licences could be revoked. The police for their part seemed rather unimpressed, if not somewhat annoyed, at my intrusion into their police station and obviously did not feel that a couple of possum poachers warranted their pressing charges. But none of that really mattered. As far as the poachers were concerned I had made my point. I was obviously a total nut case and mentally deranged, and a hundred or so possum skins to be picked up off a poison line were hardly worth being "mistaken for a deer" over. My poaching friends never came back.

With possums now fetching top dollars I could sense much more trouble brewing. I felt it would only be a matter of time before something really serious occurred and I really did not want any part of it. But by the same measure I was quite prepared to defend my territory.

Depending on the country, often my work was cut out handling eighty or ninety traps in a day. That many traps usually covered a lot of country and if that meant climbing through bush all day, then that many traps was about as much as I could handle. In the Waione though, I was working the full limit of my 110 traps. But to do it I was going like a mad thing all day, actually running from trap to trap to

Uh! Oh! On my way to Europe!

cover my line. Back in the Taringamotu I had been able to work 110 traps because all my sets were right alongside the road and I drove from trap to trap the entire distance of my line. Once again, I was working along a road, but the difference in the Waione was, a lot of my traps were down spurs that fell away from the main ridge. It was not practical trying to drive down these spurs. Instead I parked the Land Rover out on the main ridge and ran down the spurs killing and resetting as I went. On the way back up I would pick up the dead possums and load them all into the back of my Land Rover. I did not skin anything out in the bush. The entire day was dedicated to maintaining my line and keeping up the tallies. Every day I would pull up any traps that had not caught and push them into new territory. For awhile there I was catching between 90 and 98 possums a day and then gradually I started to run out of territory and the numbers began slipping back.

Usually it was quite late before I got back to camp and often it was already dark. Waiting to greet me would be a huge heap of cold possums to skin from the previous day, and now a new lot to be cached beneath the floor of my house where they could cool down ready for the next night. It took me on average an hour to skin 35 possums. So there I would be, bending over in the cold night air, sometimes in the drizzle and the rain, working to the light of a pressure lamp, for anything up to three hours without time out to straighten my back.

Usually more than an hour went into tacking out 30 possums including the turning of their tails and slinging them from the

After stunning with a whack to the head, thump your
possum fair between the eyes to kill it
Keenly watched by Kim, Bob Hannigan thumps a possum

Kim cleans up the damage
while Bob resets the trap
Bob moving between traps.
Five Mile Mill trap line

mesh. So tacking out accounted for three more hours at least. And somewhere along the way I still had to find a couple of hours for stripping boards so that I had something to tack the fresh skins onto. By now I was regularly working until 1.00am and later just trying to keep up to par.

Most mornings I began the day eating the dinner that I had been too tired to eat the night before. Then I would try and clear a few more boards before heading out in the bush to give me a bit of a head start for when I got back that night. The work load was such that I was always running behind time and at the same time I was probably pushing it just a little too far. Usually I was too exhausted to get up to an early start and so it was often after 9.30 am before I got away from camp in the morning. This became a vicious circle, racing to get round my line before dark, getting back to camp later and later in the evening, all adding to the pressure of trying to get everything accomplished before getting to bed.

I had just cleaned up a huge pile of possums outside the camp one drizzly night and as I straightened up to start piling the skinned carcasses into the back of the Land Rover for dumping out in the bush next day, my back gave out. I went down in a heap on the ground. That, effectively, was the beginning of the end of my trapping career.

Fortunately it was late in the season and there wasn't a great deal needed doing before I closed down my line and started cleaning up for the winter.

I was in sheer agony the next day but I still had to go back up in the bush and spring all my traps. There was nothing I could do about the possums I had caught. My pain was their good fortune, every one of them liberated.

By the end of the day, my back could no longer support the weight of my body. I felt my way along the Land Rover to the steel mill gate and nearly fainted as pain shot through my spine trying to lift it open. Somehow I got it closed again behind the Land Rover and back at Ruamata I collapsed onto my bed and remained there, a complete cripple for the next couple of days.

End of the line

A few days later I was back in the Waione, finishing off where I had been so rudely interrupted, but this time I was taking it easy and really just mopping up. I knew that I would never again be able to handle huge trap lines and skin great piles of possums.

Skins are hung over ropes to air out.
Final job before shipment, they need to be gently brushed and combed. Skins are baled flesh to flesh, fur to fur, and sprinkled with napthalene, 300 to the bale.

Sometime after the September sale, Bill Broadfoot came bouncing into my camp a mixture of excitement and trepidation.

"What was your top price?" he asked.

" Sixteen Dollars," I replied.

"You bloody beaut!" he exclaimed. "I've beaten the both of you. I've got the top price! Odey only got $16.50 and I got $18. I've got the new world record! I was worried you might have beaten me. I can't get over it. I've finally beaten Dave Odey and knocked him off his perch."

"What was your average price?" I asked.

"About four-fifty," said Bill.

"What about Odey? What did he average?"

"About the same as me," Bill replied. "Why?"

"Because, you bloody beaut! I averaged $7.60 and I've just beaten the both of you. And that also has to be a new world record!"

Leading fashion model, former Miss Wellington, Frances Probert, models a beautiful possum fur coat valued at the time at US$800. It was made from a selection of furs trapped by Wayne Blake. (photo and text from a leading fashion magazine 1970)

CHAPTER 28

Mopping Up

Seasons come and seasons go, and time keeps moving on!

The experiences recorded in this book have come and gone. So has the era from which they are derived. Several of the good men — trappers, hunters and co — mentioned herein have also come and gone. A few more are getting on and struggling. The rest of us are still around and kicking, but time keeps moving on.

Even the landscape keeps changing. Stumps and trees have been burned, bush cleared, monoao and silver tussock ploughed into the ground, mill houses removed, possum camps bulldozed, farmlands broken in, sheep, cattle and cows. Forests of pine have been planted, grown up, matured and even harvested in some of the areas where I once lived, trapped native and wrote about.

Times have changed and things are different. But the spirit of adventure still burns deep in many a young, and not so young, good

The end of an era. Dave Odey's camp

Kim remained faithful to the end

Kiwi bloke. And from that point of view, things have not really changed at all. I get the occasional letters from budding young trappers, asking me how to do this and how to do that. One young fellow was just 14 years old when he first wrote. I help where I can and he keeps in touch. He's out in the bush every chance he gets and is as keen as mustard. Reminds me of when I was a boy. Another of my mates is a young trapper well up in his 70's. Not so long ago I showed him how to cover his traps. Now he is running lines, skinning and plucking possums, hunting deer and trying to talk me into getting back into it myself.

This book is written as a tribute to all these blokes; past, present and future.

I trust that the information recorded herein regarding trapping and fur handling will prove helpful to any who are keen to learn. If it is something relating to hunting, rifle safety, taking your boots off in a boat or just a bush recipe then I am likewise more than pleased if you gleaned something from it. But more than all else, if it helps inspire another generation of young New Zealanders to grab a rifle and pull on a pair of boots then my mission has been well accomplished.

My old mate, Dave Odey, always liked to have the last word. I guess he always will! His Memorial Plaque sums it up nicely for all of us....

DAVID ODEY

19 JULY 1918
29 NOVEMBER 1991

HE LOVED THE BUSH

Glossary of Terms

alimony	regular payment of money made to a divorced or separated person by that one's spouse
Anson (boots)	(trade name) tramping/hunting boots
berko	berserk
billy	metal pot for boiling water and cooking food over a camp fire
bivvy	a 'make do' rough shelter, often beneath an overhanging rock
block (of bush)	area allocated to a hunter or trapper
bob (or two)	shilling, ten cents, loosely translated — a bit of money
bollocky	naked
bonus shooting	deer cullers who were paid only for the tails they produced, also referred to as bounty hunting
boofhead	semi retarded, moronic
bounty hunting	refer to 'bonus shooting'
brew	drink of tea
bush lawyer	a woody climbing plant richly endowed with sharp hooked prickles that forms an impenetrable and nigh inextricable tangle throughout portions of the forest
bush tram	carriage running on rails that transported logs from bush to mill
camp oven	cast iron pot used for stewing, roasting and baking over a camp fire
chocker	full, full up
chompers	teeth
choumollier	leafy plant grown as winter crop for sheep and cattle

cobber	friend
cocky	farmer
condy	condensed milk
crabs	crayfish, rock lobsters
culler	professional hunter employed by the Forest Service to eradicate various species of introduced animals
culling	eradicating noxious animals in the employ of the Forest Service
cwt	one hundredweight (see weight conversion — end of Glossary)
Dimp	insect repellent
Dollar equivalent	In 1968/69 the NZ$ had about 30 times the buying power of a NZ$ in 2005 (i.e., What you could pay $1 for in '68/69 you would pay $30 for in 2005
dunger	old clapped out (boat)
fathom	six foot
fly camp	temporary camp away from base
fonged	intoxicated, inebriated, drunk
gear	clothing
geek	look
gin trap	steel jawed possum trap
glassing	searching with the aid of binoculars
goolies	boulders
Government hunter	deer culler, also called a Government shooter
greasy (noun)	camp cook
greenbone	butterfish, excellent eating fish that lives in kelp
green skin	skin that is fresh and not yet started to dry out
gunga	backside, buttocks

gunnel	the upper edge around the hull of a ship
half a crown	two shillings and sixpence, decimal equivalent = 25c
helicopter shooter	professional shooter employed to shoot game from a helicopter
hick	unsophisticated and uninformed person
hocked off	sold
horopito	red leafed pepper tree, pungent small tree common throughout New Zealand forest
huhu grub	edible wood boring grub of the huhu beetle
hut builder	worker employed by the Forest Service to build deer culler's huts in the mountains and bush
inanga	whitebait, small freshwater fish
joey (possum)	baby possum, can also refer to the young of certain other species — for example a baby chamois
jacksie	anal sphincter
jug	prison
kahikatea	native white pine
kamahi	common lowland forest tree
karked out	died, dead
kina	sea egg
king hit	knock unconscious with one well directed blow
kitten (possum)	immature, ¾ grown
koitareke	marsh crake, small marsh bird
koura	crayfish
kutu	head louse
Lee Enfield	.303 British military rifle
long johns	long underwear
lug, lugging	carry, carrying

lurk	a scheme or proposition
LWB	long wheel base
maimai	duck shooter's hiding place
meat shooter	professional venison hunter (not operating from helicopters)
mocker	clothes
mokopuna	grandchild
monoao	common Central Plateau native heather like plant
mooching	loitering or hanging around
morepork	native owl
NZFS	New Zealand Forest Service
office wallah	person involved with office work
pakeha	common Maori expression for European person
pakihi	South Island West Coast swamp land
parry	Paradise Duck
paua	native abalone
perk	a benefit (not necessarily entirely law abiding)
pikau	canvas bag, tied at the top and carried on the back
plaster	shoot dead
podocarp	shrub or tree of the podocarpus genus found in tropical and subtropical lands
pokey	small
ponga fronds	leaves of the silver tree fern
possum	Trichosurus vulpecula dense furred Australasian arboreal marsupial, phalanger
possum pad	visible track or pathway made by possums
potted	betrayed to police
pound (money)	twenty shillings, decimal equivalent = $2

privatee	private shooter, weekend sports shooter
pup tent	small two man A-frame sleeping tent
rewarewa	native honeysuckle
ring (up the)	anus (up the)
ragwort	noxious weed
ratchety	broken down and poorly maintained
rock bivvy	a 'make do' rough shelter beneath a rock
rousie	rouseabout, person employed to do odd jobs
run holder	owner or leaser of farm land
Sako Vixen	name and model of a rifle manufactured in Finland
scoofter	pig
scree	wide expanse of loose stones fanning down a mountain slope
SF (90)	State Forest (#90)
shearing longs	Thick woollen trousers reinforced for holding sheep while shearing. Ideal wear for possum skinning.
Sixty Bar Eight	(60/8). Survey Block 60, Planting Camp #8. Planting camps were numbered and identified in this manner when Kaingaroa was being initially planted during the Great Depression. Most camps were removed after planting was completed, but 60/8 was added to and retained as a Forestry camp.
sloshed	intoxicated
smersh/smershing	smug smile/smiling smugly
S.M.L.E.	.303 British military rifle (usually pronounced 'smelly') Stands for: Short Magazine Lee Enfield
snig track	track along which logs were hauled from the bush
sooling	encouraging a dog to attack

stone (weight)	fourteen pounds, 6.36kg
stroppy	obstreperous, a noisy uncontrolled smart ass
supplejack	very tough woody vine
swannie	(Swanndri) hooded, knee length bush shirt
Swanndri	(trade name) hooded, knee length bush shirt, (swannie)
SWB	short wheel base
tamariki	children
tawaki	Fiordland crested penguin
token	tail and ears off a shot animal — produced as evidence of a kill
thermos	Thermos flask, vacuum flask for hot drink
Three O	.303 rifle
track cutter	worker employed by the Forest Service to cut tracks through the bush
treble-two	.222 calibre rifle
tree tomatoes	old name for tamarillos
Trekka	NZ made light 4 wheel drive vehicle with transverse leaf suspension
tussie	tussock
tweak	to look sneakily
umu	Maori earth oven
winkle-pickers	shoes with very pointed narrow toes, popular in the mid-20th century
whacky baccy	marijuana
whitebait	Inanga, small (delicacy) translucent fresh water fish
wop-wops	outback, remote area
yakker	work (usually modified with the word "hard" yakker)

zeddie	small spoon shaped fishing lure
Dollar comparison:	Purchasing power: 1966 — $1: 2005 — $30 (i.e. what you paid $1 for in 1966, you paid approximately $30 for in 2005

Weight (conversion)

one pound (1lb)	454 grams
2.2 lbs	1 kilogram
hundredweight (cwt)	112 pounds, 51kg
20cwt	1 ton
1 ton	2,240 lbs
stone	14 lbs, 6.36kgs

Measurement (conversion factors)

Inch (")	2.54 millimetre
Foot (')	0.305 metre
yard	0.914 metre
kilometre	about .62 mile
mile	about 1.61 km
nautical mile	about 1.85 km
12 inches	1 foot
3 feet	1 yard
5,280 feet	1,760 yards / 1 mile
22 yards	1 chain
10 chains	220 yards / 1 furlong
8 furlongs	1 mile
acre	4,840 square yards (4,046.86 sq metres)
square mile	640 acres